Astronaut Conrad (or Gordon) took this magnificent photograph on September ___ during the ___ the ___ was 225 nautical ___ miles, and by using a super wide-angle lens he was able to include the entire Fertile Crescent. At the lower left appears part of the Agena target vehicle which is docked to the Gemini spacecraft.

The breath-taking view, looking northeast, is from over the region of Asyut, Egypt. In the center is the Sinai Peninsula, jutting into the northern end of the Red Sea. One of the peaks in the granite range is Jebel Musa ("The Mountain of Moses"). In the foreground are the eastern desert of Egypt (called the Arabian Desert in Greek and Roman times) and the Gulf of Suez. Clearly visible is the Suez Canal including the Bitter Lakes and Lake Timsah (partially obscured by clouds). The Great Rift extends north from the Gulf of Aqaba through the Arabah, the Dead Sea (with the light-colored Lisan ("Tongue") projecting from the eastern shore), the Jordan Valley, the Sea of Galilee, and on up through Lebanon.

In the upper-left corner the entire coast of the eastern Mediterranean can be seen, even to the region of Tarsus just beyond the Gulf of Alexandretta (Iskanderun). The harbors of Haifa and Beirut, and the bay north of Tripoli are very distinct. The dark patches extending east from the Sea of Galilee indicate the basalt areas of the Jebel Druz region. Just beyond the basalt area and to the right of the Sea of Galilee lies Damascus. At the top center appears the confluence of the Khabur River with the Euphrates. In the upper-right section a massive plume of black smoke casts its shadow for miles. This column resulted from the burn-off of the lake of oil formed by a pipeline break. Beyond is modern Iraq where the dark areas indicate the Tigris and Euphrates Valleys. At the edge of the photo is the region of ancient Ur, the birthplace of Abraham. Clouds over the Zagros Mountains appear in the background.

Moses,
The Servant of Yahweh

Moses,
The Servant of Yahweh

DEWEY M. BEEGLE

Professor of Old Testament
Wesley Theological Seminary

WILLIAM B. EERDMANS PUBLISHING COMPANY
Grand Rapids, Michigan

*Gemini 11 photo on front endsheets used by
courtesy of the National Aeronautics and
Space Administration*

In Memory of My Mother

GLADYS JULIETTE (SMITH) BEEGLE
1896-1947

Along with her example
of faith and devotion,
She taught me the necessity
of asking honest questions

Foreword

When the people of Israel in their sacred convocations rehearsed the mighty acts by which the God of their fathers redeemed them and made them his people, the name of one man stood out above all others in the record:

> *He made known his ways to Moses,*
> *his acts to the people of Israel.*

In Egypt, at the Sea of Reeds, at Sinai and at Kadesh, Moses is their leader. I am rather more sceptical about literary source-analysis in the Pentateuch than Dr. Beegle is; but from Egypt onwards, however many strata of tradition may be discerned in the narrative, Moses the man of God is there throughout as judge, guide, legislator and intercessor, Yahweh's incomparable prophet and spokesman, whom he knew face to face and with whom he spoke "mouth to mouth." This fact can be interpreted in more ways than one: Martin Noth, for example, judges that "since the Pentateuch narrative was compiled step by step from a series of originally independent themes, the regular appearance of Moses in most of these themes cannot be original but must be the result of later assimilation." To me, the evidence points in exactly the opposite direction. Since he appears in most of the Pentateuchal themes, the man Moses bestrode the whole complex of historical events as decisively as he pervades the whole literary structure. His Egyptian name roots him in Egypt so far as the beginning of his career is concerned; the undisputed (though unidentified) location of his tomb among the mountains of Moab, "in the valley opposite Beth-peor," fixes the geographical terminus of his career equally firmly.

Dr. Beegle's vividly presented account of Moses, for which archaeological evidence has supplemented the literary data, recognizes Moses' towering stature and does justice to the biblical portrayal of his decisive presence with Israel at

7

every crucial stage of its migration from the Nile to the Jordan. He acknowledges the complexity of the problems raised by the narrative, and reckons judiciously with the chief divergent solutions that have been propounded, but rightly links Moses with that "representative group of tribes" which shared the experiences of the Exodus, Sinai, Kadesh, and Transjordan. Above all, he underscores Moses' paramount role as the communicator of divine revelation to his people, from the burning bush onward, and the true secret of his greatness in the personal relationship which the God of Israel established and maintained with him. For these and other reasons I am happy to commend this work to its readers, of whom I hope there will be many.

F. F. BRUCE

Contents

Preface

The dominant spirit of western civilization today is that man has come of age. The new sophistication tends to demean the past as a period of adolescence to be played down or forgotten. This attitude has permeated religious circles as well, so that in many instances the achievement of a sense of history is rather low on the list of priorities. But the Judaeo-Christian faith is rooted in history, and anyone who ignores the biblical insights is doomed to the frustration of trial and error in attempting to rediscover the ultimates of life.

There is, on the other hand, a minority with a concern for understanding Scripture; yet more often than not those with this devotion to learn about the meaning of the past do not have the training to read the biblical sources with discrimination. The Bible is the result of a long and complicated process of transmitting, collecting, and editing of accounts and teachings associated with the history of Israel and the early Church. The chief problem is one of interpretation. A genuine understanding of how God worked in history through his people cannot be gained by a simplistic reading of Scripture. Accordingly, the need is to learn basic ways of studying the Bible. A very encouraging fact is that much incisive work can be done with recent translations of the English Bible.

The purpose of this book is twofold: (1) to encourage an interest in biblical study in those open-minded persons who, for a variety of reasons, have not had a meaningful experience with Scripture; and (2) to instruct all those who have the desire but lack the knowledge to interpret the Bible effectively. This educational process is made more meaningful by being focused on the life of Moses, one of the greatest personalities of the Old Testament. To understand this past we will have to dip into the book of Genesis a number of times, and since his life spans the books of

Exodus through Deuteronomy we will be examining most of the Pentateuch ("Five Books"). Moreover, adequate handling of some of the problems will necessitate reference to the books of Joshua and Judges; therefore in tracing the life of Moses the reader will receive a good deal of practice in interpreting biblical sources.

The difficulty with much of the study of the Bible has been the failure to apply the biblical insights to contemporary life and problems. This abstract, ivory-tower approach has resulted in an antiquarian attitude dulling ethical sensitivity to theological relevance. Accordingly, one aspect of this study of Moses will be the attempt to relate his life and times to our day.

Much of the pertinent material of the story is noted or quoted in the book, but for the greatest understanding the reader should have a recent translation of the Bible at hand. Use of the map will enhance the study by helping the reader follow in the footsteps of Moses. The first chapter of the book goes into some detail to show the various approaches to biblical study and to give some criteria for checking the interpretations of scholars. Later chapters refer to these technical features, and so the reader is advised to work through the first chapter carefully before moving on to the rest of the book.

The chasm between scholars and laymen (both in and out of the church) is widening. This book is an attempt to bridge that gap. It is not bedtime reading because the issues are complex; yet the searching, inquiring person (regardless of his religious background) can participate in the exciting experience of biblical research. If churches, Sunday schools, Bible schools, and even theological seminaries are to nullify the charges of obscurantism or biblical ignorance they must be willing to study the Bible in the light of all new knowledge. The thrill and challenge of a more accurate understanding of Scripture are key factors in the renewal of the church, and hopefully they will play genuine roles in the renewal of society.

The frequent references to Professor William Foxwell Albright (1891-1971), formerly W. W. Spence Professor of Semitic Languages, The Johns Hopkins University, will be some indication of the extent to which I am indebted to my late teacher. It is an honor to help perpetuate remembrance of him and his work.

Professor F. F. Bruce, Rylands Professor of Biblical Criticism and Exegesis, Manchester University, England, graciously consented to write the foreword, and hearty thanks go to him for his interest in the book and its purpose.

Dewey M. Beegle

Washington, D.C.

Chapter 1

Moses and History

Few historical figures have evoked such wide-ranging reactions and opinions as has Moses. For centuries he was considered the author of the first five books of the Old Testament, including the so-called prophetic account of his own death. Very conservative Jewish and Christian groups still contend for the Mosaic authorship of the Pentateuch, but few would argue that Moses wrote the passage about his death. Yet the basic inference from this assumption is that all the details pertaining to Moses and the Israelites are firsthand reports and that as such they are historically accurate.

At the opposite end of the scholarly spectrum is the point of view expressed by the late German scholar Martin Noth (1902-1968). For him the most concrete fact about Moses was the tradition concerning his tomb in the region of Mt. Nebo in Transjordan. Accordingly, Noth was willing to grant that Moses probably had something to do with the preparations in Moab for the occupation of Canaan, but beyond this point he was very pessimistic. Noth did not deny a historical core to the Exodus and Sinai traditions, but he believed that these events were experienced by two different groups and that the stories were transmitted independently of each other. Thus any reference to Moses in the Exodus and Sinai stories was interpreted by Noth as a late editorial addition to the text. In other words, the biblical story about the Israelites resulted from an editor weaving separate themes or traditions together around a main character Moses, who was actually an obscure person from Moab.

These extremes, plus a number of views in between, make the question about Moses a very confusing issue. Alert laymen in the Jewish and Christian tradition ask, "Whom are we to believe? Is there no way of settling the issue

more precisely?" While archaeology has greatly increased
our knowledge about the peoples and cultures of biblical
lands, we are still dependent on biblical sources for any
story about Moses and the Israelites. The chief problem,
therefore, is one of interpretation (exegesis).

There are two basic reasons why the same biblical narrative has been interpreted in so many ways: (1) the text
is very complex and ambiguous at times; and (2) every
student of the Bible brings some presuppositions to the
task of interpretation. As a result all interpretations are
to some extent subjective. Some have declared the situation hopeless because they claim there is no way of ascer-
taining the truth of the matter. In fact, however, some
interpreters (exegetes) are far more objective than others,
and it is possible to come closer to the reality of the issue.
In order to check on the accuracy of the various interpretations it is necessary to know some of the basic theories and
criteria by which the interpreters make their judgments.

Literary Criticism

Modern critical study of the Bible began in the eighteenth
century A.D. The basic clue was a variation in the designations for God. It was observed that some narratives of the
Pentateuch had *Elohim,* the general term for deity (translated "God" in most English translations). Other passages
had *Yahweh,* the personal name for the God of Israel. The
latter designation appears as "Jehovah" in the American
Standard Version (ASV) and "Lord" (with small capital
letters) in the King James Version (KJV), Revised Standard Version (RSV), New English Bible (NEB), and New
American Bible (NAB). At times *Yahweh* appears with
Adonay ("Master, Lord" with lower-case letters) and at
other times with *Elohim;* thus *Adonay Yahweh* is translated "Lord God" instead of "Lord Lord," and *Yahweh
Elohim* becomes "Lord God." The basic rule is: wherever
in English translations a designation for God appears in
small capital letters the Hebrew text has *Yahweh.*

In order to explain this divergent use of divine names
the early critics theorized that two separate sources, E and
J, had been united in the biblical text. Later on the critics
isolated units which seemed to come from priestly traditions
and these were called the P source. Since the book of Deu-

teronomy had many characteristics similar to the book of
Jeremiah and the reform of Josiah (while differing from
the books Genesis through Numbers), scholars concluded
that Deuteronomy was based on the scroll found in the temple at Jerusalem in 621 B.C. The point of view expressed
in Deuteronomy and various parts of Joshua, Judges, Samuel, and Kings was assigned the designation D. The dates
for these literary sources have varied somewhat among the
critics, but the following outline is typical:

J (Yahwistic source)
    about 950 B.C., in Solomon's reign or
    about 850 B.C., in Jehoshaphat's reign
E (Elohistic source)
    about 750 B.C., in the reign of Jeroboam II
D (Deuteronomic source)
    about 615 B.C., in Josiah's reign
P (Priestly source)
    about 550 B.C., in the Babylonian exile

The J source was dominant in the southern kingdom
where Judah was the leading tribe and Jerusalem the capital city. The E source, on the other hand, was the point
of view of the northern kingdom where Ephraim was the
main tribe. The accidental combination of the J's and E's
is a very helpful mnemonic device for remembering and
relating the two older sources.

Evolutionary Development

A new approach to the critical study of the Old Testament
came in 1876-77 when the German scholar Julius Wellhausen published his views. He accepted and refined the
JEDP theory noted above, but his main proposal was not
in the realm of literary criticism. Rather he forced the various sources into a philosophical theory of development which
affirmed that religious ideas and customs had simple, prim-
itive beginnings and in time they evolved to ever higher
and more complex forms. Wellhausen believed that the
exalted monotheistic view of God found in the Old Testament was the work of the prophet Amos and his successors.
The religious ideas associated with the Patriarchs and
Moses were too advanced for those times, so he claimed,
therefore some editor must have projected them back into

the narratives of the earlier periods of Hebrew history. Moses was considered a very nebulous figure at best and the Patriarchs as individuals were denied any historical basis. For a number of years Wellhausen's views dominated the study of the Old Testament. At the same time, the literary or source critics carried their research to such minute details the four major sources were subdivided into four strands: the original source and three editorial strands of revision added at later times. The new designations of J, for example, were J, J^1, J^2, and J^3. The result of this activity was that at times single verses were split up into four or five sources.

Form Criticism

The excesses of Wellhausen and the literary critics resulted in a reaction. In 1901 Hermann Gunkel discussed the sagas in the book of Genesis. He contended that the form of the stories indicated that the present prose narrative derived from very ancient folk tales which had been handed down from generation to generation in poetic form. Hugo Gressmann made a similar study of Exodus, and thus the two German scholars initiated the type of critical approach known as "form criticism" or "form history" (*Formgeschichte*).

Until recently, however, there has been some ambiguity in the definition of terms and in the application of method. The term "form" has been used to indicate the structure or pattern of a unit, but secondarily it has been equated with the German term *Gattung*, which is concerned with the type or genre of the biblical passage. In modern society the letter is a basic type of literary expression. Moreover, it has a specific structure: greeting, content of communication, and closing. Although structure is helpful in determining the broad category, the precise life situation is determined by the content. When a letter begins "My Darling," it is quite evident that it is not a communication between business concerns. Custom dictates that it is inappropriate to close a formal letter of invitation with "Lovingly."

The basic insight of form criticism is that life situations develop their own specific types of expression. The ideas, symbols, and customs of a wedding differ greatly from those of a funeral. A court trial is easily distinguished from a love scene. Ancient society was just as precise in developing specific terms, expressions, and structure for communicating in various situations of life; therefore it is possible in biblical study to identify such types as sayings, narratives, poems, prayers, songs, sermons, and laws.

Another facet of form criticism is tracing the history of the various types of literature (*Gattungsgeschichte*). Life moves on and new types emerge out of the vestige of older types. These flourish for a while and then in turn pass into oblivion. The type of communication called "prophetic speech" seems to have originated with Amos (about 750 B.C.). Over the years there were changes in detail (Ezekiel, for example), and finally by 400 B.C. the prophetic spirit ceased to exist and the category of prophetic oracle disappeared.

While form criticism cannot solve all the biblical problems, it has made two major contributions to the understanding of the Bible: (1) it has been a check on literary criticism by showing that excessive subdividing of the text into different sources does violence to biblical units which come from a single life situation; and (2) in many instances it has determined the origin and setting in life (*Sitz im Leben*) of biblical passages.

Evolutionary Development and Literary Criticism

Wellhausen's evolutionary theory of the Old Testament was formulated before the rise of modern archaeological method and the subsequent discoveries. After World War I it became increasingly clear that this theory did not accord with the facts, and after World War II it could be declared that Wellhausenism was dead. Conservatives welcomed this trend and went on to imply that literary criticism had been dealt a death blow as well. But this was wishful thinking. The mediating scholar William F. Albright was foremost in declaring the death of Wellhausenism, but he never doubted or repudiated the basic insights of the literary critics. It is a fact that literary criticism was formulated before Wellhausen, and it has continued since his influence passed. That Wellhausen took the source or documentary theory and forced it into his evolu-

tionary theory in no way means that the source theory died
with the evolutionary theory.

Reaction to Literary Criticism

One of the foremost opponents of the source theory
of literary criticism was the late Jewish scholar Umberto
Cassuto. His counterarguments appear in *The Documentary Hypothesis and the Composition of the Pentateuch*
(1961), a translation by Israel Abrahams of the original
Hebrew edition (1941). He states that the literary or
documentary theory rests on five pillars: (1) differenti-
ation of names as sources; (2) language and style; (3)
contradictions and divergences of view; (4) duplications
and repetitions; and (5) composite sections. He treats each
of these five topics in detail and attempts to show that
the so-called pillars turn to dust when examined thoroughly. He concludes that the pillars are imaginary, and he reduces his argument to simple mathematics by observing
that $0 + 0 + 0 + 0 + 0 = 0$.[1] But Cassuto's sweeping
claims are too neat and all-inclusive to be convincing.

With respect to the use of divine names he claims that
the variation between *Elohim* and *Yahweh* is not due to
sources, but to the intention of the compiler of the Pentateuch. The name *Yahweh* was used when the writer wished
to express the personal, awe-inspiring, ethical God of Israel,
whereas *Elohim* was employed to depict the abstract, transcendent, impersonal, and universal aspects of God's being.
But when Cassuto applies his theory to the data of the
biblical text he finds exceptions which he must rationalize
away. Genesis 20, for example, is normally assigned to the
E source. Cassuto explains the use of *Elohim* in verse 3
as due to the editor because Abimelech was an alien to
Yahweh and it would not have been proper to use the personal name for God in this context. Yet in verse 17 the
text reads, "Then Abraham prayed to God; and God healed
Abimelech, and also healed his wife and female slaves so
that they bore children." Abraham built an altar to *Yahweh*
(Gen. 12:7), and in a vision he addressed God (in what
amounts to a prayer) as *Adonay Yahweh* ("Lord GOD")

---

[1] Umberto Cassuto, *The Documentary Hypothesis and the Composition of the Pentateuch,* tr. Israel Abrahams (Jerusalem: Magnes,
1961), p. 101.

(15:2, 8). It is indeed strange why the editor did not have Abraham praying to *Yahweh* in 20:17.

In Genesis 1:27 *Elohim* "created man in his own image," but in 2:7 *Yahweh Elohim* "formed man of dust from the ground, and breathed into his nostrils the breath of life." Both verses share the concept of man's close relationship to his creator, but why did the editor shift names? Another example is Genesis 6:5, where *Yahweh* "saw that the wickedness of man was great in the earth, and that every imagination of the thoughts of his heart was only evil continually." In 6:12, however, *Elohim* "saw the earth, and behold, it was corrupt; for all flesh had corrupted their way upon the earth." The term "man" seems more personal than "flesh," but the essential content of the two passages is the same. It is extremely dubious to theorize that the editor made a conscious shift from *Yahweh* to *Elohim*.

Cassuto recognizes that the details become rather complex, and so he tries to protect his theory with the following generalization: "Sometimes, of course, it happens that two opposite rules apply together and come in conflict with each other; then, as logic demands, the rule that is more material to the primary purport of the relevant passage prevails."[2] But the basic issue of this claim is "Whose 'logic' is to be followed?" Cassuto's theory determines his logic just as clearly as the theory of the literary critics shapes their logic. Some of Cassuto's arguments point up the weaknesses of the extreme literary critics, and in this respect he has done a service. But his theory is just as vulnerable in the other four topics as in the use of divine names. Whenever the data do not fit his presuppositions his ingenuity is quick to supply reasons for the variations. His sweeping claim that the biblical details "can always be explained without difficulty"[3] on the basis of his rules is going too far. The five "pillars" have not crumbled to dust at the touch of Cassuto's finger.

In 1943 Oswald T. Allis, Cassuto's counterpart in the United States, published *The Five Books of Moses*.[4] There are a number of similarities in the argument, but there

2 *Ibid.*, p. 32.

3 *Ibid.*, p. 41.

4 Oswald T. Allis, *The Five Books of Moses* (Philadelphia: Presbyterian and Reformed, 1943).

seems to be no direct dependence. Allis never mentions or
quotes from Cassuto, and it is difficult to imagine such an
oversight had he known of the work of his ally in Palestine.
Although he approaches the problem from a more rigid
theological point of view than Cassuto, Allis also makes
a good case against the excesses of the literary critics. His
claims that they reason in a circle and that they tend to
doctor the evidence are certainly valid at times; but when
the biblical data go against his theory Allis, like Cassuto,
resorts to mental gymnastics (another form of doctoring)
in order to harmonize the evidence.

One of the most able of the current opponents of the
documentary hypothesis is K. A. Kitchen. In *Ancient Orient
and Old Testament* (1966) he covers briefly the basic arguments of Cassuto and Allis, but then he breaks new
ground by appealing to various styles in ancient texts whose
literary unity is beyond all doubt. "The biographical inscription of the Egyptian official Uni (*c.* 2400 BC)," Kitchen
observes, "includes flowing narrative (like 'J', 'E' ?), summary statements ('P' ?), a victory-hymn ('H' ?), and two
different refrains ('R$_1$', 'R$_2$' ?) repeated at suitable but varying intervals. Yet there can in fact be no question at all
of disparate sources here, in what is a monumental inscription composed and engraved as a unitary whole at the volition of the man whom it commemorates."[5] While the illustration shows that various styles were employed in ancient
texts composed by single authors, the inscription of Uni
is not completely analogous to difficult biblical passages. It
is granted that matters of vocabulary and style are very
slippery criteria and that the data can be made to argue
both ways. The more decisive factors are the sudden shifts
in point of view, logic of argument, and grammatical sequence between adjacent blocks of material. As we shall
see later, the narratives of Exodus swarm with difficulties
of this nature and Kitchen's arguments do not really answer
the tough literary problems of such passages.

Sources and Tradition History

After claiming to have destroyed the source theory of the

---

[5] K. A. Kitchen, *Ancient Orient and Old Testament* (Chicago:
Inter-Varsity, 1966), p. 125.

literary critics, Cassuto relates in survey fashion how he thinks the Bible came to have its present form:

> It is no daring conjecture, therefore, to suppose that a whole world of traditions was known to the Israelites in olden times, traditions that apparently differed in their origin, nature and characteristics. Some of them preserved memories of ancient events, and some belonged to the category of folk-lore; some were the product of the Israelite spirit and some contained elements that emanated from pagan culture; a number of them were handed down by the general populace and others were subjected to the close study of the exponents of the Wisdom literature; there were stories that were given a poetic and consequently a more fixed form, and others that were narrated in prose that was liable to suffer changes in the course of time; there were simple tales and complex, succinct and detailed, lucid and obscure, unpretentious and most sublime. From all this treasure, the Torah selected those traditions that appeared suited to its aims, and then proceeded to purify and refine them, to arrange and integrate them, to recast their style and phrasing, and generally to give them a new aspect of its own design, until they were welded into a unified whole.[6]

Thus while Cassuto denies the sources of the critics, he declares that numerous traditions have come together. The Torah (Pentateuch) did not assemble itself; therefore the process of selecting, refining, arranging, recasting, and integrating the various traditions was done by one or more compilers.

What Cassuto was apparently reacting against was the impression given by some critics that the various editors had written sources in front of them and that their compilation consisted in taking units, verses, and phrases from one source and mixing them with elements from other sources in a rather mechanical, scissors-and-paste method. But the better literary critics have long since given up such an idea. It is being increasingly recognized that J and E are so thoroughly mixed in certain units that it is impossible to separate the two. The most probable explanation for this fact is that this mixture took place during the long period of oral transmission and that when the so-called J source

---

[6] Cassuto, *op. cit.*, p. 102.

was put in written form during Solomon's reign (if not in the latter part of David's) this mixture was already present.

It is a well-known fact that no two people viewing the same event will report all the details, nor will they have them in the same order. Few people have photographic recall; therefore the personality, background, and interests of the observers or participants are factors in determining what they see and how they interpret the event. The complex, frightening events of the plagues and the deliverance from Egypt were experienced by many people from differing vantage points, and it is virtually certain that variations appeared as they first recounted the stories. Those with priestly interests would relate the accounts as seen through their perspective, and the same would be true of those inclined to the wisdom and prophetic traditions. Surely the laymen and the uneducated saw things from still different points of view. Moses and those who assisted him probably helped shape and standardize the series of stories, but other points of view must have persisted.

As will be noted later, it was Moses who designated the name *Yahweh* (known for some time in other circles) as the personal name of the God of the Hebrews. His assistant Hoshea was renamed Joshua (where *Jo* represents a shortened form of *Yahweh*), and probably *Yahweh* became the preferred designation for the ritual of official worship services. But *El*, the old designation for deity, and *El Shaddai* ("God of the Mountain"), traditionally translated "God (the) Almighty," the name of the God of the Patriarchs, had great sentimental attachment, and they continued to be revered. Since it had become the practice to use the plural of a god's name as a claim for his or her being a supreme god with all the characteristics of deity, the Hebrews shifted from *El* (through the variant form *Eloah*) to the plural form *Elohim* as the general designation for their Supreme God. Accordingly, as the stories of the Exodus and Sinai were formulated and recited, the tendency was to choose one or the other of the two basic names depending on the preference of the group or the composer.

In the Old Testament which has come down to us, the earliest portions are in poetic form. One of the basic features of early Hebrew poetry was to express the same idea in parallel lines using similar words. Since in such instances the composer or the one who helped standardize the poems had to use both *Elohim* and *Yahweh,* preference was indicated by placing that name in the first line. This same principle was applied to the Psalms. Psalm 40:17, for example, reads:

As for me, I am poor and needy;
but the Lord (Adonay, *perhaps a substitute for* Yahweh)
takes thought for me.
You are my help and my deliverer;
do not tarry, O my God!

The parallel verse in Psalm 70:5 has:

> *But I am poor and needy;*
> *hasten to me, O God!*
> *You are my help and my deliverer;*
> *O Yahweh, do not tarry!*

The reason for this inversion of the designations for God is that Psalm 40 is in the Yahwistic group of Psalms (1-41 and 84-150) while Psalm 70 is in the Elohistic group (42-83). This decided preference is so persistent that in the Yahwistic Psalms the name *Yahweh* occurs 584 times while *Elohim* appears only 94 times. In the Elohistic Psalms the situation is almost exactly reversed: *Elohim* occurs 210 times with *Yahweh* appearing only 45 times.

While the kingdom of Israel was united under David and Solomon, the theological preference of Jerusalem was for *Yahweh,* and thus it was the dominant designation for God. But when Israel, the northern kingdom, split off from Judah, the southern kingdom, King Jeroboam and his religious leaders returned to the preference for *Elohim.* It is thus much more probable that the E source dates from around 900 B.C. instead of the standard date of 750 B.C. Moreover, it was a revision based on a point of view which had persisted throughout the periods of the wilderness wanderings, the Judges, and the united monarchy.

A point of view related to the E source or tradition is that expressed in D. The scroll found in 621 B.C. (probably most of the book of Deuteronomy) was very likely composed in the northern kingdom about 750 B.C. When

Israel fell in 722/21 the scroll found its way down into Judah where it was stored in the temple. Josiah was so shocked at his and the people's ignorance of the contents he apparently authorized someone to issue a history of Israel from Moses down to their time in order that the people might be educated about their past. This history, as Martin Noth correctly observes, appears in the books Deuteronomy through 2 Kings (with the exception of the book of Ruth). From the available records (the newly found scroll and blocks of material from Israel and Judah) the historian compiled the story, but in addition he inserted many comments which interpreted events in line with the viewpoint of the temple scroll.

The dominant priests at the temple in Jerusalem were those from the Zadokite line. They claimed direct descent from Aaron, and it is undoubtedly this group which preserved the material found in the P source. Thus, while the J and P lines of tradition were current in Judah, the E and D traditions were being maintained up north in Israel. Apparently the scrolls containing the northern traditions were preserved by removing them from Samaria and/or Bethel before the northern kingdom fell. Although the four major sources JEDP were edited at different times they all had roots going back into the beginnings of Israelite history, and in general it can be said that *they are essentially recensions or variations of the same story.*

Tradition History

Cassuto was nearer the truth when he wrote, "The stream of this (biblical) tradition may be compared to a great and wide-spreading river that traverses vast distances; although in the course of its journey the river loses part of its water, which is absorbed by the ground or evaporates in the air because of the heat of the sun, and it is also increasingly augmented by the waters of the tributaries that pour into it, yet it carries with it, even after it has covered hundreds of miles, some of the waters that it held at the beginning when it first started to flow from its original source."[7] While many details of the original biblical events were lost during transmission of the stories, tributaries of

---

[7] *Ibid.*, pp. 102-103.

comment and explanation found their way into the tradition.

Just as certainly as people see an event from different points of view, they tend to focus less clearly on the details as the period of time widens between the event and their recollection. The proverbial "fish story" is pertinent at this point. Every time the fisherman tells the story about the fish that got away, the size of the fish tends to increase. While exaggeration is sometimes intentional, more often than not it is an unconscious expression of human nature. Distance and time do lend enchantment, and when the memory blurs, the essence of an experience is expressed in new ways with varying details.

This was just as true of the Israelites. Exodus 14:21 explains that "Yahweh drove the sea back by a strong east wind all night, and made the sea dry land." Yet the very next verse states that when the Israelites went across on the dry ground the waters were "a wall for them on their right hand and on their left." How could the Israelites walk into the fury of an east wind so powerful it caused a wall of water on both sides? The strong wind, which was the original explanation, was described in poetic fashion as the blast of Yahweh's nostrils piling the water in heaps (Exod. 15:8). When later generations recapitulated the miraculous event in their ritual they interpreted the poetic, hyperbolic statement as literal fact, and so this comment was included within the growing tradition about the Exodus.

It is quite evident, therefore, that the biblical narratives or sagas are a combination of history and faith. The duty of every serious student of the Bible is to isolate the layers of tradition wherever they occur. In this way it is possible to show the development of the traditions. This concern to trace the history of traditions *(Überlieferungsgeschichte)* is actually an outgrowth of form criticism. One of the major contributions of this method of studying Scripture has been as a corrective to Wellhausen's tendency to date the contents of biblical passages in the period of their compilation. Because the P source seemed to have been compiled during the Babylonian exile, Wellhausen considered the tabernacle and much of the priestly regulations as creations of the priests while in exile. It could just as well be argued that a history of George Washington written in twentieth-

century American prose proves that Washington dates from
the twentieth century.

On the other hand, tradition history, like literary and
form criticism, has tried to prove too much and thus taken
the method to unwarranted extremes. Martin Noth, an
initiator and leader in this approach, is a pertinent example. By doubting the authenticity of most references to
Moses and by rejecting the continuity between the Exodus
and Sinai experiences, he slighted the fact that these elements appear in the J, E, and P sources. His claim that
an editor doctored the traditions in order to create the colossal figure of Moses requires as much credulity as is
necessary to believe that Moses wrote the entire Pentateuch. The truth, as usual, is somewhere between.

Redaction Criticism

Originally, research into the history of traditions included both oral and written tradition. But since the transmission of written sources has some features which distinguish it from oral transmission, the history of editions
or redactions *(Redaktionsgeschichte)* has developed as another specialized approach to the study of Scripture. The
editors (redactors) responsible for the biblical text collected oral traditions and put them in written form. Yet
they were more than compilers because in making their
sources relevant for their time they incorporated some of
their interpretations in the documents. Later editors dis-
agreed at times and so they changed the text. A classic
example is where the Chronicler doubts the written tradition that Yahweh in anger incited David to take a census
(2 Sam. 24:1). To him it was inconceivable that God would
do such a thing, and so he substituted "Satan" for "Yahweh" (1 Chron. 21:1).

Rhetorical Criticism

A more recent approach to biblical research is the method
of studying the style of the passage. Otto Eissfeldt and
W. F. Albright, leaders in this approach (called "rhetorical
criticism" by James Muilenburg[8]), have shown that the
earliest fragments of the Bible are in poetic form and that

---

[8] James Muilenburg, "Form Criticism and Beyond," *Journal of Biblical Literature*, LXXXVIII, 1 (March 1969), 1-18.

the arrangement or style of the elements has a structure which later generations did not understand. By close scrutiny to details of poetic form and syntax it is possible to show the development of varying styles over the centuries. With this method many of the sections which Wellhausen dated late can be shown to be among the earliest parts of the Bible.

The Role of Archaeology

Careful use of literary, form, tradition, redaction, and rhetorical types of criticism enables scholars to reconstruct the growth and development of many aspects of the Bible (for example, customs, ideas, ritual, and written sources). The result is a series of sequences in which the relative order of the items is fairly well established. What is lacking, however, is a time line by which the various phases of the historical process can be dated. This is precisely where archaeology comes in. While developing their own relative sequence of peoples and cultures of the Near East, archaeologists observed that some ancient kings listed eclipses (both of the sun and the moon) as the outstanding events for certain years of their reigns. By the use of astronomical data the actual year (B.C.) of these eclipses was determined. When the sequence of empires (reckoned from the various king lists) was aligned with these historical pegs, it was possible to date persons and events before and after the eclipses. Consequently, there has been constructed a framework of ancient history which (with only a few years' possible error) is quite accurate as far back as 2000 B.C.

Moreover, archaeological research has been able to piece together enough details that the broad outlines of ancient Near Eastern history stand out clearly. By matching the details of biblical passages with similar features in the historical mosaic it is possible to date many events described in the Old Testament. In this process of checking the biblical statements from external evidence, the most reliable criterion is pottery. Pieces (sherds) of broken ceramic vessels are found at every site occupied by man after the invention of pottery. Since form and styles (unpainted, incised, painted, etc.) vary in different places and at different times, a remarkably accurate pottery chronology has been

worked out. With this knowledge, surface or survey archaeologists like the late Nelson Glueck (1900-1971) have been
able to locate sites of human occupation and to determine
(without excavation in many instances) the periods in
which people resided there. Such information is exceedingly
helpful in checking geographical and historical references
in the Bible. Because the results of archaeological research
are rather objective and precise they serve also as checks
on the findings of scholars who work largely with the literary or internal data of Scripture.

This survey has attempted to show that each type of
critical study of the Bible has an element of truth. The
basic error of past generations has been to think that its
specific approach to Scripture held the answer to the
formation of the Bible. Any one-stringed approach to criticism is doomed to failure. The serious biblical critic must
give due weight to literary, form, tradition, redaction, and
rhetorical approaches to criticism as well as to the data
supplied by archaeology.

Difficulty of the Moses Story

The task of attempting to reconstruct the actual story of
Moses is very difficult. In fact, it can be done only in broad
outline. Even with our modern techniques of reporting and
information gathering it is difficult to get an accurate picture of the total personality of our great leaders and in-
tellectual giants. Both biography and autobiography are
imperfect attempts to capture in words the totality of
human personality. It is the conviction of this writer
that there was a Moses. Without him and the God who
called him there would have been no group of persons
known as Israel. Moses, furthermore, like all great persons,
was a very complex personality. Facets of his gifts and
temperament shine through some of the biblical passages,
but at best our information is tantalizing. Later traditions
have attempted to fill in some of the gaps, and at times
these are overdrawn. Aside from the main experiences at
Sinai and Qadesh-barnea it is impossible to reconstruct
with any degree of certainty what happened during most
of the years in the wilderness. Notwithstanding these difficulties, however, an attempt will be made to sketch the
story of "Moses, the servant of Yahweh" (Deut. 34:5).

Chapter 2

The Hebrews in Egypt

The story about Moses begins in Egypt. From the book of Exodus we learn that he came from a group of people called Hebrews and that they were slaves of the Egyptian Pharaoh. Who were these Hebrews? Why and when did they come to Egypt? How many were there originally? Where did they settle and how long had they been there? These may seem to be irrelevant questions, but the man Moses was part of a larger story; therefore if we are to understand him we must see him in the larger historical context of which he was a part.

The Hapiru

From about 2500 to 1150 B.C. various inscriptions from the regions of the Fertile Crescent (Mesopotamia, Syria, Palestine, and Egypt) refer to groups of people called *Hapiru (Habiru)* in Mesopotamia or *Apiru* in western Syria, Palestine, and Egypt. This term, meaning "dusty," designated a class of people and clearly had nothing to do with race or ethnic origin. Feelings about the Hapiru were mixed. Sometimes they served a useful function and at other times they were a threat. While they were not nomadic like the true Bedouin, they did travel about a great deal. At present the most probable explanation is that the Hapiru were associated generally with the donkey caravans which followed the great trade routes. The head caravaneers rode the lead donkeys while the drivers walked along with the loaded animals assigned to their care. Albright holds that *Apiru* means "Dusty Ones," thus explaining why their social status was quite low. When trade was poor and few caravans moving, the Hapiru had to look for other ways of making a living. Some took up robbery or smuggling, while others turned to warfare by hiring out as mercenary troops. Still others sold their freedom for the protection and security of slavery.

Ur, Center of Commerce

The city of Ur in Babylonia became the commercial capital of the Third Dynasty of Ur (about 2060-1955 B.C.). The main caravan route led northwest to Haran, on the Balikh River, in northern Syria. The name Haran is the Hebrew and English spelling of *Harran* ("Caravan City"), a most fitting designation for one of the major outposts of the whole caravan system. It was a stopover point on the route between Assyria (northeastern Mesopotamia) and Cappadocia (central Asia Minor) as well as the start of the route running southwest to Egypt. The chief god of the kings of Ur was the moon-god Sin, and the temple of Sin at Haran was probably built by them. This tremendous commercial empire collapsed for a few years when the Elamites swept in from the east (about 1955 B.C.) and conquered lower Babylonia. But the trade routes were restored during the Dynasty of Larsa, and they continued until after 1700 B.C.

Abraham and Caravans

It is exceedingly interesting that the Bible states that Terah left Ur with his son Abram (Abraham), his daughter-in-law Sarai (Sarah), and his grandson Lot, and that they settled in Haran. Perhaps Terah was involved with the caravan business and his move to the "Caravan City" was in the line of duty. In any case, it was there that Abraham received his call to go to the land of Canaan. He journeyed through the country until he came to the ancient holy place at Shechem. The inhabitants of the area were called *Bene Hamor* ("Sons of the Ass"), which probably meant that they were associated with donkey caravans. Moreover, Shechem was a key city in the caravan system because it controlled the east-west trade route running between Mt. Ebal and Mt. Gerizim, and the north-south route along the ridge of the Palestinian hill country. Other towns along this route to Egypt were Bethel, Hebron, and Beersheba, and the Genesis account tells us that Abraham spent some time at each place. Still another city where he spent a good deal of time was Gerar, in the southwestern part of Canaan. It was on the route running southeast from Gaza to the Arabian Peninsula.

In mourning over the fact that he was still childless, Abraham noted that the heir of his house was Eliezer of Damascus (Gen. 15:2). This is a strange bit of information because Damascus has not been mentioned previously in the narrative. How could anyone from that city be Abraham's heir? Although the biblical account does not tell us the precise route which Abraham took from Haran to Canaan, almost certainly he came through Damascus. It was the most important trade center en route to Egypt, and many caravan routes intersected there. In order to protect their investments ancient bankers or moneylenders used to be adopted into the family of the man receiving the loan, so that in case of the latter's premature death the banker would inherit the estate and thus be assured of recovering his principal and interest. It appears that Abraham needed funds for his activities in Palestine; therefore he borrowed from Eliezer in Damascus and as a guarantee of the loan he adopted him as heir.

Genesis 14 is a distinctive source which differs in many respects from the other narratives about Abraham. In verse 13 he is called "the *Ibri*," which has traditionally been spelled "Hebrew" in English translations. The original Mesopotamian form *Hapiru* (Egyptian *Apiru*) was later spelled *Habiru (Abiru)*, and from this came the designation Hebrew. Since this latter spelling had the same consonants as the verb "to cross over," the popular definition of a Hebrew was "one from beyond (the river)." It is significant, therefore, that when the Bible calls Abraham "the Hebrew" it is designating him as one of the Hapiru.

Another bit of evidence in this direction is the statement that when Abraham heard of Lot's capture he set out in pursuit with 318 "trained men, born in his house." Since the biblical narrative notes that Abraham had many flocks, tradition has conceived of him as a wealthy shepherd or herdsman wandering from place to place looking for more pasture land. It is doubtful that a herdsman would have such a large retinue. As William F. Albright has suggested, it is far more probable that Abraham needed such a large number of retainers to care for the donkeys and to supervise and guard his caravans.[1]

Another indication of Abraham's activity is the frequent mention of the Negev (spelled *Negeb* in most English translations). He was dwelling there when famine overtook the land, and from there he went down to sojourn in Egypt. After his return from Egypt he settled in the Negev for a while with his numerous flocks and herds (Gen. 13:1-2). When Hagar fled from Sarah's wrath she wandered in the wilderness toward Shur, where she found a spring of water. This well was near Qadesh-barnea, and here Isaac dwelt at a later time (Gen. 24:62; 25:11). After the destruction of Sodom, Abraham returned to the Negev, dwelling between Qadesh and Shur (Gen. 20:1). With the return of Sarah's jealousy, Hagar and Ishmael were sent out to wander in the wilderness of Beersheba (Gen. 21:14). It was from Beersheba that Abraham departed for Moriah, the land where he expected to sacrifice Isaac (Gen. 21:33; 22:2, 19).

All the references in the Abraham stories to the Negev and the wilderness seem very strange for a person with numerous flocks and herds to water. Some scholars have frankly rejected the information as secondary and unreliable. A series of archaeological surveys conducted by Nelson Glueck found evidence that various peoples occupied the Negev down through the centuries. Remains of many cisterns and several dams (some still holding water) witnessed to ancient attempts at preserving every possible drop of the six-to-ten-inch annual rainfall of this region. At numerous settlements discovered in the plains of the northern Negev around Beersheba and also in the highlands of the central Negev, extending down to Qadesh-barnea, the pottery was of a uniform type found elsewhere in the twentieth and nineteenth centuries B.C. Of equal importance is the fact that for many centuries preceding and following this period the Negev was largely uninhabited. No pottery from these earlier and later cultures has been found! Therefore, if the details of the biblical narrative are to be

---

[1] W. F. Albright, "Abram the Hebrew: A New Archaeological Interpretation," *Bulletin of the American Schools of Oriental Research,* 163 (October 1961), 36-54.

taken seriously, Abraham must be dated somewhere between 2000 and 1800 B.C.

The biblical record states that Abraham had some camels. If so, he was one of the first to domesticate the camel. After the great period of donkey caravans in the nineteenth century B.C. it was learned that hybrid mules were stronger and could carry larger loads. Gradually the horse was trained for use in caravans; but the ideal animal for caravans, especially for the shortcut routes through the desert, was the camel. Aside from a reference to camels as being among the domesticated animals of the Egyptians (Exod. 9:3), camels are not mentioned in the Bible between the Patriarchal stories in Genesis and the story of the camel-riding Midianites in Judges 6. It is quite possible that Abraham had some camels, but it is doubtful that he used them extensively in his caravans. The places mentioned in the Negev indicate that he took the route extending from Mamre (Hebron) in the southern hill country via Beer-sheba and Qadesh-barnea to Egypt. This inland trail across the northern part of the Sinai Peninsula was ideally suited for donkeys since there were many watering stations along the way and the donkeys could carry heavy loads over the rocky terrain. Camels, on the other hand, were suited for the sandy desert route along the Mediterranean coast where there were few good water holes. Had Abraham used this route the narrative would certainly have mentioned sites in the region of Gaza and the coast.

Further evidence for the tradition of the inland route is the fact that Jacob and his family "set out from Beer-sheba" (Gen. 46:5) on their journey to Egypt. As will be noted later, Moses apparently knew of this direct route because at Qadesh-barnea he instructed the spies, "Go up into the Negev yonder, and go up into the hill country" (Num. 13:17). In summary, the evidence seems to support the biblical claim that Abraham was a Hapiru (Hebrew). He probably earned his basic livelihood as a caravaneer. His reputation was so great his successors passed on the stories of his activities, and evidently they continued to be called Hebrews.

Why Did the Hebrews Come to Egypt?

Since the Nile River was fairly dependable in its annual

overflow, Egypt had far fewer periods of famine than the regions of Syria and Canaan. It was such a situation which caused Abraham to spend some time in Egypt, and the records of Egypt tell of many such periods when Semites from the Near East sought sustenance for themselves and their flocks there.

At times, however, Egypt suffered along with its Asiatic neighbors. The Bible tells of a severe famine which overtook all the Near East; but fortunately Joseph, a Hebrew, had been warned of it and the king of Egypt authorized him to store up food for the period of crop failure. News of food reached Canaan, and Jacob sent his sons there to get provisions. Joseph recognized his brothers and eventually made arrangements for his father and the whole family to reside in Egypt for a while.

How Many Hebrews Came to Egypt?

It is impossible to say with certainty how many of the biblical Hebrews were in Egypt originally. Genesis 46:5 states simply that Jacob came with his sons and their wives and children. Verses 6-7 (presumably from a different source) view the situation from the standpoint of Jacob's "offspring," that is, his sons, daughters, grandsons, and granddaughters (thus ruling out the wives of the sons and grandsons). The story continues in verse 28, and it is most likely that originally there was no attempt to give the number of the immigrant Hebrews. In time, however, there grew up the tradition that seventy descendants of Jacob came into Egypt. At that time the number 70 was used as a round number meaning "quite a few," but later tradition interpreted the number literally. Accordingly, a later editor inserted verses 8-27 in an attempt to name precisely the seventy who came to Egypt. The basic list he used named the descendants according to their mother. Thus the offspring of Jacob who came from Leah totaled thirty-three. Zilpah was credited with sixteen, Rachel with fourteen, and Bilhah with seven. The total comes to seventy, but a granddaughter and four great-grandsons of Jacob were included to reach the magic number.

The editor knew, however, that the list of Jacob's descendants was not accurate for the purpose intended in Genesis 46 because it included Judah's sons Er and Onan, who had died in Canaan, and Joseph and his two sons, who were already in Egypt. This left a total of sixty-five. On the other hand, the editor felt that Dinah, the daughter of Leah, should be included in the count. Therefore he added the statement, "All the persons belonging to Jacob, who came into Egypt, who were his own offspring, not including Jacob's sons' wives, were sixty-six persons in all" (Gen. 46:26). But this was not the end of the additions because someone else noted in verse 27 that if Jacob, Joseph, and his two sons were included, "all the persons of the house of Jacob, that came into Egypt, were seventy." Exodus 1:5 seems to stem from the tradition of the original list in Genesis 46 because it states, "All the offspring of Jacob were seventy persons."

It is clear that the number 70 has been superimposed on both the list of the descendants of Jacob and the list of the Hebrews who came into Egypt. It is an approximation at best because ancient genealogies tended to list only the males. It was the exceptional female who was considered worthy of mention. The combined list in the unit 8-25 includes only one daughter and one granddaughter, but there must have been many more since verse 7 refers specifically to daughters and granddaughters.

Where Did the Hebrews Settle in Egypt?

According to the biblical account, Joseph settled Jacob and his family in "the land of Goshen" (Gen. 45:10). It was a section suitable for flocks and herds, and apparently it was somewhat isolated from the centers of Egyptian population inasmuch as shepherds were "an abomination to the Egyptians" (Gen. 46:34). About fifty miles northeast of modern Cairo there is a valley called Wadi Tumilat. This fertile valley is about five to six miles wide and extends eastward about thirty miles to Ismailiah on Lake Timsah (now a part of the Suez Canal). There is every indication that this is the region in which the Hebrews lived. The Septuagint (the Greek translation of the Old Testament) was made in Egypt during the reign of the Greek Ptolemies, and in place of "the land of Goshen" there appears "the land of Gesem of Arabia." We normally think of the Arabian Desert as being the mammoth peninsula extending southeast of Palestine, but the classical geographers in the Greek and Roman periods called the part of Egypt east of the Nile River the Arabian Desert. One of the districts of northeast Egypt was called "Arabia," and so the translator of Genesis in the Septuagint was apparently equating Gesem with Goshen and locating it in the general region now called Wadi Tumilat.

When Did the Hebrews Settle in Goshen?

One line of evidence for dating the settlement in Goshen comes from the literary features of Genesis 37-50. The story of Joseph is decidedly different in character from the Patriarchal narratives, and this is apparent even in the English translations. The stories of the Patriarchs are usually condensed, and there are many archaic elements in the text. The Joseph story, however, is very long and in good Hebrew prose. In 1959 J. Vergote published his study of the Joseph narrative, and he showed conclusively that the story was accurate in its use of Egyptian names and customs. He was inclined to date Joseph in the fourteenth century B.C. and to assign the formation of the story in the thirteenth century. There were probably later revisions because the present form of the story seems to date from the tenth century B.C. The question, then, is whether the composition in the thirteenth century was relatively near the events described, or whether it was a more or less modernized form of an ancient narrative which had been passed on by oral tradition. In short, the argument from the literary evidence must be checked by other sets of data.

The fact of Joseph's sudden rise to power as the second in command in Egypt has led other scholars to associate Joseph with the Hyksos, an Egyptian term meaning "Rulers of Foreign Countries." These invaders were apparently mixed in racial origin, but according to the names which happened to be recorded most of the leaders were Semitic. They came from Syria-Palestine about 1730 B.C. and conquered Egypt with ease since they had the latest and best equipment for war: horse-drawn chariots and powerful composite bows. The Hyksos settled in the northeastern part of Egypt and their capital Avaris (known as Zoan in Hebrew and Tanis in Greek) was located about twenty-five miles north of Wadi Tumilat. An editorial comment in

Numbers 13:22 states, "Hebron was built seven years before Zoan in Egypt." Inasmuch as Hebron was adjacent to Mamre, one of the towns where Abraham lived, and where he was buried, it is very difficult to account for the detailed information of the editorial note without recognizing that there must have been some kind of contact between the Hebrews and the Hyksos. It is much easier to account for Joseph's rise to power if the king was a Hyksos and not a native Egyptian. Furthermore, when Joseph informed his father and brothers that they would be in the land of Goshen he commented, "and you shall be near me" (Gen. 45:10). In other words, Joseph's administrative center was near Goshen. This was true of the Hyksos capital Avaris, but not of Memphis and Thebes, the administrative centers of the Egyptians.

The Date of Abraham

A related factor in dating Joseph is consideration of the biblical data concerning the time spans back to Abraham and forward to Moses. During the years 1925-1931 excavations at Nuzi, east of the Tigris River, unearthed clay tablets with Hurrian (biblical Horite) records and laws dating from the fifteenth century B.C. Since customs noted in these tablets have clarified many obscure passages in the Abraham narratives, some scholars have jumped to the conclusion that Abraham lived between 1500 and 1400 B.C. But customary law at Nuzi could well have had its origin much earlier in Mesopotamia. The archaic names in the Abraham stories come from the period of 1900 B.C. and following. Moreover, it has been pointed out above that the episodes about Abraham in Ur, Haran, and the Negev fit into the period 2000-1800 B.C. and not later.

Although caution must be exercised in using figures noted in Genesis, the biblical tradition states that it was 215 years from Abraham's entry into Canaan until Jacob went to Egypt. If this total is added to 1720 (the approximate time of Joseph), it indicates that Abraham's entry into Canaan was about 1935 B.C. While this date should not be pressed too far, it is fairly close to the period toward which most of the data about Abraham point.

In choosing between the early or late date for Abraham there is a basic principle of logic: it is far easier to explain how ancient features and details of Abraham's time could have been maintained at later times than it is to explain how later scribes could have antiqued a story by incorporating details which fit a historical context centuries prior to the composition of the narrative. Some later *ideas* have been projected back by the biblical writers, but this is far different from the minute archaeological and linguistic details which are embedded in the Abraham narratives. Ancient scribes did not do such minute research as is carried on today, and it is virtually certain that the network of accurate data about Abraham stems from the nineteenth century B.C.

How Long Were the Hebrews in Egypt?

There are two statements in the Bible which relate to the period of the Hebrew sojourn in Egypt. In a vision Yahweh informs Abraham that his descendants "will be oppressed for four hundred years" (Gen. 15:13). Exodus 12:40 notes, "The time that the people of Israel dwelt in Egypt was four hundred and thirty years." Some scholars have rejected this information on the grounds that the genealogical lists usually have only four generations from those who came into Egypt to those who left in the Exodus (for example, Levi, Kohath, Amram, and Moses). But there is the interesting statement in Genesis 15:16 that the oppressed descendants of Abraham would return to Palestine "in the fourth *dor*." The Hebrew word *dor* has usually been translated "generation," but this gives the impression that the narrative is confused. On the contrary, *dor* and its Semitic cognates mean primarily "duration, time span, age," and only secondarily do they mean "generation." Apparently the text was originally understood to mean "in the fourth life span." In the light of this fact the reference to 400 years makes tolerable sense. It should also be pointed out that while many of the genealogies have only four names from the period of Jacob to that of Moses, some list from seven to ten names. In other words, it is quite probable that the lists are selective. It may be that the preference for four names was due to later editors taking *dor* to mean "generation" instead of "life span."

It is recognized that 430 years is a very long time for the Hebrews to have stayed in Egypt, but there is some nonbiblical evidence supporting this claim. Excavations at Avaris (Tanis) uncovered a stele (upright stone monument) with an inscription by a vizier named Sethos commemorating the four hundredth anniversary of the rule of the Egyptian god Seth as king. Since Seth was adopted as the god of the Hyksos, the stele probably celebrates the founding of Tanis as well. The vizier later became Sethos I, who reigned as king of Egypt about 1316-1304 B.C. Projecting back 400 years would date the building of Avaris about 1730-1720 B.C., the proposed date for Joseph. It could well be that the Hebrews knew of this memorial or the calculation involved, and that the extra thirty years took account of the time from the erection of the stele until the exodus from Egypt. In any case, it is interesting that the various lines of evidence tend to support the biblical figure of 430 years.

It should be noted that in Exodus 12:40 the Septuagint translation reads, "The time that the people of Israel dwelt in Egypt and in the land of Canaan was four hundred and thirty years." Apparently the translator was allowing the traditional 215 years for the stay in Canaan and another 215 years for the sojourn in Egypt. It is tempting to adopt the Septuagint figure for the stay in Egypt because 215 years seems far more reasonable, but the problem is not settled quite that easily. The burden of proof is on the scholar who accepts the shorter period. This means that all the data pertaining to the Joseph and Abraham periods must be relocated in other historical contexts where the biblical data fit. This is indeed a difficult task, and all attempts thus far have had to ignore or twist certain elements of biblical evidence.

Enslavement of the Hebrews

The peace and prosperity of the Hebrews continued until "there arose a new king over Egypt, who did not know Joseph" (Exod. 1:8). The implication is not simply the rise of another king, but the beginning of another dynasty or kingly succession which had no knowledge of Joseph, or which refused to grant the Hebrews special status. The rule of the Hyksos came to an end about 1550 B.C. when Amosis I gained control. It is highly probable that this native Egyptian, who founded the Eighteenth Dynasty, was the new king who did not know Joseph. He certainly had every reason to be suspicious of a group of people who had been favored by the Hyksos. He could well have said, "Come, let us deal shrewdly with them, lest they multiply, and, if war befall us, they join our enemies and fight against us and escape from the land" (Exod. 1:10).

Verse 11 poses a problem, however, because after noting that taskmasters were put over the Hebrews the text states that the people built the store-cities Pithom and Raamses for the Pharaoh. This could not have been true for Amosis I and his successors because the Eighteenth Dynasty Pharaohs hated the memory of the Hyksos so much they considered the region around Avaris as more or less desecrated, and there is no evidence that these kings had any major building operations in this part of Egypt.

It was a different story, on the other hand, with the Nineteenth Dynasty. Ramses (also spelled Ramesses) I, the founder of the Dynasty, had some affinity for the Hyksos, and it seems that his lineage involved some mixed marriages between the Hyksos and Egyptians. In any case, he and his son Sethos I did not have the aversion to the Avaris region, and so they began reconstruction of the towns and moved their capital there. The major building activity there, however, came during the early part of the long, powerful reign of Ramses II (1304-1237 B.C.).

The narrative in Exodus 1:8-11 seems to relate events fairly close together; therefore if Sethos I is taken as the oppressive king who built Pithom and Raamses, Ramses I would appear to be the king who did not know Joseph. But this interpretation of the passage fails to explain why a dynasty of kings with some attachment to the Hyksos would be ignorant of Joseph and the Hebrews, while the previous dynasty, with its hatred of the Hyksos and suspicion of the Hebrews, would have left them unmolested. It would seem wiser to designate Amosis I as the Pharaoh who did not know Joseph, Ramses I and Sethos I as the builders of Pithom and Raamses, and Ramses II as the Pharaoh of the Exodus. This implies that the biblical text passes over other Eighteenth Dynasty kings (for example, Tuthmosis III and Amenophis III) who also were probably oppressive with the Hebrews, and thus the story moves immediately into the historical context of Moses.

The Location of Pithom and Raamses

The name Pithom derives from the Egyptian designation *Per-Atum* ("House of Atum"), later pronounced *Pitom*. The god Atum or Tum was a form of the sun-god. There are two major sites in Wadi Tumilat: Tell er-Retabeh, toward the west, and Tell el-Maskhutah, to the east. The latter is the largest mound of ancient ruins east of Raamses (Tanis), and some scholars consider this site to be ancient Pithom. Others, however, locate Pithom at Tell er-Retabeh, and in turn they designate Tell el-Maskhutah as ancient Succoth (Egyptian *Tjeku* or *Theku*). The evidence from Egyptian records is very complex and somewhat ambiguous. Some scholars feel that Succoth was the designation for a district as well as a city. While the debate is interesting, it is not necessary for us to settle the matter here. In either case, Pithom is located in Wadi Tumilat, the biblical land of Goshen.

Raamses is clearly the Hebrew designation for the Egyptian name *Per(Pi)-Ramses* ("House of Ramses"). Most scholars consider this site to be Ramses' reconstruction of the Hyksos capital Avaris. Excavations at the thirty-two-acre site (which has been identified also with biblical Zoan, Greek *Tanis*) have unearthed the ruins of a mammoth temple and some gigantic obelisks. Apparently only the great capital complex at Thebes (the southern capital used by the Eighteenth Dynasty Pharaohs) surpassed Per-Ramses in splendor. But here again there is a dispute. Some scholars prefer to locate Per-Ramses near the modern village of Qantir where a palace of Ramses II has been excavated. Others contend that since Qantir is only twelve miles south of Tanis, the whole area was considered Per-Ramses with the palace at Qantir and the administrative and religious buildings at Raamses (Tanis). Recent excavations just south-southwest of Qantir have unearthed a site which may be Avaris, the original Hyksos capital. Notwithstanding the uncertainty concerning the identification of these sites, all of them are relatively close to each other and there is no problem in accepting the biblical claim that the Hebrews were used as state slaves. Moreover, the broad

outlines of the historical situation are clear. A few years
prior to 1300 B.C. the Pharaohs of the Nineteenth Egyptian
Dynasty began extensive building operations in the region
of Avaris and the land of Goshen. It was this fact that
enabled the P tradition of the Joseph story to modernize
the text by calling this area "the land of Ramses" (Gen.
47:11). This same understanding is found in Psalm 78:12
where the Hebrews are located "in the plain (fields) of
Zoan (Tanis)."

Hebrews and Apiru

Earlier in Palestine the Hebrews turned more and more
from caravaneering to other pursuits such as animal hus-
bandry. Thus Jacob and his family settled in the land of
Goshen because they had flocks and herds. Egyptian records
of the fifteenth century B.C. refer to Apiru in the Delta
region of the Nile who tended vineyards and made wine.
While these groups were not necessarily Israelites, they
were Asiatics or Semites who had become state slaves of
the Egyptians. It is quite possible that in the process of time
the Hebrews in the Goshen area also took up this occupation. Memory of the relation between donkey caravaneering
and wine making may be preserved in the old blessing given
to Judah: "He tethers his donkey to a vine, his purebred
colt to the choice vine" (Gen. 49:11).

From about 1550 to 1450 B.C. the Egyptians worked
copper and turquoise mines at Serabit el-Khadim in the
Sinai Peninsula. The laborers were state slaves with a mixed
Semitic-Egyptian culture. There was a temple to the Egyptian goddess Hathor, who was called "The Mistress of Turquoise," and one of the gods worshiped by the slaves was
Tirshu (Hebrew *tirosh,* "wine") ("The Lord of the Wine
Press"). Inscriptions carved in rocks of the area are in
a western Semitic dialect, indicating that these slaves were
similar in ethnic origin to the Apiru in Egypt proper. It is
clear, therefore, that the Eighteenth Dynasty kings had
many state slaves, and almost certainly the Hebrews in the
land of Goshen did not escape these oppressive measures.
The massive building program of Ramses II meant the continuation of slavery, and so his records have numerous
references to Apiru, some of which were used as transport
workers. Whether the biblical Hebrews were part of these

Apiru is uncertain, but at least they experienced the same misery as the other Apiru.

How Many Tribes Were in Egypt?

According to biblical tradition Jacob had twelve sons and all of them came to live in Egypt. Inasmuch as Jacob's name was changed to Israel the standard biblical designation for his descendants is "the children of Israel." But there are portions of the Old Testament which indicate that the actual events were not quite as simple and neat as the normative biblical tradition suggests. Usually Ephraim is described as one of the sons of Joseph, and thus a grandson of Jacob. Ephraim is said to have been born in Egypt (Gen. 41:52), and the presumption is that he died there. Yet in a genealogy of the Ephraimite tribe (1 Chron. 7:20-27) there is a little narrative about Ephraim's daughter who was responsible for founding the towns of Lower and Upper Bethhoron. These were in Palestine in the territory which the tribe of Ephraim was to occupy during the time of Joshua. The implication is that the towns were built during the lifetime of the tribal Patriarch Ephraim. Clearly the events are prior to the conquest described in the book of Joshua because nine generations later Joshua, the son of Nun, is listed.

One can say with the older liberals that Chronicles is late and the information is not trustworthy, but more recent investigation has shown that the compiler of the books of Chronicles used ancient sources, even some which the Samuel-Kings history had not utilized. If, as the evidence seems to indicate, this bit of information is correct, then there was a man in Palestine named Ephraim and from him a clan began. There is no indication that any of this group went down into Egypt. Perhaps Joseph named his second son after the man back in Canaan.

In Genesis 34 Jacob's sons Simeon and Levi are given credit for the capture of Shechem. Two men could not have taken such an important town by themselves. Most certainly it was the *tribes* of Simeon and Levi that conquered the city. Genesis 48:22 seems to speak of the same event, and yet Israel (Jacob) tells Joseph that he took Shechem with his sword and bow. The formation and development of the various Hebrew tribes was a long, complex process, and we have only tantalizing bits of information about what actually happened.

The tribe of Levi, for example, was originally a very warlike tribe. They were involved in the capture of Shechem, and when Jacob left his testament with the various tribes he cursed the fierce anger of Levi (Gen. 49:5-7). In the early days they were in no sense a priestly tribe, and they were listed along with the other tribes which came from Leah: Reuben, Simeon, Levi, Judah, Zebulun, and Issachar (Gen. 35:23). Later on when Levi assumed the priestly function, the tribe could not be counted with the others, and so there were only eleven tribes. This raised a problem, however, because the ancient world used the sexagesimal system of mathematics (based on the number 60) and many cultures had federations of twelve or six tribes. Inasmuch as the Hebrews shared this view, another tribe had to be added to make a twelve-tribe league. The problem was solved by having Jacob adopt Joseph's sons Manasseh and Ephraim as his own sons (Gen. 48:5). Accordingly, whereas Joseph is listed as a single tribe when Levi is included, Manasseh and Ephraim are raised to the status of full tribes when Levi assumes the priestly duties. But this shift did not completely solve the problem either. When Levi was set aside as a special group this meant that the old six-tribe federation of Leah was reduced to five. To maintain the conventional number 6, Gad, the son of Zilpah (Leah's maid), was pulled up and listed in Levi's place (Num. 26:15).

In the biblical account of the conquest of Canaan by the Israelites there is a reference to a southern campaign in the territory later occupied by Benjamin and Judah, and then an expedition up north against Hazor, but there is absolute silence about the central part of the country. This is the territory occupied by the Joseph tribes, Manasseh and Ephraim, and it appears that they moved into the area without a fight. Shechem, the ancient caravan center and holy place, was located in Manasseh, and excavations at the site have found no destruction level dating from the thirteenth century B.C. It was at Shechem that all the tribes gathered before Joshua in order to renew the covenant with Yahweh, and there also that the mummy of Joseph was buried in a field purchased by Jacob. Joshua was buried in Timnath-serah in the hill country of Ephraim, and Shiloh, where a sanctuary and the ark were located, was in Ephraim. It can be said that the twelve-tribe confederacy or amphictyony centered in the hill country of Ephraim and Manasseh.

It is indeed strange that the Bible makes no mention of this area in the story of the Israelite conquest. It is hardly possible that the Israelites would have forgotten about military action in this area had they been involved in such a campaign. In short, some other explanation must be found to account for the biblical evidence.

The Apiru in Canaan

About 1550 B.C., when the Hyksos control of Egypt was broken, Amosis I extended his control throughout Canaan, destroying most of the major cities, Shechem included. From that time on, the local rulers (sometimes called "kings" as in the book of Joshua) were under Egyptian supervision and control. A number of these petty kings wrote letters to their Egyptian overlords affirming their own loyalty, but complaining about other rulers who threatened the stability of the region. One of the main topics of these Amarna Letters (written about 1380-1350 B.C.) was the threat posed by the Apiru, especially in the central hill country. Their leader was Labayu, and Shechem (which came under his control) may have been his capital. His sons succeeded him and kept the region in turmoil. It is no accident that the precise area controlled by the Apiru is the area which is passed over in silence in the narrative of the conquest. In other words, the Israelites did not have to fight for the area because some of their relatives were already there.

There is no direct evidence to show how they got there. Perhaps some of the descendants of the Ephraimites who stayed in Canaan were part of Labayu's forces. On the other hand, it is hardly likely that all the members of the various tribes remained in Egypt after the threat of famine was over. There was constant contact between Palestine and Egypt during the Hyksos period because they controlled both areas, and the same was true of the Egyptians during the Eighteenth and Nineteenth Dynasties. Perhaps some members of the Hebrew tribes shuttled back and forth during their lifetime depending on which area offered the most advantages.

The Sons of Israel

In various passages in Genesis and Exodus the Hebrews in Egypt are called literally "the sons of Israel." The expression is translated in some versions as "the children of Israel," and "the people of Israel" in others. This designation stemmed from the traditional belief that all twelve tribes were in Egypt and that the patriarchs of the tribes were the literal sons of Jacob, whose name was changed to Israel.

As noted above, it is quite clear that some of the Hebrews were in Canaan and some in Egypt. A number of the tribal names have forms which were common in the eighteenth century B.C., and there is every reason to believe that members of these groups resided in Egypt for a while. But it is impossible to state with certainty how many of the twelve early tribes had representatives in Egypt during the oppressive reign of Sethos I.

Martin Noth contends that "Israel" was the designation of the precise twelve-tribe amphictyony which was formed at Shechem when Joshua presided over the covenant ceremony binding the people to Yahweh.[2] His major contention is that some of the tribal names developed at a later period, and so they could not have been known earlier. Ephraim, for example, is a place name, according to Noth, and not a personal name.[3] Therefore, the tribe must have taken its name from the hilly country called Mt. Ephraim, the region in which it lived. This is a rather strong argument but, as noted above, there is some biblical evidence that people from a group called Ephraim were in Palestine while the Hebrews were in Egypt. Some scholars, accordingly, still contend that the region got its name from the tribe.

William F. Albright takes a more moderate view concerning the formation of Israel. He suggests that the twelve tribes were formed at Mt. Sinai when Moses, at the sug-

---

[2] Martin Noth, *The History of Israel*, 2nd ed. (New York: Harper, 1960), pp. 91-93.

[3] *Ibid.*, p. 60.

gestion of Jethro, his father-in-law, organized the people into groups (Exod. 18:21).[4]

Most certainly some of the descendants of Israel, the Patriarch, were in Egypt, and in a broad sense one can speak of the Hebrews as "the sons of Israel" or "the Israelites." Yet it is equally clear from biblical evidence that some of the refugees at the Exodus were from oppressed groups other than the biblical Hebrews. It was this "mixed multitude" (Exod. 12:38) which was organized by Moses. Most of those who went through the Exodus and Sinai experiences died in the wilderness, and so their children had, in many instances, to accept those events on the basis of their testimony. At Shechem other groups of Hebrews were absorbed into the covenant, and evidently the process continued, so that all along the line there were additions to the people of Israel. In fact, then, God's covenant people were in a fellowship, and most of them entered literally "on confession of faith." Later on the racial lines were drawn tight, but in the earlier years the concept of a pure race was not a concern of the people of God.

Noth and Albright stress two different stages in the long development of the people called Israel; and if the expression "the sons of Israel" is understood in a broad sense, one can apply it to the early stage, the Hebrews in Egypt.

It is unfortunate that no records have come down to us about the 430-year stay in Egypt. There must have been many changes, and yet there must have been a continuity which preserved the stories of the past, otherwise our Bible would never have had the book of Genesis. The important fact is that Yahweh was faithful to his covenant with Abraham, and therefore he liberated the enslaved Hebrews in Egypt in order that they might return to Canaan, rejoin their brethren, and as a united group make a covenant to do his will.

---

[4] Albright, *The Biblical Period from Abraham to Ezra* (New York: Harper, 1963), pp. 33-34.

Chapter 3

Moses — the Prince and the Fugitive

According to the biblical tradition, one of the fears of the Pharaoh who did not know Joseph (Amosis I) was that there were "too many" Hebrews. A large minority on the very edge of the northeastern border of Egypt posed a real security problem, especially in the event that another enemy like the Hyksos should come out of Syria-Palestine. Various Pharaohs set the Hebrews to oppressive tasks in order to break their spirit and in turn to minimize their growth in numbers. Sethos I had them build Pithom and Raamses, "But the more they were oppressed, the more they multiplied" (Exod. 1:12).

Male Hebrew Babies Ordered Slain

The next part of the drama is described in 1:15-21, a unit usually assigned to the E source. Here the ruler of Egypt is called "king," and not "Pharaoh." He attempts to solve the problem by dealing personally with the Hebrew midwives Shiphrah ("Beauty") and Puah ("Splendor"). Somehow he has the impression that they will obey him, and so he requests that all boys be slain on the birthstool, but that the girls be spared. The midwives fear God *(Elohim)* more than the king, therefore they spare the boys as well as the girls. On learning of this fact the king calls the midwives and demands an answer. The Hebrew women, so they report, are more vigorous than the Egyptian women, and before a midwife can get there the child is born. Nothing is said concerning the king's reaction, but the implication is that he is satisfied because attention shifts to God's reward of "daughters" to the midwives.

It should be noted in passing that since the names of the midwives are Semitic in form, and since the name Puah is found in the fourteenth-century Ugaritic tablets, this part of the story has an authentic ring. At the same time, however, the implication of this source is that the number of the Hebrews was not very large because two midwives could care for the newborn children.

Traditionally, 1:22 has been interpreted as the king's drastic second attempt to slay the male babies inasmuch as he has been foiled by the midwives. From the standpoint of literary features, however, verse 22 is related to 2:1-10. It serves as the basis for the story of Moses' birth, and throughout this unit (usually attributed to J) the Egyptian ruler is called "Pharaoh," not "king." All the Egyptians are commanded to cast any male Hebrew babies into the Nile. The directive is rather unexpected because there were so many other more efficient ways of accomplishing Pharaoh's purpose. Nevertheless, such an order would have been feasible since at that time the eastern branch of the Nile passed just west of the land of Goshen.

The Birth and Rescue of Moses

Notwithstanding the differences in details and points of view of the J and E sources, the clear-cut fact is that any newborn Hebrew male was in danger of having his life snuffed out. This is true whether one interprets the two accounts as successive measures of Pharaoh, or whether they are two traditions about Pharaoh's determined attempt at genocide. What trauma there must have been at the birth of every child! A young couple, both from the house of Levi, came up to their moment of truth. Due to his patriarchal culture, in which the males were primary in matters of lineage and inheritance, the husband must have had an unconscious yearning for a son; but fear probably transformed that desire into a wish for a daughter. The joy which would normally have come with the news "You have a son!" was now suppressed with the shadow of death. But the boy was a beautiful child and the mother decided to hide him.

Yet one can hide a healthy, crying child just about so long, and so after three months Moses' mother took "a basket made of bulrushes, and daubed it with bitumen and pitch; and she put the child in it and placed it among the reeds at the river's bank" (Exod. 2:3). She knew that this eastern branch of the Nile ran north, passing along the western edge of Sethos' palace grounds and capital. Perhaps someone would hear the child crying and take care of him. The anxious mother had Moses' sister follow the small ark to see what would happen. Little did the mother realize that Pharaoh's daughter would come to bathe in the Nile that day. This situation must have caused a lump to come in the throat of Moses' sister — "What if the princess finds the basket and recognizes that the baby is a Hebrew?"

As her fears were realized she came closer rather than running away. When she saw that Pharaoh's daughter had pity on the crying baby, even though she knew it was a Hebrew child, she inquired whether she should get a Hebrew woman to nurse him. The idea sounded good to the princess and she told the girl to do so. There was only one Hebrew woman who should nurse the boy and that was his mother. Accordingly, Moses' mother came to get the child, and the princess said, "Take this child away, and nurse him for me, and I will give you your wages" (2:9). Notwithstanding the royal order to slay the newborn Hebrew males, the princess had decided to adopt the beautiful boy. His life would be spared and his mother would have him back for a little while, even being paid for rearing her own son.

It should be observed that in this fascinating story the names of the parents and the sister of Moses are not given. Had the original composer known the names he would most likely have used them. It is a notation in Exodus 6:20 (a P source) which states that Amram and Jochebed were the parents of Moses and Aaron, and it is not until Exodus 15:20 that Miriam is identified as the sister of Aaron, and thus implicitly as the girl who walked along the bank of the Nile. The quick shift in Exodus 2 from verse 1 to 2 implies that Moses was the first child, but according to Exodus 7:7 Aaron was three years older than Moses, and Miriam must have been older still if she watched the basket and made the suggestion to the princess. Tradition made the association between the anonymous characters in chapter 2 and the names of Moses' parents and sister. While there is no clear-cut evidence to disprove the association, the interpretive process would be much easier had the story in Exodus 2 used specific names.

The Birth of Sargon I

Another factor which must be considered in the interpretation of the story is the fact that over a thousand years before Moses there was another famous Semite, Sargon I, who was saved from death by being placed in a basket on the Euphrates River. The legend concerning Sargon's birth relates how his mother, due to some unknown change in status, had to bear him in secret and then to put him on the Euphrates in a basket of bulrushes sealed with bitumen. The river carried the baby boy downstream where Akki, the drawer of water, noticed the basket and rescued Sargon. Akki took him as his son and reared him. Later on he was assigned by Akki to care for the garden, and it was there that Ishtar, the moon-goddess, noticed him and granted him her love.

In spite of many differences in detail, the similarities between the birth stories of Sargon and Moses are obvious. In view of this fact, most Old Testament scholars believe that after Moses became famous the account about the basket on the river was inserted into the story about Moses on the grounds that such a person of destiny must have had a remarkable beginning similar to that of Sargon. The technical name for this process is "aetiology." This term (deriving from the Greek word *aitia*, "cause") means the attempt to give an explanation why certain things were true. In answer to the query "Why was Moses so important?" someone suggested that he must have had a miraculous beginning like Sargon I. This line of reasoning is certainly possible since the ancestors of Moses came from Mesopotamia and they could well have retained this remarkable story in their tradition. On the other hand, if Moses' parents knew of this tradition it is equally possible that they would resort to the same method in order to save their son. There is insufficient evidence to be dogmatic either way; therefore a decisive judgment on the issue must be understood to be a *value judgment* made on the basis of the critic's presuppositions.

The Meaning of the Name "Moses"

Moses was weaned by his mother and then returned to Pharaoh's daughter as her adopted son. The princess named the boy "Moses" because she had "drawn him out of the water" (2:10). This is another form of aetiology known as "popular etymology." The Hebrew form of the name Moses is *Mosheh,* and since it is very similar to the Hebrew verb *mashah* ("to draw out"), the rescue of Moses from the Nile is taken as the reason for the name.

The Hebrew Bible is filled with popular etymologies. The original form of the name Babylon was *Bab-ilu* ("The gate of the god"). In Hebrew it became *Babel.* Inasmuch as the infamous tower described in Genesis 11 was there, the biblical editor noted, "Therefore its name was called Babel, because there Yahweh confused the language of all the earth" (vs. 9). The Hebrew word *balbel,* another form of *balal* ("to confuse"), was considered close enough to *Babel* to have a cause and effect relationship, even though there is no true relationship between the two words. An even more extreme case of popular etymology is 1 Chronicles 4:9. A mother names her son Jabez because she "bore him in pain." The Hebrew word for "pain" is *oseb,* and Jabez is actually *Yabes* in Hebrew. The letters "s" and "b" are interchanged in the two words, and yet popular etymology was not stopped by such a minor difficulty. The ancient mind reasoned that there was an explanation for every name, and if the meaning was not explicit some well-intentioned scribe could always find one.

The real question in the case of Moses is whether the popular etymology is an example of primary aetiology (the whole story created to explain the name Moses), or whether the aetiology is secondary (Moses was actually rescued from the Nile, but then the event employed to explain the name). Here again it is difficult to speak with dogmatism, but in either case it is virtually certain that the name Moses is the Egyptian form *mose* (earlier *mase*) ("is born"). Inasmuch as the name Tuthmosis, for example, means "(The god) Toth is born," the original name of Moses must have been longer. Perhaps when he threw his lot in with his own people he dropped the name of the Egyptian god. However, even the Egyptians of Moses' time shortened this type of name to "Mose." Had the editor of Exodus 2 known the true meaning of Moses' name he would most likely have given it. Another indication of the secondary nature of the popular etymology is that it depends on knowledge of the Hebrew language. The implication is that the

Egyptian princess was an expert in Hebrew, but this is doubtful.

Moses — An Egyptian Prince

The biblical story jumps from the naming of Moses (2:10) to a time when Moses has "grown up" and decided to visit his own people, the Hebrews. There is no indication how old he was at the time, but the story implies that he was a young man, probably in his twenties. A later tradition, which was current in the New Testament Church at the time of Stephen, thought that Moses was forty years old at the time (Acts 7:23). This interpretation is most certainly a guess based on the idea that the three phases of Moses' life were about equal in length. Since he is reported to have died at 120 and he spent forty years wandering with the Israelites, that would mean he was a prince in the court of Pharaoh's daughter about forty years and a sojourner in Midian for another forty.

Another tradition from the first century A.D. was that "Moses was instructed in all the wisdom of the Egyptians, and he was mighty in his words and deeds" (Acts 7:22). It is doubtful that this statement was based on any primary source material stemming from the period of Moses. More than likely it is an inference from the biblical narrative that the Egyptian princess took Moses and reared him. It is certainly nearer the truth than the assumption that Moses was forty when he went to visit his people.

Regardless of his exact age, Moses is pictured as a young adult. He must have had years of training in the language, customs, literature, and art of the Egyptians. He knew that he was a Hebrew and evidently he learned his mother's tongue as well. It is reasonable to assume, furthermore, that due to the international character of the court Moses learned other languages and much about the geography of the great empire controlled by the Egyptians.

Moses Kills an Egyptian

In spite of his royal position and training, blood was "thicker than water" and Moses could not resist paying a visit to his own people. While on his inspection tour he saw the oppressive measures the Hebrews were under. When he found an Egyptian taskmaster beating (Hebrew verb *hikkah*) a Hebrew, probably to death, he could control his sense of justice no longer. Moses looked both ways to see whether anyone was watching, and when he thought he was in the clear he slew (Hebrew verb *hikkah*) the Egyptian.

This story implies a good deal about Moses. Not only did he have a deep sense of loyalty to his own people, but he had a burning sense of justice. He was a volatile man of action, therefore he took justice into his own hands. Apparently he felt he could handle the tough Egyptian overlord because as a prince he was in excellent physical condition and he knew the latest methods of warfare and hand-to-hand combat.

Moses must have had a strong ego as well, because the flush of victory pulled him back the next day. He had removed one threat to his people and perhaps he could be of assistance again. This time, however, he found two Hebrews fighting. He stopped the fight and asked the offender why he had started the brawl. But Moses, the mediator, was jolted with two questions: "Who made you a prince and a judge over us? Do you mean to kill me as you killed the Egyptian?" (2:14). In that moment the confidence of the self-appointed judge turned into cowardice. His sense of justice and his concern for his own people vanished as fear seized him. One of his own people knew his "secret" and soon Pharaoh would too. He would have to flee for his life!

Moses and the Tale of Sinuhe

In typically crisp fashion the biblical narrative states, "Moses fled from Pharaoh, and stayed in the land of Midian" (2:15). Nothing is said about the difficulties involved in his escape, but we can get some idea from the story of a fugitive many centuries before Moses.

The first of the great kings of the Twelfth Dynasty in Egypt was Amenemhet (Amenemmes) I, about 1990-1960 B.C. During the last decade or so of his reign his coregent was his son Senusert (Sesostris) I, about 1971-1928. Nefru, the daughter of Amenemhet and wife of Senusert, had an attendant named Sinuhe. On one occasion Sinuhe accompanied Senusert on a military expedition against the Libyans to the west of Egypt. While the army was returning from this campaign, King Amenemhet died. News was rushed to Senusert in order that he might return to the capital and secure his throne before some pretender learned of the death. Sinuhe happened to be near enough to overhear the message. As attendant to Nefru he had had close contact with both rulers and there should have been no anxiety on his part, but apparently he had done something which he thought would displease Senusert and he feared that in the transfer of power he would be imprisoned or slain. "My heart was distraught," he said, "my arms spread out in dismay, trembling fell upon all my limbs. I removed myself by leaps and bounds to seek a hiding place for myself. I placed myself between two bushes, in order to cut myself off from the road and its travel."[1]

Sinuhe worked his way back along the western edge of the Delta, and crossed the Nile at a point near the site of modern Cairo. Then he fled northeast, probably skirting along what is now Wadi Tumilat, until he came to the "Wall of the Ruler," a line of fortresses at the eastern border, approximately where the Suez Canal is located. Sinuhe reports, "I came up to the Wall of the Ruler, made to oppose the Asiatics and to crush the Sand-Crossers. I took a crouching position in a bush for fear lest the watchmen upon the wall where their day's duty was might see me."[2] He moved on in the evening, and at daybreak he was past the forts and in the eastern part of the Bitter Lakes region. "An attack of thirst overtook me. I was parched, and my throat was dusty. I said, 'This is the taste of death!' "[3] As he was at the point of despair he heard some cattle lowing, and on inspection he found a band of Asiatics. The sheikh recognized him, gave him a drink of water, and took him to his tribe. He was passed from tribe to tribe until finally he settled with Ammi-enshi, a ruler in Syria. Sinuhe married his eldest daughter, had a number of children, and became the ruler of a tribe in a very fertile portion of the country. Years later Senusert heard about Sinuhe's success, urged him to return to Egypt, and restored him as a courtier among the nobles.

---

[1] James B. Pritchard, ed., *Ancient Near Eastern Texts Relating to the Old Testament*, 3rd ed. (Princeton: Princeton Univ., 1969), p. 19.

[2] *Ibid.*

[3] *Ibid.*

The Location of Midian

Although the stories of Sinuhe and Moses do not end
the same way, there are many similarities between them.
Moses too must have had a difficult time escaping past the
line of fortresses at the eastern border. Once they were past
the danger point, however, they took different routes. Sinuhe
worked his way up through Palestine, but Moses stayed
clear of that area because Egyptian officials were too plentiful there. Rather, he fled to Midian. If only the narrative
had specified the precise location in relation to known geographical areas it would have made much scholarly debate
unnecessary. Midian proper was east of the Gulf of Aqaba,
in the northern section of Hejaz in Arabia, but there is
evidence that some of the Midianite clans crossed over the
Arabah (the great valley south of the Dead Sea) at the
head of the Gulf of Aqaba and settled in the eastern and
southern sections of the Sinai Peninsula.

Moses Marries Zipporah

While Moses was resting by a well in Midian, seven girls
came there, drew water, and filled troughs to water their
father's flock. Then shepherds arrived and drove the girls
and their flock away in order to water their own thirsty
flocks. Moses, with his sense of justice, came to the rescue
of the girls. His prowess as a warrior must have been outstanding because he took on the shepherds (maybe with
the help of the girls) and routed them. That job done, he
drew water and finished watering the girls' flock.

On arriving home their astonished father, the priest of
Midian, wanted to know why they had been able to return
so soon, and so they explained what the "Egyptian" had
done for them. "And where is he?" said the father. "Why
have you left the man? Call him, that he may eat bread"
(2:20). Moses must have been trailing the girls because
the very next sentence states, "Moses was content to dwell
with the man." Since the priest of Midian apparently had
no sons, he was glad to have a man around, even an Egyptian, and so he gave his daughter Zipporah as a wife for
Moses. In time Zipporah, which means quite literally "Lady
Bird," presented Moses with a son. Moses, according to
tradition, named him "Gershom," explaining "I have been
a sojourner (Hebrew *ger*) in a foreign land." Evidently

"Gershom" was associated with *ger sham* ("a sojourner there").

Reuel and Jethro

The story of Moses' initial experiences in Midian has been considered as coming through the J tradition. The "priest of Midian" is not named at first, but in verse 18 he is called "Reuel." The same name appears in Numbers 10:29, yet in Exodus 3:1 (partially attributed to the E source) Moses' father-in-law is called "Jethro." As a whole, literary critics have treated the two names as J and E variants applying to the same person. Although, as noted above, Reuel occurs only two times, the name was hardly invented, and so it must go back to an early tradition. William F. Albright has suggested that Reuel was the patriarch of the clan to which Jethro belonged, and that originally the story had, "They came to their father (Jethro, the son of) Reuel."[4]

The King of Egypt Dies

Moses assumed responsibility for the flock of Jethro, and he roamed the Midian wilderness "many days" seeking pasture for the flock. Then the story flashes back to Egypt with a notice that the king of Egypt is dead. The Hebrews had hoped that their slavery would end when Sethos I died, but his son Ramses II was even more tyrannical. They groaned under the desperate conditions and cried out for help. When God heard their moans he "remembered his covenant with Abraham, with Isaac, and with Jacob" (2:24). In this way the biblical narrative alerts the reader to the fact that God is finally going to deliver the Hebrews.

The Burning Bush Episode and Literary Criticism

The narrative about Moses at the burning bush is found in Exodus 3:1-4:17. Martin Buber, the late Jewish scholar, rejected the idea that this unit of material could be regarded as "a compilation from varying sources and documents." He claimed that with the removal of a few additions, "a homogeneous picture" emerges. "Any apparent contradiction can be accounted for," he affirmed, "by the fact that the text has not been fully understood." This challenge to the claims of the literary critics needs to be considered,

---

4 Albright, *Yahweh and the Gods of Canaan* (Garden City, N. Y.: Doubleday, 1968), pp. 38-42.

and there is no more appropriate place to investigate the matter than the complex section 3:1-18. In general, the critics have reconstructed E and J as follows:

E	J
Now Moses was keeping the flock of his father-in-law, Jethro, the priest of Midian; and he led his flock to the west side of the wilderness, and came to Horeb, the mountain of God (1). God called to him out of the bush, "Moses, Moses!" And he said, "Here I am" (4b). And he said, "I am the God of your father, the God of A-braham, the God of Isaac, and the God of Jacob." And Moses hid his face, for he was afraid to look at God (6). "And now, behold, the cry of the people of Israel has come to me, and I have seen the oppression with which the Egyptians oppress them. Come, I will send you to Pharaoh that you may bring forth my people, the sons of Israel, out of Egypt." But Moses said to God, "Who am I that I should go to Pharaoh, and bring the sons of Israel out of Egypt?" He said, "But I will be with you; and this shall be the sign for you, that I have sent you: when you have brought forth the people out of Egypt, you shall serve God upon this mountain." Then Moses said to God, "If I come to the	And the angel of Yahweh appeared to him in a flame of fire out of the midst of a bush; and he looked, and lo, the bush was burning, yet it was not consumed. And Moses said, "I will turn aside and see this great sight, why the bush is not burnt." When Yahweh saw that he turned aside to see (2-4a), then he said, "Do not come near; put off your shoes from your feet, for the place on which you are standing is holy ground" (5). Then Yahweh said, "I have seen the afflic-tion of my people who are in Egypt, and have heard their cry because of their task-masters; I know their suffer-ings, and I have come down to deliver them out of the hand of the Egyptians, and to bring them up out of that land to a good and broad land, a land flowing with milk and honey, to the place of the Canaanites, the Hit-tites, the Amorites, the Perizzites, the Hivites, and the Jebusites (7-8). Go and gather the elders of Israel together, and say to them, 'Yahweh, the God of your fa-thers, the God of Abraham, of Isaac, and of Jacob, has

people of Israel and say to them, 'The God of your fathers has sent me to you,' and they ask me, 'What is his name?' what shall I say to them?" God said to Moses, "I AM WHO I AM." And he said, "Say this to the people of Israel, 'I AM has sent me to you.'" God also said to Moses, "Say this to the people of Israel, 'Yahweh, the God of your fathers, the God of Abraham, the God of Isaac, and the God of Jacob, has sent me to you': this is my name forever, and thus I am to be remembered throughout all generations" (9-15).

appeared to me, saying, "I have observed you and what has been done to you in Egypt; and I promise that I will bring you up out of the affliction of Egypt, to the land of the Canaanites, the Hittites, the Amorites, the Perizzites, the Hivites, and the Jebusites, a land flowing with milk and honey.'" And they will hearken to your voice; and you and the elders of Israel shall go to the king of Egypt and say to him, 'Yahweh, the God of the Hebrews, has met with us; and now, we pray you, let us go a three days' journey into the wilderness, that we may sacrifice to Yahweh our God'" (16-18).

The older critics assigned 3:1 to E because of the mention of "Jethro," "Horeb," and "God = *Elohim*," but this left J without a proper introduction. More recent scholars, like Martin Noth, have considered the J account to be the earliest and the most complete of the traditions, therefore 3:1 is assigned as follows:

> J Now Moses was keeping the flock of his father-in-law, the priest of Midian; and he led his flock to the west side of the wilderness.

> E And (Moses) came to Horeb, the mountain of God.

Noth accomplishes this revision by dropping "Jethro" as a late addition of some editor influenced by the E tradition.

Chapter 3, however, holds more difficulties for the source critics. Noth, for example, concurs in the judgment that E uses "the king of Egypt," while J speaks of "Pharaoh." Yet the reverse is true in verse 11 (where "Pharaoh" appears with *Elohim*) and verse 18 (where "the king of Egypt" appears with *Yahweh*). These and other inner discrepancies are a warning that this unit of material is a

very complex mixture of J and E. Since this probably occurred during the period of oral transmission of the story,
it is *not* possible to unravel all the threads that have gone
into making the tapestry.

Martin Buber attempts to explain this situation as "the
fruit of a highly cultivated dialectic and narrative art."[5]
There is evidence from nonbiblical texts to show that some
of the ancient scribes composed their narratives with duplicate units using synonymous terms. But this "dialectic" art
cannot account for some of the sudden shifts in the biblical
narrative. The truth of the matter is somewhere between
Buber (and Cassuto, whom he followed) and Noth. Buber
and Cassuto are correct in their claim that the text is more
than a compilation by a later editor, but Noth and the
literary critics are right in declaring that variant traditions have come together to form the present biblical text.
Many people over a long period of time had a hand in
shaping the narrative as we have it now.

The warning against taking the source analysis too literally has further implications because scholars have inferred rather refined theologies and points of view from
the sources. In E, for example, God speaks to Moses directly from the bush, and later on he says, "Come." This
implies that God was enshrined at the mountain. In J,
however, Yahweh is conceived of as residing in heaven;
consequently he must "come down" to get into action. E
pictures Moses as an envoy sent by God to deliver the
people of Israel. In J it is actually Yahweh who delivers the
people, while Moses is the messenger who carries Yahweh's
authoritative word to the elders of Israel and the king of
Egypt.

In some cases the characteristics of J and E are com-
plementary and the difference is one of emphasis rather
than of contradiction. While E understands God as sending
the envoy Moses to deliver the people of Israel, it is implicit that God is the ultimate power who has the authority
to send Moses and to deliver the people. On the other hand,
when J speaks of Yahweh as the deliverer and Moses
as his messenger, it is equally implicit that Moses is sent

[5] Martin Buber, *Moses, the Revelation and the Covenant* (New
York: Harper, n.d.), p. 39.

with authority and that he is the agent through whom
Yahweh will work. The power of the combined story lies
in the fact that the two points of view often strengthen
each other.

At the same time it is recognized that the biblical text
has some clear-cut disparities. This is far more evident in
4:18-28, and some of the problems will be noted later.
Such a condition is to be expected because not all the details which the traditions acquired were in accord with the
actual historical facts. In cases of discrepancy the interpreter must give attention to source analysis in order to
isolate the traditions as far as possible and to determine
which tradition is the most accurate.

From the standpoint of method it should be pointed out
that some of the so-called assured results of critical study
are actually based on very slippery, subjective reasoning.
A far-reaching inference which Noth, for example, draws
from the source analysis in 3:15 is that the J tradition did
not know the location of the burning bush, nor did it associate that experience of Moses with the Horeb-Sinai
region. Only later on were the two connected when someone noticed that *seneh*, the Hebrew word for "bush," was
similar to Sinai. Such a massive assumption is hardly justi-
fied by the silence of the J tradition. It is far more probable
that the threefold mention of the bush was J's way of saying that Yahweh's appearance to Moses in the *seneh* was
a foretaste of what Yahweh would do in the same place
when Moses returned to Sinai with the people of Israel.

Oral tradition was neither inerrant nor completely naïve.
It made its mistakes, but archaeology has shown that biblical tradition is essentially reliable. When critical reconstructions like Noth's call in question most of the traditional judgments the burden of proof shifts to the critic.
No one doubts the ingenuity of these radical theories, but
ingenuity does not have a very high correlation with truth.

The Mountain of God

As a prelude to the story about the burning bush, the
Hebrew text notes that in order to find sufficient pasture
for Jethro's flock Moses went "back of the wilderness." The
King James Version (KJV) translates "to the back side
of the desert." Most recent translations, including the Re-

vised Standard Version (RSV), interpret this to mean "to the west(ern) side of the wilderness." But the New Jewish Version (NJV) has "into the wilderness." The ambiguity of the Hebrew text precludes any dogmatic claims as to the precise meaning, but the most common view, as the translations indicate, is that Moses moved from a portion of Midian east or north of the Gulf of Aqaba to a western section on the Sinai Peninsula.

In any case, Moses came to "the mountain of God." There is no indication in the story that he realized that the mountain was sacred. He was tending to his business as a shepherd, and not on some spiritual retreat. But after his experience at the burning bush he knew it was sacred, and it is only natural that tradition would later refer to the peak as "the mountain of God."

The specific identification "Horeb" comes at the very end of the Hebrew sentence, and Noth may well be right in considering it as a later addition. The real question, however, is whether this tradition was correct in equating "the mountain of God" with "Horeb." Noth denies this, but there is much evidence to show that tradition was right. The interpretation of the burning bush experience does not hinge on the answer to this problem; and since it will be much easier to consider the data in connection with the covenant at Sinai, the issue will be postponed until then.

Chapter 4

Moses — the Prophet

While Moses was tending his flock at "the mountain of God," suddenly he noticed a flame of fire coming from a bush. He had seen brush fires before, but something was strange about this incident — the bush was not consumed!

The Burning Bush

Tradition interpreted the flame as "the messenger (angel) of Yahweh." In Genesis "the messenger of Yahweh" appears in the form of a man, and only later do the biblical characters realize that the person was a "theophany," that is, an appearance of God. At the burning bush, however, there is no indication that Moses saw the form of a person. He looked, but he could not believe his eyes — "the bush was burning, yet it was not consumed." The story makes it quite evident that Moses had no idea of the spiritual implications of the sight. He was simply intrigued by what he saw, and therefore he thought, "I will turn aside and see this great sight, why the bush is not burnt." It is most important to observe that the flame (the messenger) is a manifestation of Yahweh.

The first part of Exodus 3:4 is ambiguous: "When Yahweh saw that he turned aside to see, Elohim called to him out of the bush." This shift of subject in the middle of a sentence is rather strange. The Septuagint indicates that the Hebrew text which the translator used had Yahweh in place of Elohim, but why repeat the name of the subject in such a short sentence? The literary critics seem to have the better of the argument here when they assign the first clause to J and the second to E. Later on, Yahweh is quoted as saying, "I have come down." The implication is that Yahweh is at the scene of the burning bush; therefore both traditions are agreed that God spoke to Moses from the bush. An important aspect of the story is the clear-cut distinction between God and his manifestation. While it is the flame (Yahweh's manifestation) which attracts Moses' attention, it is Yahweh himself who speaks to Moses.

Numerous attempts have been made to explain the burning bush. At certain times of the year various bushes of the Near East are brilliant with flamelike blossoms, but this cannot be the explanation. Moses had spent some time in the wilderness and he most certainly had had the experience of viewing some bushes aflame with blossoms and others aflame with fire. The flame of this bush looked like fire, but mysteriously it did not consume the bush. It is tempting to interpret the event as a vision (like Yahweh's appearance to Abraham in Gen. 15:1) in which the "seeing" and the "hearing" are within the person. Yet tradition believed that Yahweh attracted Moses' attention by an external object.

In the temple of Horus at Edfu, between Luxor and Aswan in Egypt, there is recorded a story which says of the great falcon deity, "Lo, you are a flame inspiring fear ... which lives on in a mound of *kk*-bushes." Although the inscription dates about a thousand years after Moses and the type of bush is uncertain, it is very interesting to have the remnant of a tradition that deity manifested himself by an awesome flame in a cluster of bushes. The origin of this tradition is uncertain, yet the similarity with the biblical story is apparent. Even though the explanation of the burning bush is not within our grasp, the important fact is that God confronted man and made his will known.

God Confronts Moses

Visual means are employed to attract the attention of Moses, but they are simply preparation for the real encounter through the spoken word. God addresses Moses in a fatherly way, calling his name twice, and Moses answers with a childlike "Here I am," just as Samuel would do years later (1 Sam. 3:4). The shock of being called by name must have stopped Moses in his tracks; but lest he still try to satisfy his curiosity about the bush he is warned, "Do not come near! Take off your shoes from your feet, for the place on which you are standing is holy ground" (3:5). Ancient man believed that it was not possible for a

human being to see or touch God and live; thus Moses dare
not come any closer to the bush. Even where he is, the
ground is holy and he has to remove his sandals in order
that his bare feet touch the sacred earth. No man-made
protection is to desecrate the creature's humble approach
to his Creator.

It is implicit that Moses obeyed the instructions, because
immediately after the warning God goes on to identify himself: "I am the God of your father, the God of Abraham,
the God of Isaac, and the God of Jacob." If the Hebrew
text is literally accurate, then God claims to be the God
of Moses' father. In 3:15, however, a similar passage has
"the God of your fathers," after which the three great
Patriarchs are named. Although it is unlikely that God
identified himself as the God of Moses' father, it does raise
the issue of faith and worship among the Hebrews in Egypt.

The Faith of the Hebrews

The only reference to any religious belief on the part of
the Hebrews is the statement that "the midwives feared
God" (Exod. 2:17, 21). In 2:23-24 God hears the pathetic
cries of the Hebrews, but there is no statement that the
pleas were addressed to him. There is no explicit reference
to any priesthood, place of worship, or ritual of worship.
It is almost as if the suffering of the people had eliminated
all aspects of worship. But this can hardly have been true
because persecution usually results in strengthening the
faith of the committed.

It would appear from the biblical narrative that Moses
was taken back to the Egyptian princess soon after he was
weaned. He would hardly have remembered anything from
this age, and so the fact that he knew he was a Hebrew
implies that he had learned of his origin during his years
in the Egyptian court. His curiosity, which is so evident
at the burning bush, must have been aroused to the point
that he checked on the history of his people. Since this was
a religious history, and since the ancestral deity of a clan
was very important to the ancients, it is hardly conceivable that Moses was ignorant of "the God of the Fathers"
and the names (*El Elyon*, "God Most High," and *El Shaddai*, "God of the Mountain," perhaps meaning "God of the
Hill Country" in Palestine) by which he had been known.

He must have known of God's special relationship with
Abraham and the promise which came out of this covenant relationship. Tradition, at least, was convinced that
Moses was knowledgeable in this area; otherwise he would
not have been able to understand which God was talking
to him.

The Commission of Moses

When Moses realized that the God who had called Abraham was speaking with him, he "hid his face, for he was
afraid to look at God." Like Elijah, centuries later, Moses
probably "wrapped his face in his mantle" (1 Kings 19:13).
God informs the fearful Moses that he has seen the affliction of the Hebrews and heard their cries. With great
empathy Yahweh says, "I know their sufferings." Then he
declares his intention of taking immediate action to deliver
them from the Egyptians.

As Moses waits for further information about God's
plans, he is stunned — "Come, I will send you to Pharaoh
that you may bring forth my people, the sons of Israel, out
of Egypt" (3:10). Moses had been trained at the court
of Pharaoh and he knew the customs and thought patterns
of the Egyptians. Of all the Hebrews he was the best quali-
fied to be God's agent of deliverance. At one time he had
even expressed great concern for his people. God knew what
he was doing, but at the thought of the staggering assignment Moses denies his qualifications: "Who am I that I
should go to Pharaoh, and bring the sons of Israel out of
Egypt?" At first glance the objection seems to be quite
humble in spirit, but most likely the piety was a cover
for fear. News did not travel as fast in ancient times, but
word got around. The death of Sethos I and the succession
of his son Ramses II must have spread to the most isolated sections within the Egyptian sphere of influence.
Moses had fled from one Pharaoh and he does not relish
confrontation with a more ruthless one. Apparently God
senses his fear because he does not chide him — he just
reassures him: "But I will be with you."

Such a marvelous promise should have calmed the trou-
bled soul of Moses, but the nagging doubt was still there.
He did not ask for a sign, as Gideon would many years
later (Judg. 6:36-40); yet his uneasiness must have shown

on his face because God said, "This shall be the sign for
you, that I have sent you." What follows seems to be the
sign: "When you (singular) have brought forth the people out of Egypt, you (plural) shall serve God upon this
mountain" (3:12). Such a sign, however, would require
a great deal of faith because the assurance of his commission would not come for some time. On the one hand,
it hardly seems like the kind of assurance an uneasy person would want. Some scholars have considered the bush
as the sign, while others have thought of it as being Moses'
rod. On the other hand, it was probably God's intention
that the prediction (that Moses and the people of Israel
would some day worship him at the sacred mountain) would
stimulate his hope to the point where he would accept the
challenge.

The Name of God

In the ancient world a person's name was thought to represent his character and personality. One could never know
another person until his name was known. This was even
more crucial when it came to the names of the gods. Moses
anticipated that the people would question him thoroughly
on this point, and so he asked, "If I come to the people
of Israel and say to them, 'The God of your fathers has
sent me to you,' and they ask me, 'What is his name?'
what shall I say to them?" (3:13).

The present Hebrew text states that God answered Moses,
"I shall be what I shall be." This is clearly the revelatory
statement about the character of the God talking to Moses.
But what does it mean? The King James and American
Standard Versions read, "I AM THAT I AM," and the Revised Standard Version translates, "I AM WHO I AM." The
margin of the ASV suggests, "I AM BECAUSE I AM," and the
margin of the RSV offers, "I AM WHAT I AM." The Septuagint interpreted the expression to mean, "I am the One
who exists," but this has philosophical overtones which
stemmed from the Greek training of the translator. The
Hebrews and the other Semites did not think in speculative
philosophical terms. The issue of pure being or existence
never arose. The Hebrew language was one of action, and
the God of the Hebrews was understood as One who acted.

But within the limits of Hebrew thought there are a

number of possible interpretations. Buber, for example, takes a clue from Exodus 33:19, "I will show mercy on whom I will show mercy"; therefore he interprets the passage to mean, "I am and remain present that I shall be present."[1] He understands this answer as a rebuke to the Egyptian magicians who threatened the gods if they did not answer when invoked. Yahweh is and will be the friend of the Hebrews, and so they have no need to invoke or conjure him. An equally probable and more straightforward meaning is, "I shall be whatever I will." Be that as it may, the answer which God gave Moses was intended to reveal his character; therefore it is reasonable to assume that his personal name would stem from the affirmation. Perhaps the meaning of the name "Yahweh" will help clarify the intent of the revelatory statement.

The Meaning of the Name "Yahweh"

Some inscriptions dating about 1800-1600 B.C. have preserved the Amorite (West Semitic) personal name *Yahwi-el*. The latter part of the name is El, the old generic term for deity and the title of the father-god far off in his heaven. The first part is a causative form of the verb *hawah (hayah)* ("to be"), meaning "May he cause to be (bring into existence)." Thus the old name probably meant "May El bring into existence." Some scholars have objected to this interpretation of the name on the grounds that the causative form of "to be" was too speculative for the Semitic mind. But this concept has nothing to do with Greek philosophy. From earliest times man has made things. He learned from experience that he could create things, that is, cause them to be. Egyptian inscriptions from the pyramids of the Fifth and Sixth Dynasties (about 2400 B.C. and following) employ the causative form of the verb "to become" with the meaning "to bring into existence, create." In Babylonia the causative of "to be" occurs in inscriptions of the Old Kingdom (1800 B.C. and down).

Inasmuch as God's claim, "I shall be what I shall be," is based on the Hebrew verb *hayah* ("to be"), it is virtually certain that the name Yahweh derived from *hawah*, the Old West Semitic spelling of the same verb. Moreover, the

---

[1] Buber, *Moses, the Revelation and the Covenant*, p. 52.

nonbiblical examples of the causative forms of "to be" make it highly probable that the name Yahweh meant "He who creates (brings into existence)."

This would indicate perhaps that God's original answer to Moses was in the causative as well. In this case God would have been saying, "I create what I bring into existence." This change involves only the shift of one vowel in the Hebrew — *ehyeh* to *ahyeh* — and since the vowels were not added to the Hebrew manuscripts until after A.D. 700, there could well have been a change during the long period of oral transmission of the vowels. Inasmuch as God was making the declaration about himself it is natural that he used the first person. In the ancient Near East, however, the verbal forms in personal names were almost always in the third person; therefore in conformity with this practice Moses would have rephrased the statement, "He who creates what comes into existence." This would have meant a change from *ahyeh* to *yahyeh*, which in the older spelling would have been *yahweh*.

The present Hebrew text states that while Moses was still pondering God's revelation to him, God told him, "Say to the people of Israel, 'I SHALL BE has sent me to you.' " In other words, God took the first part of his revelatory statement and used it as a personal name. If the shift is made to the causative form and to the third person, then Moses would have told the people, "HE WHO CREATES has sent me to you." This is precisely the meaning of "Yahweh," and so Moses probably told the Hebrews, "Yahweh has sent me to you."

In shortening the longer statement to form the personal name for God the object of his creative power was dropped, and this left a sense of incompleteness. As a result there developed a number of longer titles for God in which the personal name Yahweh was included. An excellent example is *Yahweh Sebaoth* (1 Sam. 4:4), which is usually translated "LORD of hosts." Originally "hosts" probably referred to the sun, moon, planets, and stars, and thus God's title meant, "He who has created the heavenly bodies." Later on, as a designation of the God who led Israel into battle, it meant, "He who brings armies (hosts of warriors) into existence." Rather appropriately, the name appears as "Lord

Sabaoth" in the second verse of Luther's hymn "A Mighty Fortress Is Our God."

After making his character known to Moses and designating his personal name, God clarified the whole matter by equating his name with "the God of the Fathers": "Say this to the people of Israel, 'Yahweh, the God of your fathers, the God of Abraham, the God of Isaac, and the God of Jacob, has sent me to you': this is my name forever, and thus I am to be remembered throughout all the generations" (3:15). In essence, then, God's claim reveals to Moses that "the God of the Fathers" was actually the sovereign Lord over all the universe and mankind. He had created the heavens and he would keep his promise to Abraham. Neither Moses nor Pharaoh would thwart his purpose!

When Was the Name "Yahweh" First Used?

Inasmuch as the unit 3:9-15 has all the characteristics of the E tradition (which prefers Elohim to Yahweh), the explicit use of the name Yahweh seems to indicate that the E tradition believed that it was to Moses that God first revealed his personal name. It is interesting to note that the P tradition had the same belief. In Exodus 6:2-3 the text reads, "And God said to Moses, 'I am Yahweh. I appeared to Abraham, to Isaac, and to Jacob, as El Shaddai, but by my name Yahweh I did not make myself known to them.'"

In contrast, the J tradition states that as early as the time of Seth and Enosh (the son and grandson of Adam), "men began to call upon the name of Yahweh" (Gen. 4:26). J claims also that when Abraham first came into Canaan Yahweh appeared to him (Gen. 12:7). In fact, Yahweh appears a number of times to Abraham and to Isaac and Jacob as well. Martin Buber follows the J tradition quite literally in believing that the Hebrews had knowledge of the name Yahweh and that they used it. Accordingly, he contends that when Moses asked, "What is his name?" he meant, "What is the meaning and character of his name?" In rejecting the apparent meaning of Exodus 3:15 and 6:3, Buber comments, "What is said is not that the patriarchs made no use of the name of YHWH *(Yahweh)*, but only that they did not know him in the quality characterized by this name."[2] As usual, the issue hinges on the interpretation of an ambiguity. When the J tradition uses the name Yahweh, is it declaring that the actual name was used in early times, or that the same God, who was well known later as Yahweh, was worshiped by Seth and the later Patriarchs?

From all the evidence related to the name Yahweh it is quite clear that Abraham, the other Patriarchs, and the Hebrews in Egypt could have known about the name Yahweh. In this sense Buber is probably correct in declaring that the name was not brand new when it was used at the burning bush. On the other hand, that is not saying very much when Exodus 6:3 says explicitly, "By my name Yahweh I did not make myself known to them." When Buber has to interpret this to mean that God had not made himself known "in the quality characterized by this name," is he not saying that God had not lived up to the capacity which the name implied? Why reveal a name with great meaning and then not measure up to it? Such action would have led to great disillusionment. The main point is that Moses marked the beginning of a qualitatively superior understanding of the nature of the God of the Hebrews. The God who appeared to Moses was the same God who appeared to Abraham, but he appeared with another personal name. Therefore Moses was given the privilege of understanding that God in a much deeper way.

Personal Names with "Yahweh"

From the point of view that the name Yahweh was revealed first to Moses, the most compelling evidence of all comes from the use of the name in longer personal names. The styles and forms of names varied from period to period, but one of the most common types was the use of a name for a god, a verbal element, and an object of the verb. An excellent example is Nebuchadrezzar (or more commonly Nebuchadnezzar), the name of the famous king of Babylon (Jer. 21:2). The Babylonian form of the name is *Nabu-kudurri-usur*, meaning "O Nabu, protect my boundary stone," or, as suggested by others, "Nabu, protect my succession-rights." The Babylonian god Nabu was the son of

---

[2] *Ibid.*, p. 49.

Marduk (Bel), and both are mentioned in Isaiah 46:1 as Nebo and Bel. Mt. Nebo in ancient Moab (modern Jordan) was evidently a site where Nabu was worshiped.

In like manner the names El and Yahweh were used in names of persons in the biblical tradition. One of the sons of King Josiah of Judah was Eliakim. The Hebrew form *El-yakim* means "God raises up" or "God establishes." His name was changed to Jehoiakim (2 Chron. 36:4; Hebrew *Yeho-yakim*, "Yahweh raises up"). Yahweh was shortened to Yahu, and the contracted form appears in names as Yeho. The reason most of the names in the English translations have the letter "J" instead of "Y" is that in continental Europe (where the names were first printed in Latin letters) the "J" was pronounced like a "Y."

The form Yeho (Jeho) was often shortened to Yo (Jo). The name *Jo*nathan ("Yahweh has given") comes from the longer form *Jeho*nathan. *Jeho*shaphat ("Yahweh has judged") appears in the shortened form *Jo*shaphat. At other times the form Yahu was shortened to Yah and placed at the end of the name instead of the beginning. The son of Jehoiakim was Jehoiachin (Hebrew *Yeho-yachin*, "Yahweh establishes [or, is loyal]"), but in 1 Chronicles 3:16 the name (with the same meaning) appears of Jeconiah (Hebrew *Yechon-yah*). The nickname or shortened form Coniah appears in Jeremiah 22:24.

This rather detailed explanation will help in understanding Numbers 13:16: "And Moses called Hoshea, the son of Nun, Joshua." The longer form of Hoshea seems to have been *Hoshe-el* ("Save, O El"). When Moses changed his name he substituted Yahweh for El, and thus the new form was *Hosha-yah* ("Save, O Yahweh"). It was apparently this form which was shortened to Hoshea. On the other hand, Joshua (from which the name Jesus comes) is the shortened form of *Jeho*shua ("Yahweh is salvation"), in which the name Yahweh is placed at the beginning of the name instead of at the end. In other words, when Moses decided to make a shift, he changed both forms of the name (with the name of God at the end and at the beginning) by substituting Yahweh for El.

In Exodus 6:20 the mother of Moses is called Jochebed, and it would appear that Jo is the shortened form of Yahweh. But the vowel pattern of the rest of the name does not fit in with the types of names using Yahweh. Therefore, it is probable that the name derives from some other form. If it should prove later on, however, that Jochebed is a personal name using Yahweh, it is probably a revised form of the name of Moses' mother because its appearance in Exodus 6:20 follows soon after the claim in 6:3 that Yahweh made himself known first to Moses. In either case, then, Joshua is the first clear-cut example of a biblical name to use Yahweh as one of its components.

If the name Yahweh had been known in earlier times with any marked degree of understanding, it is incomprehensible why the name was not used in personal names just as El was. The E and P traditions agree that the name Yahweh, as a revelation of God's character, was given first to Moses, and the personal names of the Bible confirm this judgment in a very compelling way. It would seem, then, that the J tradition projected the name Yahweh back into the earlier narratives on the conviction that the God of Seth, Abraham, Isaac, and Jacob was the same as the God of Moses.

The interpretation of the meaning of Yahweh rests quite heavily on the sequence of events noted in 3:14-15. It is frankly admitted, however, that the condensed nature of the answers appears unnatural. Within less than four lines the text states, "God said to Moses ... And he said ... God also said." God's third statement seems to be the most logical and complete answer to Moses' question in verse 13, while verse 14 appears to be an explanation of the name Yahweh which is in 3:15. Many scholars consider verse 14 to be a later addition to the text; therefore when the scribe inserted it he had to add the word "also" in 3:15.

This interpretation of the text could well be true, but God must have given Moses some kind of explanation of the name Yahweh or else he would have had difficulty in understanding the personal name. If the original story skipped over this part of God's discourse with Moses, tradition would feel that some explanation should be included. In any event, the insertion is an early one, and it is the only revelatory statement in which God is pictured as making known the nature and character back of the name Yahweh. Even though added later, it is a very important

statement and it is likely an accurate understanding of
what took place between God and Moses.

Moses the Prophet

After God reveals himself to Moses, he gives orders for
the implementation of his plans: "Go and assemble the
elders of Israel together, and say to them, 'Yahweh, the
God of your fathers, the God of Abraham, of Isaac, and
of Jacob has appeared to me.' " "Go ... assemble ... and
say" — Moses is to be God's chosen messenger. The normative Hebrew word for "prophet" is *nabi,* which comes from
a verb meaning "to call." The verb is used many times in
Amorite and Akkadian personal names where it is clear
that a god is calling a man. In Hebrew tradition, therefore,
a prophet was a man called by God and authorized to
speak for him. Moses' essential role, accordingly, is that of
a prophet, many years before the classical prophets of
Israel and Judah. Hosea, one of these later prophets, wrote,
"By a prophet Yahweh brought Israel up from Egypt,"
thus echoing the voice of tradition that Moses was indeed
a prophet.

According to the Hebrew text of Genesis 20:7, God says
of Abraham, "He is a prophet," but originally the Hebrew
word was most likely a passive verb form, not the noun
"prophet." In this instance Abraham does not have an
authoritative word of God to proclaim. Rather, God is explaining to Abimelech, "He has been called by me." Abraham was certainly a prophet in the sense that he had been
called, but Moses was the first true prophet — one called
and authorized to speak for God. On the other hand, this
does not mean that Moses shared in all the characteristics
which the later prophets exhibited. Samuel, for example,
was a true prophet, and in recognition of his call from
God the people referred to him as "the man of God" (1
Sam. 9:6). But he was called a "seer" also, and Samuel
referred to himself as such (1 Sam. 9:19). It was this gift
which led Saul to Samuel in hopes that he could tell him
where the lost asses of Kish, his father, were. Moses did
not have the power of a seer, and this feature of later
prophecy never played a role in his period of leadership.
But in the basic meaning of "a called spokesman," Moses
was the prophet *par excellence,* and features of his call and

life would shape the narratives and messages of the later prophets, especially Isaiah and Jeremiah.

Whereas most of the classical prophets are messengers of judgment and doom, Moses is given Yahweh's message of hope: "I have observed ... I promise ... I will bring you up out of the affliction of Egypt to ... a land flowing with milk and honey." Egypt was a land flowing with milk and honey, but as state slaves of Ramses II the Hebrews were not free to have and enjoy the abundance of the land. The prospect of going to a land where they could have a good diet was "good news" indeed, and the message was intended to start Moses' heart beating with expectation. Even the elders will listen, Moses is told, "and you and the elders of Israel shall go to the king of Egypt and say to him, 'Yahweh, the God of the Hebrews, has met with us; and now, we pray you, let us go a three days' journey into the wilderness, that we may sacrifice to Yahweh our God' " (3:18).

The description of the pleasant land as "the land of the Canaanites, the Hittites, the Amorites, the Perizzites, the Hivites, and the Jebusites" (both in verses 8 and 17) is actually a standardized description of the land of Canaan which resulted from a list of the major enemies the Israelites had to face when they came into the land. Even if one grants that Yahweh knew about all the people in the land of Canaan, it is doubtful that he would have bored Moses with such details. Some editor in the J tradition felt it necessary to add the description because the land of Canaan was mentioned.

The unit 3:19-22, which is usually attributed to the E tradition, is quite pessimistic in tone: "I know that the king of Egypt will not let you go." There is advance notice that God will have to perform "wonders" to free his people, and then instructions given that the Hebrew women ask the Egyptians for gold and silver jewelry, and clothing in order that the Israelites not go out of Egypt empty-handed. This will be possible because God will give them favor in the eyes of the Egyptians. Apparently the idea is that some of the Egyptians will feel sorry for the Hebrews and give them jewelry (which could be worn and used in trade) and clothing (for their depleted wardrobe) as a sort of reparations payment for all the days of slave labor.

No doubt Moses needed some briefing on what to expect and to say, but the details in the passage appear more like a scribal preview of what is to come. This judgment is strengthened by the fact that 3:19-22 breaks into the dramatic story of Yahweh's interaction with Moses. The narrative of 3:18 is clearly continued in 4:1. Moses has some doubts about the openness of the elders, in spite of Yahweh's assurance, and so he replies, "But behold, they will not believe me or listen to my voice, for they will say, 'Yahweh did not appear to you.'" The form and content of the unit 3:19-22 break up the true, and psychologically sound, sequence of events.

The Reluctant Prophet

When Moses expresses doubt that the elders will believe his story and his message, Yahweh gives him some "signs" (4:2-9) which he can perform in order to convince them. Like most shepherds, Moses has a rod in his hand, and when Yahweh tells him to cast it down it becomes a snake. Moses flees in fright, but Yahweh instructs him to take the snake by the tail. He does so and it becomes a rod. Magic with serpents was practiced by the Egyptians many years before Moses, and even today there are persons in Egypt with the gift of smelling out cobras. By pressing back of the head they can paralyze the snake and it becomes like a rod. When it is thrown down, the jolt removes the effect of the paralysis and the snake slithers off. This process (snake-rod-snake) is well known, but Moses' experience reversed the conditions (rod-snake-rod), and this takes a little doing.

Just in case the Hebrews do not believe the first sign, Moses is given a second. He is instructed to put his hand "into his bosom," and on withdrawing it the hand is "leprous, as white as snow," according to the standard translations. The technical Hebrew word is actually a general term covering a wide range of diseases or conditions affecting persons, garments, and houses. Leviticus 13:1-46 deals with such symptoms as swellings, sores, pustules, and white or reddish-white spots on the skin, as well as discoloration of the hairs. Actual leprosy (Hansen's Disease) was known in the ancient world, but in most cases the biblical use of the term refers to such varied diseases

as psoriasis, vitiligo, ringworm, and syphilis. Leviticus
13:47-59 even describes the "leprosy" of garments made of
wool, linen, or animal skin. The greenish or reddish symptoms probably refer to the deterioration of the garments
through mold, mildew, or worms. Still another category is
the "leprosy" of houses (Lev. 14:33-53). Here greenish
spots are signs of mold which would weaken walls made
of mud-brick or stone with mud mortar, thus endangering
the inhabitants. The reddish spots apparently indicate ter-
mites or rot in the wooden columns of the house.

In the case of the sign to Moses, perhaps something like
psoriasis was involved. The proof of Yahweh's authority
is that on returning his hand to his bosom it is healed. This
too is quite a trick and surely the people will believe, but
as an extra precaution Moses is given the third sign: water
from the Nile will become blood red on the dry ground.
This latter sign anticipates in essence the first plague, and
since there is no biblical statement that this happened prior
to that time, 4:9 is most likely a later addition.

Whatever the signs were which Yahweh gave to Moses,
they did not overcome his reluctance, and so finally he
comes to one of his deep-seated fears, "Oh, my Lord, I am
not eloquent, either heretofore or since you have spoken
to your servant; but I am slow of speech and of tongue"
(4:10). Moses knows he has fast hands (as the Egyptian
and the shepherds found out), but how can he serve as
Yahweh's messenger with a "slow tongue"? He could not
speak well before Yahweh appeared to him, and his condition has not improved during the burning bush experience.
In effect, Moses is thinking, "If Yahweh wants to make
me a messenger, why doesn't he correct my difficulty?"

Yahweh counters the objection with a barrage of questions: "Who has made man's mouth? Who makes him dumb,
or deaf, or seeing, or blind? Is it not I, Yahweh?" Prior
to the exile the normative view in Israel was to attribute
everything that happened to Yahweh. Thus in Isaiah 45:7
Yahweh is quoted as saying, "I make weal and create woe."
Yahweh knows that he has made Moses a stammerer, but
he is going to use him anyway: "Now therefore go, and I
will be with your mouth and teach you what you shall
speak." Paul understood God's method when he wrote,
"God has chosen what is weak in the world to shame the

strong,... so that no human being might boast in the presence of God" (1 Cor. 1:27, 29).

Aaron Made Spokesman

Moses is still stunned by the awesomeness of the assignment, and he makes one last desperate plea, "Oh, my Lord, send, I pray, some other person." This classic "dodge" is so true to human nature everyone can stand "barefooted" with Moses. Yet he fails to realize that his cry for deliverance proves to Yahweh that his objection is invalid. If he can speak well enough to protest against Yahweh's wishes, certainly he can speak for Yahweh. Yahweh's patience gives out, therefore, and he answers Moses angrily, "Is there not Aaron, your brother, the Levite? I know that he can speak well." Then Moses learns that Aaron is on his way to meet him. This is a sudden shift of events because there has been no evidence of any contact between Moses and his family. How does Aaron know where to go? The answer comes from a later passage where Yahweh instructs Aaron, "Go into the wilderness to meet Moses" (4:27). The fact that Aaron is designated "the Levite" may indicate that some ritualistic role has been assigned to him. Moses knew that he came from the tribe of Levi, and it would make little sense to identify Aaron as coming from that family.

After mentioning the approach of Aaron, Yahweh continues relating his plans to Moses: "And you shall speak to him and put the words in his mouth; and I will be with your mouth and with his mouth, and will teach you what you shall do. He shall speak for you to the people; and he shall be a mouth for you, and you shall be to him as God" (4:15-16). This is an amazing turn of events. Yahweh is angry with his stubborn prophet, but he is not going to bypass him. In order to remove the last objection of Moses, Aaron will be commissioned as the spokesman for Moses. In reality, then, Aaron will become the prophet and Moses will play the role of God. Yahweh could choose to make his will known directly to Aaron, but Yahweh is determined to have Moses, therefore he will speak the authoritative words through him.

After this marvelous concession to Moses, he is told to take "this rod" with which he shall do "the signs." In the

J tradition Moses has his own rod, and it is used only for the sign of the snake. Accordingly, the literary critics assign verse 17 to the E tradition.

The Return to Egypt

The account of Moses' return to Egypt occurs in 4:18-28. This section is a difficult mixture of J and E, and as noted earlier it has a number of inner difficulties. Moses returns to Jethro first to ask permission to go back to Egypt. He gives as his reason his desire to see whether his kinsmen are still alive. Evidently he did not confide in Jethro about his experience at the burning bush, nor did he tell him that he was now a prophet under Yahweh's command. In any event, Jethro answers with a gracious, "Go in peace." Moses is informed that it is safe to return to Egypt because the men who were seeking his life have died. He takes his wife and sons and starts back to Egypt. Thus far we have been told only about Gershom, but the E tradition in Exodus 18:4 lists Eliezer as the other son.

On the way back Yahweh informs Moses that he must be sure to perform all the miracles in Pharaoh's presence, but he is warned that Yahweh himself will harden Pharaoh's heart so that Pharaoh will not let the people go. This briefing session continues when Yahweh instructs Moses to say to Pharaoh, "Israel is my firstborn son, and I say to you, 'Let my son go that he may serve me'; if you refuse to let him go, behold, I will slay your firstborn son." Pharaoh will be a tough one, and only the most drastic of measures will make him give way. Here for the first time is the explicit teaching about the fatherhood of God. The Israelites are his people, and if necessary death will be used to free them. The prophet Hosea had to care for his own children while his wayward wife was gone, and through this experience he sensed anew what God's love must have been like: "When Israel was a child, I loved him, and out of Egypt I called my son" (11:1).

The difficulty of these verses is not so much about the content, but the question, as in 3:19-22, "How much of the material is scribal addition?" The threat against Pharaoh's son never plays a part in Moses' argument to get the release of the people. Moses needed some instruction about the earlier part of the confrontation rather than about the last plague. One can always find reasons for the presence and sequence of the passages, but difficulties so far outweigh the reasons that one gets the feeling that the rationale is that of the editor and not the original sequence of events. The purpose of this study, in so far as it is possible, is to see Moses as he was and not what various periods of tradition attributed to him.

Bridegroom of Blood

The unit 4:24-26 is one of the most difficult passages in the whole Bible. It is extremely archaic, and very little of it can be interpreted with certainty. At a lodging place somewhere en route to Egypt, Yahweh meets Moses and attempts to kill him. There is no indication how he tried to take his life, but some serious illness must have come over Moses. "Then Zipporah took a flint and cut off her son's foreskin, and touched his feet with it, and said, 'Surely you are a bridegroom of blood to me!' So he let him alone. Then it was that she said, 'You are a bridegroom of blood,' because of the circumcision." For the ancients the true wilderness was haunted, and travelers took great care lest a night demon attack them. Perhaps such an event was originally described in this story, and when it was associated with Moses' journey through the wilderness, Yahweh was considered the attacker.

The scribal note at the end of the passage seems to associate the circumcision with marriage. Depending on the culture, the people of the Near East performed circumcision at infancy, puberty, or marriage. The first problem is that Moses has been married for some time. The fact that Yahweh wants to kill him implies that he has sinned grievously against him. The passage which the editor apparently has in mind is the P tradition, which held that Abraham and his household were circumcised as an outward sign of God's covenant with them. Failure to observe the custom would be disastrous: "Any uncircumcised male who is not circumcised in the flesh of his foreskin shall be cut off from his people; he has broken my covenant" (Gen. 17:14).

There is no biblical indication whatsoever that Moses was circumcised, and perhaps this would account for Yahweh's severe attack. Zipporah takes quick action to spare the life of Moses, but surprisingly she circumcises her son. This would imply that Yahweh was angry because Moses had not permitted his son to be circumcised. Since this story is from the J tradition, which refers to Moses' sons earlier, it raises the question of which son, Gershom or Eliezer? Later Jewish tradition said it was the younger; but this only compounds the problem, because if one child had been circumcised, why not the other, and if neither had been circumcised, why not both that night? Zipporah (like Joshua in Josh. 5:2) uses a "flint" as the knife because custom decrees that this sacred act not be performed with a modern tool made of metal.

Another ambiguity is the statement "his feet." Almost certainly "feet" is the ancient euphemism for "genitals," just as the seraphim in Isaiah's vision use two of their six wings to cover their feet = genitals (Isa. 6:2). The foreskin came from the child's genitals, so apparently the reference is to Moses' genitals. Inasmuch as Moses was uncircumcised, perhaps the touch of the child's bloody foreskin was a symbolic circumcision. Thereby Zipporah could save the life of Moses and consider him as her actual "bridegroom of blood." But one must be careful about doing interpretive handstands. Older commentators went to great lengths to make the text literally true in all respects. The old German scholar Franz Delitzsch, for example, quotes Kurtz as follows: "Moses had been as good as taken from her by the deadly attack which had been made upon him. She purchased his life by the blood of her son; she received him back, as it were, from the dead, and married him anew; he was, in fact, a bridegroom of blood to her." Be that as it may, Zipporah's actions were effective and Yahweh let Moses alone.

The short story ends, and the implication is that Moses continued on to Egypt with his family. Yet the J tradition never refers to the wife or sons in Egypt. On the other hand, the E tradition states that at Moses' return to the sacred mountain after the Exodus, Jethro brought Zipporah and the two boys to him. The reason they happened to be with Jethro was that Moses had sent them away, and they naturally returned to her home. Evidently it was after the circumcision incident that Moses sent them back.

Not only does the unit 4:24-26 swarm with difficulties,

but the precise reason for the placement of the story is a mystery too. If circumcision was the real concern back of Yahweh's wrath, why wasn't the issue raised at the burning bush? It would seem that if the editor had taken Genesis 17:14 seriously, the logical place for the incident was in Midian before the burning bush experience, because how could Yahweh call and commission a Hebrew who was outside the covenant relationship? Apparently the original incident was associated with some lonely lodging place along the desert trail between Midian and Egypt, and the story was inserted into the biblical account at the point where Moses would have passed the general area of the lodging place.

Moses Meets Aaron

While Moses is en route to Egypt, Yahweh instructs Aaron, "Go into the wilderness to meet Moses." He does so, and he happens to meet Moses at "the mountain of God." He greets him with a kiss, and then Moses reports "all the words of Yahweh" concerning his commission and his power to perform signs. It is very strange, however, that Moses does not inform Aaron that he is to be his spokesman. Furthermore, Moses has been on his way back to Egypt for some time, and yet the meeting place is back at the sacred mountain.

A number of scholars feel that the references to Aaron's going into the wilderness to meet Moses (4:14, 27) are priestly additions in order to put the priesthood on a level with prophecy. Since these passages note also that Aaron would be glad to meet Moses and that on meeting he kissed him, other scholars interpret the statements as a priestly recognition of the leading role which prophecy played in Israel's history.

It should be evident by now that the story of Moses' return to Egypt is a very mixed text. Its brevity compounds the difficulty of interpretation. But notwithstanding all the hazards of interpretation, certain facts stand out: in spite of a threat to his life, Moses, the fugitive prince and Hebrew, returned to Egypt as a prophet with the authority of Yahweh's call and commission in order to rescue his enslaved people from the harsh cruelty of Ramses II.

Chapter 5

"Let My People Go"

On returning to Egypt, Moses and Aaron go directly to the land of Goshen, and there they assemble "all the elders of the people of Israel" (4:29). The narrative does not indicate whether they had any difficulty getting back or not. The presumption is that since those who had sought the life of Moses were dead, entry was made in regular fashion at one of the border stations.

Moses and Aaron Report to the People of Israel

Aaron, as the spokesman, reports "all the words which Yahweh spoke to Moses." There is no mention of any disbelief, and so the event seems to agree with the assurance of 3:18, "They will hearken to your voice." Yet in addition, according to the present Hebrew text, Aaron does "the signs in the sight of the people" (4:30). This is unexpected, and it seems to be at variance with the story thus far in two respects. First, Aaron has been authorized to serve only as the spokesman. It was Moses who was given the authority to perform the signs, and the assumption is that he would do so in Egypt. In the second place, the signs were given to Moses as an answer to his claim, "They will not believe me or listen to my voice." If the elders and the people did not need the assurance of the signs, why perform them? A third difficulty is the shift in the text: the words seem to be addressed to the elders, but the signs are done before the people. Further evidence that the "signs" may be a secondary addition is found in 4:31, where the people believe on the basis of what they "heard," not what they "saw." In any event, as a result of the activities of Moses and Aaron the people "bowed their heads and worshiped."

The unit 5:1-6:1 recounts the results of the first confrontations with Pharaoh. Verses 5:1-2, 4 tell of the attempt by Moses and Aaron to get the release of the people of Israel. In 5:3, 5 the elders seem to be involved since 5:3 is the same request which Yahweh gave Moses at the burning bush (3:18), with the instructions that the elders go with him to the king. The third request is made by the Hebrew foremen assigned by the Egyptians to oversee their own people (5:15-19). The shifts between the variant accounts are evident in the combined story, but the traditions agree essentially: Pharaoh became more tyrannical as a result of the requests.

"Who Is Yahweh?"

With the assurance that the elders and the people are back of them, Moses and Aaron head for the conference with Pharaoh. Once they are there they lose no time in getting to the issue: "Thus says Yahweh, the God of Israel, 'Let my people go, that they may hold a feast to me in the wilderness'" (5:1). Ramses, like all the Pharaohs, claimed to be divine, and his name, meaning "(The sun-god) Ra has begotten him," bears this out. As a god in human form Ramses was not accustomed to taking orders from lesser gods, let alone an unknown like Yahweh. "Who is Yahweh," he asks, "that I should heed his voice and let Israel go? I do not know Yahweh, and moreover I will not let Israel go" (5:2).

Who Was Ramses?

In order to understand more fully the difficulties which Moses faced as Yahweh's representative, it is necessary to know what kind of person Ramses was. His mummy is on display at the Egyptian Museum in Cairo; and as one views the little body with sandy-red hair, hooked nose, and long neck it is hard to believe that he could have reigned over Egypt for sixty-seven years. He began his reign as a teenager about seventeen or eighteen, and during his long life he fathered more than a hundred sons and perhaps as many daughters. Twelve of his sons preceded him in death, so that his successor Merneptah, his thirteenth son, was quite old when he came to the throne. Egyptian records do not indicate that Ramses was either wise or gifted as a ruler. What he had was a colossal ego and the will to prove himself.

One of the turning points in his career came in the fifth year of his reign. The Hittites from Asia Minor had moved down to control Syria, and Ramses determined to remove this threat to the north. He led his army through Palestine into Syria, where he challenged the army of the Hittite king Muwatallis. With confidence greater than his military skill he led his forces into a trap which had been laid for him at Qadesh on the Orontes River. By sheer personal bravery and with the aid of reinforcements he was able to fight his way out of the military noose, thereby saving his own life and most of his army.

In the light of Ramses' purpose, the battle at Qadesh was an utter failure. But a god does not have defeats, and so the alchemy of the divine myth turned a drubbing into a glorious victory. With every step of his homeward journey the story grew in his mind. He alone had won the victory. When confronted with 2500 chariots (each with three warriors), he invoked the aid of the god Amun and made his enemies "heaps of corpses." The cowardly Muwatallis watched the battle from a distance, and when he saw his troops going down to defeat he sent in another 1000 chariots. Ramses charged them and strewed the plain of Qadesh with their bodies. On his return to Egypt this bombastic tale was his report to the nation.

As a salve to his wounded ego, Ramses expanded his building operations into a massive program. He would prove to his people that he was greater than any of his predecessors. His capital near the land of Goshen was enlarged and beautified. A temple to Amun was on the west, one to Seth on the south, Astarte's to the east, and Uto's to the north. Ships came and went from the wharves on the river front, and the city was full of food and provisions. No one had a lack, and the young men walked the streets in their best attire with sweet oil on their coiffured hair. Singers, trained at Memphis, sang sweetly, and ale, beer, and wine flowed freely.

Ramses built temples at Luxor, Karnak, and the Ramesseum in the region of the old capital at Thebes. Many more were built along the Nile, the most distant being the one at Abu Simbel, about 800 miles from his capital in the

Delta. This temple was carved out of a red sandstone cliff, and the façade featured four sixty-five-foot statues of Ramses seated on his throne. On the walls of these various temples were chiseled the inscriptions and scenes depicting his "victory" at Qadesh. His gigantic figure dwarfed the Hittites and even his own troops. Before his long reign would end, the boast of his "smashing success" at Qadesh would literally fill acres of wall space.

It was probably only three or four years after the Qadesh disaster that Moses approached Ramses, and so he was dealing with a young man about twenty-six years of age. Since Ramses' wounded vanity was still sensitive it is quite evident why he threw down the gauntlet, challenging Yahweh to a test of will and power. Moreover, his extensive building operations in the Delta region demanded more and more labor. He could not afford to let the Hebrews go if he were to maintain his construction schedule and his mode of gracious living.

The Hebrews' Burdens Increased

After Ramses' stern refusal to grant the request of Moses and Aaron, another request (probably by the elders) is made. In order to impress Pharaoh with the urgency of their demand they express their fear that Yahweh will deal harshly with them if they do not sacrifice to him in the wilderness (5:3). Ramses is still unmoved by the appeal to Yahweh. People who have time to think of going on a spiritual retreat must be lazy, and so the way to solve the problem is to occupy their spare time. Ramses decides that the best way would be to withhold straw binder for making bricks, thus requiring the people to gather their own straw or stubble while still producing the same quota of bricks each day. The fiendish plan is announced, and the people scatter over the countryside early in the morning trying to find enough binder for the necessary number of bricks. The Egyptian taskmasters keep warning the people, "Complete your work, your daily task, as when there was straw." As weariness overtakes the slaves and their production drops, their fellow Hebrews assigned as foremen are beaten and asked, "Why have you not done all your task of making bricks today, as before?"

The foremen realize that the demand for the same num-

ber of bricks is impossible, and so they take their case to
Pharaoh: "Why do you deal thus with your servants? No
straw is given to your servants, yet they say to us, 'Make
bricks!' And behold, your servants are beaten; but the fault
is in your own people" (5:15-16). The foremen are suggesting that Ramses' subordinates are responsible for the
chaotic situation. An alternative translation of the last
clause (based on early translations of the Hebrew) is, "And
you do wrong to your own people." In this case the foremen would be claiming that they are really Pharaoh's people and that he is at fault. But their appeal, just like the
others, falls on deaf ears. Ramses still insists that the
people are lazy and that no straw will be given them. The
foremen know they are in trouble when they are instructed
on parting, "You shall by no means lessen your daily number of bricks" (5:19).

As the foremen leave their interview with Ramses they
meet Moses and Aaron, who are waiting for them. This
would imply either that Moses had a hand in sending the
foremen to Pharaoh, or that he had been informed of the
new bargaining session. In either case, they are vitally interested to know the outcome. They get the answer immediately with a verbal slap in the face: "Yahweh look upon
you and judge, because you have made us offensive in the
sight of Pharaoh and his servants, and have put a sword
in their hand to kill us" (5:21).

Moses pours out his frustration to Yahweh, "Why have
you done evil to this people? Why did you ever send me?
For since I came to Pharaoh to speak in your name, he
has done evil to this people, and you have not delivered
your people at all" (5:22-23). What Moses has failed to
see is that some of the Hebrews, like the foremen, are still
in the ambiguous situation of trying to respect Ramses and
worship Yahweh. In this all-out struggle there can be no
middle-of-the-road stance. Yahweh realizes that the irrationality of Ramses' demands will drive the people to the
point of genuine commitment, and so he informs Moses
implicitly that the situation is getting better because it is
getting worse: "Now you shall see what I will do to Pharaoh; for with a strong hand he will send them out, yea,
with a strong hand he will drive them out of his land"
(6:1). With this statement the J narrative is setting the

stage for the plagues and Yahweh's contest with Pharaoh.

The Priestly Account of Moses' Call
and Aaron's Appointment

The unit 6:2-7:7 is a priestly version of the same story recounted by the mixed JE traditions in 3:1-6:1. The style, vocabulary, and point of view are decidedly different in this section, and the fact that a number of incidents found in the JE story are repeated here makes it virtually certain that the unit is a variant account of the story. That it is a priestly version is quite evident in the number of priestly concerns which are highlighted. The most obvious fact is the preeminence given to Aaron. In many instances he is the one in the spotlight, not Moses.

The editor who put the story in the form we have it now probably thought that Moses, in his depressed mood, needed another revelation from God, and since the P version of the story started with God's appearance to Moses he inserted the account at this point. There is no reference to Horeb or Sinai, and thus implicitly the P tradition remembered Moses' call as coming in Egypt.

God's first words to Moses are, "I am Yahweh," and then he makes the declaration, which we considered earlier, that he had not made himself known to the Patriarchs by the name Yahweh. Yahweh informs Moses that he has heard the groaning of the people and that he intends to keep his covenant promise by bringing his people to the land of Canaan. Moses is instructed to tell the people the good news that Yahweh will deliver them from their miserable bondage "with an outstretched arm and with great acts of judgment" (6:6). He will take them to himself as his own people, and he in turn will be their God. Almost as an oath to verify his promises, Yahweh twice reiterates, "I am Yahweh." In the experience of the deliverance they will *know* that Yahweh is their God. Moses relays Yahweh's message of hope to the people, but they do not listen "because of their broken spirit and their cruel bondage" (6:9).

Then Yahweh instructs Moses to go to "Pharaoh, king of Egypt" (the combination of the single designations in JE) and tell him to let the people of Israel go out of the land. Moses replies, "Behold, the people of Israel have not listened to me. How then shall Pharaoh listen to me, who am a man of uncircumcised lips?" (6:12). The expression "uncircumcised lips" is a priestly way of having Moses say, "My lips are inadequate." In essence this is what Moses was saying at the burning bush, when he declared, "I am slow of speech and of tongue" (4:10).

Moses' objection is repeated in 6:30, and on inspection it is evident that 6:28-30 is a recapitulation of 6:2-12. In other words, 6:13-27 is a later addition. The editor had material which he wanted to preserve; therefore at a place which seemed appropriate he inserted the new material into the narrative. In order for the reader to pick up the thread of the story the editor summarized or repeated the narrative at the point where it was broken. This practice was observed by Harold M. Wiener, a British jurist, in the 1920's while doing research to counter the documentary theory of the literary critics. As a result he developed the "Repetitive Resumption" theory to account for much of the literary phenomena in the Pentateuch. While Wiener's theory does not explain the development and transmission of the various oral traditions, it does indicate some of the editorial steps in compiling the text as we have it. The Israeli scholar Shemaryahu Talmon has continued research along the lines suggested by Wiener, and in a paper (yet to be published) he claims to have found over 100 examples of repetitive resumption. In Exodus 1:6, for example, the reference to the death of Joseph picks up the narrative of Genesis 50:26. Therefore, the list of the "sons of Israel" is an editorial addition at a later time. The fact that 1:6 refers back to 50:26 is a clear indication, moreover, that the books Genesis and Exodus are artificial divisions of what was once a continuous story.

The section 6:13-27 must have been inserted by a priestly editor because the main topics are Aaron and his genealogy. Furthermore, it seems to have been inserted in the wrong place since Aaron is not mentioned as the spokesman for Moses until 7:1-2. In any case, the list begins with Reuben and his sons, and continues down the traditional order with Simeon. Levi follows him, but there the genealogy of the twelve tribes stops because the specific purpose is to trace the line of Aaron. In 6:20 Aaron and Moses are listed as the sons of Amram and Jochebed. The line of Moses is dropped at this point, but the lineage of Aaron, the elder son, is carried on through Eleazar to Phinehas, whose name is Egyptian and means "The Swarthy One." The genealogy is followed by a note in 6:26-27 explaining that the Aaron and Moses (in that order) of the genealogy were the persons whom Yahweh instructed to go to "Pharaoh, king of Egypt."

After the Aaronite genealogy, the repetition of Moses' objection picks up the narrative which was cut at 6:12. Then Yahweh answers, "See, I make you as God to Pharaoh, and Aaron your brother shall be your prophet" (7:1). This is a more explicit statement of what the J tradition has in 4:16. Moses' role as the prophet of God is shifted to Aaron; and in the contest with Pharaoh, Moses will act in the place of God. Moses will receive instructions from Yahweh and pass them on to Aaron, who will then be the actual spokesman before Pharaoh.

Moses is warned that Yahweh will harden Pharaoh's heart so that he will not listen in spite of many "signs and wonders." Pharaoh's refusal will be the occasion for Yahweh's action: "I will lay my hand upon Egypt and bring forth my hosts, my people the sons of Israel, out of the land of Egypt by great acts of judgment" (7:4). A new expression, which is distinctive to the P tradition, is the description of the sons of Israel as "my hosts." Another distinctive feature is the priestly idea that the plagues will be "judgments" (6:6; 7:4; 12:12). Furthermore, the whole contest between Yahweh and Pharaoh will be a teaching experience: "And the Egyptians shall know that I am Yahweh when I stretch forth my hand upon Egypt and bring out the people of Israel from among them." In the process of this experience both the Israelites (6:7) and the Egyptians (7:5) will learn who Yahweh really is. The unit closes with a scribal note that at the time Moses was eighty years old, but Aaron was eighty-three.

Literary Criticism of the Story of the Plagues

Literary critics have long recognized that the story of the plagues is a combination of different traditions. The normative analysis of the account is as follows:

Plague	J	E	P
1. Blood-red water	7:14-18, 20c-21a,	Parts of 7:15, 17, 20 with	7:19-20a, 21b-22

		23-25	"Moses' rod"	
2.	Frogs	8:1-4, 8-15		8:5-7
3.	Mos- quitoes			8:16-19
4.	Flies	8:20-32		
5.	Animal plague	9:1-7		
6.	Boils			9:8-12
7.	Hail	9:13-35	Parts of 9:22, 23,24,25,35 "Moses' rod"	
8.	Locusts	10:1-20, 24-26, 28-29	Parts of 10:12, 13,14,15,20	
9.	Darkness		10:21-23, 27	
10.	Death of firstborn	11:4-8	11:1-3	11:9-10

According to this analysis, J has seven plagues, E refers to five, and P describes five, but no single tradition includes all ten of them. Moreover, the fourth and fifth plagues appear only in J, the ninth only in E, and the third and sixth only in P. It should be observed that the portions assigned to the E tradition are very fragmentary, often being only a clause about Moses' rod. Somehow the older critics got the idea that any reference to a rod in the hand of Moses had to come from the E tradition. In the passage 4:2-4 Moses had a rod (Hebrew *matteh*) in his hand, and the section is clearly J. Yet the same word in 7:15, 17, 20 is assigned to the E tradition. This kind of nit-picking makes mincemeat of the text, and there is no need for it. With the exception of 9:30 (where "Yahweh Elohim" occurs) Yahweh is the consistent designation for God throughout the story. And even in 9:30 some of the early texts and translations omit "Elohim." As Noth observes, this is practically conclusive evidence against attributing any of the plague story to E.[1]

The question arises, then, whether all the portions assigned to E should be reassigned to J. Noth assigns 7:15,

---

[1] Martin Noth, *Exodus* (Philadelphia: Westminster, 1962), p. 70.

17, 20 and 11:1-3 to J, but practically all those in chapters 9 and 10 to P.[2] When Yahweh instructs Moses, "Stretch out your hand" (9:22; 10:12, 21), it is implicit that he has a rod in it; and this is made explicit in 9:23 and 10:13, "Moses stretched forth his rod." There is no doubt that in the P tradition Aaron has a rod, but the question is whether the priestly point of view would have remembered about Moses having a rod. By attributing the passages just noted to P, Noth is affirming that in the P tradition both Moses and Aaron have rods.

Characteristics of the J and P Traditions

Since the name Yahweh is used consistently in both the J and P traditions, Noth is certainly correct in declaring that the story of the plagues is a combination of J and P only. Some of the characteristics of these traditions are as follows:

J	P
1. In most cases, Moses alone is sent to Pharaoh, and he speaks for himself (verbs in the singular indicate this: 7:14-16; 8:1);	1. Moses works with and through Aaron; therefore a common expression is, "Say to Aaron" (7:9; 8:5, etc.);
2. Yahweh is identified as "the God of the Hebrews" (7:16; 9:1; 10:3);	2. Yahweh speaks of his people as "the sons (people) of Israel" (7:2, 4, 5; 9:35; 10:20);
3. Moses repeatedly makes the demand, "Let my people go" (7:16; 8:1, 20; 9:1, 13; 10:3);	3. The contest between Yahweh and Pharaoh is considered a power struggle. Aside from instructions in 7:2, no demands are made of Pharaoh;
4. When Pharaoh refuses, the plague is announced;	4. The plagues take place unannounced. They are viewed as signs of power and their description is brief;
5. The plagues take effect without human intervention (8:24; 9:6, etc.) or	5. The plagues take effect through the action of Aaron (7:10; 8:6, etc.);

[2] *Ibid.*

Moses, not Aaron, gives
the signal (7:20; 9:22; 10:
12, 21);

6. Magicians never men-
tioned;

6. Magicians mentioned a
number of times (7:11,
22; 8:7, 19, etc.);

7. Forms of the Hebrew verb
kabed ("to be heavy")
used to indicate Pharaoh's
"stubborn" heart;

7. Forms of the Hebrew verb
hazaq ("to be firm,
strong") used to indicate
Pharaoh's "hard" heart;

8. Tends to close with the
formula, "Pharaoh did not
let the people go" (8:32;
9:7, etc.).

8. Tends to close with the
formula, "Pharaoh would
not listen to them as Yahweh had said" (7:13, 22;
8:19, etc.).

Evaluation of the Literary Analysis

It has been noted that the older literary critics went
too far in attributing isolated portions of verses to the
E tradition. On the other hand, there is clear-cut evidence for a combination of the J and P traditions in the
story of the plagues. But what does this mean? Is the complete story of the events found in the combination of the
traditions, or is one of the traditions more accurate and
the other an elaboration due to oral transmission of the
story? How much of a historical base is there to the plagues?
How relevant are the variant details found in the traditions?

Scholars have ranged widely in answering all of these
questions. Up to the time of World War II the most common view was a fairly radical one. One remnant of this
approach found expression as late as 1952 in one of the
standard commentaries on the Bible.[3] The accounts of the
plagues are "fantastic stories," according to this scholar,
and any attempt to explain them "betrays a concern for
historical veracity or congruity at the cost of meaning and
truth." He grants that some of the plagues "rest on actual
events that facilitated the escape of the Israelites," but
that the stories as we have them are "a series of piously
decorated accounts" whose value "is symbolic rather than

---

[3] J. Coert Rylaarsdam, "The Book of Exodus," *The Interpreter's
Bible* (Nashville: Abingdon, n.d.), I, 839.

historical." Is it necessarily true that "historical veracity" must be pitted against "truth"? Fanciful additions do not mean that the whole account is unreliable. Why is it impossible, then, to discover the historical core of the stories? These questions have been taken into account in a thorough study of the plagues, published in 1957-58 by Greta Hort,[4] formerly of Prague and now at Aarhus University, Denmark. This study claims that all the plagues have a historical core, and that there is a cause and effect relationship between the plagues (except one) in the very order in which they appear in the combined story. Hort accepts the fact that variant traditions have come together to form the story, but that at the same time the combined story is the actual sequence of events. In telling the story of the plagues we will be drawing upon this study quite often.

Preparation for the Plagues

As a prelude to the actual plagues, the P tradition has the story in which Moses and Aaron prove themselves by performing a "wonder" (also translated "miracle"). Yahweh warns them that when Pharaoh says, "Prove yourselves by performing a wonder," then Moses is to instruct Aaron to cast his rod down at the feet of Pharaoh and it will become a serpent (Hebrew *tannin*). This Hebrew word is used most often in the sense of a "dragon" (either on land or in the sea). This is in contrast to the J account of 4:3 where Moses' rod turned into a *nahash* ("snake").

After Pharaoh and his servants watch Aaron's rod turn into the formidable serpent, Pharaoh calls for his wise men, sorcerers, and magicians. They duplicate the trick, but Aaron proves that Yahweh is superior because his serpent swallows the Egyptian serpents. In spite of this amazing event, Pharaoh's heart is hard and he will not listen to Moses and Aaron. The story is rather fanciful, and it is difficult in this instance to know what actually did happen. It should be noted, however, that this sign or wonder by Aaron in the presence of Pharaoh may have influenced an editor to suppose that Aaron did some signs before the

---

[4] Greta Hort, "The Plagues of Egypt," *Zeitschrift für die alttestamentliche Wissenschaft*, LXIX (1957), 84-103, and LXX (1958), 48-59.

people as well, and thus he inserted in 4:30 "and he did the signs in the sight of the people."

The First Plague: The Blood-red Nile

The accounts of the first plague appear in the section 7:14-24. Inasmuch as Pharaoh's heart is still stubborn, Yahweh instructs Moses to go to the river bank in the morning and wait for Pharaoh as he comes down (perhaps to bathe). When he arrives, Moses reminds him that he has not obeyed Yahweh's demand "Let my people go," and then he conveys Yahweh's warning: "By this you shall know that I am Yahweh: behold, I will strike the water that is in the Nile with the rod that is in my hand, and it shall be turned to blood, and the fish in the Nile shall die, and the Nile shall become foul, and the Egyptians will loathe to drink water from the Nile" (7:17-18). Since Yahweh is the subject of the sentence, he is claiming to have a rod in his hand with which he will strike the water. This is indeed strange, because nowhere else is Yahweh pictured as using a rod to bring about the plagues. The original statement of Yahweh probably said, "I will strike the water that is in the Nile and it shall be turned to blood." Since the rod of Moses and Aaron is employed in most of the plagues, perhaps someone felt that Yahweh had to have a rod and so he inserted "with the rod that is in my hand." Later on Moses strikes the Nile with his rod and the Nile turns blood-red. Because they could not drink the water of the Nile the Egyptians "dug round about the Nile for water to drink" (7:24).

In the P version the plague extends throughout Egypt so that all surface sources of water turn to blood: not only the main river, but the canals, ponds, pools, and even "in the trees and in the stones" (7:19). The RSV interprets this to mean "both in vessels of wood and in vessels of stone." But it could mean that the sap of the trees and the springs from the rocks were affected as well. Even though the precise meaning is uncertain, the passage is part of P's claim that every bit of surface water in Egypt turned to blood. Later on P states, "The magicians of Egypt did the same by their secret arts" (7:22). If all the surface liquid of Egypt had already been turned into blood, how could the magicians perform the same miracle? The theme of the magicians is greatly enhanced with the express purpose of showing the power of Yahweh. They will be able to repeat the first few plagues, but finally they will be outclassed and frankly admit to Pharaoh, "This is the finger of God" (8:19). With this understanding, therefore, the actions of the magicians should not be expected to fit logically into the sequence of events. Putting aside for a while the issue of the extent of the plague, the basic feature common to both traditions is that the water of the Nile turned blood-red. The essential problem, therefore, is to determine whether such a condition ever existed.

Annual Flooding of the Nile

The biblical witness that the Nile turned blood-red is supported by a nonbiblical Egyptian text which refers to a blood-red Nile as one of the plagues which will come upon Egypt in an evil period of time. It is very unlikely that such a fantastic idea would ever have found expression either in or out of the Bible had there not been some basis in fact.

The sources of the Nile in Egypt are the White Nile and the Blue Nile. The White Nile originates in the lake region of east-central Africa, known today as Uganda. The fairly consistent equatorial rains swell the river until it is a large stream. It loses much of its water supply, however, as it flows through the swamps that have been formed in the plains of eastern Sudan. The Blue Nile, on the other hand, originates in the headwaters of the Ethiopian highlands. There are no swamps because the stream flows swiftly down its gorge until it joins the White Nile at Khartoum. While the White Nile is fairly steady in its flow, the Blue Nile varies from a small stream to a raging torrent. It is at its highest in September because of the summer monsoon rains and the melting snow of the mountains. At this time of the year the swollen Nile flows north over the outcropping of granite known as the Sixth Cataract. Before it reaches the Fifth Cataract it is enlarged still further by the Atbara, a seasonal river flowing (like the Blue Nile) from the Ethiopian highlands. This tremendous increase in water flow was the reason for the annual flooding of the Nile.

The Route of the Nile

From the point of the confluence with the Atbara, the Nile flows in the shape of a gigantic letter "s" covering the northern part of Sudan (ancient Nubia, meaning "Gold") and roaring over four cataracts (Fifth-Second). In ancient times the river flowed another 250 miles down to the First Cataract, the traditional southern boundary of Egypt where the outpost town of Syene (modern Aswan) was located. This portion of the river is now a lake because the High Dam at Aswan has backed Lake Nasser all the way to the Second Cataract.

From Aswan (only 295 feet above sea level) the Nile flows gently through its narrow valley for about 500 miles. At times the desert and the surrounding hills come to the river's edge on both sides, while at other places the valley widens out a few miles. Just south of modern Cairo, at the site of Memphis, the ancient capital of northern Egypt, the Nile valley widens out into a "v" shape and the river separates into a number of channels forming the Delta region. This northern section of Egypt from Memphis to the Mediterranean Sea has traditionally been called "Lower Egypt" because it is the lowest in altitude, while the narrow ribbon of arable land stretching south from Memphis to Aswan has been called "Upper Egypt." The climate and living conditions of the two regions have always been different, which in turn have resulted in varying customs and points of view among the people of the two areas. The problem of uniting the different groups was a perpetual concern for the Pharaohs. This age-old difference is preserved in the Hebrew name for Egypt, *Misraim*, meaning "Two Regions," and this fact will have some bearing on understanding the plagues.

Various Colors of the Nile

In the past (as now) the water of the White Nile was white for most of the year due to decomposed matter picked up in the swampy regions in the Sudan. But when the water lowered, the White Nile began to pick up fresh vegetable matter and the color changed to a cabbage green. As the vegetable matter decayed, the water acquired a foul odor and taste. During those years in which the summer rains of Ethiopia failed to materialize, the water of the

Nile proper consisted largely of the supply from the White Nile. Over the centuries, therefore, it was learned that when the water of the Nile became green and undrinkable it was the sign of an extremely difficult year because there would be little, if any, flooding of the Nile.

Because the biblical account refers to the foul water of the Nile which the people were loathe to drink, older scholars attempted to interpret the first plague as a period when the Nile was below normal. But this explanation is invalid for two basic reasons: the water would have been greenish, not blood-red, and although undrinkable the water would not have killed the fish. The explanation of the biblical plague must be sought, therefore, in exceptional events associated with the flooding of the Nile.

During most of the year in ancient times, as now, the water of the Blue Nile was a crystal blue, as the name implies. But when the river became a torrent the color changed to the color of the soil picked up along the way. The Ethiopian highlands had a thick covering of very bright red soil (almost carmine in color) which formed a very fine dust when it dried out. During the average rainy season the Blue Nile picked up the loose particles which had accumulated along the edges of the river valley since the last year, and thus it became pinkish in color. During the excessively heavy rains, however, more red earth washed off the slopes of the hills, and the river, raging down its course at an exceptional height, scoured additional tons of the red earth from the walls of the valley. At the confluence of the two rivers the terrific flow of the Blue Nile (now blood-red) almost blocked off the flow of the White Nile, so it did very little to reduce the intense red color. Further downstream the Atbara poured more red water into the river. Inasmuch as there were no dams to restrict its flow, the Nile flooded blood-red all the way to the Mediterranean because some of the fine particles of red earth remained in suspension.

An excessively high flooding of the Nile was just as disastrous as no flood, but in a different way. Since Egypt, to all extents and purposes, consisted mainly of the valley of the Nile, a very high flood inundated most of the valley. The wells and irrigation ditches with their sluice gates were ruined, and pools of water settled where there had been none for years. Egyptian records speak of such conditions as "the vast abyss," or "a veritable sea." With this understanding of the situation the claims of the P account do not appear to be as exaggerated as most scholars have claimed. The biblical narrative, it should be noted, does not claim exemption for the land of Goshen because it too would have felt the impact of the high flood. During the time of Ramses there was an all-water route from the Nile, near Memphis, to the Gulf of Suez. It ran through Wadi Tumilat, and just west of Lake Timsah it turned south, skirting the western edge of the Bitter Lakes and finally connecting with the Gulf. The canal, therefore, would have been blood-red with silt and algae. Furthermore, the pollution of the wells of those who normally lived some distance from the river would explain why the Egyptians (and presumably the Israelites) had to dig wells at the edge of the high flood in order to get the drinkable water which had filtered through the soil.

Mountain Algae

While the high Nile accounts for the blood-red color of the water and the reason for digging wells at its edge, it does not explain the death of the fish, the stench of the water, and its undrinkable quality. The German botanist Gessner has suggested that the torrential rains causing the high Nile brought mountain algae (known as flagellates) and their bacteria from Lake Tana and the surrounding region. These algae are brilliant red and would have given the water an even more blood-red appearance. They give off a great deal of oxygen during the day, but at night they absorb an even greater amount. This great fluctuation of oxygen, above and below the normal level for fish, would gradually weaken the fish and finally kill them. It is doubtful that the dead fish were evenly distributed throughout the surface water, because they would tend to collect in eddies and clumps of reeds or brush. Accordingly, the undrinkable quality of the water was probably due primarily to the flagellates, and the stench of the water was due to the bacteria associated with the flagellates.

The Historicity of the First Plague

An exceptionally high flooding of the Nile accounts for

all the essential conditions described in the biblical narrative of the first plague; thus one can be reasonably assured that an actual historical event lay back of the story. While the plague itself was a rare, but natural, event, this fact does not detract from the sense of wonder. The miraculous element consisted in the timing. That an event, which occurs only once every century or so, should take place just as Moses was negotiating with Pharaoh is a remarkable coincidence indeed, and it is not hard to see why the Hebrews considered it to be the hand of Yahweh striking the Nile. There are additions and exaggerations, but these (like the references to the magicians) came with oral tradition and do not negate the essential truth of the story.

One of the most recent results of associating the first plague with the flooding of the Nile is that it is possible to determine rather closely the time of the year in which it occurred. The Blue Nile and the Atbara begin flooding in July and August. They reach their peak in September and fall rapidly during October and November. Allowing for the distance the flood crest had to travel, the month of August was probably the onset of the first plague, and its immediate effects continued into November.

Some scholars have assumed that the original description of the first plague mentioned its sudden cessation, but that an editor deleted the statement. This argument from silence is too dependent on the assumption that all the plagues had been standardized into a regular pattern. There are a number of variations in the accounts which indicate, from the form critical point of view, that tradition did not force the plague stories into a rigid mold. There is a pattern in the J and P traditions, to be sure, but this does not eliminate the distinctive details which tradition remembered. The biblical narrative says nothing about the cessation of the first plague because it continued for some time. Only as the Nile fell to its usual level and fresh water from the White Nile washed the algae out to sea would the plague abate, and fish and human life return to normal.

The Second Plague: Frogs

The accounts of the second plague appear in the section 7:25-8:15. Seven days after Yahweh brought on the first plague by striking the Nile, he instructs Moses to go to

Pharaoh and ask in his name, "Let my people go, that they may serve me." He is warned that if he refuses, frogs will swarm out of the Nile and get into every part of the houses, even into the kitchen area. Pharaoh's palace, like the regular homes, will be alive with the creatures. It is implicit that he refused Moses' request because the frogs swarm over the land. This experience gets to Pharaoh more than the first plague, and he calls for Moses and Aaron. "Entreat Yahweh," he pleads, "to take away the frogs from me and from my people; and I will let the people go to sacrifice to Yahweh" (8:4). Pharaoh has come "to know" the power of Yahweh, and for the time being he is willing to recognize the God of Israel. In order to rub it in a little bit, Moses says, "Be pleased to command me when I am to entreat for you," and Pharaoh answers, "Tomorrow." It will be done as he requests, Moses explains, so that he may know that there is no one like Yahweh. Moses prays to Yahweh, and at the appointed time the frogs "die out of the houses and courtyards and out of the fields" (8:13). They are gathered in piles and the land reeks with the stench of decayed flesh.

In the P tradition Aaron stretches his hand with the rod over the waters of Egypt and frogs come up and cover the land. Again, the magicians are given credit for repeating the plague. From ancient times the Nile has swarmed with little frogs. Late in September and on into October, when the annual flood is receding, they come up on the dry land along the edge of the river. Yet this cannot be the explanation because it is a regular event. Furthermore, the second plague occurred in August, just a week after the first plague started.

Most likely the dead fish washed to the edges of the river and got caught in eddies and clumps of reeds and brush. They attracted various insects and became infected with the spores of anthrax bacillus carried by the insects from the land along the river. While frogs do not eat fish, they too became infected by anthrax spores contaminating the water and the air along the edges of the river because that was their natural habitat. Finally, the pollution caused by the bacteria and decomposing fish forced the frogs to leave the river. Not liking direct sunlight, they sought out shady places with some moisture. This would explain why they came into the homes. Within a short time they would die, all within a day or two, because they were infected with anthrax about the same time. There were so many frogs the people simply made heaps of the dead bodies while they were collecting them. Due to the virulent nature of anthrax the heaps of flesh began to decompose before the people could dig holes and bury them, and so the stench permeated the whole country.

The fact that the basic details of the biblical narratives in both the first and second plagues follow a definite cause and effect relationship is hardly to be attributed to some ancient storyteller trying to get across a spiritual truth. There are too many details and they mesh too nicely to be an accident or contrivance of an editor. The stories came into being because the plagues actually occurred. Again, it should be noted that the land of Goshen was not exempted because the frogs were all over Egypt.

Pharaoh's Stubborn Heart

One of the major themes in the contest between Yahweh and Pharaoh is the persistent refusal of the king to grant the request of Moses. Even though he pleaded with Moses to ask Yahweh for deliverance from the frogs, when the frogs died and he had relief from the plague "he caused his heart to be heavy" (8:15). This is a literal translation of the J tradition statement, which uses the causative form of the verb *kabed* ("to be heavy"). The standard translations have "he hardened his heart," but others use "stiffened," or "made stubborn, obstinate," to distinguish *kabed* from the P tradition verb *hazaq* ("to be firm, strong, hard"). The important factor in this J tradition statement is that Pharaoh was the one making his heart stubborn or obstinate. The same expression occurs in 8:32 and 9:34. Yet in 7:14 and 9:7 J employs the ambiguous expression, "Pharaoh's heart was heavy," without stating explicitly who made his heart heavy.

A further complication is the J statement in which Yahweh says with respect to Pharaoh, "I have made his heart and the heart of his servants heavy, that I may show these signs of mine among them" (10:1). Had Pharaoh yielded to Moses' request after the first plague and let the people go, there would have been no more oppor-

tunity for Yahweh to do his "signs." No Pharaoh would
have granted Moses' demand so readily, however. Least
of all would this have been true of Ramses II. His ego,
empire, and way of life were threatened, and although
he yielded temporarily under the pressure of the plagues
he reverted to type when the pressure was off. The continual vacillation depicted in the biblical narrative makes
sense psychologically because Ramses II would have acted
in just this manner. The J tradition recognized Pharaoh's
part in his stubborn refusal to grant the request, but since
Yahweh was ultimately responsible for all actions of men
and nature, the drawn-out series of plagues was interpreted as the work of Yahweh. In this way tradition thought
that Yahweh had lengthened the negotiations in order to
punish Pharaoh for daring to ask, "Who is Yahweh?"

The same point of view is found in the P tradition. The
ambiguous statement "Pharaoh's heart was hard" occurs
in 7:13, 22; 8:19; 9:35, but "Yahweh hardened Pharaoh's
heart" appears in 9:12; 10:20, 27. The fact of Yahweh's
initiative is made clear in 11:9 where Yahweh says to
Moses, "Pharaoh will not listen to you; that my wonders
may be multiplied in the land of Egypt." The view that
Yahweh used Pharaoh as a puppet in order to prove
himself and vindicate his own ego is quite foreign in an
age which stresses freedom of the human will, and many
readers of the Bible have been perplexed. In trying to
understand such Old Testament interpretations of events,
it must be remembered that the people of the ancient
biblical world did not make a distinction between primary
and secondary causes. Most interpreters of the Bible today
would say, with the three passages in J, "Pharaoh made
his heart heavy." His ego and whole way of life were
at stake, and in order to save face and maintain his control he exercised his own will, refusing to let the people
of Israel go. In other words, the primary reason for this
stubbornness was Pharaoh himself. Yet in the broader
context of the ancient world, God created Pharaoh with
a strong ego determined to defend itself. While Pharaoh's
part was not ignored, God himself was considered (in a
secondary sense) as responsible for Pharaoh's actions.

The Third Plague: Mosquitoes

The third plague is described in just four verses (8:16-19). Aaron, at the command of Moses, strikes the dust on the earth and these particles of soil become *kinnim* "throughout all the land of Egypt." On the basis of an older interpretation the King James Version translated "lice," but this is very unlikely. The Septuagint has a Greek word which seems to mean "gnats," and this is the translation in the RSV. Yet Origen, who lived in Egypt and became one of the great scholars in the early Christian Church, interpreted the term to be "small stinging insects." Gnats can bite, but most likely Origen's reference was to "mosquitoes," and this is what the American Translation has.

During the normal flooding of the Nile, pools of water were left as the river receded. Mosquitoes laid their eggs in the pools, and within a short time thousands of young mosquitoes hatched. This occurred annually during October and November, while the pools were drying up. Those who normally lived some distance from the Nile were not affected as much as those near the water. But during an exceptionally high flood there were pools all over Egypt and everyone was pestered by the insects. The excessive amount of water over a longer period meant an enormous multiplication of the pests, and they tapered off gradually only as the pools dried up. The third plague occurred during October and November, just like the normal appearance of the mosquitoes, but the intensity and extent of the scourge were so much greater than usual the people interpreted the event as one of Yahweh's "signs." And why not, since it grew out of the conditions of the first plague? Moses and Aaron must have been scratching along with Pharaoh, because the land of Goshen was not exempted from the mosquitoes.

An interesting feature of the narrative describing the third plague is the failure of the magicians to produce mosquitoes. Why this should be more difficult than the first two plagues is not indicated. The sky was swarming with mosquitoes. Surely, the magicians could have used their "secret arts" to claim that some of the insects were their own creation. But they didn't, and in awe they say to

Pharaoh, "This is the finger of God." He will not listen, however, because his heart is hard.

The Fourth Plague: Flies

The unit describing the fourth plague is 8:20-32. Moses is instructed by Yahweh to get up early in the morning and confront Pharaoh again at the water's edge: "Let my people go, that they may serve me." He is warned that a refusal will bring on swarms of flies, and then he is told, "But on that day I will set apart the land of Goshen, where my people dwell, so that no swarms of flies shall be there; that you may know that I am Yahweh in the midst of the earth. Thus I will put a division between my people and your people. By tomorrow shall this sign be" (8:22-23).

The flies swarm on schedule, and soon Pharaoh makes his first concession, "Go, sacrifice to your God within the land" (8:25). Pharaoh is willing to let the Hebrews have a few days of rest in order to serve Yahweh, but he wants to keep them within his grasp, to be put back to work when the vacation is over. Moses understands his intentions, and he uses a clever argument in refusing the offer. Pharaoh's idea would not be good because their sacrifices would be "abominable to the Egyptians," and so they would stone the Hebrews. Just how many Egyptians would be watching the proceedings in the land of Goshen is a question, but Moses uses the argument anyway and returns to the original demands, "We must go three days' journey into the wilderness and sacrifice to Yahweh."

Apparently Pharaoh's will power is weakening somewhat, because on hearing Moses' adamant request he answers, "I will let you go to sacrifice to Yahweh your God in the wilderness; only you shall not go very far away. Make entreaty for me" (8:28). Pharaoh is ready to let the people sacrifice in the wilderness, but he wants them to stay pretty close to the border. In this way his frontier guards can keep an eye on them. Moses is willing to play the game because his basic demand has been met; therefore he offers to pray to Yahweh in Pharaoh's behalf. Just in case he is tempted to forget his bargain, Moses warns him that he should not "deal falsely again" by refusing to let the people go. Moses prays and Yahweh removes the flies from Pharaoh and the Egyptians. The narrative adds, with finality, "Not one remained." But when the plague is gone he makes his heart obstinate again. With such a short memory, the warning goes with the flies and Ramses backs down on his agreement.

There is a type of fly known as *Stomoxys calcitrans*. It comes late in the fly season and it bites, usually the lower extremities of animals and men. In tropical climates it multiplies rapidly. The eggs are laid in rotting vegetable matter (sometimes mixed with dung), and within a month or so a whole new generation of flies comes into existence. But when the vegetable matter has decayed or dried up, the flies disappear. It was apparently this type of fly which appeared as the fourth plague. Toward the end of October, when the Nile was in the process of recession, land along the river's edge had quantities of decaying vegetation. Eggs laid there hatched in late November, and this new generation in turn laid more eggs in the decaying vegetation of the last stage of the Nile's recession. The second generation appeared in late December and early January, and after their short life span the flies suddenly disappeared.

This cycle of flies occurred in Upper Egypt, where the temperature is very hot even in November and December; but in Lower Egypt at this time of the year the cool breezes from the Mediterranean produce a temperate climate which would not have permitted the scourge of flies. The biblical narrative is correct, therefore, in claiming that the Hebrews in the land of Goshen were spared this plague. One problem arises, however. All the Egyptians in the temperate climate of Lower Egypt should have been spared this plague as well, including Ramses and all the Egyptians of his capital complex. Either oral tradition assumed that since the Hebrews had been spared, all the Egyptians were plagued, or it made the general distinction of associating Lower Egypt with the Hebrews and Upper Egypt with the Egyptians, inasmuch as most of the Egyptians lived between Memphis and Aswan. Although the present form of the narrative overstates the case, it is essentially correct in remembering that the fourth plague was different because the Hebrews were spared.

One further matter of interpretation needs to be considered at this point. Inasmuch as the third plague is entirely assigned to the P tradition and all the fourth plague is J, a number of scholars have been saying for years that the two accounts are really variant descriptions of the same plague. This is a tempting solution. If the two were equated, then the failure of the magicians to produce insects would mean that they tried to return the favor by bringing insects on the Hebrews, but could not because Yahweh spared them. On the other hand, the Hebrew name of the insect is different in each case. Moreover, P understands the plague to extend "throughout all the land of Egypt," while J remembers that it was all of Egypt, except Goshen. Both of the zoological explanations make sense of the biblical data, and it would seem that until more definitive evidence is forthcoming it would be wiser to treat the accounts in P and J as separate plagues.

The Fifth Plague: Death of the Livestock

The account of the fifth plague appears in 9:1-7, which is one definite unit of material. It looks like J, but it is varied in the pattern of its presentation. As usual Moses is instructed what to say to Pharaoh, but in the middle of the sentence Yahweh's quotation shifts from the first person (as in 8:21) to the third person (9:3). Moreover, the typical negotiating session with Pharaoh is dropped completely. Yahweh's threat this time is a severe plague (murrain) on "the cattle which are in the field." The term "cattle" is used in the general sense of "livestock," and so a list of specific animals follows: horses, asses, camels, and herds (regular cattle or oxen) as "big stock," and flocks (sheep and goats) as "little stock." Yahweh will make a distinction again because the cattle of Israel will not die. Implicitly Pharaoh refuses to let the people go, the murrain comes, and "all the cattle" of the Egyptians die. Pharaoh sends an inspection party to Goshen, and they report that "not one of the cattle of the Israelites was dead" (9:7). Still, Pharaoh does not let the people go because his heart is stubborn.

The crucial piece of information concerning this plague is that the murrain would be on the livestock "in the field." During the period June through December (that is, the time spanning the annual inundation of the Nile) livestock were kept within their stalls. In the early part of January, when portions of the flooded land had dried out, some of the livestock were let out into the fields. As they roamed they grazed where the heaps of frogs had been. In doing so they consumed anthrax spores with their food, and in time they died just as the frogs had. When the narrative says that "all the cattle" died, it means all the animals that had been "in the field." The livestock of the Hebrews were still in their stalls early in January because the draining and drying process was slower in Lower Egypt and the livestock would have mired into the soft earth. This prevented the animals from contracting anthrax, and thereby they were spared.

The Sixth Plague: Boils

The narrative about the sixth plague is the section 9:8-12. It is entirely from the P tradition, but the usual form of narration has been altered. As in the J tradition, Moses is the chief actor, and Aaron and his rod fade into the background. Yahweh instructs Moses and Aaron, "Take handfuls of ashes from the kiln, and let Moses throw them toward heaven in the sight of Pharaoh. And it shall become fine dust over all the land of Egypt, and become boils breaking out in sores on man and beast throughout all the land of Egypt" (9:8-9). They take ashes and Moses throws them toward heaven. Even the magicians get the boils, and they cannot "stand before Moses." Again, Pharaoh refuses to let the people go because Yahweh has hardened his heart.

The sixth plague is definitely related to the fourth. The pestiferous flies undoubtedly investigated the areas where the frog heaps had been, and in doing so they became carriers of anthrax spores. As they bit the legs of men and beasts (in late December and early January), their hosts contracted skin anthrax with its boils and blains. Since the flies were limited to Upper Egypt, it is implicit that the skin anthrax was limited to the same region. Since the P tradition never gives any hint as to what is happening in Goshen, a statement about an exemption for the Israelites would not be expected. Some scholars have considered the mention of "beasts" as proof of a contradiction with the fifth plague. As noted above, however, some of the livestock of Upper Egypt were kept in their stalls. They were spared death from internal anthrax, but the flies could carry skin anthrax to them. Inasmuch as the flies tended to bite the feet and legs, it is quite understandable why the magicians could not "stand" before Moses. The narrative makes no mention of a sudden cessation of the plague because it would take weeks to get rid of the infectious anthrax. The boils probably started early in January and continued on into February.

As in the case of the mosquitoes and the flies, some scholars have contended that the fifth plague (all J) and the sixth plague (all P) are variants of the same plague. Anthrax and animals are common to both, but in the fifth plague only animals are involved and the infection is internal, resulting in death. In the sixth plague, both men and beasts are involved, but the infection is not fatal because it is on the skin. There is every reason, therefore, to consider the plagues as separate events. It is much easier to explain the biblical data if one holds that in transmission of the stories J and P each dropped one of the events in each of the pairs of similar plagues, rather than to ignore the genuine differences in the narratives and consider them variants of the same plague.

The Seventh Plague: Hail

The account of the seventh plague, largely J, occurs in 9:13-35. Moses confronts Pharaoh "early in the morning" and makes the same request, "Let my people go." As a veiled threat Yahweh is quoted as saying, "For this time I will send all my plagues upon your heart, ... that you may know that there is none like me in all the earth." The meaning is uncertain. It seems to indicate that a climax of Yahweh's activity is near, but the plague of hail, while awesome, is not the last of Yahweh's signs. Perhaps Yahweh intends that Pharaoh rehearse the plagues seriously and "take to heart" their meaning. Yahweh tells Pharaoh that he could have struck him down, but that he saved his life so he could witness his power. The stories of the signs and wonders will spread to other nations so that Yahweh's name will "be declared throughout all the earth."

Since Pharaoh is still "exalting" himself, he is warned that his refusal will result in very heavy hail "such as never has been in Egypt from the day it was founded until now" (9:18). Yahweh goes a step further by warning Pharaoh, and indirectly all the people of the court, to bring their slaves and animals under cover. Here for the first time "the servants of Pharaoh" are given a chance to express their faith in Yahweh, and some do so, even at the risk of infuriating their king. Moses points his rod toward heaven and Yahweh sends thunder and hail. Fire runs down to the earth, and everything in the field is pelted with the phenomenal hailstones. The people in Goshen are spared, however, since there is no hail there.

Pharaoh calls for Moses and Aaron and confesses, "I have sinned this time; Yahweh is in the right and I and my people are in the wrong" (9:27). He pleads for Yahweh's mercy and promises, "I will let you go, and you shall stay no longer." Then Moses answers, "As soon as I have gone out of the city, I will stretch out my hands to Yahweh; the thunder will cease, and there will be no more hail, that you may know that the earth is Yahweh's. But as for you and your servants, I know that you do not yet fear Yahweh" (9:29-30). Heretofore Moses has waited until the next day to petition Yahweh, but this time he does so as soon as he is outside the capital city of Ramses. The hail stops, but Pharaoh sins once more by refusing to let the Hebrews go.

A scribal note in 9:31-32 is of prime importance in dating the seventh plague: "The flax and the barley were ruined, for the barley was in the ear and the flax was in bud. But the wheat and the spelt were not ruined, for they are late in coming up." The addition is awkwardly placed because it fits logically after verse 25, where the hail damage is described, but its value is not impaired by this dislocation. Thunderstorms with hail are rare in Upper Egypt, yet they do occur. An important factor is that they are not seasonal in this region; consequently they can appear at any time. In the more temperate climate of Lower Egypt, on the other hand, hailstorms normally occur in late spring and early autumn. A rare storm may appear in the summer, but never between November and March.

The normal schedule of planting and reaping in Egypt was as follows: barley, wheat, and spelt were sown in August, but barley grew faster and was harvested in

February, while wheat and spelt were not ready until the end of March; flax was planted at the beginning of January and it flowered in about three weeks. Allowing for a delay of two weeks or so due to the extra high flood, flax was probably planted in mid-January that year, and thus in flower just at the time that the barley was ready to reap. The hail ruined both of these crops, but the wheat and spelt were not up far enough yet to be harmed.

Accordingly, the seventh plague came in February. It must have been a frightful storm racing up the Nile valley from the Mediterranean, for when the cool, moist air encountered the very hot, dry air of Upper Egypt, lightning streaked to the earth ahead of the mammoth hailstones. The inhabitants of the upper valley, accustomed to cloudless skies, must have watched in awe at the devastation of the hail and the display of fireworks and roaring thunder. Goshen and the Israelites probably got plenty of rain from the storm, but the temperature was too cool there to form any hail. The biblical narrative assumes that Pharaoh and his servants were subject to the hail, but the Egyptians in the Delta region were undoubtedly spared as well. When Moses walked out of the city to pray to Yahweh, he may have gotten wet, but he was not struck with hail.

The Eighth Plague: Locusts

The section 10:1-20, largely J, is the account of the eighth plague. Before instructing Moses what to say to Pharaoh, Yahweh warns him that he has made Pharaoh's heart stubborn. This time his servants will join him in his obstinacy, so that Yahweh may show his signs among them. Another purpose of Yahweh's action is that Moses may tell his son and grandson (the Septuagint has "children and grandchildren") how Yahweh "made sport of the Egyptians" (10:2). Moses and Aaron confront Pharaoh and say, "Thus says Yahweh, the God of the Hebrews, 'How long will you refuse to humble yourself before me? Let my people go, that they may serve me.'" Refusal will mean an exceptional plague of locusts covering the land, filling the houses, and eating all the vegetation left over from the hail. Then Moses turns and walks out.

Some of Pharaoh's servants are not impressed with his obdurate handling of the problem, and with all common sense they ask, "How long shall this man be a snare to us? Let the men go, that they may serve Yahweh their God; do you not yet understand that Egypt is ruined?" (10:7). Pharaoh accepts their suggestion and has Moses and Aaron brought back. "Go, serve Yahweh your God," Pharaoh commands, but then he asks, "Who are to go?" Moses reports that all of the people and their livestock will go: young and old, sons and daughters, flocks and herds. Pharaoh accuses them of having an "evil purpose," and he swears that he will never let the "little ones" go. He knows that the adults will never run away if the children are still in Egypt. Then Pharaoh makes his offer, "You men go serve Yahweh, for that is what you want" (10:11).

But Moses wants more, and so he stretches out his rod over the land. Yahweh sends "an east wind" that blows all day and night, and in the morning the earth is covered with the swarming locusts. Moses and Aaron are summoned quickly and Pharaoh confesses again, "I have sinned against Yahweh your God, and against you. Now, therefore, forgive my sin, I pray you, only this once, and entreat Yahweh your God only to remove this death from me" (10:16-17). Locusts are fearsome enough at any time, but this tremendous army is terrifying to behold. Moses senses the emergency, and apparently he prays just after leaving the palace. In answer to his entreaty, "Yahweh turned a very strong sea breeze, which lifted the locusts and drove them into the Reed Sea; not a single locust was left in all the country of Egypt" (10:19). But Pharaoh's hardened heart refuses to let the children of Israel go.

Locusts were nothing new to the Egyptians. Every so often a black cloud of them would fly in from the southeast. Their ultimate origin seems to have been down in the Sudan. In September the mature locusts migrated to regions around Port Sudan, on the west side of the Red Sea, and Jidda, across the Sea on the Arabian Peninsula. Eggs deposited in these regions during September hatched out in winter, and by February and March they were mature enough to migrate on their own. They usually flew north following the Red Sea. If the winds were more from the southwest, the locusts were driven to Palestine, but if a Sirocco (a hot wind from the Arabian Peninsula) came up, the locusts were blown over Egypt, mostly in the northern section.

The exceedingly wet summer in Ethiopia, which sent the Nile on its rampage, must have brought more moisture to the Port Sudan and Jidda areas as well. Thus there must have been a bumper crop of young locusts in late February. As they winged their way north the Sirocco caught them and drove them over Egypt. Within a short time the munching army had stripped the land bare. Normally the Sirocco winds blow across the Sinai Peninsula, up the Gulf of Suez, and into the Delta region. This would have meant that most of the plague was in Lower Egypt; yet the account says that all of Egypt was involved.

Deliverance from the locusts came with "a very strong sea breeze." In Palestine this would have meant a west wind, but in Egypt it would have meant a north or northwest wind. It is a question, then, of how to interpret the expression "sea breeze." Most translations have "west wind," on the assumption that the Palestinian understanding of the expression was intended, but it is quite possible that the expression originally had an Egyptian orientation. In that case, a strong Mediterranean breeze drove the locusts south, and they denuded the countryside en route. The only difficulty with this interpretation is the claim that the locusts were driven into the Reed Sea. Most translations have "Red Sea," but this is impossible, as we shall see in the next chapter. The Reed Sea was to the east or northeast of the land of Goshen; therefore a west wind would have cleared only the northern part of Egypt. Hort suggests that the words which now mean "Reed Sea," originally read "right hand." Inasmuch as the ancients were "oriented" (that is, the points of reference were determined by facing east), the expression "right hand" meant "south." With this understanding, the biblical narrative claims that during February a very heavy Mediterranean storm drove the locusts south, up the Nile valley, and eventually out of the country. The uncommon feature of the plague was not the presence of locusts. Rather, it was their intensity and the extent of their devastating activity which led the people to consider the scourge as the hand of Yahweh.

The Ninth Plague: Thick Darkness

The ninth plague appears in very abbreviated form in 10:21-23 (mostly P), and the final negotiations with Pharaoh (mostly J) appear in 10:24-29. Yahweh instructs Moses to stretch out his hand toward heaven "that there may be darkness over the land of Egypt, a darkness to be felt." Moses does so, and there is a "thick darkness in all the land of Egypt three days," except that "all the people of Israel" have light where they dwell. The darkness is so bad no one leaves his place because it is impossible to see anything.

Beginning in March, strong winds blow off the Sahara desert from the south and southwest. These hot winds are called the *Khamsin,* meaning "fifty," which is an abbreviation of the Arabic description, "the fifty-day wind." For two or three days at a time these driving winds pick up sand and dust until the sky is a thick yellow fog with the sun peeking through as a pale disk. Their period of intensity is about fifty days, thus the Arabic name.

After the plague of locusts the thick layer of red silt, which had been laid down by the flood, had no vegetation to hold it in place and the hot sun dried it out until it became dust. Early in March, when the first storm of the *Khamsin* came off the Sahara, it swept across the barren, flat surfaces of the Nile valley picking up the fine red particles until the darkness was so thick the sun was obliterated. The stinging particles in the driving wind were felt, and most certainly the heat was felt, but the biblical statement seems to have a psychological overtone in that the awesome, uncanny aspects of the storm got to the Egyptians. The storm lasted for three days, and no one dared go outside.

Inasmuch as the Israelites were in the far northeast corner of Egypt and somewhat protected by the hills on the south side of Wadi Tumilat, the winds were not as strong there. Furthermore, the layer of red silt would not yet have dried out as much there. Undoubtedly some of the storm hit the land of Goshen, but the winds did not pick up enough particles to darken the sky, and so the Hebrews had enough light to perform the regular duties around their homes.

As a result of the darkness Pharaoh calls for Moses and says, "Go, serve Yahweh; your children also may go with you; only let your flocks and your herds remain behind" (10:24). He reasons that the Hebrews will not leave permanently if their animals are still in Egypt. "Not a hoof shall be left behind," Moses replies, because the people will not know until they get into the wilderness what animals, and how many, will be required for the sacrifices to Yahweh. Because Pharaoh does not want to cut that last hold on the Israelites, he refuses to meet all of Moses' demands. His obstinacy turns to anger, and he drives Moses away with a threat, "Get away from me! Be careful never to see my face again, for in the day you see my face you shall die" (10:28). "As you say!" Moses agrees, "I will not see your face again." And with this final comment the negotiations with Pharaoh come to an end.

Literary Criticism and the Plagues

The evidence noted above seems to indicate that the story of the nine plagues (Exod. 7:8-10:29) is an essentially accurate account of what happened during the extended confrontation between Moses and Pharaoh. The implication is that neither the J nor the P tradition relates the entire story. This raises the problem of how the editor was able to take the pieces of the two traditions and connect them in the correct order. The explanation of the older literary critics was that the variant traditions were duplicate accounts of a shorter series of plagues. But this answer is not adequate if Hort's reconstruction of the plague sequence is accurate. On the contrary, Hort's conclusion seems to side with conservative scholars in arguing for the unity of the story.

Yet recognition of the essential unity of the account does not explain the decided shifts in vocabulary, style, and point of view. Regardless of the designations given, there is a definite contrast between the material in Exodus 3:1-6:1 and 6:2-7:7, and between the two ways of describing the plagues. The assumption of the literary critics was that such a sudden shift could not have occurred within one writer. The logical outcome of this premise was the theory that different traditions gave rise to the variant accounts. Whereas conservative scholars have done a service in noting the excesses of the literary critics and in showing that at times ancient writers consciously employed contrasting styles within the same document, they have not developed a theory which can adequately account for the abrupt shifts in content and logic.

While the theory of variant traditions is hard put to explain all the biblical data, there is enough evidence (in the opinion of this writer) to show that the history of the Israelites was passed on through different groups within Israel, thereby producing variant recensions or traditions of the story. In spite of the difficulty posed by Hort's study of the plagues, the support for two traditions in Exodus 3:1-10:29 is stronger than the argument that one person composed the entire story essentially as it is. The definitive answer to this and other problems of the biblical narrative has not been given, and perhaps a completely satisfactory solution will never be found.

Chapter 6

The Passover

The preceding chapter has indicated that the story of
the nine plagues (Exod. 7:8-10:29) is a literary unit com-
bining the J and P traditions and that the long series of
negotiations between Moses and Pharaoh extended over
a seven-month period (August-March). Both traditions
interpreted the protracted bargaining sessions as the work
of Yahweh in hardening Pharaoh's heart so that he might
show his signs and wonders before Pharaoh and the Egyptians. In fact, however, the numerous encounters resulted
from a genuine struggle between two strong-willed persons.

One of the recurrent themes in the contest is Moses'
demand that the people be allowed to go three days' journey
into the wilderness to serve Yahweh. In the light of Yahweh's intention of delivering his people so that they can
possess the land of Canaan, the request is really a subter-
fuge. Why did Yahweh not have Moses give Pharaoh the
real reason for requesting the release of the Israelites?
Perhaps it was thought that Pharaoh would be more
amenable if a request was made in line with an Egyptian
custom. While there is no ancient evidence for a custom
of praying in the wilderness because of conditions of the
Nile, there is good evidence from the Arab period. Records
tell of four times between A.D. 1359 and 1450 when the
Nile was too high or too low and the Sultan ordered the
people to go into the desert and pray that Allah would
lower or raise the Nile. Certainly the ancient Egyptians
must have prayed to their gods when the Nile was ab-
normally high or low, because life depended on a normal
inundation. Perhaps Moses thought that a request along
this line would have more impact on Pharaoh. It failed
to make an impression, however, and from the very start
Pharaoh was distrustful. Thus the stage was set for a

long struggle between a suspicious ruler with a super ego
and a prophet with a superior understanding of Yahweh
and his ways of working.

From start to finish the actions of Pharaoh are precisely those of a proud man defending his prestige, power,
and way of life. As a god he represents the Egyptian
pantheon of gods; therefore he can tolerate nothing which
threatens his status or that of the gods. No unknown
like Yahweh can come in and give orders. The Israelites
are not the only disgruntled slaves, and if he agrees to
let them go and serve Yahweh, then the other groups will
ask for the same privilege. Soon a chain-reaction revolt
will get started, and so the only thing to do is to suppress
the slave rebellion before it gains headway. Yet the plagues
are so terrific that Pharaoh cannot help being uneasy. As
the pressure builds up he begins to acknowledge Yahweh,
but only grudgingly.

Finally he sees that it would be expedient to yield a
point or two in order to restore order. He tries to get
the people to sacrifice in Goshen (8:25). When this fails
he has to yield a bit more, and so he offers to let them
serve Yahweh near the edge of the Egyptian border (8:28).
But Moses insists on a three-day journey into the wilderness. Pharaoh is on the spot again. If he refuses, Yahweh
will apply more pressure. The only sensible thing to do
is to yield a half point. He will allow the men to make
the journey (10:11), but the women, children, and animals cannot since they must be the pledge to guarantee
the return of the men. Moses rejects this offer as well,
and Egypt is hit with the army of locusts. Pharaoh does
not want to lose face, but under Yahweh's blows he is
reeling like a punchy boxer. He will try to escape a knock-
out by backing up one more step. Let all the people go
serve Yahweh, but leave the livestock (10:24). Moses is
a hard bargainer, however, and he insists on taking every
animal. Pharaoh knows that this is the end of the line.
If he yields on this point, he loses face by admitting that
Yahweh is greater than the gods of Egypt. He would
rather go down swinging, and so with anger he drives
Moses from his presence with a warning never to come
back again.

The other crucial factor in this struggle of wills is Moses the prophet. He has felt the presence and power of Yahweh, and he has been called to deliver the people of Israel from slavery. He is frustrated after his first encounters with Pharaoh because everything turns against the people and their situation is worse than ever. He doubts his call and wonders why Yahweh has been so slow in taking action against Pharaoh. Then Yahweh replies, "Now you shall see what I will do to Pharaoh" (6:1). When the Nile turns blood-red and overflows the land, Moses can see the "strong hand" of Yahweh. Now he understands that Yahweh is going to use convulsive extremes in his created world to humble Pharoah. He will use his rod as a symbol of that power, but not as a diviner, like the magicians. As the plagues develop in a cause and effect way he is enabled to interpret the awesome series of events, and he uses each of them as an opportunity to press for the release of the Hebrews. With every evasive move of Pharaoh there is the prophetic word of Moses. After nine rounds Egypt is ruined and on the verge of collapse, yet Pharaoh will not yield that last point. When his stubbornness turns to anger, Moses has to leave. It appears that he is no nearer his goal of freeing the Israelites than he was at the beginning, but he evidences no despair. Apparently he has an inner assurance that Pharaoh will not have the last word. Somehow Yahweh will be victorious.

Chapters 11-14 and Biblical Criticism

Yahweh's final act against Pharaoh in order to get the release of the Israelites is the death of the firstborn. This tenth plague is tied in very closely with the description of the Passover, the Feast of Unleavened Bread *(Massoth)*, and the Exodus. These crucial events were the touchstone of Israel's faith, and it is apparent from the complex collection of material in chapters 11-14 that the stories were reworked many times. The E tradition reappears and is worked in with the J and P traditions. There is even evidence of the D source.

While there is general agreement from the literary point of view that there is a difference between the material in chapter 11 and chapter 10, there is wide variation in the interpretation of this evidence. Noth, for example, holds that the section dealing with the Passover and the death of the firstborn is the earliest material and that the story was preserved and passed on by the cult of Israel; that is, the annual celebration of the event was part of the religious calendar.[1] He believes that the stories about the plagues are a separate tradition and that they developed as an outgrowth of the attempt to explain what had happened before Yahweh's decisive action. In other words, Noth considers the plague stories as aetiology since they did not actually happen as the prelude to the Passover and the death of the firstborn.

From a different perspective, Dennis McCarthy contends that the story of the crossing of the Reed Sea (14: 1-31) has the same characteristic words, phrases, and motifs as the plague stories (7:8-10:29), and that the two units form one narrative.[2] This story (developed from material in the various traditions) claims that Israel escaped secretly from Egypt when she saw that Pharaoh was unyielding in spite of the plagues. McCarthy recognizes that this view of the Exodus contradicts the story in chapters 11-13; therefore he believes that the crossing of the Reed Sea is independent of the Passover tradition. Moreover, since the triumphant poem of Exodus 15 was undoubtedly sung at the annual celebration of the Exodus, the crossing of the Reed Sea was probably viewed as the climax of Yahweh's activity against Pharaoh. Accordingly, McCarthy believes that in reenacting the triumphal crossing the stories of the plagues were gradually developed to heighten the suspense of the drama. Thus he agrees with Noth in an aetiological explanation of the plague stories, even though he starts with the Reed Sea tradition instead of the Passover tradition.

There can be little argument with the theory that many of the traditions found in the Bible were preserved and passed on through the ritual of Israel's cult. The real question is how much of the material stems from actual events in the early history of Israel and how much was developed later on by the cult of Israel. The discussion of the nine

---

[1] Noth, *Exodus*, p. 88.
[2] Dennis J. McCarthy, "Plagues and Sea of Reeds: Exodus 5-14," *Journal of Biblical Literature*, LXXXV, 1 (June 1966), 137-158.

plagues has shown that in all probability these were actual events; therefore the aetiological explanation of Noth and McCarthy is unwarranted. There are most certainly additions to the traditions and a number of inconsistencies, if not outright contradictions, but these accretions resulted in large measure during the process of transmitting the stories. Unless there is good evidence to the contrary, the wisest procedure is to give the benefit of the doubt to tradition. During the last half-century the radical theories of the critics have not stood the test of archaeological findings nearly as well as the biblical text.

The Institution of the Passover

Yahweh informs Moses that he will bring "one more plague," and then Pharaoh will drive the people away completely. There is no indication as to the nature of the plague. Then Moses is instructed to have the people ask their Egyptian neighbors for silver and gold items (probably jewelry). In this instance clothing is not mentioned and both the men and women are to participate in the collection, whereas in 3:22 only the women were involved and clothing was included in the items to be gathered. This will be possible because the people have "favor in the sight of the Egyptians." One of the major reasons for this kindly attitude is given: "The man Moses was very great in the land of Egypt, in the sight of Pharaoh's servants and in the sight of the people" (11:3). The servants and the people are standing in the sandals of the Israelites, as it were, and they sense the injustice of their situation and the irrationality of Pharaoh's actions with Moses. Accordingly, they will be ready to grant the request.

The narrative jumps from instructions to Moses to a statement by Moses: "Thus says Yahweh: About midnight I will go forth in the midst of Egypt, and all the firstborn in the land of Egypt shall die, from the firstborn of Pharaoh who sits upon his throne, even to the firstborn of the maidservant who is behind the mill, and all the firstborn of the cattle. And there shall be a great cry throughout all the land of Egypt, such as there has never been, nor ever shall be again" (11:4-6). To whom is Moses speaking? In verse 2 he is instructed to speak to the people of Israel, and the implication is that the warning about the death of the firstborn is addressed to them as well. On the other hand, verses 7-8 seem to indicate that Moses was talking directly with Pharaoh: "But against any of the people of Israel, either man or beast, not a dog shall growl, that you may know that Yahweh makes a distinction between the Egyptians and Israel. And all these your servants shall come down to me, and bow down to me saying, 'Get out, you and all the people who follow you.' And after that I will go out." Then the narrative adds, "And he went out from Pharaoh in hot anger." This is very strange because Pharaoh has threatened Moses with death the next time he shows his face around the palace, and there is no indication that Pharaoh has changed his attitude.

Following this difficult passage is the standardized refrain of the P tradition: "Then Yahweh said to Moses, 'Pharaoh will not listen to you, that my wonders may be multiplied in the land of Egypt.' Moses and Aaron did all these wonders before Pharaoh, and Yahweh hardened Pharaoh's heart, and he did not let the people of Israel go out of his land" (11:9-10). The death of the firstborn constitutes one plague or wonder; therefore P's reference to "wonders" indicates that at one time this refrain was in a different context. In any case, it leads up to the priestly instructions concerning the observance of the Passover (12:1-13).

Yahweh's first statement to Moses and Aaron is: "This month shall be for you the beginning of months; it shall be the first month of the year for you." There is evidence that in the reign of Solomon the Israelites had a solar-lunar calendar with the year beginning in September (as it does with the New Year's festival *Rosh Hashanah* in the current Jewish calendar). It was not until the seventh century B.C. that Judah adopted the lunar-solar calendar of the Mesopotamians with the year beginning in Nisan (March-April). "This month" in the priestly instructions refers clearly to Nisan, and it is an indication that the whole verse is a later addition to make it absolutely clear that the Passover was at the beginning of the ritual calendar. Moses and Aaron are to instruct "the congregation (Hebrew *edah*) of Israel" (12:3). This is the first appearance in the Bible of this specialized term of the P tradition (which is never found in J, E, or D). The fact that it is used here instead of the normal word "people" is another indication that the present form of the passage in 12:1-13 stems from a later period. The Hebrews in Egypt were not organized in the precise cultic fashion that "the congregation" was in Palestine.

As preparation for the Passover the people are to take a young animal of the flock on "the tenth day of this month" (meaning Nisan) for each household. If the family is too small to consume a whole animal, it is to join with a neighbor's family so that very little, if any, of the meat will be left over. The animal can be either a sheep or a goat, but the lamb or kid must be a perfect year-old male (that is, it was born during the last calving season). The choice animal is to be kept until the fourteenth day of the month when "the whole assembly of the congregation of Israel shall kill it between the two evenings" (12:6). Later Jewish interpretation understood "between the evenings," another technical expression of the P tradition, to mean 2:30-3:30 P.M. According to this understanding of the passage, evening started when the sun passed its zenith at noon. The first evening was the two-and-a-half-hour period 12:00-2:30 P.M. and the second 3:30-6:00 P.M. Even though the meaning cannot be determined with certainty, it is highly unlikely that such precise instructions were given for the first Passover because conditions were in such a turmoil. It appears that again some of the refinements of later times have been projected back into the narrative. The reference to "the whole assembly" means that collectively each household or group of families was to sacrifice its animal at the same time.

Then some of the blood was to be put on the lintel and two side frames of the doors of the homes where the sacrificial meals were to be eaten. While the killing of the passover animal was in the afternoon of the fourteenth of Nisan, the actual passover meal was on the fifteenth because the day was reckoned as beginning at ·sundown. Probably the roasting was still going on when the new day began. The whole animal was to be roasted: head, entrails, and all. In preparation for the meal the people were to be fully clothed with sandals on and a staff in hand. They were to eat the roasted meat with unleavened bread

and bitter herbs. None of the meat was to be eaten raw
or boiled in water. The latter instruction is in direct contradiction to the D regulations for keeping the Passover:
"And you shall boil it and eat it at the place which Yahweh
your God will choose" (Deut. 16:7). The meal was to be
eaten in haste, apparently in case orders should come suddenly to move out. Any of the animal left over after the
feast was to be burnt before morning.

It is Yahweh's Passover (Hebrew *pesah*) since he will
soon "pass over" (Hebrew *abar*) the land of Egypt and
kill all the firstborn "both of man and beast." In doing
so Yahweh "will execute judgments on all the gods of
Egypt" (12:12). He affirms his intention with the authoritative claim, "I am Yahweh." When Yahweh sees the
blood he will pass over the house so that no plague shall
fall upon them "to destroy" them.

The original meaning of the Hebrew verb *pasah* seems
to have been "to limp, dance." It is used in the story of
Elijah on Mt. Carmel, where it says that the prophets
of Baal "limped about the altar which they had made"
(1 Kings 18:26). The Hebrew noun *pesah* (from which the
Greek *pascha* and English "paschal" are derived) is from
the same verb, but it is difficult to relate the idea of limp-
ing or dancing. Whatever the original meaning of the term,
the biblical text clearly interprets it as the feast eaten
while Yahweh "passes over" the land of Egypt, and thus
the feast of Passover. This same meaning is given in the
J account: "For Yahweh will pass over (Hebrew *abar*)
to slay the Egyptians; and when he sees the blood on the
lintel and on the two doorposts, Yahweh will pass over
(Hebrew *pasah*) the door" (12:23).

Inasmuch as Pharaoh represents the Egyptian pantheon
of gods, Yahweh will execute judgment on all the gods,
even the divine son of Pharaoh. From earliest times Egypt
was divided into districts (later called "nomes"), each one
with an animal or plant representation of its chief deity.
Eventually there were twenty districts in Lower Egypt
and twenty-two in Upper Egypt. The totemic symbol was
shown on the standard or ensign of each district. Some
of the animals involved in the plagues were the object
of worship (for example, the frogs), and older scholars
were inclined to interpret the plagues as specific attacks

directed at certain gods, but it is doubtful that such specificity was involved. Rather, the series of plagues was intended to show that Yahweh was master over Pharaoh and the whole Egyptian pantheon.

The J instructions concerning the Passover are found in 12:21-27. After giving the warning of 11:4-6, Moses calls for the elders of Israel and instructs them. The basic procedures for protecting the Israelites are essentially the same as in the P regulations, but there is no reference to the passover meal. A new item is the use of a bunch of "hyssop," an aromatic plant, to apply the blood to the lintel and the doorposts. No one is to go out the door until the morning, that is, after Yahweh has passed over. As Yahweh sees the blood he "will not allow the destroyer to enter" the house (12:23). When the people get to the land Yahweh has promised, they are to commemorate the event annually. If the children ask, "What do you mean by this service?" the parents are to answer, "It is the sacrifice of Yahweh's passover, for he passed over the houses of the people of Israel in Egypt, when he slew the Egyptians but spared our houses" (12:27).

The Meaning of the Passover

The J version is concerned solely with the procedure of keeping death away from the homes. This negative aspect is certainly important, but in terms of the exodus from the country, P's concern for the festal aspect of the event is equally important. The people of Israel were on the verge of a very arduous and enervating experience, and once they were protected from death they needed to be fortified both physically and spiritually. The bounteous feast with plenty of meat would strengthen their bodies, and the fellowship of eating together would add to the anticipation of being delivered from their cruel bondage as well as quell some of the worries of the fearful. This was the moment they had been looking forward to, and they should eat the meal with joy and thanksgiving for Yahweh's mighty deeds. All future generations would look back to this night as the beginning of deliverance.

Although the regulations about the Passover appear in the biblical narrative as completely new instructions from Yahweh, there are some details imbedded in them which indicate that a very old custom has been adapted for specific use by the Israelites. In the J tradition, Yahweh says that he will not allow "the destroyer" to enter the houses with blood on the doors. Thus far there has been little hesitancy in the biblical narrative of describing Yahweh in manlike (anthropomorphic) terms. He strikes the Nile and it turns blood-red. In the P narrative he is the one "seeing" and "passing over." Why does Yahweh need a helper named "The Destroyer"?

This bit of information seems to refer to an old ceremony in which an animal was killed and the blood put on the flaps of the tents and the gates of the folds in order to prevent the messenger of death from slipping in at night and killing some of the family or flocks. The P tradition may have a remnant of the same idea because Yahweh says that no plague will fall on the Israelites "to destroy" them. The Hebrew verb is the same root as that back of the noun "destroyer." It is conjectured that this old custom took place in the spring when the shepherds began moving from the winter pastures to the summer fields. This was a dangerous time for the shepherds and the flocks, because the newborn had to be guarded carefully, especially the firstborn. The instructions to be ready for quick departure and to burn the meat which remained over probably came from the old custom. Later in their history the Israelites will borrow many forms and customs from their neighbors, but in each case a new meaning will be given to it. There is no reason for reluctance in recognizing an old custom back of the Passover. The power of Yahweh and the drama of the deliverance will give *the* Passover a unique meaning never to be rivaled.

After the Israelites entered Canaan they probably celebrated the feast of Passover in their homes as they had in Egypt. With the centralization of worship there were periods when it was treated as a pilgrimage feast. Joseph and Mary made annual trips to Jerusalem to celebrate the feast of Passover (Luke 2:41), and when Jesus was twelve he was left behind because he was discussing theological issues with the teachers in the temple. Later, on the Mount of Transfiguration, Moses and Elijah appeared with Jesus and talked of his departure (Greek *exodos*), which was to occur at Jerusalem (Luke 9:31). Although the last supper of Jesus was probably eaten a day before the actual feast, it was clearly understood by the disciples as the paschal meal. The blessing, the breaking of bread, the drinking of the wine, and the singing of a hymn were undoubtedly parts of the passover ritual at that time.

Ever since the destruction of the temple in A.D. 70, the passover meal has been celebrated mainly in the home. The Seder, the passover service celebrated by Jews today, retains the essential features of the ancient custom. The ritual makes the family commemoration a very personal experience, and the secret is found in one of its counsels, "It is incumbent on every Israelite, in every generation, to look upon himself as if he had actually gone out from Egypt. . . . It was not only our ancestors that the Most Holy redeemed from Egypt, but us also did he redeem with them." Accordingly, the participants can say, "He brought *us* out from Egypt."

St. Paul reported the tradition that at the last supper Jesus instructed the disciples to continue eating the bread and drinking the wine in "remembrance" of him (1 Cor. 11:24-25). Thus the passover meal of the Exodus was transformed into a celebration commemorating the death and exodus ("departure") of Jesus. Both the Passover and the Lord's Supper will continue because they are rooted in historical events of ultimate significance.

The Feast of Unleavened Bread

The section 12:14-20 is the P tradition's understanding of the Feast of Unleavened Bread *(Massoth)*. It is a rather repetitious passage, and scholars differ as to the meaning of the first verse: "This day shall be for you a memorial day, and you shall keep it as a feast to Yahweh; throughout your generations you shall observe it as an ordinance forever." Does "this day" refer back to the time of the Passover, or does it point ahead (as usual in biblical usage) to the first day of Massoth? Some scholars include 12:14 as part of the unit dealing with the Passover, but most treat it as part of the following instructions. Everyone is to eat unleavened bread for seven days. Anyone eating "what is leavened" will be "cut off from Israel."

On the first and seventh days no work is to be done and the people are to gather in holy assemblies. Yahweh instructs the people, "You shall observe the feast of unleavened bread, for on this very day I brought your hosts out of the land of Egypt" (12:17).

Then Yahweh gives the specific instructions for the timing of the feast: "In the first month, on the fourteenth day of the month at evening, you shall eat unleavened bread, and so until the twenty-first day of the month at evening." By referring to the fourteenth, this regulation seems to include the time for killing the passover animal. If this ruling were taken literally, Massoth would be an eight-day feast. But the additional specification "at evening" probably was intended to mean that Massoth began on the fifteenth with the passover meal. Therefore, this ordinance is equating the passover night with the first half of the first day of Massoth.

The J version concerning Massoth is found in 13:3-10. When the people are in Canaan they are to remember the day in Abib (meaning "ear of grain," and thus the old agricultural name for the first month, Nisan) when Yahweh brought them out of Egypt. For seven days no leavened bread is to be eaten. The seventh day is to be a feast day, but nothing is said of the first day, as in the P tradition, where the first and last days are for rest and holy assemblies. The people are to explain to their sons, "It is because of what Yahweh did for me when I came out of Egypt" (13:8). Succeeding generations would be able to give the same testimony because at each commemoration of the Passover and Massoth the re-creation of the marvelous events would be so genuine the worshipers could experience them by faith. They could tell their children that they had been in Egypt with Moses. In a real sense this is the goal of all reading and study of the Bible. For those who have the daring and the desire, it is possible to relive these truly great moments of history. It takes some daring, however, because it might mean a confrontation with Yahweh at the burning bush and a call to challenge some modern Pharaoh for the release of his slaves.

This ordinance or teaching of Yahweh is to be observed "at its appointed time from year to year," and it is to be as a "sign" on the hand and as a "memorial" between the eyes (13:9). The terms "sign" and "memorial" were similes and not intended to be taken literally. They point to older customs, however, in which a brand or tattoo on the hand was the designation of membership in some cultic group and an amulet worn on the forehead probably served to charm away evil spirits. The same idea is expressed in connection with the consecration of the firstborn (13:16), except that the more specific word "frontlets" (Hebrew *totaphoth*) is substituted for "memorial." Later on the Jews took this metaphorical language literally and made leather bands with phylacteries (small black leather cubes with passages from the Torah inscribed on strips of parchment). One cube was worn on the inside of the left arm and the other in the middle of the forehead.

The Meaning of Massoth and Its Relation to Passover

At first glance the connection of unleavened bread with the paschal feast seems rather incongruous. The explanation of the relationship is given in two verses of the J account. Since the Egyptians were sending the Israelites out as fast as possible, "the people took their dough before it was leavened, their kneading bowls being bound up in their mantles on their shoulders" (12:24). On their journey out of Egypt they stopped at Succoth and "they baked unleavened cakes of the dough which they had brought out of Egypt, for it was not leavened, because they were thrust out of Egypt and could not tarry, neither had they prepared for themselves any provisions" (12:39). In their rush to get out of Pharaoh's grasp they probably took little time for cooking, and so the unleavened bread had to last for a few days. Whether it was exactly seven days is immaterial. The Israelites did have an experience of a diet consisting largely of unleavened bread, and later tradition settled on seven days inasmuch as seven was the perfect number.

The crucial question, as always, has to do with the historicity of the J account. Did the Israelites actually exist on unleavened bread for a few days, or is the story an explanation to account for the fact that in Palestine the feast of Massoth was associated with the Passover? Noth, like a number of other scholars, holds that the feast of

Massoth was "a cult feast in the agricultural tradition of Palestine at the beginning of the grain harvest, at which the first produce of the land was offered for the cultic consecration of the harvest and eaten still uncontaminated by the addition of leaven." Accordingly, he considers the feasts of Passover and Massoth as having completely independent origins; therefore the J account is aetiology to explain why they happened to be celebrated in Palestine at the same time.[3]

There is no reason to doubt that there was some kind of feast at the beginning of the grain harvest in Palestine, and it is certainly obvious that details related to that feast have influenced the biblical regulations, but does this fact prove that the J tradition touched up the story in order to make it fit with later practice? The narrative about eating unleavened bread makes good sense in the context of the Exodus, and it is just as probable that the basic motivation for the feast of Massoth came from this experience. Later on, of course, the ritual calendar of the Canaanites would have its influence, and some of the detailed instructions in the present narratives have certainly been projected back due to later developments in Palestine. The interpretation of the problem hinges solely on the presuppositions of the scholar. Noth convinced himself that there was little material of historical worth in the biblical narratives up to the time of the covenant ceremony in Joshua 24. With this bias, his judgments were bound to be very pessimistic.

The prejudice of the author of this book on Moses is that the crucial episodes of the Old Testament were in fact actual events in which Yahweh, the God of Israel, made himself known in special ways. If there never was an exodus from Egypt, then the Old Testament is a hoax. But the issue of Massoth is not one of those crucial events. If it should be proven that the J account is indeed aetiology, that fact would not alter the main foundation of Yahweh's activity, and this writer would have no trouble in accepting the data. The attempt to show historical probability does not stem from a fearful uneasiness that faith will evaporate when the facts are known. Rather, concern

---

[3] Noth, *Exodus*, pp. 89, 97.

to show the alternative probability is intended as a check on the mammoth leaps involved in some of Noth's assumptions. Much of his work in the realm of criticism is beyond dispute, but some of his conclusions in the realm of tradition history involve too many gaps to be considered final. Noth's most pessimistic judgments are still theory, and they should be understood for what they really are.

The Consecration of the Firstborn

One of the most ancient beliefs of mankind was that the firstborn of man and animals had to be dedicated to the god of fertility. This was to insure more children and stock, and to guarantee their health and well-being. In many instances this meant the sacrifice of human beings. It was this old custom which led Abraham to determine to sacrifice Isaac. He had hoped and prayed for a son by Sarah, and now that he had that precious son would he be willing to sacrifice him to El Shaddai in faith that this God would give him more sons and prosperity? This was the struggle going on in Abraham's heart, and he settled it in an act of faith. Just as he was about to take the life of Isaac he heard a noise behind him, and turning he saw "a ram caught in a thicket by his horns" (Gen. 22:13). He realized that God had provided the ram for the sacrifice, and so he "offered it up as a burnt offering instead of his son." He heard God say to him, "Now I know that you fear God, seeing you have not withheld your son, your only son, from me" (22:12). In that traumatic experience Abraham learned that his God would never require the death of firstborn sons. They would still be dedicated to God, but they would be redeemed instead of sacrificed.

The passover animals were not required to be the firstborn. Apparently the regulations concerning firstborns (13: 1-2, 11-16) were attached to the passover account because the blood of the paschal lamb or kid protected the firstborn of the Israelites. The people are told that when they come to the promised land they are "to set apart to Yahweh all that first opens the womb." All the male firstlings of the livestock will be Yahweh's. One exception is noted: "Every firstling of an ass you shall redeem with a lamb, or if you will not redeem it you shall break its neck" (13: 13). Since the ass was solid-hoofed, it was excluded from the list of clean animals (those which chew the cud and have cloven hoofs). It could not be sacrificed and eaten; therefore it had to die with a broken neck or be redeemed with a lamb (which was then slain). All firstborn sons were to be redeemed as well. When inquisitive sons ask, "What does this mean?" the rationale of the regulation is to be given: "By strength of hand Yahweh brought us out of Egypt, from the house of bondage. For when Pharaoh stubbornly refused to let us go, Yahweh slew all the firstborn in the land of Egypt, both the firstborn of man and the firstborn of the livestock. Therefore I sacrifice to Yahweh all the males that first open the womb, but all the firstborn of my sons I redeem" (13:14-15). Compliance with the regulation shall be like a "sign" on the hand and "frontlets" between the eyes.

The Passover and the Beginning of the Flight

The J account of the Passover is given in 12:29-39 and the P account (with related matters) occurs in 12:40-51. At midnight, according to J, Yahweh smites the firstborn of Egypt, from the Prince, Pharaoh's son, all the way down to the son of the prisoner in the dungeon. The firstborn of the livestock die as well. "There was not a house where one was not dead" (12:30). Perhaps some infection related to the anthrax of the previous plagues was responsible for further death among the children and the animals. That the plague involved only the firstborn and that it hit every home is probably due to the selectivity of tradition. Many children and animals probably died, but the most grievous part of the experience would have been the sorrow concerning the firstborn. Remembrance of this and empathy for their sorrowing neighbors highlighted this aspect so that it overshadowed the other deaths.

Pharaoh and the Egyptians detect the deaths during the night, and there is great wailing over the land. Moses and Aaron are summoned, in spite of Pharaoh's previous threat, and told, "Rise up, go out from among my people, both you and the people of Israel, and go, serve Yahweh as you have said. Take your flocks and your herds, as you have said, and be gone; and bless me also" (12:31-32). With the death of the Prince, Pharaoh is momentarily shaken, and he asks for a blessing from Moses, which is really a request for Yahweh's blessing. This is not the same young king who asked arrogantly, "Who is Yahweh?" The Egyptians say, "We are dead men," and they urge the Hebrews to leave as quickly as possible.

As they leave, they take not only the unleavened dough, but the jewelry and clothing which they are wearing. Here and in 3:22 this event is referred to as the "despoiling" of the Egyptians. Some scholars have interpreted the story to mean that the Hebrews purposefully deceived the Egyptians by asking for a loan of items when they fully intended to walk off with them. It is hard to believe that there would have been that many credulous Egyptians. These people were not fools either. As noted earlier, there must have been a number of Egyptians who sympathized with the Israelites and who thought very highly of Moses. During the long series of plagues they must have sensed that things were building up to a climax, and they certainly knew that it was the intention of the Israelites to leave. If the Hebrews got any jewelry and clothing from the Egyptians, it was because the Egyptians wanted to give them, not that they were fooled. Later tradition may have interpreted the act as "taking spoils" from the Egyptians, but the likelihood, as noted earlier, is that the people gave their clothing and jewelry as a kind of reparations for the maltreatment and slave labor of the Hebrews.

The P tradition makes the historical reference, "At the end of 430 years, on that very day, all the hosts of Yahweh went out from the land of Egypt" (12:41). Although this is an exceedingly long stay in Egypt, it seems to have been true (as we have noted) for some of the Hebrews. Since the passover night was "a time of watching by Yahweh, to bring them out of the land of Egypt; so this same night is a night of watching kept to Yahweh by all the people of Israel throughout their generations" (12:42). Yahweh, who neither slumbers nor sleeps (Ps. 121:4), was very watchful on passover night to protect his people and to bring them out of Egypt. Therefore, it was only fitting that future generations should commemorate the night by being watchful in attitude and thankful to Yahweh.

In 12:43-49 the P tradition, with its concern for regulations, inserts the ordinance concerning participation in the passover feast. The law of circumcision (Gen. 17:9-14) will be the standard. Only those who have been circumcised are within the covenant fellowship; therefore only they can participate in the feast. The foreigner, the sojourner (foreigner living permanently in the land), and the hired servant are excluded from participation on the assumption that they worship other gods and would not be interested in being circumcised and worshiping Yahweh. But if the purchased slave (who is part of the family) desires to express his faith in Yahweh by submitting to circumcision, then he is eligible to share in the Passover. The same is true of the sojourner as long as all the males in his household submit to circumcision along with him. Since 12:51 is a recapitulation of 12:41-42, the section 43-50 is clearly a later addition.

The Date of the Exodus

The P account concerning the departure of the Israelites closes with the refrain that "on that very day" (that is, 430 years after entering Egypt) Yahweh brought the people of Israel out of the land. In chapter 2 it was concluded that the Exodus occurred most likely in the early part of the reign of Ramses II. There is no further biblical evidence to determine the date more precisely, but some data from Egyptian records and excavations may shed a little more light on the subject.

Excavations at the Ramesseum (the mortuary temple of Ramses II) in Thebes uncovered a number of wine jars. These had stamped inscriptions telling the source of the wine, the names of the wine makers, and the year of Ramses' reign. Most of the place names were of towns in northeastern Egypt, where most of the vineyards were, and the personal names were a mixture of Egyptian and Semitic names. A total of seventy sealings was found for the sixth year of Ramses' reign, but there were 244 for the seventh year. The figure dropped to 146 for the eighth year, and then plummeted to eleven for the ninth year. Assuming that the excavated jar seals represent the proportion of wine consumed during those years, the dramatic rise probably means that Ramses moved his retinue to Thebes during the two years. Thebes was the winter capital in normal times because the weather was nicer there than at the capital in the Delta. Therefore, it was possible to shift bases of operation fairly quickly.

After routing Ramses at Qadesh, about 1300 B.C., the Hittites kept the pressure on him by encouraging the city-states in lower Syria and Palestine to rebel. The revolt started in the sixth year of Ramses' reign, and extended down to Ashkelon (Ascalon) in southern Palestine in the summer of the seventh year. This would have been the reason why Ramses shifted his capital to Thebes. W. F. Albright has suggested that perhaps in the spring of the eighth year, when the revolt was at its highest, the Israelites took advantage of the situation by fleeing from the country.[4] If this be true, the date of the Exodus was about 1297 B.C. Even if Albright's suggestion should not be accurate to the year, the proposed date cannot be wrong by much.

Merneptah, the son of Ramses II, was victorious over the Libyans in the spring of his fifth year (about 1233 B.C.). A "Hymn of Victory" commemorating the event was composed, and at the end was attached a shorter hymn telling of Merneptah's victories over the Asiatics. Included in the list is Israel, the first mention of the name in non-biblical inscriptions. Merneptah boasts, "Israel is laid waste, his seed is not." Obviously, Merneptah had some of his father in him because he did not obliterate the Israelites. It was the practice in Egypt to use a determinative sign with names to indicate whether the names represented people or lands. In the Merneptah Stele the name Israel is classified as a people, whereas all the other names are designated as countries. This would indicate that the Israelites were in Palestine in sufficient numbers to constitute a threat to Merneptah, but that they had not settled down on a specific section of the country long enough to be considered indigenous. If the Egyptian scribe was accurate in his designation, it would mean that in 1233 B.C. Israel was still in the process of gaining control of the land of Canaan. Thus a date of Albright's suggestion, 1297 B.C., down to 1290 would allow for the years

[4] Albright, *Yahweh and the Gods of Canaan*, p. 159.

in the wilderness, the time in Transjordan, and the period of getting a foothold in Canaan.

Another bit of biblical information about the date of the Exodus is found in 1 Kings 6:1: "In the 480th year after the people of Israel came out of the land of Egypt, in the fourth year of Solomon's reign over Israel . . . he began to build the house of Yahweh." The fourth year of Solomon's reign was close to 960 B.C., and if the 480 years are added, the verse seems to claim that the Exodus occurred about 1440 B.C. For many years this date was considered to be accurate, but it runs counter to practically all the archaeological evidence. Palestine in the mid-fifteenth century was recovering from the Egyptian destruction about a century earlier. There is no widespread destruction in the area at that time. In the thirteenth century, however, there is evidence of violent destruction at many of the sites in Palestine, and a 1290 date for the Exodus would mean that the Israelites were probably responsible for the devastation.

Moreover, the biblical evidence of 1 Kings 6:1 must be viewed in connection with the reference about Pharaoh using the Hebrews to build Pithom and Raamses (Exod. 1:11). The latter fact could not have been true in 1440 during the reign of Tuthmosis III; therefore unless the biblical evidence is contradictory there must be some other explanation for the 480 years. It so happens that the genealogical tables list twelve generations from Moses to Solomon, and if a scribe allowed forty years to a generation (as was done at times), then he would arrive at the figure 480. Since a generation is actually nearer twenty-five years, the twelve generations would mean a span of about 300 years. Figuring back from 960 would put the Exodus at about 1260 B.C. This may be a bit late, but it is far nearer the truth than 1440.

The Number of the Israelites

When the people of Israel hurried out of their dwellings in Goshen, "a mixed multitude also went up with them, and very many livestock, both flocks and herds" (12:38). Some of the other oppressed groups in the region decided to throw in their lot with the Hebrews and escape at the same time. Moses had insisted on taking all their animals with them, and the people did so even though it would slow down the speed of their exit. The narrative adds the note that the number of the Israelites was "about 600,000 men on foot, besides women and children" (12:37). The expression "men on foot" probably refers to the men of fighting age, that is, twenty years old and up (Num. 1:18; 26:2). Thus the total would exclude the old men as well as the women, teen-agers, and children. According to this information, then, the total number of Israelites was approximately 2 million.

There are two other passages which explicitly list the warriors of Israel by tribe. Numbers 1 is designated as a census of men of fighting age taken during the stay at Mt. Sinai. The tribe of Levi is exempted, by the command of Yahweh, because it is to function in connection with the tabernacle and the priestly duties (Num. 1:47-53). The list begins with Reuben, which has "46 *eleph* 500." The total of the twelve tribes comes to "603 *eleph* 550" (1:46). It is quite clear that the editor of this section of the Bible understood the Hebrew word *eleph* to mean "1,000," and thus in adding the various totals of the tribes he arrived at the total of 603,550. The same is true of the census taken of the second generation in the plains of Moab. The total comes to 601,730 (Num. 26:51), excluding the tribe of Levi. The 600,000 of Exodus 12:37 seems to be a rounding off of these census totals from a later period.

From all available evidence, the total population of Egypt at its largest (about the time of the Eighteenth and Nineteenth Dynasties and again in the Roman period) was not much in excess of 7 million. In other words, if the biblical statement is taken literally the Israelites constituted more than a quarter of the total population of Egypt. In recent times Wadi Tumilat has not supported more than about 12,000 people, and the population of the Sinai Peninsula has been around 5,000. It is certain that the land of Goshen and the region around Mt. Sinai could never have supported 2 million people along with their animals.

Furthermore, the narrative gives one the impression of a much smaller group. The Hebrews have only two official midwives, and Moses and Aaron call *all* the people to-

gether to report what happened at the burning bush. Anyone who has been in a crowd of 100,000 people and seen
the difficulty of handling such a mass of humanity, even
with loudspeaker systems and policemen, can hardly imagine how Moses could have controlled a massive group twenty
times that size. The population of greater Washington, D.C.,
including the city and its environs, is over 2 million. When
one contemplates the size of the water system needed to
accommodate this number, and then realizes that Moses
quenched the thirst of the people by water from a rock
in the wilderness, it becomes obvious that something is
wrong in the understanding of the biblical passage. At
Sinai "all the people" will watch Moses as he enters the
"tent of meeting." Moreover, Jethro will find Moses trying
to adjudicate all the disputes of the people. He will not be
able to do so, but the fact that he tries indicates a much
smaller group of people.

One of the early attempts to deal with the problem was
the idea that the 603,550 in Numbers 1 came from a numerical interpretation of the expression "the children of
Israel." Inasmuch as the letters of the Hebrew alphabet
are used to designate numerals as well (the first letter
aleph is 1, the second letter *beth* is 2, etc.), the numerical
total of the letters in "the children of Israel" comes to
603. But this ingenious idea does not account for the 550
men left over, nor does it explain the allotment of the totals
to the various tribes. It is strictly an accident that the
numerical value of the expression multiplied by 1,000
happens to approximate one of the census totals.

A far more probable explanation is the suggestion by
W. F. Albright. The two census lists are reasonable for
the military manpower of Israel during the Golden Age
of David and Solomon. Since they were undated, a later
editor understood the reports to refer to the censuses which,
according to tradition, Moses took at Sinai and in Moab,
and so he inserted them into the narrative at the appropriate places.[5] This explanation has the merit of treating
the reports as authentic census lists while accounting for

[5] Albright, *From the Stone Age to Christianity*, 2nd ed. (Baltimore:
Johns Hopkins, 1957), p. 253.

the difficulty by a well-intentioned scribe who misunderstood his sources.

Another possibility was suggested by Sir Flinders Petrie, the father of modern biblical archaeology. He contended that the clue to the problem was the understanding of the Hebrew word *eleph*.[6] When Yahweh calls Gideon to deliver Israel from the Midianites, he answers, "Pray, Lord, how can I deliver Israel? Behold, my *eleph* is the weakest in Manasseh, and I am the least in my family" (Judg. 6:15). The meaning "1,000" does not make sense in this verse. Clearly, the term refers to a clan or tribal subgroup, with no reference to numerical size. In the light of this information the listing for Reuben would mean "46 groups having a total of 500 warriors." The following chart shows the two censuses according to this explanation:

Tribe	Numbers 1		Numbers 26	
	Groups	Warriors	Groups	Warriors
Reuben	46	500	43	730
Simeon	59	300	22	200
Gad	45	650	40	500
Judah	74	600	76	500
Issachar	54	400	64	300
Zebulun	57	400	60	500
Ephraim	40	500	32	500
Manasseh	32	200	52	700
Benjamin	35	400	45	600
Dan	62	700	64	400
Asher	41	500	53	400
Naphtali	53	400	45	400
Total	598	5550	596	5730

Since the average for each group runs about 9.3 in the first census and 9.6 in the second, Petrie suggested that each group was a tent group consisting of two grandparents, two parents, three children, and two herdsmen or persons from the "mixed multitude."[7] But all three references to the number of the Israelites have implicit or explicit references to military men, and it would seem that this fact should not be ignored. The total for the first

---

[6] W. M. F. Petrie, *Researches in Sinai*.

[7] Petrie, *Egypt and Israel*, p. 44.

census, therefore, would best be understood as meaning 598 groups with a total of 5,550 men of fighting age. Allowing for the old men, women, teen-agers, children, and the tribe of Levi, a total of about 16,000 would be fairly accurate.

Still another interpretation of the census lists is suggested by George E. Mendenhall.[8] He concurs with the biblical text, contrary to Petrie, that military men, not the entire population, are listed. On the other hand, he does not consider the lists as authentic documents from the time of Moses. They are tribal military lists from about 1125-1100 B.C., with Numbers 1 being slightly older than Numbers 26. However, since the total population was considerably greater than 16,000 around 1125, Mendenhall considers the lists as quotas for the tribes, not the total census of men of military age. *Eleph*, he explains, "originally referred to a subsection of a tribe; the term was then carried over to designate the contingent of troops under its own leader which the subsection contributed to the army of the Federation," that is, during the Judges. This old system broke down early in the monarchy, when the "royal army included units of approximately a thousand men under the command of an officer appointed by the king. This system was naturally read back into the census lists of the federation period, yielding impossibly high figures."

Mendenhall's explanation of the editorial misunderstanding of *eleph* is beyond question, and since "Nahshon the son of Amminadab" (Num. 1:7) seems to be the same person noted in David's genealogy (Ruth 4:20), his date of 1125 B.C. for Numbers 1 may be correct. Yet, as will be noted later, some of the names of the twelve tribal leaders assigned as census takers are very old forms, and they seem to be accurate for the period of Moses. Furthermore, there seems to have been a tradition that Moses took two censuses. Accordingly, the lists in Numbers 1 and 26 may still be authentic reports from the wilderness years, just as Petrie contended.

While the date of the census lists cannot be fixed con-

---

[8] George E. Mendenhall, "The Census Lists of Numbers 1 and 26," *Journal of Biblical Literature*, LXXVII, 1 (March 1958), 52-66.

clusively, it is clear that the Israelites did not total more than about 16,000 in the time of Moses. Anyone who thinks that this estimate is reducing the miraculous element of the Bible should try to lead such a group through the Sinai wilderness. The biblical text must not be interpreted to say more than it actually does. Certainly, the power of Yahweh is not enhanced by contending for an impossibility. On the other hand, the fact that Moses did lead a sizable group out of Egypt and through the Sinai wilderness is a witness to Yahweh's concern and special aid.

Chapter 7

Through the Reed Sea

When Pharaoh learned of the death of the firstborn, he summoned Moses and Aaron "by night" and ordered them and all the Israelites to leave. Since the Egyptians helped rush them out, the presumption is that they started their departure early in the morning of the fifteenth of Nisan (about April 1), before sunrise. Since the months began with a new moon, the fifteenth was a full moon. This was fortunate for the Israelites because they had moonlight to assist them in gathering their goods and animals, and in forming their ranks for the march. Those who had died in Egypt would have to be left behind. There was one exception, however. Joseph had made the Hebrews promise to take his remains with them when God would visit them with deliverance from Egypt. Because of his high status, Joseph was embalmed and his body put in a mummy-case or sarcophagus (Gen. 50:26). His mummy was enshrined in the land of Goshen as a constant reminder to the people of the oath which they had sworn. Moses made good on the vow and took the body of Joseph with him. There is nothing said about its location in the line of march, but the most logical place for the famous forebear would have been the place of honor at the head of the procession along with Moses. Much later the biblical narrative states that the mummy of Joseph was "buried at Shechem, in the plot of ground which Jacob had bought" (Josh. 24:32).

The Route of the Exodus

The first specific information about the route of the Hebrews states that they "journeyed from Rameses to Succoth" (12:37). Inasmuch as they did not live at the capital of Raamses, the reference to Rameses must mean

144

the district, which presumably included the land of Goshen.
Moses led the people to Succoth, but here again the mean-
ing is not clear. As noted earlier, some scholars locate
Succoth at Tell el-Maskhutah in the eastern part of Wadi
Tumilat, but the Anastasi Papyri V and VI refer to slaves
escaping past the frontier wall at Tjeku (Succoth) and
Shasu (nomads from Edom) being admitted at Tjeku.
These statements seem to be more specific than a reference
to the district of Succoth; therefore it appears that Tjeku
means one of the main forts in the Wall of the Ruler
(Prince). In this case Succoth was somewhere near the
present site of Ismailiah, just north of Lake Timsah.

Moses must have had some apprehension whether the
frontier guards had received the order to release the Israelites, or whether they would believe the report. It is
unlikely, therefore, that Moses stopped at this Egyptian
outpost. Accordingly, the biblical reference to Succoth probably means the district. In any event, the Israelites were
near the eastern border of Egypt. There, at some distance
to the east of Goshen, the people baked the unleavened
dough and made bread for that and the following days.

Four Routes from the Border of Egypt

The stopover at Succoth was more than a bakeout, however, because Moses had to decide which would be the
best way to take the people. There were four possibilities.
To the north, beginning at Sele, near modern Qantarah,
was the coastal route to Palestine. It headed toward the
Mediterranean and then along the southern edge of Lake
Sirbonis (modern Lake Bardawil, named after King Bald-
win of the Crusades). This lake (about ten to fifteen
miles across and fifty miles long) was separated from the
Mediterranean Sea only by a narrow strip of land, some
of it with quicksands; therefore the main route had to
go south of the lake. It continued on past Wadi el-Arish
to Gaza in southwestern Palestine. This route was about
140 miles long, and aside from a few wells along the way
most of it was waterless desert. Notwithstanding these
difficulties, it was the shortest route, and thus it was used
regularly by ancient businessmen and warriors who, like
their modern counterparts, seemed to be in a hurry. This
was especially true during the Eighteenth and Nineteenth

Dynasties, when caravans and the great armies of the warrior Pharaohs made it the "superhighway" between Africa and Asia. No doubt Ramses had troops stationed along the way to guard against the revolt which the Hittites were backing.

The second route available to Moses from the district of Succoth was the inland trail across the Sinai Peninsula, the lower Negev, and into Beersheba. In the Bible the wilderness to the east of Egypt is called "the wilderness of Shur" (Exod. 15:22). Since "Shur" means "wall," this was the desert region to the east of the Wall of the Prince. The Abraham narratives refer to "the way of Shur" (Gen. 16:7), and most certainly this middle route was the one used by Abraham and Jacob in their travels to Egypt. Moses could have headed in this direction by going north or south of Lake Timsah.

The third possibility for Moses was the southern route running across the middle of the Sinai Peninsula and crossing into Arabia at the head of the Gulf of Aqaba. The start of this trail was from the Lake Timsah region also, but it headed southeast whereas the middle route went almost due east.

The fourth choice was to go south from Lake Timsah. After joining the overland route from Memphis at the head of the Gulf of Suez, this route went along the east side of the Gulf and then inland to the mines at Serabit el-Khadim. It was this route which Moses knew best. One of the assurances to Moses, according to the narrative, was that he would some day worship at the mountain of God with the people of Israel. Even if one should doubt the authenticity of the passage, Moses must have cherished for the Israelites his experience at the mountain, and so he probably had in mind leading them there on a pilgrimage.

With respect to the coastal route, the biblical narrative (the first material from the E tradition since Exod. 5:4) makes the interesting comment, "God did not lead them by way of the land of Philistines, although that was near; for God said, 'Lest the people repent when they see war, and return to Egypt' " (Exod. 13:17). Apparently the Israelites were so weary and beaten down they would return to Egypt rather than fight their way along the coast.

The reference to "the land of the Philistines" is an anachronism ("against time") because the Philistines did not occupy the region around Gaza until after 1200 B.C.; thus the area could not have been given that title in 1290.

Red Sea or Reed Sea?

Rather than send the Israelites by the coastal route, God "led the people round by the way of the wilderness toward the Reed (Papyrus) Sea (Hebrew *yam suph*). And the people of Israel went up out of the land of Egypt equipped for battle" (13:18). Most translations have "Red Sea" instead of "Reed Sea," but this is a misunderstanding which originated in the Hebrew Bible and then was expanded in the Septuagint translation. In Numbers 33:10 *yam suph* is used to describe the Gulf of Suez, and in 1 Kings 9:26, a passage about Solomon's fleet, it refers to the Gulf of Aqaba. The Greeks considered the Gulf of Suez and the Gulf of Aqaba as part of the Red Sea proper, and since these were called *yam suph,* it was a natural step for the translators to use "Red Sea" for every occurrence of *yam suph.*

The Hebrew word *suph* seems to have come from the Egyptian word *tjufe* ("papyrus, reed"). The Anastasi III Papyrus refers to "Papyrus Lake," which furnished papyrus (a reed for making "paper," and thus the source of our word) for the city of Raamses. The same inscription makes reference to "Horus Lake" (Hebrew *Shihor*), which produced a tougher variety of reeds. Since papyrus is strictly a fresh-water reed, it could not have grown in the very salty water of the Gulf of Suez, nor in the brackish water of Lake Timsah and the Bitter Lakes. The Papyrus Lake, therefore, was a fresh-water swamp. Although its exact location is not known, it was to the east of Raamses (Tanis) and probably in an area now forming one of the bays of Lake Menzaleh. Whether this specific Papyrus Lake was the biblical *yam suph* will have to be considered later with other data about the route of march.

Horus Lake and the Pelusiac Nile

Horus Lake (Shihor) is mentioned in Joshua 13:3 as being at the east of Egypt. 1 Chronicles 13:5 considers the Lake the southern boundary of David's empire. It was probably north of Lake Timsah (Crocodile Lake), and together with the latter and the Bitter Lakes it comprised part of the Wall of the Prince, the line of forts and lakes forming the eastern border of Egypt. Jeremiah refers to the "waters of Shihor" as though they were the Nile (Jer. 2:18). There are other indications that about the ninth century B.C. the eastern branch of the Nile (flowing past the site of the city of Raamses) gradually silted up until it overflowed the high levees and cut a new course further east. Perhaps it ran into Horus Lake and then cut a path on the other side to the Mediterranean. A number of towns formed along the edge of the new branch just as they had along the old one. Since the town on the Mediterranean was called Pelusium (mentioned in Ezek. 30:15, 16 under the name Sin), the Greeks called this the Pelusiac branch of the Nile. It too silted up, and about the fourteenth or fifteenth century A.D. the Nile found another route further west, leaving the former river towns stranded. The important fact is that the Pelusiac branch was not formed until after the thirteenth century B.C., and so the Israelites did not have to cross any branch of the Nile in their flight from Egypt.

The itinerary of the Israelites continues in Exodus 13:20 with the notation that they "moved on from Succoth, and camped at Etham, on the edge of the wilderness." The fortress Thel (Sele), where the coast route began, was designated *hetem* ("fort") in Egyptian. Accordingly, some scholars think that *Etham* (Greek *Othom*) means "Fortress," and they locate it at Serapeum, a fort of Ramses II between Lake Timsah and the northern Bitter Lake. As noted earlier, there was an all-water route from the Nile to the Gulf of Suez. Just west of Lake Timsah it turned south, skirting the western edge of the Bitter Lakes and finally connecting with the Gulf. Thus the fort at Serapeum probably served double duty as an entry station and a guardpost for the canal to the west. If Etham was Serapeum, then Moses went southeast, between the canal and Lake Timsah, to the very edge of the wilderness.

The Pillar of Cloud and of Fire

As to the means of guidance which Moses had, the narrative states, "Yahweh went before them by day in a pillar (column) of cloud to lead them along the way, and by night in a pillar (column) of fire to give them light, that they might travel by day and by night" (13:21). Inasmuch as the first few nights of the Exodus were in full or three-quarters moon, there was little need for light to travel by. The important fact about the biblical comment is the element of divine guidance.

It is quite likely that what is referred to was a brazier of burning wood carried on a long pole so that it could be seen for some distance. The Persian armies did this, and when Alexander the Great found out that the trumpet was not an effective signal, he shifted to the fire signal. The Arab caravans did the same thing later on. The column of smoke was visible during the day and flame at night; therefore it could serve as a signal for a full twenty-four hours. When Yahweh made known to Moses when and where to move, he gave instructions to those carrying the fire and they moved out. When the destination was reached the movement of the fire was halted. For most of the Israelites, therefore, the column of smoke (or flame) was taken as a manifestation of Yahweh's divine guidance because they moved and stopped in accordance with the fire.

A recent study by George E. Mendenhall has thrown a great deal of light on the complex issue of manifestations of deity.[1] As a basic premise he declares, "It seems to be almost a universal in the history of religion that certain aspects of reality experienced by persons are identified as manifestations of that which is proclaimed in the sacred tradition. Such identification bridges the transcendent and the immanent, the past and present, the sacred and the secular." This issue of "religious identification," as Mendenhall labels it, usually focused at the center of religious, political, and military power — the king. He had a natural body, but he was regarded as having a divine nature as well. As early as the Fifth Dynasty in Egypt the symbol of Pharaoh Sahura (about 2500 B.C.) was the winged sun disk (a fusion of the sun-god Re and the falcon-god Horus). This symbol was equated with the name of the

---

[1] Mendenhall, "The Mask of Yahweh," chap. 2 in *The Tenth Generation* (Baltimore: Johns Hopkins, 1972).

king and regarded as his image. At the same time it was the image of the gods Re and Horus.

Well over 2,000 years later the same essential concept appears in some myths inscribed in the temple of Horus at Edfu. Horus is traveling in the solar boat with Re when they confront the forces of the enemy god Seth. He asks permission to attack and with Re's consent rises into the heavens as a great winged disk. As the "great flyer" he throws the enemy into such confusion they can neither see nor hear, and so they destroy each other. The historical event back of this myth is not apparent, but it is clear that the reigning Ptolemy is Horus, Lord of Heaven, and that his manifestation is the winged sun disk.

Variations of this dual identity of royalty and deity have been found all the way from Greece to India. Two specific words used in Babylonia are very helpful in understanding the idea of manifestation. *Melammu* is a dazzling halo or luminous cloud surrounding anything divine or associated with deity (temples, weapons, symbols, or objects worn by the images of the gods in the temple ritual). As the representative and likeness of the gods, the king was endowed with a *melammu* at his coronation. Moreover, the *melammu*, as the manifestation of divine nature, served as a mask to hide the natural body of kings, gods, and demons. The related term *puluhtu* designates anything which inspires fear and awe, and at times it refers to a garment of flame surrounding a god or king. The latter was probably a red garment or cloak which, like the mask, was used in ritual or cultic activities.

The term traditionally translated "cloud" in Exodus 13:21 is the Hebrew word *anan*. Insight into its meaning has come from six uses of this Semitic word in the fourteenth-century-B.C. tablets from Ras Shamra (ancient Ugarit). Although some of the texts are marred, it is clear that *anan* is something closely identified with divine beings, either as a substitute for their names, or an aspect of their person. In short, it appears to be a semantic equivalent for Babylonian *melammu*, and this conclusion is borne out when the biblical uses of the word are examined.

There are about eighty-six occurrences of *anan* in the Old Testament, spanning many centuries, and of course there is a shift in meaning. The basic fact, as Mendenhall points out, is that "all of the references to the *anan* of Yahweh as an active agent in past experience of human beings have to do with the Exodus and Wanderings traditions regardless of the literary 'source', L, J, E, D, or P, and it occurs in contexts assigned to all of these. There is no usage of the word in a narrative context after the death of Moses, and the only passages in which it is referred to as any kind of presently empirical reality in later contexts have to do with the Jerusalem cultus." During the Bronze Age (3000-1200 B.C.) the *melammu/anan* aspect of deity was associated with a wide range of natural and empirical phenomena (storms, heavenly bodies, exercise of royal dominion, war, disease, etc.), of which "cloud (smoke)" was only one of the symbols.

A key verse in understanding the older meaning of *anan* is Exodus 14:24: "In the morning watch Yahweh, in the pillar of fire and *anan*, looked down on the camp of the Egyptians, and he confounded the camp of the Egyptians." Contrary to 13:21, which seems to refer to two separate pillars, this passage is correct in noting that there was just one pillar. This strengthens the suggestion that the brazier on the long pole was the basis for the column, which appeared as smoke (cloud) during the day and fire at night. Yahweh was immanent in the column, but the smoke and fire served as a mask or covering to hide him. These symbols, then, were assurances to the Israelites that Yahweh was actively engaged in the struggle against the Egyptians.

Another very instructive passage is 14:19: "The messenger (angel) of God who went before the host of Israel moved and went behind them; and the pillar of *anan* moved from before them and stood behind them." The two halves of the verse are clearly variant statements describing the same event. The "messenger of God," like the "messenger of Yahweh" in Exodus 3:2, is obviously a manifestation of Yahweh, and so is the "pillar of *anan.*" It is quite evident, therefore, that the messenger and the *anan* represent two different ways of expressing the manifestation of Yahweh in the exercise of his authority and sovereignty. Whereas the use of *anan* as "epiphany," manifestation of deity, was lost after the period of Moses, the idea of a messenger (angel) carried on for centuries as the basic means of describing a manifestation of Yahweh (see, for example, Josh. 5:13-15; Judg. 13; and Acts 7:38, 53).

A later use of *anan* is found in 1 Kings 8:10-11: "And when the priests came out of the holy place the *anan* filled the house of Yahweh so that the priests could not stand to minister because of the *anan;* for the glory *(kabod)* of Yahweh filled the house of Yahweh." At the thrilling moment of bringing the ark of the covenant of Yahweh into the most holy place of the new temple built by Solomon, the priests undoubtedly burned a great deal of incense on the altar of incense so that the holy place was filled with the aromatic smoke. In this instance *anan* means "cloud, smoke," and it is equated with Yahweh's glory. Although the incense smoke is understood as an expression of Yahweh, it is not *anan* in the older sense of the mask of Yahweh's active presence.

In Isaiah's vision in the temple "the house was filled with smoke (Hebrew *ashan*)" (Isa. 6:4). The smoke of incense filled the temple, but Isaiah does not refer to it as *anan* even though it is certain that the smoke was a manifestation of the Lord who was "sitting upon a throne, high and lifted up" (6:1). It is evident, therefore, that by the eighth century B.C. the original meaning of *anan* had been lost, and when the classical prophets wanted to express the idea of Yahweh's manifestation they used *ashan* ("smoke") in its place because the ritual use of incense made smoke one of the most common ways of indicating the presence of Yahweh. Since *anan* had acquired the specific meaning "cloud," this idea was read back into all the older passages.

The Location of the Reed Sea

When the Israelites were at Etham, on the edge of the wilderness, Yahweh told Moses, "Tell the Israelites to turn back and camp in front of Pi-hahiroth, between Migdol and the sea, in front of Baal-zephon; you shall camp opposite it, by the sea" (Exod. 14:2). The "sea" is apparently a reference to the Reed Sea, and so the location of the three sites named should be helpful in determining where the Israelites crossed. An inscription from about 1575 B.C.

mentions a town Pi-hathor (which could be the biblical
Pi-hahiroth) in connection with Avaris, and it is clear from
the context that it was on the far northeastern border of
Egypt, but more precision is not possible.

Migdol, meaning "tower," was the name applied to a
number of places which were primarily forts. Ruins of a
"tower" fort of Ramses II have been found on Jebel Abu
Hasan, a hill with a view east over the canal and the valley
between the southern Bitter Lake and the Gulf of Suez.
Some scholars locate the Migdol of 14:2 here. On the other
hand, a far more prominent site named Migdol is the one
at modern Tell el-Heir. This is about twelve miles northeast of Tell Abu Seifah, the site of Sele where the coast
route began. In other words, this Migdol was probably the
first main stopover along the short route. Ezekiel 29:10
and 30:6 indicate that Migdol was the first important place
on entering Egypt at the northeast corner. It is referred
to in Jeremiah 44:1 and 46:14 in connection with Tahpanhes. A Phoenician letter from the sixth century B.C.
speaks of "Baal-zephon and all the gods of Tahpanhes."
This is very interesting because it tells us that the town
which Jeremiah associated with Migdol had a sanctuary
where Baal-zephon was worshiped as the chief god of the
pantheon.

The name Baal-zephon means "Lord of the North," but
there was a specific peak which the eastern Mediterranean
world associated with the residence of this god. North of
Ras Shamra (Ugarit) and southeast of Antioch in Syria
is a striking conical peak which rises majestically out of
the Mediterranean Sea. It is the dominant feature for
many miles around, and it was the first point of land
ancient mariners picked up when they returned from a
trip to the west. It is little wonder that seafarers worshiped Baal-zephon as their patron god, because his residence was on the peak which was such a welcome sight.
The fame of Baal-zephon was carried around the Mediterranean, even down to Egypt. The patron of mariners
in the Greek and Roman periods was Zeus Casius. Independently Otto Eissfeldt and W. F. Albright showed that
this god was Baal-zephon and that his residence was the

same peak, Mons Casius.[2] The Ugaritic tablets refer to Baal-zephon and associate him with the mythical phoenix bird and with a sacred bark or sailing vessel. An Egyptian inscription from the fourteenth century lists Baal-zephon as a foreign deity, and an inscription from the reign of Ramses II lists Baal-zephon along with two other Semitic gods who were worshiped in Egypt.

The Theory of a Southern Crossing

Clearly, then, the biblical reference to Baal-zephon means a place primarily noted for a sanctuary dedicated to the worship of that deity. F. M. Abel and other scholars locate Baal-zephon at the northern end of the Gulf of Suez. They estimate that Pi-hahiroth was a marshy region to the west of the Bitter Lakes, and that the Israelites came south between this area and the hills to the west. The plain between the southern Bitter Lake and Jebel Abu Hasan was where they camped "between Migdol and the sea." Another basic feature of the southern-crossing theory is that a shallow body of water extended from the southern Bitter Lake all the way to the Gulf of Suez. With water barring any route to the east and hills restricting their movement south or west, the only feasible alternative was to retrace their steps and leave Egypt across the isthmus of land between the northern Bitter Lake and Lake Timsah. This situation would explain why Pharaoh, on hearing the report about the Israelites, thought, "They are entangled in the land; the wilderness has shut them in" (14:3).

Since the ancients did not indicate direction precisely by using the intermediate points northeast, southeast, etc., the "strong east wind" (14:21) which Yahweh used to clear the Reed Sea was probably a northeast wind. Thus, according to this theory, the strong wind combined with a strong ebb tide cleared a shallow portion of the channel, enabling the Israelites to cross over "on dry ground" (14:22). After they were across, the cessation of the wind and a strong

---

[2] Eissfeldt, *Baal Zaphon, Zeus Kasios und der Durchzug der Israeliten durchs Meer*, 1932, and Albright, "The North-Canaanite Epic of 'Al'êyân Ba'al and Môt," *The Journal of the Palestine Oriental Society*, XII, 4 (1932), 192.

flood tide brought the water back to drown the Egyptians (14:27).

This theory of a southern crossing seems quite plausible, but there are some serious difficulties. One of them is the assumption that the southern Bitter Lake was connected with the Gulf of Suez. In essence this is the theory which commentators in the late nineteenth and early twentieth century used to explain why the Septuagint translated "Red Sea" for all the occurrences of *yam suph*. But the contention that the Gulf of Suez actually extended another thirty miles to the northern end of the Bitter Lakes means either that the water level of the Gulf lowered at a later time or that the land rose.

In 1947-48 W. F. Albright discovered some ruins at Merkhah, about five miles south of the modern port of Abu Zeneimeh. Excavation produced much fifteenth-century pottery, and since the edge of the site was only about 350 feet from the Gulf of Suez, it was quite evident that this was the port for the Egyptian mining operations at Serabit el-Khadim. Most important of all, however, was the fact that the lowest part of the old seaport town was six and a half feet above the high tide level. In other words, the level of the Gulf of Suez is much the same as it was in the fifteenth century B.C. This is what would be expected because the Sinai Peninsula has a granite base which reduces any upward or downward movement to a minimum. Inasmuch as the level of the Gulf of Suez has not changed appreciably since the time of Moses, the only alternative for the theory of a southern crossing is that the valley floor between the Bitter Lakes and the Gulf of Suez rose at some later time. This is highly unlikely since it is so close to the base of the Sinai Peninsula; therefore a southern crossing seems rather dubious.

It is true that there are marine shells along the valley north of the Gulf of Suez. These can be accounted for without assuming a body of water there in the time of Moses. The shells were probably deposited in prehistoric times when the Gulf did extend north to include the Bitter Lakes. A further difficulty for the theory of a southern crossing is that no papyrus could have grown in this region. If the Reed Sea of the biblical narrative refers to a papyrus lake, as the name *suph* implies, then a southern route is impossible.

The Theory of a Northern Crossing

While the proponents of a southern crossing locate Baal-zephon near the northern end of the Gulf of Suez, it seems very unlikely that this sanctuary would have been located anywhere except at a seaport on the Mediterranean. There are two possibilities. First is Casium (Greek *Kasion*) along the strip of land between the Mediterranean Sea and Lake Sirbonis. Scholars differ as to its location along the strip of land, but at least they agree it was a seaport on the Mediterranean. The name Casium is clearly related to (Zeus) Casius, the Greek and Roman designation for Baal-zephon. Eissfeldt and Noth contend that this was the location of the biblical Baal-zephon. Accordingly, when the Israelites camped "in front of Baal-zephon" they were in "the neighborhood of the western shore of Lake Sirbonis." In order for this camp site to fit the description "between Migdol and the sea," the "sea" must be the Mediterranean, not the Reed Sea. Hemmed in by Lake Sirbonis on the east and the Mediterranean on the north, the Israelites would have been entangled in the wilderness, and thus it would be a temptation for Pharaoh to pursue them. When the Egyptians approached, the strong east wind of Yahweh emptied a lagoon of Lake Sirbonis allowing the Israelites to cross.

This view of an extreme northern crossing and exodus along the coastal route is in direct contradiction to Exodus 13:17, and W. F. Albright disagrees with the theory for a number of reasons.[3] Since Casium is never mentioned prior to the Greek and Roman periods, it was probably not in existence at the time of Moses. On the contrary, the Phoenician letter from the sixth century B.C. indicates that at that time Baal-zephon was the chief god at Tahpanhes, and the implication is that this deity had been worshiped at this place for some time. The town received its name Tahpanhes, meaning "The Fort of Phinehas," in the early eleventh century B.C., when a strong Theban general named Phinehas came to the Delta region to suppress

---

[3] Albright, "Baal-zephon," *Alfred Bertholet Festschrift*, 1950, pp. 1-14.

a rebellion. He did such a good job that a number of places incorporated his name as a part of their new names. It is quite probable that the older name for Tahpanhes was actually Baal-zephon, as in the biblical narrative, since this deity was known and worshiped in Egypt as early as the fourteenth century B.C. Later on when the Greeks were prominent in Egypt the name Tahpanhes was transcribed as Taphnas, and then finally spelled Daphnai like the Greek name of Daphne. The location of the old seaport is marked by the modern Tell Defneh, ruins along the southern edge of Lake Menzaleh, about five miles west of Qantarah.

When all the evidence with respect to Pi-hahiroth, Migdol, and Baal-zephon is taken together, the result is a cluster of towns located in the far northeast corner of Egypt in the very region of the Papyrus Lake of Ramses II. It is rather surprising to have the Israelites leaving the edge of the wilderness at Etham and heading north, and Moses must have been equally shocked to be headed in the opposite direction he intended going. In any case, Yahweh's instructions to him were: "Tell the people of Israel to turn back and camp in front of Pi-hahiroth, between Migdol and the sea, in front of Baal-zephon; you shall camp opposite it, by the sea" (14:2). The puzzle becomes more complex with the information in Numbers 33:7 that the Israelites "set out from Etham and turned back to Pi-hahiroth, which faces Baal-zephon, and they camped in front of Migdol."

Of the three sites, Baal-zephon was the furthest west. Migdol was about seventeen miles to the northeast, and Pi-hahiroth somewhere in between because it faced Baal-zephon and was between Migdol and the sea. According to the combined evidence of both verses, the Israelites camped "in front of" all three sites. Either some of the original information has dropped out in the transmission of the story, or the narrators were using "in front of" in a very general way. Exodus 14:2 can be interpreted to mean that Pi-hahiroth was on the eastern side of the Papyrus Lake and thus "between Migdol and the sea." If the Israelites camped on the western side of the Lake "against" or "in front of" Baal-zephon, then they were opposite Pi-hahiroth, thereby being "in front of" it. However, the camp was "in front of Migdol" (Num. 33:7) only in the broadest sense.

It is quite apparent that every theory concerning the route of the Exodus has its share of problems. In a real sense the scholars are just as entangled in the evidence as the Israelites were in the wilderness. Notwithstanding some difficulties, however, the theory which places the Reed (Papyrus) Sea between Tahpanhes and Migdol still has the preponderance of evidence in its favor.

Through the Reed (Papyrus) Sea

The purpose of the instructions in Exodus 14:2, according to the P tradition, was to entice Pharaoh so that reports of the Israelites' whereabouts would cause him to think, "They are entangled in the land; the wilderness has shut them in." Yahweh will harden his heart and he will pursue them. In so doing Yahweh will "get glory over Pharaoh and all his host." Then follows a very puzzling verse: "When the king of Egypt was told that the people had fled, the mind of Pharaoh and his servants was changed toward the people, and they said, 'What is this we have done, that we have let Israel go from serving us?' " (14:5). Thus far the narrative (both J and P traditions) has made it quite plain that Pharaoh knowingly and willingly drove the Israelites out of his country. The use of "king of Egypt" and the fact that he had to be told "that the people had fled" seem to be part of a tradition which explained the Exodus as a secretive flight.

Pharaoh, according to the latter part of 14:5, knows that the Israelites are gone, but he and his servants miss their services and so they have a change of mind. Therefore Pharaoh readies his own chariot and heads out with his army plus "600 picked chariots and all the other chariots of Egypt with officers over all of them" (14:7). He pursues the Israelites as they are "going out with a high hand," that is, "going out defiantly." This too seems to be a bit of the tradition which remembered the Exodus as a defiant, secretive escape. In any event, "all Pharaoh's horses and chariots and his horsemen and his army" overtake the Israelites "camped at the sea, opposite Pi-hahiroth, in front of Baal-zephon" (14:9). There is no mention of

Pharaoh himself being there. He probably led the army out a few miles and then turned back.

The people are in great fear at the sight of the Egyptians, and they vent their fears on Moses: "Is it because there are no graves in Egypt that you have taken us away to die in the wilderness? What have you done to us, in bringing us out of Egypt? Is this not what we said to you in Egypt, 'Let us alone and let us serve the Egyptians'? For it would have been better for us to serve the Egyptians than to die in the wilderness" (14:11-12). The wilderness is technically within Egypt's borders, but as far as the grumblers are concerned it is outside the inhabitable areas like the land of Goshen. Although the complaint is not described by the usual expression "murmured against," the content of the people's objections definitely makes this the first of a long series of murmurings which border on rebellion against Moses. In answer he challenges their lack of faith in Yahweh with a strong statement of assurance: "Fear not, stand firm, and see the salvation of Yahweh, which he will work for you today; for the Egyptians whom you see today, you shall never see again. Yahweh will fight for you, and you have only to be still" (14:13-14).

Yet the P tradition recalls that Moses had some uneasiness too. Yahweh answers him, "Why do you cry to me? Tell the people of Israel to go forward. Lift up your rod and stretch out your hand over the sea and divide it, that the people of Israel may go on dry ground through the sea" (14:15-16). Then the "messenger of God," that is, the "column of manifestation," moves from the front of the Israelites to their rear, "coming between the host of Egypt and the host of Israel. And there was the manifestation and the darkness, and it lit up the night without one approaching the other all night" (14:20). The Hebrew text is very difficult to interpret. It seems to say that the flaming brazier was moved from the front of the Israelite camp to the rear so that it would light up the sky between the two forces, thus preventing the Egyptians from a sneak attack during the night. The Greek translation has, "And the night passed without one approaching the other all night." Since the translator took *anan* to mean a literal cloud, he probably thought that the dark cloud settled down separating the two camps. In spite of the difficulties, one thing is clear: the two camps settled down for the night in preparation for the battle in the morning.

After receiving instructions from Yahweh, Moses stretches out his hand over the sea and Yahweh drives the sea back "by a strong east wind all night" (14:21). The strongest type of east wind would actually have been a Sirocco from the southeast, thus driving the shallow water of the papyrus swamp to the northwest. Early in the morning Moses leads the Israelites through the emptied basin of the swamp "on dry ground." The hot, dry air would have dried up much of the moisture, but it is doubtful that they went over on perfectly dry ground. The statements that the waters were "divided" and "a wall on the right hand and on the left" are certainly elaborations of later tradition. As noted earlier, they came from a literal interpretation of the poetic imagery found in the triumphal song of Moses and Miriam: "At the blast of your nostrils the waters piled up, the floods stood up in a heap; the deeps congealed in the heart of the sea" (15:8). The terrific storm is viewed as the exhalation of an indignant God. Obviously, however, the people could not have crossed while the storm was piling the water in heaps.

As the Israelites pass through the swamp basin the Egyptians follow in hot pursuit: horses, chariots, and all. Yahweh, who watched over his people during the passover night (12:42), has been on guard stationed "in the column of fire and manifestation" (note the inversion of the two aspects). In the morning watch (the last of the three periods of guard duty into which the night was divided) Yahweh sees the Egyptians pursuing and he decides to take action. The Hebrew verb *hamam* can mean "confuse, frustrate, rout," and the account seems to include aspects of all these meanings. The Hebrew text of 14:25 says that Yahweh "removed" the wheels of the Egyptian chariots, but all the early translations have "bound, clogged." Evidently the chariot wheels mired up to the hubs in the soft soil at the bottom of the basin. In any case, the Egyptians say, "Let us flee from before Israel, for Yahweh fights for them against the Egyptians." While they laboriously try to run out of the basin, Moses raises his hand and just about sunrise the waters return to the basin. The "chariots and the horsemen and all the host of Pharaoh" are covered so that "not so much as one of them remained" (14:28). The frequent references to "all, every" and "none, not one" in the Exodus narratives is an enhancing of the stories which comes from later tradition. The same tendency occurs in other portions of the Old Testament (for example, the flood and conquest stories), thus indicating that these covering statements are to be taken generally, not literally.

The Meaning of the Crossing

The people of Israel realize how marvelously Yahweh has saved them when they see the corpses of the drowned Egyptians lining the shore of the lake. Then the narrative states, "Israel saw the great work which Yahweh did against the Egyptians, and the people feared Yahweh; and they believed in Yahweh and in his servant Moses" (14:31). Yahweh has indeed made himself "known" to the Egyptians and to his own people. Never again will Ramses say in disdain, "Who is Yahweh?" His task force has been riddled, and he is ready now to let the people go and serve Yahweh. It has been a long school of hard knocks, but finally he has learned his lesson. There will be no songs of triumph and no inflated boasts emblazoned on the walls of the temples because this utter defeat occurred in the land, not some distant country. For Pharaoh and the decimated Egyptian families, this will be a day to forget.

The biblical narrative claims that Yahweh performed his wonder of deliverance by natural means of his own creation. Here, as in the case of the plagues, the miracle is in the timing. The wonder of Yahweh's deeds in history is well expressed by Martin Buber:

> The concept of miracle which is permissible from the historical approach can be defined at its starting point as an abiding astonishment. The philosophizing and the religious person both wonder at the phenomenon, but the one neutralizes his wonder in ideal knowledge, while the other abides in that wonder; no knowledge, no cognition, can weaken his astonishment. Any causal explanation only deepens the wonder for him. The great turning-points in religious history are based on the fact that again and ever again an individual and a group attached to him

wonder and keep on wondering; at a natural phenomenon,
at a historical event, or at both together; always at something which intervenes fatefully in the life of this individual and this group. They sense and experience it as a
wonder....
    The real miracle means that in the astonishing expe-
rience of the event the current system of cause and effect
becomes, as it were, transparent and permits a glimpse of
the sphere in which a sole power, not restricted by any
other, is at work. To live with the miracle means to recognize this power on every given occasion as the effecting
one.[4]

The wonder of the awesome deliverance by Yahweh
turned to joy, and so "Miriam, the prophetess, the sister
of Aaron, took a timbrel in her hand; and all the women
went out with her with timbrels and dancing" (15:20).
Then Miriam sang to them, "Sing to Yahweh, for he has
triumphed gloriously; the horse and his rider he has thrown
into the sea." This poetic couplet is one of the earliest
portions preserved in the Old Testament, and its present
form is not far from the original words sung by Miriam.
She is called the prophetess because she used music and
rhythm to lead the women in stirring the Israelites to an
ecstatic expression of praise to Yahweh. It is rather puzzling, however, why Miriam is identified as the sister of
Aaron, and not of Moses and Aaron. Aaron was the elder
of the two, but Moses, as the genuine prophet, outranked
him; therefore the omission of his name may indicate that
this tradition did not consider Miriam as the sister of Moses.

The Song of Moses and Miriam.

The ecstasy of Miriam is shared by Moses, and he leads
all the people in a hymn of triumph (15:1-18). This national anthem of the Israelites, which came through the
J tradition, is similar in type to the other victory songs
of the thirteenth century: Ramses' false victory at Qadesh;
and Merneptah's triumph over the Libyans. After the repetition of Miriam's refrain, 15:2 has a description of Yahweh with great theological content:

> *My strength and my song is he,*
> *and he has become my salvation;*

---
[4] Buber, *Moses, the Revelation and the Covenant*, pp. 75-78.

> *This is my God whom I praise,*
> *my father's God whom I exalt.*

The God who appeared at the burning bush as the "God of the fathers" (Exod. 3:6) has shown his power in saving his people from the Egyptians; accordingly, Moses expresses his thanksgiving to Yahweh for his sustaining power, his deliverance, and his faithfulness over the generations.

Verse 3 reads literally, "Yahweh is a man of war; Yahweh is his name." The biblical writers talk of God in very anthropomorphic terms (his hand, arm, eyes, nostrils, etc.), but they do not call him "man." Accordingly, Albright suggests taking the name in its original causative sense, "He brings warriors into existence."[5] Even if "a man of war" was taken as a description of Yahweh, it was certainly not characterizing Yahweh as a war-god. Inasmuch as it was Yahweh who fought the battle against the Egyptians, the Israelites realized that he was the one leading them to victory. Their duty was to trust and be "still" while he fought for them.

After the two verses of adoration and praise of Yahweh, the hymn returns to the victory at the sea. Pharaoh's chariots and officers go down into the depths "like a stone" (4-5). Then follows a refrain in the typical style of repetitive parallelism (abc:abd), which is found in the Ugaritic literature almost a century before Moses:

a	b	c
Thy right hand,	O Yahweh,	is awesome in power,
a	b	d
Thy right hand,	O Yahweh,	crushes the enemy.

Verses 7-10 form a unit or strophe about the defeat of the Egyptians, then the second refrain appears in a slight variation (abc:adb) of the same repetitive style:

a	b	c
Who is like thee,	among the gods,	O Yahweh?
a	d	b
Who is like thee,	awesome	among the holy ones?

This refrain is clearly an old Canaanite couplet with the

---

[5] Albright, unpublished manuscript.

name Yahweh substituted for Baal, the Lord of the Canaanite pantheon. But in adapting the form for his own use
Moses did not adopt the concept of polytheism. There was
only one God, and he was Yahweh. The reference to the
"gods" was understood in the sense that God had a council of created beings who were authorized to carry out
his will and thus liable to judgment if they failed to do
so. This concept is very explicit in Psalm 82:1-2: "God
has taken his place in the divine council; in the midst of
the gods he holds judgment: How long will you judge
unjustly and show partiality to the wicked?" God's judgment is given in verses 6-7: "You are gods, sons of the
Most High, all of you; nevertheless, you shall die like men,
and fall like any prince."

Verses 12-16a form another strophe about Yahweh's
deeds. He stretched out his right hand and "the earth
swallowed them." This statement seems out of place since
it was the sea which swallowed the Egyptians. However,
the expression is really an idiom for death because burial
in a grave or pit was the normal way of caring for the
dead. Verse 13 summarizes Yahweh's way of dealing with
his people:

> *Thou hast led with thy steadfast love,*
> *the people whom thou hast redeemed,*
> *Thou hast guided them by thy might*
> *to thy holy pasture.*

The word "pasture" (Hebrew *naweh*) is usually translated
"abode" and then taken to mean the land of Canaan, but
the verbs in this verse are in the past tense; therefore "pasture" refers to the area through which Yahweh, their
shepherd, has led them. The inhabitants of Edom, Moab,
and Canaan have heard of Yahweh's mighty deeds and
they will tremble in fear:

a	c	b
Until thy people,	O Yahweh,	pass by,
a	d	b
Until the people	whom thou hast created	pass by.

Thus, the last half of verse 16 is really the third refrain
of the hymn.

Verse 17 looks to the future and definitely refers to

the hill country of Palestine which Yahweh has allotted
(by his promise to Abraham) for his people and where
Yahweh will establish his abode:

> *Thou wilt bring them in,*
> *and plant them in thy allotted mountain,*
> *The dais of thy throne,*
> *which thou hast made, O Yahweh,*
> *The sanctuary, O Yahweh,*
> *which thy hands have created.*

Scholars have tended to interpret the latter part of the
song of Moses and Miriam (verses 13-18) as a composition
dating from Israel's residence in the land of Canaan.
There is some indication of later influence, but in general the statements have so many archaic expressions and
terms (for example, *naweh*, "pasture," and *makon*, "dais"),
and the style of poetry is so true to early Canaanite poetry, that the original poem certainly dates from the thirteenth century B.C. The statements looking into the future
are of such a general nature Moses could easily have made
them on the basis of his knowledge of Yahweh's promise
to Abraham and the route he intended to follow.

While many scholars have come to recognize the strong
Canaanite influence on the style of the song, they attribute this to the period of David and Solomon when
the architectural, musical, and ritual forms of the Canaanites were borrowed in great numbers. But this point of
view ignores completely the Canaanite influence which
Moses received indirectly in Egypt. The Delta region had
very close ties with the Canaanites along the eastern shore
of the Mediterranean. The influence of their culture and
religion was so strong the Egyptians adopted some of the
Canaanite gods and goddesses into their pantheon. We
have noted how Baal-zephon was worshiped in Egypt, and
the same was true of Qudshu, Astarte, and Anath. Since
Moses was reared in the court of Pharaoh, he probably
learned the Canaanite language, because it was very similar to the language of the Hebrews. He had opportunity to
read some of the literature of the Canaanites; therefore it
should come as no surprise that Moses knew about Canaanite styles of poetry.

In fact, then, the poem of victory in chapter 15 is essentially an eyewitness account of the victory at the sea. As such it is an older and more authentic witness to what happened than is the prose version in chapter 14. The dominant feature is the storm of Yahweh which cleared the path for the Israelites and resulted in the destruction of the Egyptians. This arrangement of a prose version followed by a poem is precisely the situation in Judges 5, where the poetic form of the song of Deborah is older and more accurate than the prose version of the story found in chapter 4.

After the exhilarating expression of praise to Yahweh for his deliverance at the sea, the Israelites had to turn their faces toward the wilderness of Shur. Freedom from the tyranny of Ramses was intended to mean freedom to serve Yahweh. But freedom is always risky business because it involves the uncertainties of moving out from security. The Israelites were beaten and weary in Egypt, yet they had water and food. The journey ahead would test the depth of their trust and commitment. Fortunately for them they did not realize that the three days' journey into the wilderness would stretch into two and a half agonizing months.

Chapter 8

Bread from Heaven

Since the fourth century A.D. the traditional site of the burning bush has been in the granite mountains in the southern tip of the Sinai Peninsula. How much older the tradition is no one can say for sure.

The Mountain of God

Monks found their way to the desolate mountains of Sinai and worshiped God on Jebel Musa ("The Mountain of Moses") (about 7,500 feet high). In a deep valley on the northern side of the mountain they found a bush which they revered as "the burning bush." Tradition says that St. Helena, the mother of Emperor Constantine, had a church built around the sacred bush. She visited the Holy Land about A.D. 327, and showed great interest in building churches and restoring holy places. It is quite possible that she heard of the monks in the Sinai desert and ordered that the church be built. Inasmuch as there are numerous reports of people who made pilgrimages to the area in the fourth century, there can be no question that the Jebel Musa tradition is at least 1,600 years old.

Yet considering the fact that Moses had his experience at the sacred mountain about 3,260 years ago, the Jebel Musa tradition is relatively late. Noth and some other scholars doubt the accuracy of the tradition on the grounds that the picture of a mountain quaking with fire and smoke (Exod. 19:18) is the description of a volcano. Inasmuch as there is no evidence of volcanic activity in the Sinai Peninsula, they are forced to locate the sacred mountain elsewhere. The nearest region of volcanic activity in historic times is northern Hejaz, to the east of the Gulf of Aqaba, that is, the eastern portion of Midian. But the volcanic interpretation of 19:18 is unnecessary because

167

smoke (cloud) and fire were the two basic aspects of the
anan of Yahweh, and a terrific thunderstorm with lightning streaking to the top of the mountain would easily
account for the description in the J tradition.

Another reason why Noth questions the Jebel Musa tradition is the claim that the itinerary of the Israelites found
in Numbers 33 is relatively late and untrustworthy, and
that the names listed are of uncertain location. But pessimism regarding the biblical and nonbiblical traditions does
not solve the problem. Noth expresses some confidence in
a crossing of Lake Sirbonis, a confrontation with God
at a volcano in Midian, and a stay at Qadesh-barnea in
the northeastern section of the Sinai Peninsula. But the
itinerary in Numbers 33 has no relevance to Noth's proposed route; therefore he has to deny the accuracy of the
list and consider it a late attempt to make up for a defi-
ciency in the sources.[1] Even should it be shown, as Noth
claims, that some parts of the list reflect a pilgrimage
route of later times, this does not make the list inaccurate.
When Elijah fled from Jezebel he went all the way to
Beersheba in southern Judah to be sure he was out of her
reach. After a period of rest he went "to Horeb, the mountain of God" (1 Kings 19:8). This indicates that there
was a live tradition about the location of the sacred mountain, and most certainly other Israelites made pilgrimages
to the site to renew their relationship with God. Furthermore, the fact that Elijah left from Beersheba indicates
a greater probability of its location in the Sinai Peninsula
than in Midian. The number of Nabatean graffiti (inscriptions scratched into rocks) in the valleys leading to the
Jebel Musa region seem to indicate that the composers
were on pilgrimage because Nabatean caravans did not
frequent this area.

The itinerary in Numbers 33 is not perfect and undoubtedly it has suffered in transmission, but neither is it the
guess of some priestly editor who knew nothing about the
geography of the Israelites' wanderings. As will be shown
many times, the places listed make sense in the lower
Sinai Peninsula; therefore there is no good reason for

---

[1] Noth, *Exodus*, pp. 110, 156, and *Numbers*, tr. James D. Martin
(Philadelphia: Westminster, 1969), pp. 242-246.

not accepting the Jebel Musa tradition as an accurate location of the original site where Yahweh made himself known to Moses and the Israelites.

The Sinai Peninsula

The Sinai Peninsula is an elongated triangle. At its base along the Mediterranean it is about 150 miles wide. About 250 miles to the south, its apex projects into the northern waters of the Red Sea. The strip along the Mediterranean is mostly sand, but ten to fifteen miles inland gravel and limestone begin to appear. This limestone plateau, rilled with wadis (dry stream beds), continues to rise gradually as it stretches southward for 125 to 150 miles. There it gives way to a range of igneous rock, mostly granite, which rises to about 8,600 feet before it descends toward the tip of the peninsula.

This outcropping of granite is similar in makeup and texture to that in southern Jordan and northwest Saudi Arabia. In prehistoric times a gigantic valley was formed in the earth's crust running from southern Asia Minor through Lebanon and Palestine all the way down into Africa. The Gulf of Aqaba and the Red Sea resulted from this catastrophic shift in land masses. The similarity of the regions on both sides of the Gulf of Aqaba is very clear in the fantastic color photograph taken from the Gemini 11 flight (see front endsheets). This fact probably explains why the Midianites crossed over the Arabah at the head of the Gulf and spent part of their time in the Sinai Peninsula.

Unlike the marvelous granite deposits near Aswan, Egypt, the molten rock cooled so quickly at Sinai that it has a shattered appearance. The western side of the range has eroded a great deal, and the slope is more gradual because the prevailing storms, coming from the west, have unloaded their water cargo on that side. On the other hand, since the eastern part of the range has been in the rain shadow, erosion is less evident and the slope is quite steep. The view from the east is magnificent, and it is little wonder that Moses was lured in this direction while hunting new pasture land.

Although the Sinai region today is largely a desolate wilderness, it should not be inferred that the area was always devoid of vegetation and wildlife. Moses would hardly have taken his flock there had this been true. Archaeology and inscriptions found on the Sinai Peninsula indicate that in ancient times the region had more water, dwarfed trees, and bushes than at present. Wild animals such as bulls, gazelles, goats, and sheep are mentioned in the inscriptions, and presumably wild fowl, including the ostrich, inhabited the region. Over the centuries the slopes were denuded and most of the wildlife perished or moved out of the area. Similarly, in Palestine most of the barren ridges of the central hill country were forested at one time. Thus, while the Sinai Peninsula was never an easy place to maintain an existence, it was more hospitable in ancient times than at the present. The rainfall in the region has never been heavy (about five to ten inches a year), but when it was consistent over a period of years the scrub and animal life increased. Prolonged drought, however, had the opposite result, and perhaps this may be part of the reason why the Sinai Peninsula today is far more barren than it was at certain times in the past.

The Route of the Israelites

After the victory over the Egyptians, "Moses had Israel depart from the Reed Sea and they went into the wilderness of Shur; they journeyed for three days in the wilderness without finding water. When they came to Marah, they could not drink the water at Marah because it was bitter; therefore it was named Marah ("Bitterness")" (Exod. 15:22-23). A few miles down the east side of the Gulf of Suez is a small oasis called Ayun Musa ("The Springs of Moses"). It is about sixty-five to seventy miles from the proposed northern crossing near Baal-zephon. It would have taken the Israelites more than three days to cover this distance; therefore its location fits the description given for Marah. While some of the springs in the area are bitter, others are fairly palatable. The quantity and quality of the water in most of the springs in the Sinai region vary according to the season; thus a spring might be drinkable at one time of the year and not at another. After the long, weary trip through the desert of Shur, the Israelites found some relief for their thirst. But apparently there was not enough drinkable water for all, and some of the people around the bitter springs "murmured against Moses, saying, 'What shall we drink?'" In desperation Moses prayed to Yahweh, who showed him a tree. When Moses threw some of the branches into the bitter spring the water became sweet. Some Arab chiefs told Ferdinand de Lesseps, builder of the Suez Canal, that they made brackish water drinkable by putting a bitter thornbush in it. Local residents of Ayun Musa do not know how to sweeten water with tree branches, but they claim that the large sweet spring at the southern end of the oasis is the one sweetened by Moses.

Some scholars locate Marah at Ain Hawara, further down the coast of the peninsula, where there is a thicket of stunted palms rimming a brackish spring. If the Israelites missed Ayun Musa, then they had to travel another forty miles through some of the most dreary country on this earth. Only pebbles and rocks grow from the dull gray soil. There are no trees or brush clumps for shade, and even the animals have deserted the region. It is far more probable that it was at Ayun Musa that the Israelites quenched their thirst and got water for continuing their journey.

The little section of material in the last half of verse 25 and in 26 is an example of an insertion from the D tradition: "There Yahweh made for them a statute and an ordinance, and there he tested them, saying, 'If you will hearken diligently to the voice of Yahweh your God, and do what is right in his eyes, and give heed to his commandments, and keep all his statutes, I will put none of the diseases upon you which I put upon the Egyptians; for I am Yahweh, your healer.'" The stress on various laws and compliance with them indicates a theological perspective which contrasts greatly with the narrative about the journey of the Israelites. One of the key words is "test, put to the test"; therefore this section relates more to the murmuring of the people at the spring Massah ("Testing"), where they put Yahweh to the test. The reason for the insertion of the passage here seems to be the relationship of "diseases" with the "bitter water." Just as Yahweh, their healer, sweetened the water, so he will heal and protect his people from plagues if they will obey him.

From Marah the Israelites "came to Elim, where there were twelve springs of water and seventy palm trees; and they camped there by the water" (15:27). Elim means "Trees," and Wadi Gharandel, about fifty miles down the coast from Ayun Musa, fits the biblical description. The numbers twelve and seventy are too neat to be taken literally, but they indicate sufficient water and shade to meet the minimal needs of the people. There is no indication how long they stayed here, but it must have been a number of days in order to revive their bodies and spirits in preparation for the next leg of the journey.

Numbers 33:5-15 lists the stages of Israel's journey from Rameses to Sinai. It is essentially the same as that found in Exodus 12-19, but there are a few additions. One important difference is the notation in 33:10 that when the Israelites left Elim they "camped by the Reed Sea." This means the Gulf of Suez, and the most likely spot would have been the plain between modern Abu Zeneimeh and Merkhah, the fifteenth-century port for the mines at Serabit el-Khadim. After leaving the Gulf coast Moses led the people inland where they camped in "the wilderness of Sin." Exodus 16:1 locates this desert "between Elim and Sinai."

The easiest route from the seacoast to Jebel Musa is through Wadi Feiran, which runs southeast from the plain of Merkhah. The narrative in Exodus would imply that Moses took the people along this wider, more gradual ascent, but the Numbers itinerary may indicate otherwise. It adds the names "Dophkah" and "Alush" after departure from the wilderness of Sin. If Dophkah is related to *mafqat*, the Egyptian word for turquoise, then the site is somewhere in the region of the mines. Since the turquoise and copper mines of Serabit el-Khadim were not worked during the Nineteenth Dynasty, there would have been no mine activity and no Egyptian forces to impede the journey of Israel. In this case they probably followed the old route to the mines and camped on the large plain Debbet er-Ramleh ("Sandy Hill"). Wadi el-Esh, to the southeast, is perhaps the site of Alush.

Although this route is more precipitous in places, it is quite possible that Moses led the Israelites this way. The wilderness of Sin, accordingly, was in the foothills of the granite range, and directly between Elim and Sinai. The *seneh* bush grew in this region, and the name Sin could well have come from the name of the bush. Exodus 16:1 adds the interesting comment that the people came to the wilderness of Sin "on the 15th day of the second month after they had departed from the land of Egypt." Since they left on the fifteenth of Nisan, about April 1, the first month after their departure was Iyyar and the second was Sivan (May-June). Thus the fifteenth of Sivan was about June 1, two months after leaving Egypt. It is possible that "second month" refers to the length of the journey, not the calendar. In this case, the second month would have begun about May 1, and their arrival at the wilderness of Sin would have been about May 15. This latter date seems more probable in terms of the entire trip to Jebel Musa.

The Murmuring Israelites

According to the arrangement of the biblical narrative, another crisis arose in the wilderness of Sin. Apparently water was plentiful, but there was a drastic shortage of food. Therefore, "The whole congregation of the people of Israel murmured against Moses and Aaron in the wilderness, and said to them, 'Would that we had died by the hand of Yahweh in the land of Egypt, when we sat by the fleshpots and ate bread to the full; for you have brought us out into this wilderness to kill this whole assembly with hunger" (16:2-3). Reference to "the whole congregation" indicates a general rebellion against Moses and Aaron. Gnawing hunger has had two results on the people: (1) they have forgotten the exhaustion of their slavery and the sting of the lashes on their backs; and (2) as a result the minimal slave rations they had are remembered as bounteous supplies of meat and bread to satisfy the desire of everyone. The people are so hungry they are about to die, and so they wish they had died easily back in Egypt and been spared all the suffering. Whether by folly or intent, Moses is held responsible for their miserable plight.

George W. Coats has made a very careful study of all the Old Testament passages relating to the murmuring

motif.[2] With respect to this incident he comments, "Since
the people are in the wilderness, threatened with hunger. . . , it seems clear that the memory of food left in
Egypt forms the *immediate* motivation for the murmuring. But the reference to an unrealistic picture of life in
Egypt seems to put the emphasis by virtue of its exaggeration on the fact that the people had been taken out
of Egypt."[3] He comments further, "The cause for the complaint is not simply a matter of remembering food that
might have been left behind in Egypt, but the fact that
they left Egypt at all. The food seems to do nothing more
than provide the setting."[4]

Coats' concern is to show that when the need of water
and food arose, Yahweh graciously supplied them to a
trusting people who waited patiently. Coats contends that
if Yahweh acted only when the people murmured, he was
solving the problem by "submitting to the demands of
the rebels." He concludes, therefore, that "the murmuring motif has been secondarily incorporated into the more
positive narrative of the people's petition for Yahweh's
aid."[5] He believes that the murmuring tradition arose in
the priestly group in Jerusalem, and that it was directed
against the northern kingdom Israel, which had argued that
only in Bethel and Dan could one really worship the God
of the Exodus.

Undoubtedly the theological struggle between Judah and
Israel helped shape some of the traditions, but it is a
question whether the motif of Yahweh's gracious aid can
be separated so neatly from the motif of Israel's murmuring. Is it possible psychologically to say that every reference to going out of Egypt is the priestly addition to
a tradition in which all the people waited patiently for
Yahweh's sustenance? These people had not been forged
into a disciplined people of God. There were "the mixed
multitude" (Exod. 12:38) and "the rabble" (Num. 11:4),
who probably had little faith in Yahweh. They had joined

[2] George W. Coats, *Rebellion in the Wilderness, The Murmuring
Motif in the Wilderness Traditions of the Old Testament* (Nashville:
Abingdon, n.d.).
[3] *Ibid.*, p. 89.
[4] *Ibid.*, p. 90.
[5] *Ibid.*, p. 93.

the Exodus primarily to get out of Egypt, but their sufferings were more than they had bargained for. With such overriding needs as water and food, it is easy (especially if one has been in the area) to see why even the sincere Israelite would have serious doubts about Moses' wisdom in bringing the group into such a desolate region. Hunger, like thirst, reminded the people of the times in Egypt when they had both. Mention of the departure from Egypt, therefore, was most likely a reference to leaving water and food.

There are two traditions in the Old Testament with respect to the attitude of the people in the wilderness. Hosea, for example, refers to Yahweh alluring his unfaithful people back into the wilderness where he can speak tenderly to them. There they will respond as they did in the days of their youth when they came out of Egypt (Hos. 2:14-15). Clearly, Hosea (who was a prophet in the northern kingdom Israel) reflects the tradition that the Israelites were faithful to Yahweh in the wilderness years. Yet Jeremiah, a prophet in Judah, had the same idea. He is instructed to proclaim to Jerusalem in Yahweh's name, "I remember the devotion of your youth, your love as a bride, how you followed me in the wilderness, in a land not sown" (Jer. 2:2).

On the contrary, Ezekiel denied that there had ever been a honeymoon. He extended the spirit of rebellion clear back to Egypt: "But they rebelled against me and would not listen to me; everyone did not cast away the detestable things their eyes feasted on, nor did they forsake the idols of Egypt" (Ezek. 20:8). Because of this situation Yahweh says, "I will bring you into the wilderness of the peoples, and there I will enter into judgment with you face to face" (20:35). The prophet Ezekiel was definitely oriented toward the interest of the priesthood at Jerusalem, and he assimilated the priestly bias which focused on the rebellion of the people. Jeremiah was from the deposed group of priests at Anathoth; therefore in line with his training he rejected the interpretation of the Jerusalem priests and sided instead with Hosea of Israel.

Coats is certainly right in locating the strong rebellion tradition in the priestly circles at Jerusalem. The question is whether this emphasis was added at a later time, or whether it was a strand in the original story which the priests highlighted as a polemical tool against the northern kingdom. The mixture of people among the Israelites undoubtedly had both attitudes: some trusted Yahweh patiently, but others were given to rebellion. From a psychological point of view it is much more probable that both kinds of people were involved in this genuine struggle for life and that both aspects of this experience were passed on by tradition. Neat separation of the two motifs by Hosea and Jeremiah, on the one hand, and Ezekiel, on the other, is probably due to the "either-or" state of affairs which developed over the years in the struggle between Israel and Judah.

Bread from Heaven

After the murmuring of the people, Yahweh informs Moses, "Behold, I will rain bread from heaven for you; and the people shall go out and gather a day's portion every day, that I may test them, whether they will walk in my law or not. On the sixth day, when they prepare what they bring in, it will be twice as much as they gather daily" (16:4-5). The clause "that I may test them, whether they will walk in my law or not," breaks the sequence of instructions, and it appears to be another interpretation of the D tradition. Notice that the instructions deal only with "bread from heaven," an anticipatory way of referring to the manna. The original complaint in verses 2-3 stems from the P tradition and refers to fleshpots and bread. The J tradition in verses 4-5 makes no mention of meat. The P narrative continues in verses 6-13. Moses and Aaron inform the people that they will know that it was Yahweh who brought them out of Egypt because in the evening they will have "flesh to eat." In the morning they will see "the glory of Yahweh," for they will have plenty of bread to satisfy them. Then Moses and Aaron tell the people quite pointedly, "Your murmurings are not against us, but against Yahweh" (16:8).

Moses instructs Aaron to assemble the people "before Yahweh" since their God has heard their murmurings. Thus, the future priest is being groomed for his task of mediating between the people and Yahweh. There is yet no cultic shrine or tabernacle where Yahweh can manifest himself; therefore as Aaron is speaking with the people they look toward the wilderness and "behold, the glory of Yahweh appeared in the manifestation *(anan)*." Quite likely the P tradition understood this to mean a "cloud." Then Yahweh instructs Moses to tell the people, "At twilight you shall eat flesh, and in the morning you shall be filled with bread; then you shall know that I am Yahweh, your God" (16:12). Immediately the narrative states, "In the evening quails came up and covered the camp; and in the morning dew lay around the camp." Since the quails are never mentioned again until the episode in Numbers 11, and verses 14-36 deal solely with manna, it appears that the manna tradition is primary for the wilderness of Sin, while the quail tradition belongs to a camp site after they leave Sinai. Accordingly, the discussion of this act of Yahweh's grace will be deferred until then.

When the dew evaporated from the ground, there remained "on the surface of the desert a fine, flakelike substance, fine as hoar-frost on the ground" (16:14). A scribal note in 16:31 observes, "The Israelites called it manna; it was white like coriander seed, and its taste was like wafers made with honey." The surprised people ask one another, "What is it?" (Hebrew *man hu*) because they have never seen anything like it. The people very likely asked the question, but that is not the basis for naming it "manna," as the popular etymology implies. Moses informs them, "It is the bread which Yahweh has given you to eat." They are told to gather as much as they can eat, but the average is to be an omer for each person.

The people go out with various containers to collect the manna. Some gather a great deal and others less, but "when they measured it with an omer, he who had gathered much did not have too much, and he who had gathered little did not have too little, each having gathered only what he could eat" (16:18). The meaning apparently is that when all the members of one household brought in the manna which each had collected, the total measured out to be exactly an omer for each member of the family. It is presumed that each family had a more or less standardized pottery jar with the capacity of an omer. Morning after morning they gather manna, but when the sun gets hot the manna melts (16:21).

A scribal note at the end of the chapter informs the reader that "an omer is the tenth of an ephah," but if the reader does not know the capacity of an ephah he is still ignorant of the amount gathered. An ephah was the tenth of a homer, the capacity of the average load a donkey (Hebrew *hamor*) could carry. Inasmuch as this estimate varied in different parts of the Near East, there are two basic systems for defining the capacity of the various dry measures. An omer in one system is slightly more than three quarts, and just over two quarts in the other. In either case, therefore, the average allotment was very generous for a day's ration.

Yahweh's providential supply of food is not to be an occasion for greed or hoarding, however. The people must learn to trust their God day by day, and so they are not to leave any of the manna until the next morning. But some do not listen, and in the morning their manna is foul and has worms. Jesus also believed in the life of trust, and he instructed his disciples to pray solely for their "daily bread" (Matt. 6:11). He warned them, moreover, not to be anxious (that is, unduly concerned) about the next day because "tomorrow will be anxious for itself" (Matt. 6:34). The hoarding which occurs whenever there is a food shortage makes us realize that this generation cannot throw stones at the Israelites. The life of trust is still one of the last things God's people learn. Anyone can be faithful to the god of success, but it takes commitment to believe in the God of the fathers when it appears that all is going wrong and he seems to do nothing about it.

"What Is It?"

The Jewish historian Flavius Josephus, writing in the latter half of the first century A.D., states that in his day manna was still coming down in rain in the Sinai region. The monks of the Monastery of the Burning Bush at Jebel Musa linked manna to the tamarisk thickets in the valleys of the central Sinai mountains. In order to check these ancient claims, F. S. Bodenheimer, late professor of zoology at the Hebrew University, Jerusalem, went to Sinai in 1927. He soon found that two related types of scale-insects produced manna by excretion: one in the higher altitudes and the other in the lowlands.[6] Growing larvae and immature females suck great quantities of sap from plants. The sap is very high in carbohydrates, but low in nitrogen. In order to get the amount of nitrogen necessary for their metabolism the insects have to suck an excessive amount of carbohydrates. As a result they excrete the excess in the form of "honeydew." These drops are changed by the air into sticky particles varying in size from a pinhead to a pea. The color is white, yellow, or brownish.

This phenomenon occurs annually between late May and early July. Since the Israelites arrived at the wilderness of Sin between May 15 and June 1, they came precisely at the manna season. Moses must have learned of this feat of nature during his stay in the Sinai Peninsula. Perhaps he brought the people through this region because it was time for manna to appear, and since there were more tamarisks on the western side of the peninsula there would be more manna in the wilderness of Sin. Whether there was enough for an omer each is very doubtful, but there was a sufficient supply to give them some physical strength and to satisfy partially their craving for sweets.

The manna produced from the tamarisk trees is surprisingly like the biblical description: small, light-colored seeds, tasting like honey wafers (Exod. 16:31), and sticky like the gum bdellium (Num. 11:7). Inasmuch as the little globules of manna collect on the ground during the night when the ants are inactive, the morning dew covers the manna. People of many lands have called the honeydew of aphids "dew of heaven," because they, like the Hebrews, did not realize that insects were the cause. It is little wonder that the Israelites called manna "bread from heaven" (Exod. 16:4), since it appeared that Yahweh had caused it to rain from the sky with the dew of the morning (Num. 11:9).

As manna dries it gets sticky and then granular, just as honey does, but it does not spoil. The reference to the hoarded manna having "worms" is a misunderstanding because the Hebrew word so translated can include the

[6] Bodenheimer, "The Manna of Sinai," *The Biblical Archaeologist Reader, 1*, pp. 76-80.

meaning "ants." Ever-hungry ants would be sure to find any manna left over. As to manna getting foul, this is probably a later addition due to the assumption that it had worms. Another important comment with a slight misunderstanding is that the manna melted when the sun got hot. Ants do not work when the ground temperature gets below 70° F., and so they cease activity early in the evening. Bodenheimer learned that in the upper valleys the soil does not get to this temperature until about 8:30 A.M. About that time the ants get busy carrying off the manna which has collected during the night. The Israelites observed that if they waited until the sun got hot the manna disappeared, and apparently later tradition took this to mean that it melted away.

While the popular etymology *man hu* ("What is it?") is not the explanation for the term manna (Hebrew *man*), linguists are uncertain as to its exact origin. It is of interest, however, that the common Arabic word for plant lice is *man*, and honeydew is called *man es-sama* ("manna of heaven"). Even in Iraq and Iran certain insects are called *man*, and they too produce manna.

Manna for the Sabbath

On the sixth day the Israelites gather two omers of manna apiece. This worries the leaders of the congregation, and they come to report the fact to Moses. Evidently Moses had not relayed to them Yahweh's previous information that on the sixth day the manna "will be twice as much as they gather daily" (16:5). Moses then conveys Yahweh's instructions: "Tomorrow is a day of solemn rest, a holy sabbath to Yahweh; bake what you need to bake, and boil what you need to boil, and all that is left over put aside as a reserve until tomorrow morning" (16:23). The people do as told, and the next morning the manna which has been put aside is not foul and does not have worms. Moses tells them, "Eat this today, for today is a sabbath to Yahweh; you will not find any in the fields today." The doubters go out anyway and they find no manna. Then Yahweh says to Moses, in a style typical of the D tradition, "How long do you refuse to keep my commandments and my laws?" Since Yahweh has given the sabbath for his people, everyone is to remain in his place: "Let no man go out of his place on the seventh day" (16:29).

The creation account notes that God rested on the seventh day, but the first use of "sabbath" (Hebrew *shabbath*) is in verse 23 of this section. The term is related to the old Babylonian word *shabattu*, a day for "quieting the heart." The seventh, fourteenth, twenty-first, and twenty-eighth days of the month were "evil days," and the physician, the oracular priest, and especially the king were to perform no official duties at all. There is no explicit statement calling these evil days *shabattu*, but the implication is that since the officials were quieting their hearts the multiple-seven days were *shabattu* also.

Abraham and all the ancient Hebrews knew of this Babylonian practice; therefore it is easy to see why the Hebrew *shabbath* is related to the Babylonian term. While the name is borrowed, the essential meaning has been changed from a negative, fearful practice to a positive, life-affirming custom. There is no indication how the Patriarchs observed the sabbath, but the historical event of a double portion of manna is a revelation to Moses that from this time on, the seventh day is to be a day devoted to Yahweh. Yahweh has provided for the people's needs, he has given them the sabbath, and so they are to rest their physical bodies while giving thanks to him for his gracious gifts. At Sinai Yahweh will command the people, "Remember the sabbath day." But this is a call to remembrance, not the origin of the new understanding of the seventh day.

The Sample of Manna

Yahweh tells Moses, "Let an omer of it be kept throughout your generations, that they may see the bread with which I fed you in the wilderness when I brought you out of the land of Egypt" (16:32). Then Moses instructs Aaron, "Take a jar and put an omer of manna in it, and place it before Yahweh, to be kept throughout your generations." The word translated "jar" seems to mean a metal vessel, probably with a cover, rather than one of the regular pottery jars. Since the manna would not spoil and the ants could not get to it, it would last indefinitely. The writer of the New Testament book of Hebrews accepted this tradition by noting that there was "a golden urn holding the manna" (9:4) in the ark.

The narrative states that Aaron placed the vessel of manna "before the testimony." The "testimony" is a designation for the ark with the two tablets of the law; thus the statement is an anachronism. It was added at some time after the Sinai experience, when to place anything "before Yahweh" meant to put it in front of the ark. As a closing comment on the manna, the narrative notes, "The Israelites ate manna for forty years, until they reached a habitable land; they ate manna until they reached the border of the land of Canaan" (16:35).

As has been indicated, manna is produced from a wide variety of plants; therefore it is quite possible that the Israelites enjoyed it at various places in their journey. But since the phenomenon is seasonal, the people could not have had manna all year long. The biblical statement seems to be a claim that Yahweh fed his people with heavenly bread throughout the forty years of their travels. This understanding could have resulted from the emphasis which early tradition gave to manna. Those who ate manna were delighted with it and looked forward to the next season; therefore manna was probably highlighted in their recollections. The fact that the manna tradition has been expanded is quite evident from the claim in Joshua 5:12 that manna did not cease until after the Israelites observed the Passover at Gilgal in the land of Canaan.

Jesus and Manna

After feeding the 5,000, Jesus informs some of the participants that they are following him because they have bread to eat, not because they have faith in him. When they ask what they should do, Jesus tells them to believe in him, whom God has sent. They ask for a sign like the heavenly manna which their fathers ate in the wilderness. Jesus replies, "Truly, truly, I say to you, it was not Moses who gave you the bread from heaven; my Father gives you the true bread from heaven" (John 6:32). The Jews know Jesus' mother and father, and so they murmur at him because he claims to be the bread from heaven. Then he presses home the difference between himself and the manna which Moses gave: "I am the bread of life. Your fathers

ate the manna in the wilderness, and they died. This is
the bread which comes down from heaven, that a man may
eat of it and not die" (6:48-50). Jesus is not discounting
Yahweh's act of grace in the Exodus. It simply is not
comparable to the true heavenly bread which God offers
in his gift of his Son. It is ironical that some Israelites
murmured because they did not have physical bread, but
some Jews murmured because they had spiritual bread.

The Spring of Meribah

After leaving the wilderness of Sin the Israelites followed Wadi Mukattab to Alush. No incident is associated
with this site, and they probably moved on after a short
stop. A few miles from Alush their route through Wadi
Mukattab joined Wadi Feiran, one of the longest valleys
in all of the Sinai Peninsula. Following this beautiful
route, they gradually climbed higher with granite peaks
towering on both sides. Before long they came to the region of Rephidim.

There is no water to drink, so the people "find fault"
with Moses and demand, "Give us water to drink" (17:3).
Moses replies, "Why do you find fault with me? Why do
you put Yahweh to the test?" Their thirst gets worse and
they murmur against Moses, "Why did you bring us up
out of Egypt to have us, our children, and our livestock
die of thirst?" Moses is distraught, and his prayer to Yahweh shows how human he is: "What shall I do with this
people? They are almost ready to stone me" (17:4). Then
Moses is told, "Pass on ahead of the people, taking with
you some of the elders of Israel; take the rod in your hand
with which you struck the Nile, and go on. I will stand
there before you on the rock at Horeb, and when you strike
the rock, water will gush out of it, so that the people may
drink." Moses does so in the sight of the elders, and water
comes forth. The people do not see the miracle of Yahweh,
but implicitly they come later to wet their parched tongues.
Moses calls "the name of the place Massah ("Testing") and
Meribah ("Faultfinding") because of the faultfinding of
the Israelites and because they tested Yahweh by saying,
'Is Yahweh among us or not?' "

Between World Wars I and II, when the British were
governing the Palestine and Sinai regions, Major C. S.

Jarvis, Governor of Sinai, reported an incident in which water came from a rock. The Camel Corps noticed a trickle of water from the side of the valley. While picking in the gravel to find more water, one of the men accidentally hit a rock, shattering the hard outer layer and exposing the porous limestone underneath. Soon clear water began to gush from the rock. Moses probably did something similar, but there is serious question that he did it at Rephidim. There are sources of water in the granite range, because the water seeps or flows through the crevices of the shattered granite. But water does not flow from a granite rock! Numbers 20:2-13 relates another incident in which Moses gets water from a rock and the spring is called Meribah. However, this event occurs in the vicinity of Qadesh-barnea, where the rock is largely limestone. Almost certainly the Exodus account is a duplicate report of the Meribah incident, which happened to be placed at Rephidim.

Another difficulty with the Exodus account is the double name. Moses gives only one name, and Meribah would seem to be the original one. The idea of faultfinding is the key to the story. It occurs twice in 17:2 and once in 17:7. The question "Why do you put Yahweh to the test?" is tacked on to the end of verse 2, and at the end of verse 7 is the addition "and because they tested Yahweh by saying, 'Is Yahweh among us or not?' " In the blessing of Moses, Massah and Meribah (in that order) are associated together (Deut. 33:8). These could be variant traditions of one event, but most likely they are similar incidents occurring in the same region. The original form of the story in Exodus 17 related the Meribah incident, and then at a later time the name Massah was inserted along with the two passages about testing because of the strong tradition that the two springs were closely associated. In any case, Meribah is to be located in the limestone region of Qadesh-barnea, and it is highly probable that the spring Massah was in the same area.

Horeb and Sinai

Although the Meribah story about getting water from a rock is out of place, a later editor assumed that it took place at Rephidim and added the notation that the rock

was "at Horeb." In Exodus 3:1 and other passages assigned to the E tradition the name of the sacred mountain
is "Horeb." This is true of the D tradition as well. The
J and P sources, on the other hand, tend to call the mountain "Sinai." Both names are at times preceded by the
Hebrew word *har* ("mountain"), and they seem to refer
to the same location; therefore literary critics, in general,
have treated them as synonyms. Part of the difficulty may
lie in the fact that *har* can mean "hill country, range" as
well as "mountain." For some scholars, Sinai is the name
for the mountain range or massif, while Horeb is considered the designation for the specific peak called "the
mountain of God." The scribal addition "at Horeb" seems
to indicate the opposite, however, because there is no tradition that Moses brought water from the sacred mountain
itself. Accordingly, the scribe seems to consider Horeb as
a region. This fits in with the meaning of Horeb ("desolate region, wilderness"), and Sinai would then be the
specific name for the peak.

Scholars have differed radically in their explanation of
the name Sinai. The idea that the term derived from Sin,
the Mesopotamian moon-god, has proven to be baseless.
As has been noted previously, the Hebrew designation for
the burning bush is *seneh*, from which is derived the bo-
tanical term senna. *Seneh* and Sinai are from the same
root, and herein lies another problem of interpretation:
which came first? The more radical scholars have considered the whole story of Moses at the burning bush as
primary aetiology, that is, solely as an attempt to explain
the name Sinai. But such pessimism is not warranted.
Others contend that the burning bush experience occurred
elsewhere, but that it was inserted in the Sinai narratives
because of the similarity of *seneh* to Sinai. It could well
be that since the senna bush was the most common variety
in the southern part of the peninsula, the region acquired
the name of the bush. Inasmuch as the specific bush associated with Moses was at the sacred mountain, the tendency among the Hebrews would have been to associate
the name Sinai with "the mountain of God." With this
understanding the expression "the wilderness of Sinai"
would mean the area around the mountain, whereas "the

wilderness of Sin" would be the name of the northwestern portion of the granite range, where the senna bush was more plentiful. Yet in consideration of the many years of transmission of the stories, it is probably nearer the truth to say that in both the Horeb and Sinai traditions the names were sometimes understood as the range or the region, and at other times as the sacred mountain peak.

The Defeat of the Amalekites

The Amalekites were a group of desert clans ranging from the Negev down to the southern part of Sinai. Their origin seems to have been Edom. Amalek is recorded as the son of Eliphaz (the eldest son of Esau) by the concubine Timna (Gen. 36:12). He is listed also as a "chief" or "clan" in the tribe of Esau (36:15). Whereas the biblical genealogies consider the Amalekites and the Israelites as distant cousins, there was certainly no affinity of spirit. When the Amalekites saw the horde of newcomers, they knew that their supply of water, manna, and game would be threatened. The only thing to do, therefore, was to defeat them and keep them from encroaching on their territory.

About twenty-five miles west-northwest of Jebel Musa is a distinctive outcropping of granite running about three miles east and west. This range, called Jebel Serbal, has five peaks with the highest about 6,750 feet. Just north of this range, Wadi Feiran opens out into a little plain over 2,000 feet above sea level. Rising from the northern edge of the plain is Jebel el-Tahuna ("The Mountain of the Mill"). From its peak there is a spectacular view of the valley below and the majestic Serbal range to the south. The plain narrows toward the east, and some palm trees indicate the beginning of the Feiran Oasis. This paradise continues east for about three miles, winding its way through the red-granite peaks. Date palms tower over thickets of tamarisk trees, and clumps of acacia trees, with their terrible thorns, warn the passer-by to be careful. Streams appear for a while, only to disappear under the bed of the wadi. In spring the pomegranate trees along the water's edge flame with crimson blossoms. This lovely valley was apparently the home of the Amalekites, and it is very evident why they would have a showdown struggle with the invading Israelites.

Moses instructs Joshua, who appears for the first time in the story, "Pick out some men for us, and hurry out to fight with Amalek, while I will stand on the top of the hill with the rod of God in my hand" (17:9). Joshua and his men go out to fight, and Moses climbs the hill with Aaron and Hur, who also appears for the first time. Hur is with Aaron at Sinai (Exod. 24:14), but that is the last we hear of him. If the traditional location of Rephidim is accurate, Joshua and his men fought the Amalekites in the plain just west of the oasis. From the top of Jebel Tahuna the three leaders have a grandstand seat where they can watch the bitter struggle. Whenever Moses holds his hand up (presumably with the rod in it) the Israelites take the *upper hand* in the battle, but when his hand drops, the Amalekites gain the initiative. As Moses wearies under the strain of holding his hand up, Aaron and Hur get a stone on which Moses is seated, and then each of them holds up one of his hands. Perhaps this tradition about both hands being raised resulted from the idea that Moses was praying to Yahweh while watching the battle. In any event, his hands are steady until sundown, and Joshua is enabled to mow down the Amalekites with the sword.

The Historicity of Joshua

Noth, following his teacher Albrecht Alt, believes that Joshua's sudden appearance is proof that the name was inserted later. He contends that even in the account of the conquest (chapters 1-12 in Joshua) the appearance of Joshua is secondary. For Noth the first historical Joshua is the Ephraimite who convened the covenant ceremony at Shechem (Josh. 24).[7] However, Joshua appears a total of twenty-seven times in the Pentateuch (seven times in Exodus, eleven in Numbers, and nine in Deuteronomy), and about 150 times in Joshua 1-23. It is claiming far too much to say that all of these references are due to scribal activity. There are some difficulties with some of these passages, as we shall see, but the tradition of his association with Moses is too widespread to be discounted

---

[7] Noth, *The History of Israel*, p. 93.

completely. Whether or not Moses had anything to do with
the selection of his successor, the situation demanded that
somebody be prepared to assist him and to assume leadership later on. All the traditions agree that Moses died in
the hills of Moab; therefore somebody had to step into
his role. Since this person led the Israelites across the Jordan and directed the conquest from the camp at Gilgal,
his identity could hardly have been so inconsequential that
the later Joshua was projected back to take his place. The
more probable answer is that the leader succeeding Moses
was in fact the Joshua of the Shechem ceremony and that
as a young man he had been the assistant of Moses.

The Vow to Obliterate the Amalekites

After the victory Yahweh instructs Moses, "Write this
as a memorial in a book, and recite it to Joshua; for I
will utterly blot out the memory of Amalek from under
the heavens" (17:14). Another account of a battle with
the Amalekites, presumably the one at Rephidim, states,
"Remember what Amalek did to you during the journey
after you came out of Egypt, how with no fear of God
he fell upon you on the way, when you were faint and
weary, and cut off all the stragglers in your rear" (Deut.
25:17-18). The custom in the time of the Israelites was
for bitter enemies to devote the opposing forces to their
own god. This practice, called *herem* in Hebrew, meant
that the Israelites devoted the enemy to Yahweh as a sacrificial ban with the vow to obliterate them. Israel's enemies devoted the Israelites to their national gods, and so
the custom was common for that period. This "holy war"
concept incited the warriors to peaks of bravery, but of
course that was true of both sides, and so theory seldom
occurred in practice. The ruthless attack of the Amalekites probably evoked the Israelite vow to destroy them.
The two peoples were bitter enemies to the end, but that
did not come for over 600 years.

In the early years of critical study of the Old Testament
some scholars had serious doubts that Moses was capable
of writing, but such radical pessimism has been thoroughly
discredited. The better scribes of Canaan could write their
language in their own alphabetic script as well as in the
scripts of three or four other languages. From 1500 to 1200

B.C., the Late Bronze Age, there was a great deal of interchange of ideas and products between the countries of the Near East. Egypt was part of this international atmosphere, and Moses would have been well versed in various languages and skilled in writing. The vow against the Amalekites is the first of five occasions when Yahweh instructs Moses to write (Exod. 17:14; 24:4, 7; 34:27; Num. 33:1, 2; Deut. 31:9, 24). There is absolutely no reason to doubt these instances, and it is implicit that Moses recorded other facts about his experience. In no way, however, can this be interpreted to mean that Moses wrote the Pentateuch as we have it. Without Moses there would have been no group of books like Genesis-Deuteronomy, but the complex arrangement of the material with which we have been dealing indicates clearly that Mosaic traditions have been reworked and woven together by oral tradition and later editors.

Moses Builds an Altar

After Moses is told of Yahweh's vow against the Amalekites, he builds an altar which he names *Yahweh-nissi* ("Yahweh is my banner"). The literal Hebrew of the following passage reads, "Because a hand has been raised against the throne of Yahweh, Yahweh will have war with Amalek from generation to generation" (17:16). This translation assumes that *kesyah* is a shortened form of *kisse-yah* ("throne of Yahweh"). But the sudden reference to a "throne" is very odd in this setting. The Amalekites have indeed challenged the authority of Yahweh, but so had Pharaoh, and thus far there has been no reference to Yahweh exercising his authority from a throne. A more probable understanding of *kesyah* is to read it *nesyah* ("Banner of Yahweh"), inasmuch as the letters "n" and "k" could easily have been confused by a scribe in copying a scroll. The whole passage would then read, "And Moses built an altar and called its name 'Yahweh is my banner,' saying, 'A hand on the banner of Yahweh. Yahweh will have war with Amalek from generation to generation.' "

The tradition that the battle with the Amalekites depended on the position of Moses' hand sounds like magic, but there may be an important core of fact. All armies carried banners and the Israelites went out "equipped for battle" (Exod. 13:18) in case they had to fight. Perhaps the Israelite ensign was attached to the rod of Moses, which would then serve as the banner for the struggle. When it was held high Joshua and his men could see it clearly and thus be aroused to battle pitch. A fleeting sight of the banner would keep them inspired, just as Francis Scott Key thrilled to the sight of the United States flag at Fort McHenry, but when the banner lowered (because of Moses' weariness) the Israelites began to lose heart. The importance of the banner in the battle would explain the name which Moses gave to the altar. Moses knew that it was Yahweh who was really leading the people and fighting for them. Without his power and presence the battle was lost indeed.

Jebel Serbal and the Mountain of God

In the period A.D. 250-300 the monastic movement started in Egypt, and during the fourth century it became very strong. Under the influence of the teaching of the church father Tertullian, men like Paul of Thebes and Antony of Alexandria determined to mortify the flesh with all of its desires. They moved away from the towns and lived alone in caves where they could spend most of their time in meditation and prayer. As the idea gained popularity more and more young men moved out to lead the life of a recluse. As the numbers of the hermits increased, some of them moved further out in the desert. Eventually some decided to go to the mountain of God.

There must have been an old tradition about the location of the mountain because some of the monks came to the Jebel Musa area. As the numbers increased, Wadi Feiran became a well-worn pilgrimage trail. The oasis was one of the main stopover points, and Jebel Tahuna became the traditional site for the hill of Rephidim where Moses watched the battle against the Amalekites.

Gradually there arose the tradition that Jebel Serbal was the mountain of God. The fact that the region was not as far away as Jebel Musa and that it had a much better water supply probably had something to do with the new tradition. In any case, there was a tremendous growth in the population of the Serbal area during the latter part of the fourth century and throughout the fifth. The new city was named Pharan, and it became a bishopric with a cathedral church. The ruins of the church are still visible in the plain to the west of the oasis.

At first the monks lived in caves in the area, but as the population increased it was not possible to maintain the solitary life typical of anchorite monks. They began building simple quarters with two small rooms: one was the dormitory for sleeping, and the other was the oratory for saying prayers (with a little niche or apse on the east side of the cell). The ruins of many of these living quarters dot the south slope of Jebel Tahuna, and from all indications the hill swarmed with humanity. Since the monks spent much of their time meditating at the entrances to the cells, one ancient writer likened them "to a lot of rabbits at the mouths of their holes."

There were other churches besides the cathedral. One was in the saddle of a valley halfway up Jebel Tahuna, and a larger one was on the peak, where Moses, Aaron, and Hur stood. Quite clearly the monks came together for worship; therefore they had some aspects of a cenobitic or communal type of life even though they actually lived in separate quarters. Tombs were cut into the face of the alluvial cliffs which had been deposited along the edge of the valley. During the seventh century, when the Arabs gained control of the area, the cells and tombs gave the impression of burrows of field mice, and since the newcomers did not know the meaning of the name Pharan, they took it to mean Feiran ("Mice"). Thus Wadi Feiran, the modern name for the famous valley, resulted from popular etymology.

In spite of the good water supply and the popularity of the region, it is doubtful that Jebel Serbal is the mountain of God. The plain in Wadi Feiran is quite small and the big valley leading up to the Serbal range is quite steep; thus there is hardly enough camping space. Since Jebel Musa fits the biblical description of the mountain of God much more closely than Jebel Serbal, it is still the preferable location.

Jethro and Zipporah Come to Moses

Suddenly the story shifts to Jethro, Moses' father-in-law.

Somehow news has reached Jethro relating "all that God did for Moses and his people Israel, how Yahweh brought Israel out of Egypt" (18:1). Zipporah and the two boys are with Jethro because he took care of them after Moses sent them back, presumably from the lodging place where the circumcision incident took place. Gershom is named, and the same explanation is given for his name as appears in Exodus 2:22. The second boy is named Eliezer, "My God is a help," for he said, "The God of my father has been my help, in delivering me from the sword of Pharaoh" (18:4). The deliverance came after the birth of the boy; therefore the name is either a later explanation, or Moses himself renamed the boy when he saw him.

Jethro came to Moses "in the wilderness where he was camped." Tacked on to this statement is the explanation, "the mountain of God" (18:5). At the end of chapter 17 Moses is at Rephidim, and the same is true in 19:2. If Jethro came to Moses at Rephidim, the addition in 18:5 is a late interpretation. On the other hand, although the explanation seems rather awkward, it may be correct. In this case, chapter 18 has been inserted in the wrong place. The whole chapter has so many characteristics of the E tradition (Elohim occurs twelve times) that it must have come through that line. Another oddity about this chapter of twenty-seven verses is that the designation "father-in-law" occurs thirteen times, when once would have been enough. Some scholars take this to mean that the original story did not know the name of Moses' father-in-law, and so Jethro is a later addition. Others interpret the thirteen occurrences as an attempt of the narrator to highlight Jethro's family relationship to Moses rather than his role as the priest of Midian. While chapter 18 is primarily from the E tradition, the name Yahweh occurs six times. Yet all of these are within the first eleven verses, and some of them are in quotations from Jethro, in which case the E tradition would have let them stand. If this is true, then the E source remembered that Jethro came to Moses at the sacred mountain. In the last analysis, however, the exact site is not basic to understanding the two major events described.

Jethro's Sacrifice

When Moses is told that Jethro has arrived, he goes out to meet him. He bows down before him, kisses him, and then they inquire about each other's welfare. Nothing is said about Zipporah and the boys, but it is assumed that Moses was glad to see them. After being named in verses 2-4, they disappear, never to appear again in any narrative before the conquest. Gershom is mentioned in Judges 18:30, where his son Jonathan is the priest for the tribe of Dan in their new home at the southern foothills of Mt. Hermon. The Hebrew text calls this Gershom the son of Manasseh, but the manuscripts of the Septuagint and other early translations have Moses. Moses was from the tribe of Levi, and it is more probable that it was his grandson who was taken by the Danites as the representative of an authentic priestly line stemming from the founder of Israel. The fact that Gershom does not appear in the wilderness narratives certainly indicates that Moses made no attempt to set up a dynasty of succession. Inasmuch as Yahweh had called him and Yahweh would appoint his successor, Gershom would never figure prominently in the life of the Israelites.

After the cordial greetings, Moses takes Jethro into his tent and relates "all that Yahweh did to Pharaoh and the Egyptians for Israel's sake, all the hardship they encountered on the journey, and how Yahweh delivered them" (18:8). Jethro rejoices over the good news and exclaims, "Blessed be Yahweh, who delivered you from the power of the Egyptians and the power of Pharaoh, who delivered the people from under the power of the Egyptians. Now I know that Yahweh is greater than all other gods (Hebrew *elohim*), in that his power prevailed over them." While Pharaoh was a reluctant believer in Yahweh, Jethro willingly acknowledges Yahweh's superiority. After all, the facts speak for themselves!

When Jethro has finished his blessing of Yahweh, he "takes a burnt-offering and sacrifices for God." In the priestly regulations, "to take" an offering means to take the animal to the priest, who then sacrifices it (see, for example, Lev. 12:8). To whom did Jethro take the animals? It is implicit that someone was to sacrifice in the wilderness after the three days' journey, but up to this point in the narrative Moses has not officiated at any sacrifices, nor has Yahweh explicitly authorized him to do so. Aaron will be ordained priest in the future, but as yet he is not authorized to officiate at sacrifices. According to the narrative, Jethro is the only authentic priest in the group, and yet he is the one "taking" the sacrifices. It is a very confusing situation, but the implication is that Jethro officiated at the sacrifices as well as bringing the animals. If Moses did the sacrificing, it is indeed strange that the fact is not spelled out specifically and even underlined.

When the sacrificial meal is ready, Aaron and the elders join Jethro, and they eat "before God" (18:12). The location of the holy place (where God's presence was) is not given. But if this is at the sacred mountain prior to the covenant experience, then the site of the burning bush must have been the place where they ate the sacred meal. Moses must have been there, but he is not mentioned. It seems that the narrator puts Aaron, the future priest of the Israelites, into the foreground as the partner of Jethro, the priest of Midian. Undoubtedly Aaron learned a great deal about the method of sacrificing and conducting a sacred meal, and it could well be that some of the basic laws of Israelite cultic practice stemmed from Jethro.

The Kenite Theory

As will be shown later, Jethro was not only a Midianite, but he was associated with a group of Midianites known as Kenites, that is, smiths, people whose primary occupation was metal working. As contrasted with the Amalekites, the Kenites were kindly disposed toward the Israelites. Some of them occupied part of the territory of Judah, and they were apparently worshipers of Yahweh. On the basis of this and other biblical evidence, some scholars believe that Yahweh was the God Jethro served and that Moses learned about Yahweh from his father-in-law.

The late British scholar H. H. Rowley (1890-1969) was quite receptive to this view since he felt it explained many biblical passages which seem to be contradictory. In line with what we have concluded, the Hebrews in Egypt were not worshipers of Yahweh. But when Moses found such a welcome haven in the family of Jethro, he was influenced by his Yahweh-worshiping father-in-law. When Yahweh appeared to him at "the mountain of God," of which Jethro had presumably informed him, Moses was convinced that Jethro's God was sending him as a missionary and a deliverer to his own people in Egypt. On hearing the wonderful report from Moses, Jethro rejoices that his own God has proven to be superior to all the gods of the Egyptians. Rowley comments, "When Moses successfully carries this enterprise through, Jethro is filled with pride and joy in the triumph of his God and initiates the Israelite leaders into the faith and practice of Yahweh-worship, and the Israelites pledge themselves to the God who has delivered them."[8] According to the Kenite theory, therefore, Jethro's blessing addressed to Yahweh is not his conversion to the God of Moses, but elation that his own God has been so gracious to his son-in-law and the Hebrews.

Martin Buber objects strenuously to this theory.[9] He contends that if Jethro was a worshiper of Yahweh all along, it is absurd for him to confess, "Now I know that Yahweh is greater than all other gods." He sees in the word *elohim*, which can mean "gods" or "God," the crux of the narrative, because from this point on Elohim occurs, not Yahweh. Since Buber rejects the source theory, he does not take the occurrences of Elohim as resulting from the E tradition, but he interprets them as the narrator's specific attempt to say that God, not Yahweh, was the common ground of belief between the Kenites and the Israelites.

Buber claims, moreover, that "before God" means in front of Moses' tent. Jethro and Moses had talked in the tent about Yahweh's victory over the Egyptians; therefore Jethro brought the animals to the entrance of the tent. There Moses sacrificed the animals and officiated at the sacred meal. According to Buber, therefore, the absence of any reference to Moses means that the narrator specifically implied that he was in charge of the whole event. This seems to be building a great deal on silence. Moses of-

8 H. H. Rowley, *From Joseph to Joshua* (New York: Oxford Univ., 1950), p. 154.

9 Buber, *Moses, the Revelation and the Covenant*, pp. 94-97.

ficiates at many other occasions and his presence is made quite conspicuous.

Although Buber does not make use of it, one of the strongest arguments against the Kenite theory is the incomprehensible silence of Moses when he returns from his experience at the burning bush. Had he really been converted to the worship of Yahweh by Jethro, it is psychologically inconceivable that he could keep his marvelous experience from his father-in-law. The fact that he would need Jethro's permission in order to deliver his people could hardly have been the reason to hide his encounter with Yahweh. On the contrary, the authority of Yahweh's call would have been taken by Jethro as the greatest reason possible for Moses to leave him temporarily.

Rowley thinks that the Kenite theory explains the two biblical traditions about the worship of Yahweh. The J tradition, as we have noted, traces the worship of Yahweh all the way back to Seth (Gen. 4:26). Since the Kenites had worshiped Yahweh as far back as they could remember, they had no tradition of a specific time when Yahweh made himself known to them. Caleb and the Kenites were very influential in the theological development of the southern kingdom, according to Rowley; therefore their point of view became a dominant interpretation and the Yahwist who worked up the J tradition believed that Yahweh was worshiped from earliest times.

On the other hand, Moses had the crisis experience of Yahweh's revelation; therefore the people whom he led (primarily the Joseph tribes, Ephraim and Manasseh) preserved this point of view in the northern kingdom and it became the standard view of the E tradition. Yet the priests of Jerusalem believed that Yahweh made himself known first to Moses, and thus both traditions were known in the southern kingdom. It still seems preferable to this writer that the J tradition projected the name of Yahweh back into the earlier narratives because of the clear-cut tradition that the God who made himself known to Moses was indeed the God of the fathers.

Should the Kenite theory prove to be essentially correct, the role of Moses would not be reduced to that of a mere transmitter of the name. Rowley observes that in contrast to the Yahwism of the Kenites the understanding of Yahweh "was fundamentally different for the tribes Moses led by the mere fact of the unforgettable experience through which they were led to it. It was always associated amongst them with the memory of the deliverance they had experienced." Rowley declares further that Moses added some new qualities to his adopted Yahwism; for example, his understanding of the Passover.[10]

The Administration of Justice

The next day after the sacred meal with Jethro, Moses holds court for the people and they stand around him "from morning to evening." When Jethro sees what is going on he inquires, "What is this you are doing for the people? Why do you hold court all alone, with the people all standing around you from morning until evening?" (18:14). Moses replies, "Because the people come to me to inquire of God. Whenever they have a dispute they come to me, that I may decide between one man and another, and let them know the statutes of God and his decisions." "What you are doing is not right," says Jethro, "you will wear yourself out, both you and the people here with you, for the task is too heavy for you; you cannot do it alone."

Jethro knows a much better way to handle the situation, and so he suggests, "You be the people's representative with God, and bring their cases to God; instruct them in the statutes and decisions, and let them know the way in which they are to walk and what they are to do. But you select out of all the people some capable, God-fearing, honest men, who despise a bribe, and set them over the people as rulers of thousands, of hundreds, of fifties, and of tens. Let them be judges for the people on ordinary occasions, but all important cases they shall bring to you.... Thus it will be lighter for you, since they will share the burden with you. If you do this, and God so commands you, you will be able to stand it, and furthermore, all these people will go home satisfied" (18:19-23). Showing a humble spirit and willingness to accept help, Moses agrees with Jethro's wise suggestion and puts the plan into operation. Jethro has accomplished his mission, and Moses

---

[10] Rowley, *op. cit.*, p. 156.

sends him away with his blessing. Jethro returns "to his own country," and he is never heard of again.

Yet Jethro's influence lived on in the new organization for the administration of justice. It was he who helped Moses to see the difference between the sacred and civil aspects of justice. Moses had enough to do trying to ascertain the will of Yahweh for the people as a whole. When he learned the guidelines of Yahweh's purpose, then he could interpret them to his trusted officials, who in turn would oversee the implementation of justice right down the line. This is another area in which it was imperative to have a successor to Moses, and Joshua certainly functioned in this capacity. When he made the covenant with the people at Shechem he also "made statutes and ordinances for them" (Josh. 24:25).

A very practical outgrowth of Jethro's suggestion was the division of the Israelites into groups. The use of *eleph* in this context seems to mean "thousand" more than it does "clan," yet the division could hardly have ignored clan and tribal relationships. Albright may well be correct in suggesting that this was the occasion where the twelve-tribe organization had its beginnings. Those who had no precise or known relationship to the established tribes would have been grouped together as new tribal units, probably taking the name of the predominant group within the tribe.[11]

The Israelites Arrive at Sinai

After defeating the Amalekites, the Israelites probably moved into the Oasis of Feiran and recuperated from the vicious battle. If Jethro came to Rephidim, then it was here that the people were divided into groups. After refreshing themselves, they left the garden spot at the eastern end. There the valley widens out, and the scenery changes back to awesome desolation. Lines of black diorite and plum-red porphyry shoot up through the red-granite mountains like a geological fireworks. Thickets of tamarisk trees occur at times. After about fifteen miles the route turns south toward the tallest mountains in the Sinai Peninsula. Before long the valley opens out onto a gently

---

[11] Albright, *The Biblical Period from Abraham to Ezra*, pp. 33-34.

sloping plain about 4,000 feet above sea level. It is called Er-Raha ("The palm [of the hand]") because it is quite flat. Inasmuch as it extends east-west over a mile, and the average width is about half a mile, this mountain-rimmed plain is about 400 acres in area.

The view from the western edge of the plain is awe-inspiring. To the east is a cluster of peaks which is outstanding because of the deep valleys that surround it. The nearest (most western) peak is called Ras es-Safsaf, and just visible at the southeast corner of the cluster is the tip of Jebel Musa (about 7,500 feet high). To the right (south) the mountains rise to over 8,500 feet, the most famous peak being St. Catherine's. North of the Jebel Musa cluster is another large peak called Jebel ed-Deir ("Mountain of the Monastery"), and in the deep valley between the two, at an altitude of about 4,500 feet, is nestled the Monastery of St. Catherine. Here, in the Chapel of the Burning Bush, is the traditional site where Yahweh revealed himself to Moses, and where St. Helena built her church.

The biblical narrative states that the Israelites left Rephidim and came into "the wilderness of Sinai." There they camped "in front of the mountain" (19:2). The plain of Er-Raha at the foot of the Jebel Musa cluster of peaks fits the biblical description very well. The 400 acres of the plain plus additional areas in the adjoining valleys would have given plenty of space to camp, and the springs in the valleys would have quenched their thirst.

The narrative adds the comment that the Israelites came into this wilderness of Sinai "on the third new moon after leaving Egypt" (19:1). Since they left on the fifteenth of Nisan (about April 1), the first new moon would have been the first day of Iyyar, the second new moon in Sivan, and the third at the beginning of Tammuz. This was about June 15, two and a half long months of difficulties and hardship after leaving Egypt. But here at last, the sign of Yahweh has come to pass — Moses and the people are ready to serve him at the mountain (Exod. 3:12).

Chapter 9

Commandments from Mount Sinai

The story of the experiences at Mt. Sinai appears between Exodus 19:3 and Numbers 10:10. Much of this material consists of collections of laws and priestly regulations: Exodus 20:22-23:33, the so-called Book of the Covenant; Exodus 25:1-31:17, instructions for building the tabernacle; Exodus 35:1-40:38, the building and erection of the tabernacle; and all of the book of Leviticus plus Numbers 1:1-10:10, various regulations involving the priests and Levites. Thus, the basic narrative of what happened at Sinai is found in just six chapters: Exodus 19-20, 24, and 32-34.

Literary Analysis of the Sinai Narratives

Ancient tradition, both Jewish and Christian, read the Sinai narratives as a more or less unified whole composed by Moses himself, and some conservative scholars still contend that this interpretation is essentially correct. Yet such a simplistic reading of the biblical text fails to recognize that the structure of the narratives in the crucial six chapters is very complex and that the story bristles with difficulties. The Sinai experiences were of basic importance for Israel, both northern and southern kingdoms, and varying reports of what happened led to various interpretations and reinterpretations over the centuries. Ancient editors tried to harmonize some of the details, and their efforts are evident; but many disjunctions remain, and any attempt to smooth over the differences necessitates extraordinary mental gymnastics.

One of the most prominent indications of mixed traditions is the repeated reference to Moses' ascent and descent of Mt. Sinai. There are seven explicit statements that Moses "went up" (Exod. 19:3, 20; 24:9, 13, 15, 18; and 34:4), and "returned to Yahweh" (32:31) implies that he "went up." Moses "came down" four times (19:14, 25; 32:15; and 34:29), and the context of "came" in 19:7 implies "came down." One can make a reasonable case for about three or four trips up the mountain, but not more.

Suspicion of this escalator-like movement up and down Mt. Sinai is strengthened by the difference between the number of ascents and descents. This is quite evident in Exodus 24:12-18:

> 12 Yahweh said to Moses, "Come up to me on the mountain and wait there, and I will give you the tablets of stone with the law and the commandment, which I have written for their instruction." 13 So Moses rose with his servant Joshua, and Moses went up into the mountain of God. 14 And he said to the elders, "Tarry here for us, until we come to you again, and now Aaron and Hur are with you. Whoever has a cause, let him go to them."
> 15 Then Moses went up on the mountain, and the cloud covered the mountain. 16 The glory of Yahweh settled on Mt. Sinai, and the cloud covered it six days, and on the seventh day he called to Moses out of the midst of the cloud. 17 Now the appearance of the glory of Yahweh was like a devouring fire on the top of the mountain in the sight of the Israelites. 18 And Moses entered the cloud and went up on the mountain. And Moses was on the mountain forty days and forty nights.

Literary critics are almost unanimous in assigning 15b-18a to the P tradition, but opinion varies on 12-15a. Older critics tended to attribute the section to E, and Walter Beyerlin concurs, because a number of details fit in best with the tradition of the northern kingdom (for example, the appearance of Joshua, a member of the tribe of Ephraim).[1] Martin Noth, on the other hand, takes seriously the use of "Yahweh," and so he considers 12-15a as preparation for the story in chapters 32 and 34, and thus essentially J.[2] In any case, it seems clear that 24:12-18 is not a unified whole. The best way to make sense of the passage is to recognize that it is a combination of two traditions.

Another example of a break in the sequence of events

---

[1] Walter Beyerlin, *Origins and History of the Oldest Sinaitic Traditions* (Naperville: Allenson, 1965), pp. 48-49.
[2] Noth, *Exodus*, pp. 199-200.

appears in Exodus 19:7-9. After having received instructions from God on the mountain,

> 7 Moses came (down) and called the elders of the people, and set before them all these words which Yahweh had commanded him. 8 And all the people answered together and said, "All that Yahweh has spoken we will do." And Moses reported the words of the people to Yahweh. 9 And Yahweh said to Moses, "I am coming to you in a thick cloud that the people may hear when I speak with you and may also believe you forever." Then Moses told Yahweh the words of the people.

Even the ancient love of repetition can hardly explain the intrusive sentence at the end of verse 9. Moreover, although different verbs are used in the Hebrew, it is useless to seek some hidden meaning in the shift from "reported" to "told."

The most probable explanation for the difficulties is still the theory that various traditions about Sinai experiences have been woven together. But recognition of this fact alone does not solve the problem because the evidence for separating the strands is ambiguous at times. Earlier literary critics, such as S. R. Driver, assigned the first part of 19:3 ("And Moses went up to God") to the E strand because of the use of "Elohim," but they allocated verses 3b through 9 to J because "Yahweh" was employed. More recent literary critics tend to assign 3b-6 to E since the Septuagint translation indicates that the Hebrew manuscript used by the translator had "Elohim" instead of "Yahweh" in 3b. This was true also in 19:10, and on this basis the older critics assigned 10-11b to E; yet some recent critics have considered "Yahweh" of the Hebrew text as representing the original wording, and so they allocate 10-11b to J.

This shift in the separation of the strands is due to other criteria than the names of God. It is clear from the biblical narratives that Israel, the northern kingdom, and Judah, the southern kingdom, differed considerably in some of their attitudes and points of view; and some of these features have been used to help unravel the traditions more accurately (for example, the theology of Judah was dominated by priestly traditions and the unconditional covenant which Yahweh made with David, and thus tended to be more cultic and authoritarian, whereas Israel was more democratic in that the people and prophets played a greater role). One of the better reconstructions of the strands is that proposed by Murray Newman:[3]

The Elohist's Version of the Covenant

1. The announcement for the people (19:2b-6); 2. The cultic preparation of the people (19:10-11a, 14-15); 3. The theophany to the people (19:16-17, 19); 4. The people make Moses their mediator (20:18-21); 5. God announces his name and nature (20:1-2); 6. Yahweh gives his law (20: 3-17); 7. The oath of the people (24:3); and 8. The sealing of the covenant (24:4-8).

The Yahwist's Version of the Covenant

1. Yahweh makes Moses the mediator (19:9a); 2. The cultic preparation of the people (19:11b-13); 3. The general theophany (19:18); 4. Moses goes to the top of the mountain (19:20; 34:1-4); 5. The special theophany to Moses (33:18-23; 34:5); 6. Yahweh proclaims his name and nature (34:6-8); 7. Yahweh offers his covenant and his law (34:10-26); 8. Yahweh's covenant with Moses and the people (34:27-28); 9. The oath of the people (19:7-8); and 10. The sealing of the covenant (24:1-2, 9-11).

Note that Newman's reconstruction involves some rearrangement of the text (for example, he agrees with Beyerlin that originally the unit 20:18-21 preceded 20: 1-2).[4] Moreover, there is still no scholarly consensus on the assignment of certain sections. Noth and Beyerlin, for example, consider 24:1-11 as essentially E, but in doing so they do not treat the passage as a unity because they still see two different strands (both northern) woven together. It is impossible to go into all aspects of various critical unravelings of the biblical narratives and to consider the validity of these reconstructions in detail. But what can be said is that there are too many disparate details, events, and points of view to be harmonized into one unified series of experiences. A most crucial question, therefore, is whether the E and J traditions represent the experiences of two

---

[3] Murray Lee Newman, Jr., *The People of the Covenant* (Nashville: Abingdon, 1962), pp. 40-46.
[4] Beyerlin, *op. cit.*, p. 5.

completely separate groups, or whether they are varying interpretations (with later additions) of events common to both. This difficult matter will be confronted in the next chapter, but in the meantime it will be helpful to examine the Sinai narratives from other points of view than the literary approach.

The Suzerainty Treaty of the Hittites

The peoples of the ancient Near East came to realize that if their cultures were to become more civilized there had to be some way of minimizing the chance of war. The most effective means of preserving law and order proved to be treaties or covenants. By the fourteenth century B.C. the Hittites had developed a treaty form with six essential elements: (1) prologue; (2) historical survey; (3) stipulations involving a loyalty oath; (4) regulations for deposit and public reading of the text; (5) list of divine witnesses to the treaty; and (6) curses and blessings. Most of the treaties found in the Hittite archives at Boghazköy, in central Asia Minor, are not between kings of equal rank, but between a great king (suzerain) and a subordinate ruler (his vassal). Accordingly, this type of agreement has been commonly designated the "suzerainty treaty."

In the prologue the Hittite kings make it clear that the words of the treaty are granted by them, and they like to describe themselves as "the Sun-god, the great king." Then follows a historical survey of relationships between the Hittite suzerains and their vassals, with special attention being given to the kindnesses shown the underlings by the overlords. The purpose of this recital was to remind the vassal and thus create a sense of obligation to abide by the treaty. The suzerain intended that the alliance should be permanent, but at the death of the vassal king there was no assurance that the successor would show the same loyalty, and so the Hittites usually reaffirmed the treaty with the new vassal.

Following the historical survey is the list of stipulations laid on the vassal. The basic requirement is an oath of loyalty. The vassal is to make agreements with no other power, and in time of war he is to fight for the suzerain "with all his heart." He must not speak against his overlord. In fact, he is to report any seditious talk, and any rebels or enemy spoils found within his territory are to be returned to the great king. It is implied from the historical survey that the suzerain making the treaty will deal justly and honorably with his vassal, but there is nothing in writing which obligates him.

After the stipulations there are provisions that copies of the treaty be placed in the holiest temples of the chief gods of the two lands concerned. This is to guarantee that the gods have access to the stipulations of the oath sworn in their presence. To make sure that the vassal and his princes do not forget the content of the agreement, the text of the treaty is to be read in their presence each year. Obviously, the covenant is in a language that both parties can understand.

Then as witnesses to the treaty, the gods of the contracting parties are assembled and listed by name. Since the deities of the suzerain are considered to be the most powerful, they are listed first. Their duty is to take notice of the vassal's vow and to take vengeance on him if he breaks it. Following the list of the Hittite gods is a list of "former gods," which in turn is followed by "the mountains, the rivers, the Tigris and Euphrates, heaven and earth, the winds (and) the clouds." Then the gods of the vassal are called on as witnesses so that he cannot appeal to them in case he violates the agreement.

Finally the curses and blessings are noted. Should the vassal not honor his oath, the gods are to destroy the vassal "together with his person, his wife, his son, his grandson, his house, his land together with everything he owns." The threat was total destruction of what he had or was. Generally in the courts of the ancient Near East the punishment was fitted to the crime, but in the realm of international treaties the threat of total vengeance by the gods was considered a far more effective deterrent to a vassal tempted to rebel against his overlord. Honoring of the agreement meant the protection of the vassal and all that he had.

The ceremony for sealing a treaty took various forms: by eating a meal together, by drinking from a common cup, by oil and water, and by some strange procedure called "puppy and lettuce"; but the most common method was the killing of an animal with which the vassal was identified. In effect the person taking the oath was saying, "May I be cut up like this animal if I break the treaty."

The Hebrew expression for making a treaty is "to cut a covenant." A number of the earlier critics thought the expression was a mistake, but their judgment was premature. In comparing the biblical covenants with the Hittite treaties, George E. Mendenhall notes many similarities and concludes that the most probable explanation of this fact is that Moses and the Israelites knew of the suzerainty treaty form and adapted it to their own use.[5] The zenith of the Hittite empire was in the fourteenth century, just prior to the rise of Moses; and since the Egyptians were involved in some of the treaties of the fifteenth and fourteenth centuries, there is every reason to believe that Moses became acquainted with the basic forms of international diplomacy. This conclusion is strengthened by the fact that the J and E narratives use the Hebrew word *berith* ("covenant, treaty") both for the covenant with God at Sinai and for treaties between kings.

Form Analysis of the Covenant Traditions

Accordingly, the suzerainty treaty can serve as an external check to help ascertain the form of the Sinai covenant. The biblical narratives make it quite apparent that God is suzerain and that he takes the initiative. The prologue is short but explicit: "I am Yahweh, your God" (Exod. 20:2a). The historical survey is reduced to the minimum; nevertheless the basis of obligation is there because the essential act of God's kindness was delivering his people from bondage in Egypt (20:2b). The same basis of appeal is noted in the announcement of the covenant: "You have seen what I did to the Egyptians, and how I bore you on eagles' wings and brought you to myself" (19:4). God has delivered them and brought them safely to himself at Sinai; therefore they are urged to obey him (19:5). In passing it should be noted that the description of Yahweh bearing the Israelites on "eagles' wings" has some similarity

---

[5] Mendenhall, "Ancient Oriental and Biblical Law," *The Biblical Archaeologist*, XVII, 2 (May 1954), 26-46, and "Covenant Forms in Israelite Tradition," *BA*, XVII, 3 (September 1954), 50-76.

to the motif of the winged sun disk. Although understood in a different way, the winged-disk symbol is apparent in Malachi 4:2: "But for you who fear my name, the sun of righteousness shall rise with healing in its wings."

Stipulations of the Covenant

Direct (apodictic) commands, both positive ("You shall ...") and negative ("You shall not ..."), are not very common in the ancient Near East, but they do occur in some of the treaties. It is most probable, therefore, that the ten commandments constitute the stipulations of Yahweh's covenant with Israel. Just as the essential provision of the secular treaty is to have only one overlord, Yahweh demands complete loyalty by excluding all other gods.

The Oath and Sealing of the Covenant

The oath and sealing of the covenant occur in Exodus 24:3-8, a section assigned to the E tradition by almost all the critics. Newman places these features right after the listing of the stipulations; therefore his reconstruction of the E version becomes probable in view of its essential similarity to the suzerainty treaty. When Moses reports to the people the words of their God, newly revealed as Yahweh, they answer with one voice, "All the words which Yahweh has spoken we will do." After this initial oath of obedience, Moses seals the covenant with the blood from the slain oxen. Half of the blood is thrown on the altar (representing God, the covenant initiator), and when the words of Yahweh are read from the Book of the Covenant, the people reiterate their vow, "All that Yahweh has spoken we will do, and we will be obedient." To seal this vow of obedience to the covenant of Yahweh, Moses throws the rest of the blood on the people.

Deposit of the Covenant Text

The narrative sections of Exodus do not tell of the disposition of the tablets, but fortunately the instructions for making the ark have the following detail attached: "You shall put into the ark the pact *(eduth)* which I shall give you" (Exod. 25:16). The Hebrew word *eduth* has traditionally been translated "testimony," but in 1955 W. F. Albright showed that the term was actually a synonym for *berith*. After further study of the use of *eduth* in and out of the Bible, Delbert Hillers concluded that the priestly editor employed the two terms to distinguish two types of covenant: *"Berith,* 'covenant,' he uses only for God's promises, those oaths that bind God only. *Eduth,* 'pact,' he uses only for what was concluded at Sinai."[6] In the covenant with Abram (Abraham), for example, God binds himself by an oath to maintain his "everlasting covenant *(berith)"* with Abraham and his descendants (Gen. 17:7), but aside from the sign of circumcision no obligations are laid on the human partners in the covenant. At Sinai, however, the people as God's vassals take an oath of fidelity to the stipulations, but God takes an oath to nothing. It is implicit, as in the Hittite treaties, that God's merciful action in the past is the guarantee of his future dealings with Israel.

The value of Exodus 25:16 is P tradition's memory that the text of the Sinai pact (presumably on the two tablets of stone) was deposited within the ark. For this reason P calls the ark "the ark of the pact" (Exod. 25:22; 40:21), just as it is called "the ark of the covenant *(berith)"* in the other traditions (for example, 1 Sam. 4:3-4). Moreover, in P the tabernacle is designated "the tabernacle of the pact" (Exod. 38:21). Another feature of P is the belief that God was enthroned on the cherubim over the ark, and that it was there in the Most Holy Place that God would speak with Moses and his priestly successors when he wished to issue further commands (Exod. 25:22). At Sinai the Most Holy Place of the suzerain and the vassals coincided, and thus there was need for only one set of tablets; but the place of deposit followed the example of the suzerainty treaty.

Public Reading of the Covenant Text

Also missing in the E and J narratives is reference to the requirement of periodic public reading of the covenant stipulations. But such a provision appears at the conclusion of the covenant which Moses made with the new generation of Israelites in Moab: "At the end of every seven years, at the set time of the year of release, at the feast

---

[6] Delbert R. Hillers, *Covenant: The History of a Biblical Idea* (Baltimore: Johns Hopkins, 1969), p. 161.

of booths, when all Israel comes to appear before Yahweh your God at the place which he will choose, you shall read this law before all Israel in their hearing" (Deut. 31:10-11). Even though the D tradition plays a relatively late role in Israel's history, its roots go back to antiquity, and the memory of the regulation for periodic reading may go back to the Sinai covenant.

Witnesses to the Covenant

The feature of the suzerainty treaty which is least evident in the Sinai covenant is the listing of divine witnesses. The reason is obvious because the secular treaties were between human rulers, whereas at Sinai the covenant was between God and his people. Since his basic requirement was the exclusion of all other gods, the covenant itself would have been violated by calling as witnesses these excluded deities. In fact, the lack of any other deities as witnesses argues strongly for the origin of practical monotheism at Sinai. On the other hand, the feature of witnesses to the oath of obedience was a well-known element in treaties, and there is biblical evidence that within the restrictions of monotheism attempts were made to involve witnesses.

Joshua's Covenant at Shechem

After the Israelites gained control of the central hill country of Palestine they assembled at Shechem, and Joshua made a covenant with them (Josh. 24:1-27). The form, so far as it can be ascertained, is similar to the suzerainty treaty. Yahweh is identified as the "God of Israel" and the initiator of the covenant. Joshua, quoting Yahweh, recites the history of God's gracious acts (2-13), but this time the survey begins with Terah and Abraham instead of the Exodus. On the basis of this long history of God's faithfulness Joshua urges the people to fear Yahweh, to serve him in sincerity, and to put away the gods which their fathers served beyond the River (14). Then with dramatic clarity Joshua confronts the hesitant with the issue. If anyone does not think Yahweh is worthy of his loyalty, he is urged to make his choice from the pantheon of gods beyond the River, or the pantheon in the land of Canaan (15). Put so baldly there is hardly any choice, and the

people declare that they will not forsake Yahweh because
he is the one who led them out of Egypt and drove out
the people of Canaan (16-18).

Apparently Joshua still senses some duplicity, and so
he declares that they cannot serve Yahweh because he is
a jealous God. If they forsake Yahweh and serve foreign
gods, then he will consume them (19-20). However, the
people respond fervently, "We will serve Yahweh." Joshua
informs them, "You are witnesses against yourselves that
you have chosen Yahweh, to serve him," and the people
answer, "We are witnesses" (21-22). Whereupon he instructs them, "Put away the foreign gods which are among
you, and incline your heart to Yahweh, the God of Israel."
The idols, and the deities they represent, are to be de-
throned; therefore they are not suitable witnesses. In this
situation, however, there is some need for the double
check of witnesses and, psychologically speaking, the people
themselves will be much better witnesses. They probably
know which of their neighbors are secretly serving other
gods, and they can check on those who refuse to abandon
their idols after having vowed allegiance to Yahweh.

Again the people make their vow to Joshua, "Yahweh
our God we will serve, and his voice we will obey" (24).
On the basis of this oath of obedience Joshua makes a
covenant with the people. Moreover, he makes "statutes and
ordinances for them," which he writes in a book or scroll
(25-26). These stipulations are not spelled out in Joshua
24 because the writer purposes to give the description of
a covenant ceremony rather than the text of the covenant
agreement. The disposition of Joshua's instruction book
is not indicated, but most likely it was left at the sanctuary
in the care of the priests.

Apparently Joshua wanted to put greater restraint on
the covenanters, and so "he took a great stone and set it
up there under the oak in the sanctuary of Yahweh" (26).
The fathers had set up these stone pillars *(masseboth)* and
used them in worshiping God (for example, Jacob in Gen.
28:18); and since pillars were associated with the original
covenant ceremony at Sinai (Exod. 24:4), perhaps Joshua
thought a pillar witness would be effective. In any case,
he told the people, "This stone shall be a witness among

us, for it has heard all the words of Yahweh which he spoke to us. Therefore, it shall be a witness against you, lest you deal falsely with your God" (27). It is difficult to ascertain how the covenanters interpreted Joshua's words about the "hearing pillar." The more superstitious may have taken it literally, but for the majority the pillar would be a lasting reminder of the regulations of Yahweh and their oath of loyalty and obedience. Whether both types of witness were employed originally by Joshua, or whether one of them was added by a later editor, is difficult to determine, but in either case tradition recalls that witnesses played a role in confirming covenants. The D tradition asserts that Moses in Moab called "heaven and earth" to witness his warning to the people that they would utterly perish from the land of Canaan if they angered Yahweh by doing evil (Deut. 4:26).

Witnesses at the Lawsuits of God

The idea of witnesses appears quite frequently in passages where God, through his prophets, brings a lawsuit against his disobedient people. The context is clearly that of a broken covenant, therefore treaty language is employed. The so-called Song of Moses (Deut. 31:30-32:47) contrasts Yahweh's faithfulness with Israel's faithlessness, and the heavens and the earth are invoked as witnesses to the praises and the allegations of the courtroom scene (32:1). The song is certainly older than the monarchy, and so it is an early witness to the invocation of witnesses. At the very beginning of his collection of oracles, Isaiah brings the charge of rebellion against Israel, and he calls on the heavens and the earth to witness his allegation (1:2). Micah calls the mountains and the hills as witnesses (6:1-2), and Jeremiah appeals to the heavens and the dry land (2:12). Some scholars interpret such passages as a literary device of the prophets, while others consider these aspects of nature (all regarded as gods in antiquity) as delegated members of God's divine council (Ps. 82). Regardless of which way this scholarly debate is resolved, the fact that the prophets used the expressions almost certainly harks back to the common practice of invoking the various aspects of nature as witnesses to treaties.

Covenant Curses and Blessings

As a conclusion the Hittite treaties usually state the consequences of disobedience and obedience. Inasmuch as the curse was thought to be the most effective aid to obedience it often appears before the blessing, and in greater detail. In the E version, however, God takes the positive approach in his introductory words to the people, "If you will obey my voice and keep my covenant, you shall be my own possession among all peoples, for all the earth is mine, and you shall be to me a kingdom of priests and a holy nation" (19:5-6).

In the light of this constructive method of eliciting the oath of fidelity it is natural that the element of the curse is muted. Nevertheless, it is there implicitly in the ceremony of sealing the covenant. When the blood of the slain oxen spatters their faces and garments it produces the awesome sense that the fate of the animals will be theirs if they break their vow of obedience.

Other passages are more explicit in associating blessings and curses with covenant ceremonies. The book of Deuteronomy is essentially an enlarged covenant, and following the stipulations, the blessings and curses appear (28:1-68). Further evidence is found in Leviticus 26. Chapters 17-26, called "The Holiness Code" by scholars, are structured as Yahweh's message to the people through Moses. Since the speech is essentially a compilation of regulations incumbent on Israel, it represents the core of a covenant ceremony. Accordingly, the fitting close to the unit is a list of blessings and curses.

The tendency in international treaties in the first millennium B.C. was for the curses to exceed by far the number and details of the blessings. This gradual dominance of the curses is evident in the biblical material as well; therefore their restricted use in the Sinai narratives indicates an adaptation of an early form of the suzerainty treaty. This is the conclusion in the other five areas of treaty components, and the support is so broad that future studies will alter the findings only in minor details.

Sinai and Tradition History

Comparison of the Hittite suzerainty treaty has led to

the conclusion that the Sinai narratives, especially the E version, describe an actual covenant ceremony with Moses at Sinai. A date early in the thirteenth century fits in well with the known data. Yet having verified the basic form of that experience does not determine precisely the text of that covenant. What instructions, for example, were actually given to Moses at Sinai? Did he receive only the ten commandments, or were other laws given as well? What was written on the two tablets of stone — the commands of Exodus 20, or the regulations of Exodus 34? Choosing Exodus 20 does not solve the problem either, because a variant list of ten commandments occurs in Deuteronomy 5. Which listing is more accurate, or does neither collection represent what was originally inscribed on the tablets? Help in answering these and many other tantalizing questions can be found in a detailed study of the various traditions. It is often possible to ascertain the sequence of basic features, and thus to learn how the tradition grew.

The D Version of the Covenant

Although the D tradition has some late features, its account of the Horeb (Sinai) experience may help clarify some issues. After repeating the ten commandments to the people assembled in Moab, Moses comments, "These words Yahweh spoke to all your assembly at the mountain out of the midst of the fire, the cloud, and thick darkness, with a loud voice, and he added no more. Then he wrote them upon two tablets of stone, and gave them to me" (Deut. 5:22). According to D, therefore, God's first revelatory act at Horeb was his audible disclosure of the ten commandments. God inscribed these, and "no more," on two tablets of stone and gave them to Moses.

The people were terrified by the voice of God, and they felt that they would die if they heard his voice any more (25). They urged Moses, therefore, to be their mediator and to report back to them any further instructions Yahweh might have for them (27). Yahweh overheard the conversation, expressed appreciation to Moses for the reverence of the people, and then issued instructions for the people to return to their tents (28-30). In the same context Yahweh commanded Moses, "But you, stand here by

me, and I will tell you all the commandment and the statutes and the ordinances which you shall teach them, that
they may do them in the land which I give them to possess" (31). The same three categories of law are mentioned in 6:1: "This is the commandment, the statutes,
and the ordinances which Yahweh your God commanded
me to teach you." Reference to "the commandment" seems
strange after the declaration of the ten commandments,
but the intent is made clear in the following verses, where
the meaning and implications of the first commandment
are considered. The core of "the commandment" is a positive paraphrase of the first commandment: "Hear, O Israel,
Yahweh is our God, Yahweh is one, and you shall love
Yahweh your God with all your heart, and with all your
soul, and with all your might" (6:4-5).

Although Moses does not explain "the statutes and the
ordinances" until chapters 12-26, it is clear from 5:31 and
6:1 that D considered these laws as revelation to Moses
at Horeb. Since many of the laws in 12-26 are similar to
the so-called Book of the Covenant (Exod. 20:22-23:33),
D seems to reflect the E version of the covenant. Both recall that God revealed the ten commandments to the people
orally and that as a result they requested Moses to mediate for them. Then both have a collection of laws which
were understood to have been given to Moses at Sinai.
Early scholars considered D as a southern tradition because
the scroll, which was found in the temple at Jerusalem,
influenced the thought of Judah from 621 B.C. on. Inten-
sive study of Deuteronomy has indicated that the early
D tradition, as represented by the scroll, most probably
originated in the northern kingdom prior to the fall of
Israel in 722 B.C. Thus, the E and D traditions, while
varying in a number of respects, have in common the
northern understanding of the Horeb (Sinai) experiences.
D is more explicit in declaring that only the ten commandments were inscribed on the tablets.

The Ten Commandments

To determine the contents of the commandments inscribed on the tablets it is necessary to compare the E
version (Exod. 20:2-17) with that of D (Deut. 5:6-21).
The first verse in each list has the prologue and a short

historical survey. The Hebrew text of the two versions is practically the same for 20:2-7 (5:6-11). The first major difference occurs in the commandment about the sabbath: E has "Remember," whereas D says "Observe." The meaning is very similar because remembering the sabbath day implies observing it as a day separated from the rest of the week. The term "observe" occurs elsewhere in D, and very likely this favorite word found its way into this verse instead of the more original "Remember."

Another indication of editorial activity in D is the addition "as Yahweh your God commanded you" following the sabbath commandment. This is one of the favorite expressions of D, and it is inserted into the text many times, but here it breaks the continuity because 5:5 introduces the commandments as a direct quotation from Yahweh. Furthermore, D expands 5:14=20:10 by inserting "your ox, or your ass, or any of" before "your cattle," and adding at the end "that your manservant and your maidservant may rest as well as you." The greatest difference between the two traditions is the explanation for the sabbath command. The editor of E thinks Yahweh designated the day as a rest because he rested on the seventh day after six days of creative activity (20:11). D, on the other hand, finds the basis of the sabbath rest in the Egyptian bondage. There the people worked diligently for Pharaoh every day of the week with no chance for rest. Both traditions interpret the command as applying to all members of the household: children, servants, sojourners, and even animals, but D felt it necessary to be more explicit with respect to the servants and animals.

The D rationale makes the most sense in the context because the memory of slavery is fresh in their minds, whereas there is no indication in the narratives that creation is a concern of Yahweh, Moses, or the people. The explanation may have originated with Moses, but it is hardly likely that he gave the creation interpretation at Sinai and then shifted to the slavery explanation in Moab. This variation probably arose because originally only the basic command was issued: "Remember the sabbath day, to keep it holy." Later on, questions of interpretation arose, and so various elaborations were appended. It is impossible, however, to determine precisely when and by whom the comments were authorized.

Both traditions have "Honor your father and your mother," and the accompanying clause "that your days may be prolonged in the land which Yahweh your God gives you" (20:12=5:16). D expands even further, however, by inserting "as Yahweh your God commanded you" after the command, and by adding "and that it may go well with you" after "prolonged." The commands involving killing, adultery, and stealing are identical in wording (with the exception of "and" before the last two), and there are no added comments in either version. In the next command D has "vain witness" (using the same word as in 5:11), while E has literally "witness of a liar." Since a lie is vain or baseless, the intent of both traditions is clearly "false witness," and most English versions cover up the difference in the Hebrew by translating "false witness" in both instances.

The command against coveting (20:17=5:21) has some variations as well. E has the basic prohibition "You shall not covet your neighbor's house." Originally "house" was probably understood to mean anything in a man's household, and this was made explicit later by enumerating "wife, manservant, maidservant, ox, and ass," and then, to cover any loopholes, by adding "anything." On the other hand, the basic command in D reads, "And you shall not covet your neighbor's wife," with "house" coming first in the list of enumerations. Perhaps D realized that in many instances breach of the command would involve coveting the neighbor's wife, and so the general and specific terms were inverted. It is much easier, however, to see why a specific list would be added to a general term like "house" than to explain why "wife" would give rise to "house." Accordingly, it appears that E has the original wording. This conclusion is supported by D's tendency to edit the text, and it is strengthened even further in this instance by the shift from "covet" to "desire" with the list of enumerations, and the insertion of "his field" after "house" (5:21).

The fact that some of the commands have no comments or explanations at all and that in other instances the interpretations vary indicates that the original two tablets probably contained the basic commands with few, if any, qualifications. In other words, those commands which at later times were felt to be ambiguous were elaborated. This was true in the case of the sabbath command, and it is probably equally true of the command against graven images, where E and D have the same comments (Exod. 20:4b-6). Since the qualifications are in the first person, thus putting them in the mouth of God, they are probably earlier than the additions in 7b and 9-11, which are in the third person.

Still further questions about the commandments involve the number "ten" and their specific numbering. The only reference to "ten" is the comment in Exodus 34:28 that there were "ten words" (that is, commands) on the stone tablets. This verse is part of the J tradition, which will be discussed in detail later on, but the basic list in E and D seems to add up to ten. Yet the division of the text is complicated by the additions, and thus, as illustrated by the following chart, Jewish and Christian traditions vary in numbering the commandments:

Commandment	Juda-ism	Bu-ber	Rom. Cath.	Gk. Or.	Luth.	Re-formed
I am Yahweh your God	1	1	Pref-ace	Pref-ace	Pref-ace	Pref-ace
No other gods	2	2	1	1	1	1
No graven images	2	2	1	2	1	2
No bowing down	2	3	1	2	1	2
No serving images	2	4	1	2	1	2
No misuse of "Yahweh"	3	5	2	3	2	3
Remember the sabbath day	4	6	3	4	3	4
Honor your parents	5	7	4	5	4	5
No killing	6	8	5	6	5	6
No adultery	7	9	6	7	6	7
No stealing	8	10	7	8	7	8
No false witness	9	11	8	9	8	9
No coveting house	10	12	9 wife	10	9	10
No coveting wife, etc.	10	12	10 house etc.	10	10	10

Martin Buber believed that the prohibitions in 20:5a were

authentic, and that originally there were twelve commandments.[7] This corresponds to that basic number 12, the number of the tribes, and most likely this was the intent of
the editor who added the comments. The issue hinges on
the authenticity of "you shall not bow down to them or
serve them." To bow down to graven images meant to
worship them, and true worship implied serving them. It
is stretching the point to make "bow down" one command and "serve" another. Furthermore, both of these
ideas are implicit in the first commandment. In fact, therefore, 5a functions as a comment, not a separate area of
restriction. Moreover, contrary to the interpretation of
the Roman Catholic and Lutheran traditions, the comment
appended to the ban on coveting can hardly be a separate
command because the specified objects are all implied in the
general term "house, household."

Meaning of the Commandments

All of the commandments are given in the second person singular. This is of great importance because it combines very neatly the corporate and individual aspects
of Israel's thought and life. Nations rooted in western
European culture have placed too much emphasis on individual freedom so that the corporate good is often lost
sight of. Such countries, especially the United States, need
to recapture the balance of corporate and individual aspects found in the ancient Hebrew tradition. Israel was
to be a "holy nation," but this corporate goal was feasible
only if collectively each person obeyed the commands of
Yahweh. Joshua encouraged the people at Shechem with
his personal witness: "As for me and my house, we will
serve Yahweh" (Josh. 24:15). He recognized that Israel's
corporate religious life hinged on the individual fidelity
of the family or clan leaders. The individual concern of
the commandments is even more apparent in the prohibition of coveting because this gets at the motivation of
the person. There is the external object of desire, of course,
but the stress is on the inner aspects of human volition.

Eight of the ten commands are negative, and some commentators have been critical of Israel because of this "neg-

---

[7] Buber, *Moses, the Revelation and the Covenant*, p. 132.

ative" approach to religion. As Mendenhall has pointed out, however, it is much easier to list the areas of restriction and then leave the other areas open for the freedom of the individual.[8] If the Israelites were to have a stable, healthy relationship with their God and with each other, certain activities would be intolerable. It was realized that such actions would never be appropriate in Yahweh's scheme of things, and so the commands were given as permanent, unconditional prohibitions.

On the other hand, it was felt that there needed to be some recognition of constructive actions leading to the well-being of Israel. In such instances the appropriate form was the positive statement. A most fitting command would have been the one in Deuteronomy 6:5: "You shall love Yahweh your God with all your heart, and with all your soul, and with all your might." But somehow the positive commands were focused in the areas of the sabbath and duty to parents.

The first three commands deal with the relationship between Israel and Yahweh, and the emphasis is on the concerns of God. The sabbath regulation forms a transition to the concerns of man and the relationship between people.

No Other Gods

The first commandment is basic to all the others, and in a genuine sense the D tradition was correct in referring to it as "the commandment" (5:31). It is implicit that no other gods are to be ranked prior to Yahweh, but this is not the primary meaning of "before me." The Hebrew reads literally "against my face," that is, "in my presence." Because Yahweh was understood to be present in the place of worship, no images of foreign gods were to be used in Israel's cult. But this did not leave room for individual idolatry either, because freedom of the individual was always within the bounds of the corporate restrictions. Granting this Hebrew point of view, it is evident that the first command is total prohibition of idolatry. Only Yahweh exists as creator and ruler of all things.

Generally speaking, belief in the existence of only one

---

[8] Mendenhall, "Ancient Oriental and Biblical Law," *BA*, XVII, 2, 30.

god has been termed "monotheism," while preference for one god over others has been designated "henotheism" or "monolatry." Scholars have filled many pages disputing over the philosophical implications of the terms, and the origin of monotheism. Albright contended for many years that the religion of Moses was rooted in monotheism.[9] He recognized that this was a practical monotheism, not the philosophical monotheism of the Greeks. Yet for its time Israelite monotheism was remarkably appropriate. Yahweh, as his name indicates, was the creator of all things. He was never identified as the sun-god, moon-god, storm-god, or fertility-god because he was over all these aspects of his creation. He was not restricted to any one place, even Sinai. Moreover, Yahweh was thought of as being alone. He had no wife or consort, and there were no sons or daughters. He was not spiritualized because he was always described in terms of human form — hands, feet, eyes, etc. Yet the splendor of this form could not be seen; therefore Yahweh appeared in a cloud. As a consequence there were to be no images of Yahweh.

There is no doubt that some circles in Israel adapted the old idea of the council of the gods. Psalm 82 is the prime example: "God has taken his place in the divine council. In the midst of the gods he holds judgment" (1). Instead of the more normal situation with God consulting the council members, the council chamber has become a courtroom and God brings an indictment against them: "How long will you judge unjustly and show partiality to the wicked?" They have not protected the weak, the afflicted, and the destitute; therefore God decrees, "You are gods, sons of the Most High, all of you, nevertheless, you shall die like men" (6-7). Even though this psalm presupposes some superhuman beings, they are under the authority of God. It is implied that they are the creatures of God and that he endowed them with their rank as council members. This concept does not negate the essence of monotheism because the members are not objects of veneration, and thus in competition with God. There is still only one God who rules over all.

---

[9] Albright, *From the Stone Age to Christianity*, pp. 257-272.

No Graven Images

The Hebrew word *pesel* is a general term meaning any representation in three dimensions. It could be wood, overlaid wood, stone, or metal. The idea of two-dimensional drawings or paintings is not included; therefore the prohibition involves images. Attached to the basic command is the qualification, "or any likeness of anything that is in heaven above, or that is in the earth beneath, or that is in the water under the earth" (20:4). This is followed by the supplementary restrictions against bowing down and serving graven images, but foreign gods and their images are the concern of the first command. Therefore the original meaning of the second command was almost certainly the prohibition of any images of Yahweh. Worship in the ancient world was tied inextricably with idols. This mentality thought of the image as somehow interrelated with the deity represented. In most cases ancient worship meant using the idol in a magical way to gain control over the deity. Taken by itself the command to worship only one God would have been interpreted by Israel as permitting images of that God. But Yahweh was not to be led around by some magical incantations of his people. He would be in their presence, but they would see no form; therefore the age-old practice of images was to be abolished. This was a dramatic shift in point of view, and so it had to be made explicit in the covenant stipulation.

Curse and Blessing

The fact that the comments concerning graven images misconstrued the meaning of the command is further evidence that they are later additions. Yet they contain some early ideas. The feature of curse and blessing was part of the Sinai covenant, and the designation of Yahweh as "a jealous God" may well have originated during the wilderness years. Some scholars have been revolted at the idea of a jealous God and have considered it a gross anthropomorphism, but the ancient Israelites were wiser than their detractors. Notwithstanding man's claim of sophistication, if he thinks theologically he is compelled ultimately to think anthropomorphically. He cannot do otherwise because he has had no other experience than that of man.

True, men have made gods in their own image, but this does not mean that God cannot be expressed in human terms. The biblical claim is that God is a person and that man was made in his image. It is not unreasonable, therefore, to find expressions of God's being in the truest experiences of man.

There are petty jealousies which stem from man's fear and insecurity, but there is a proper jealousy in which one member of a covenant rejects the rightful claim of the other. Since Yahweh had been merciful to the Hebrews in Egypt and brought them out, he had a just claim on their devotion and obedience. A basic factor in the covenant ceremony at Sinai was the understanding that if the people broke the agreement, Yahweh's covenant (steadfast) love would turn to anger, and destruction would follow. This action was not viewed as the vengeance of a capricious God. Rather, it was the natural consequence of a broken covenant. The costliness of disobedience was emphasized by the recognition that the results of covenant-breaking carry on for generations.

The uses of "hate" and "love" in Exodus 20:5-6 seem somewhat out of place, but the answer to their meaning is in the passage itself. The last part of verse 6 is usually translated "those who love me and keep my commandments," but the original meaning was "those who love me, that is, keep my commandments." In other words, love is equated with obedience. This fact was pointed out by William Moran in a study of Deuteronomy.[10] Scholars had puzzled over Deuteronomy 6:5 and wondered how love could be commanded. The answer is in the inseparable connection between love and obedience. For the Hebrew mind, inner emotion would inevitably express itself outwardly. The validity of the suzerainty treaties was the attempt to elicit the devotion of the vassal. The Hittites were wise enough to see that the covenant had a better chance of success if it was based on the good will of the vassal and not on the fear of brute force. The same was true at Sinai. The basis of Yahweh's claim on Israel was his

---

[10] William L. Moran, "The Ancient Near Eastern Background of the Love of God in Deuteronomy," *The Catholic Biblical Quarterly*, XXV, 1 (January 1963), 77-87.

devotion and actions in their behalf. Therefore, he expected his people to return that love, both in feelings and
actions.

This understanding carries over into the New Testament: "If you love me, you will keep my commandments"
(John 14:15); "You are my friends (loved ones) if you
do what I command you" (John 15:14); and "For this is
the love of God, that we keep his commandments. And his
commandments are not burdensome" (1 John 5:3). The
concept of "hate" in Exodus 20:5 is the mirror-image of
"love," that is, those who disobey Yahweh by breaking
his covenant regulations. In this case emotion is not as
clearly involved. Covenant-breaking was possible through
lack of concern or carelessness as well as through rebellious hatred. But in the covenant relationship, whether
Old or New Testament, there is no middle ground. Jesus
expressed it well, "He who is not for me is against me"
(Matt. 12:30). Accordingly, his statement about "hating"
one's family and self does not mean anger, but refusal
to obey the counterclaims, or to put competing concerns
before those of God's kingdom (Luke 14:26).

Taking Yahweh's Name in Vain

The present form of the third command is: "You shall
not take the name of Yahweh your God in vain." Inasmuch
as the commands began as a quotation from Yahweh with
the use of the first person, the original form may have
been: "You shall not take my name in vain." Apparently
someone thought the actual name should appear in the statement prohibiting its wrong use. In any case, the difference
in wording is not significant. Contrary to the widespread
opinion of many Jews and Christians, the primary thrust
of the command is not against profanity. The Hebrew states
literally, "You shall not lift up the name of Yahweh . . . to
vanity (emptiness)." In the ancient world the name was
thought to represent the person, and great care was taken
to learn the names of people. The night wrestler asked
Jacob for his name (Gen. 32:27), and Manoah, the father
of Samson, asked the name of Yahweh's messenger (Judg.
13:17). But the name could be used in magical ways to
bewitch, conjure, bless, and curse; therefore at times the
ancients sought to hide their names. In this sense the name

was similar to the image, but since the gracious revelation to Moses at the burning bush had involved the disclosure of the name Yahweh, the name could not be banned. The only solution was to ban the misuse of the name. Thus, the breaking of any vow or trust made in the name of Yahweh would be a breach of the covenant because it would be lifting up the name as a reproach upon Yahweh.

Since names are not generally misused in magical ways in the twentieth century, a more relevant interpretation involves the use of God's name or the Bible in connection with an oath or witnessing. Some Christians who are shocked at profanity have the more sinful habit of not making good on their promises. Their Christian profession implicitly involves the name of Jesus, their Christ, and by failing to fulfil their agreements they indeed crucify Christ and hold him up for contempt (Heb. 6:6). The comment "for Yahweh will not hold him guiltless who takes his name in vain" is clearly implied in the command. It is certainly a later addition simply making explicit what is implicit in the covenant oath.

Remember the Sabbath Day

As noted earlier, the institution of the sabbath was related to the giving of manna. Since its observance had begun, the command was to continue its regular observance. The cultic year with the required feasts and celebrations was tied to a calendar involving a lunar month for the most part. The regular procession of God's luminary was a constant reminder to observe the feasts, but the cycle of seven-day weeks fit neither the lunar nor the solar calendars. Apparently the command was included to serve as a verbal reminder to keep continual track of the seventh day.

The instruction "to keep it holy" meant to observe the sabbath as a day set apart by God. As such it was to be distinguished from the regular days. The additions in 20:9-10 designate the sabbath as the seventh day and then relate the day in some special way to Yahweh. Since it was Yahweh's day, it was not to be profaned. The commandment must have been questioned, or not fully observed, at some time in Israel's history because the example of God's creative week was appended as the authentication of the observance. Egyptian slavery served the same purpose in the D tradition.

Physical well-being (cessation of work for humans and animals) and spiritual welfare (time for worship and meditation about Yahweh) were probably the prime considerations in early times. Jesus was certainly correct in declaring, "The sabbath was made for man, not man for the sabbath" (Mark 2:27). He realized that Yahweh had not intended that a long list of minute restrictions should take preference over people. Making a man whole was far more basic to his well-being than the attempt to keep him from carrying his pallet. Such concerns are surely the abiding truth of the commandment. Most Christians observe the first day of the week as "the Lord's day" because of Christ's resurrection. In complex urban culture, with so many features of life demanding constant attention, it is physically impossible for all Christians to observe Sunday, let alone the rest of humanity. The only way to benefit from the abiding truth of the command is to observe another day of the week when Saturday or Sunday is not feasible.

Honor Your Parents

This command to honor parents is the second and last of the positive statements. "Honor" is a general term with no specific indication of how respect is to be expressed. Negatively, Exodus 21:15 and 17 provide the death penalty for children who strike or put a curse on their father and mother. The exhortation to honor is hardly intended for children since the whole collection is addressed to adults. Parents with children under their authority are to honor their own elderly parents. The comment gives a reason for the command: "that your days may be long in the land which Yahweh your God gives you." It is not necessarily true that respect for parents leads to longevity of life. It is true indirectly that people who care for their elderly parents set an example for their children, who in turn may care for them, thus lengthening their lives.

Society in the ancient world was built around the clan and family; therefore elders were respected and cared for. A special command was hardly necessary to achieve this goal; thus originally the statement may have had a different meaning. There is a good deal of evidence to indicate that the ancient Semites had a belief in an afterworld. By prayers and offerings of the living, the shades or spirits of the departed could be sustained. Should their children fail to honor them in this way they would be reduced to a gloomy existence in Sheol with maggots as their only companions. It was imperative, therefore, that each generation carry on the sustenance and well-being of the previous generation. Something of this nature seems to be back of the ancient concern to honor parents. But in Israel offerings to the dead were forbidden (Deut. 26:14), and so the command was interpreted differently.

Regardless of the various ways the command was interpreted, there is a core of truth which is still relevant: respect for parents engenders and fosters the attitude in the next generation. If adults do not love and respect their parents and children as individual personalities, the children will not likely respect and honor their parents. It is tragic to see so many lonely, unwanted elderly people, but in some cases they brought on their desolate situation by dishonoring their parents and driving their children and friends away.

No Killing

In the command "You shall not kill" the Hebrew term does not imply any motivation; and since there are no explanatory clauses, the meaning of the prohibition must be ascertained from a number of passages related to the issue. In the Bible a number of Hebrew verbs are used to express the act of killing. Originally some of these were probably specific terms for indicating how the act was done (for example, cutting the throat, strangling, hitting on the head, etc.), but in time the terms acquired more general usage. Nevertheless, some verbs retained their specific character. The technical term for the death penalty is the causative form of *muth* ("to die," that is, "to put to death"), and the designation for killing an enemy is *hikkah* ("to smite"). These are employed in a whole corpus of laws associated with capital punishment and holy war, killings which were considered legitimate; therefore the commandment applied to other types of killing.

The ancients learned that the loss of blood meant the loss of life; therefore they reasoned that "the life is in the blood" (Gen. 9:4). When Cain killed *(harag)* Abel, God told him, "The voice of your brother's blood is crying to me from the ground" (Gen. 4:10). This general concern for the value of human life within Israelite society is expressed in the following command: "Whoever sheds the blood of man, by man shall his blood be shed; for God made man in his own image" (Gen. 9:6). Thus capital punishment was intended as a supplement to the command not to kill. Hopefully the threat would be a deterrent, but if that failed, then death was the penalty for breaking the command. The concept of accidental or unpremeditated killing is clearly recognized in the practice of seeking refuge at the altar of the sanctuary. The provision for homicides was enlarged later on by designating six well-placed cities of refuge: three in Canaan, and three in Transjordan (Josh. 20:7-8). The possibility of being caught and killed before reaching the place of refuge was a warning against careless actions which might lead to death.

Accordingly, the command not to kill meant the prohibition of all illegitimate killings. It is precisely at the point of the exceptions (death penalty and slaughter in holy war) that the issue is focused in modern times. For this reason it is naive to quote the command as support for pacifism or an anti-war policy. The death penalty has not proved to be a deterrent, and the practice is gradually being abandoned. In general, the "blood" of a slain man is being exacted, but it is by other means, not in kind. There is some New Testament support for this new approach to the problem, but among Christians the issue is by no means settled. There is far more agreement that the concept of "holy war" has served its purpose and should be abandoned. The issue has shifted to the relative merits of "pacificism" and "the just war." The former has strong support in the teachings and life of Jesus, but the concept is very difficult to put into practice. An excellent case can be made for defensive war, yet the burden of proof rests with those waging it to show that it is just and necessary to preserve the greater good.

It is evident from the Old Testament regulations concerning murder that only the external act was dealt with.

The traditional interpretation of the command added a clause: "You shall not kill, and whoever kills shall be liable to judgment" (Matt. 5:21). The implication was that anyone who had not committed the external act had kept the law. Apparently this was what the young man meant when he claimed, "All these (commands) I have observed from my youth" (Luke 18:21). Jesus, however, interpreted the command to include those feelings and attitudes which lead to murder. For him motivation was of ultimate concern, and perhaps the prohibition of coveting led to this insight. Insofar as the intent of the command was to stop any illegitimate taking of life, the fuller interpretation of Jesus is certainly valid. Many acts of murder would have been prevented had the roots of bitterness (anger, insult, and disdain) been cut off.

No Adultery

There is no explanatory comment attached to the command forbidding adultery, and again the reason seems to be that the issue was made very explicit in case law: "If a man commits adultery with his neighbor's wife, both the adulterer and the adulteress shall be put to death" (Lev. 21:10). The same punishment is prescribed in the D tradition: "If a man is found lying with the wife of another man, both of them shall die" (Deut. 22:22). The next two verses refer to another aspect of the prohibition: "If there is a betrothed virgin, and a man meets her in the city and lies with her, then you shall bring both of them out to the gate of that city, and you shall stone them to death." If the betrothed virgin cried for help, she was absolved of guilt, and only the rapist was put to death (25-27). Here the betrothed virgin is considered as a married woman.

In ancient custom there was an extended period (usually a year) between the betrothal and the time the husband took his bride to live with her. Even though she was a virgin during this interval she was treated as a wife because the betrothal was viewed as the consummation of the marriage. In other words, betrothal was a covenant between a man and a woman, and any illicit sexual intercourse was considered a breach of that covenant. Punishment was death for the guilty, just as infidelity to Yahweh's covenant meant being "utterly destroyed" (Deut. 4:26). It is not surprising, then, to find the command against physical infidelity as one of the examples of infidelity to Yahweh.

In connection with adultery, as with killing, Jesus goes to the level of motivation: "Whoever looks at a woman lustfully has already committed adultery with her in his heart" (Matt. 5:28). In this instance "lusting" amounts to "coveting," and so Jesus has excellent Old Testament support in the specification "neighbor's wife," which is added to the command against coveting. A different emphasis in Jesus' teaching is that he grounds marriage in the physical union of man and wife (Matt. 19:4-6), not in the covenant relationship. As his biblical basis he quotes Genesis 2:24: "Therefore a man leaves his father and his mother and clings to his wife, and they become one flesh."

The practice of giving a wife a certificate of divorce and sending her away on the slightest of whims had become a travesty on the law in Deuteronomy 24:1-4. Jesus claimed that even the Old Testament provision for divorce had not been God's intent. Rather, Moses allowed the regulation as a means of maintaining justice for women who had wrongfully been put aside (Matt. 19:8). Accordingly, Jesus took a strong stand to stop the unjust practice of cheap divorces: "Everyone who divorces his wife, except on the ground of unchastity, makes her an adulteress, and whoever marries a divorced woman commits adultery" (Matt. 5:32). If the woman has been divorced on grounds other than adultery, the union between her and her husband still exists even though they are separated. If she marries and has sexual intercourse with her new husband, she becomes an adulteress because by forming a new physical union she breaks the former bond. The man commits adultery because he shares in the new union, thus breaking the former bond.

In one instance at least, Jesus circumvented the death penalty for adultery because of the penitent spirit of the woman and the hypocritical attitude of those bringing the charges (John 7:53-8:11). While in general Christians have ignored the severe punishment prescribed in the

Old Testament, they have taken seriously the idea of marriage as a covenant. In this very complex, free-wheeling age this concept is still valid, and many young people are beginning to realize it. Jesus' strict definition of adultery poses more difficulty, but it must be realized that he stated the issue so rigidly in order to help correct a great evil. The question is whether or not Jesus would insist on a physical definition of marriage where two people, who have not been unfaithful sexually, live in a hellish state of incompatibility that infects them and their children.

Jesus generally dealt with the spirit of the law, not the letter. Would he not recognize that some marriages, not made in heaven and never really approved by God, are actually shattered by evil spirits and attitudes even though the physical bond has not been broken? Mistakes made by young people in other areas can be made right and forgiven. Is it really God's will that a mistake in marriage destine those involved to a long life of misery? What good is the fiction of a physical union when the bond of spirit, the real basis for covenant, is completely shattered? What about the person who knows that his mate has been unfaithful, but because of various legal technicalities a divorce cannot be obtained on the basis of adultery? If a divorce is not obtained on other grounds, the innocent party must abstain or become guilty of adultery because the mate has formed a new union. Many Christians have come to see the complexities and have realized that the basic good for all is best served at times by divorces on grounds other than adultery. The difficulty in taking Jesus' interpretation as the eternal norm is that it makes sinners of people who are just as sorrowful and penitent as the woman taken in adultery. The Old Testament concept of marriage as covenant is still the best guideline for today and the foreseeable future.

No Stealing

No qualifications follow the prohibition of stealing, and since no specific objects are listed it appears to be a general ban on the appropriation of anything not one's own. Yet the fact that the context deals with issues involving persons (killing, adultery, and false witness) would tend to indicate that the ban on stealing has a personal reference as well. A specific case law illustrates the point: "Whoever steals a man, whether he sells him or has him in his possession, shall be put to death" (Exod. 21:16). The severe penalty indicates the seriousness of the offense.

Although the original emphasis of the eighth command was concerned with persons, the stealing of property was implicit. Exodus 22:1-4, a series of case laws concerning stealing, makes this explicit. A man stealing animals must make fivefold restitution for an ox and fourfold for a sheep. In general, free Israelites were not to be enslaved, but if a thief could not make restitution, he was sold for the amount due. The ban on stealing (persons or property) has permanent relevance, and orderly governments recognize this fact even though they may espouse no religious cause. The principle has even been expanded to fit modern culture. Copyrights, for example, are essentially bans on stealing ideas.

No False Witness

As indicated earlier, the variant wording in the E and D versions is not significant. The technical term "witness" indicates that the command applies to the official means of carrying out justice. At Sinai this meant the hearings before the local judges appointed by Moses, and later on it had reference to the courts held at the city gates. The intent is absolutely clear and so is the meaning: in determining justice, Yahweh, the holy God, will never permit untruthful statements. In the qualification "against your neighbor" the term "neighbor" is not used in any technical sense; therefore the intent of the basic command implies the explanation. A neighbor was anyone with whom one dealt in the course of everyday life. Whether the qualification was part of the original command is difficult to determine. In either case, the expression probably stems from Exodus 18:16, where Moses is explaining to Jethro his attempt to settle all the disputes "between a man and his neighbor." Again, the ban has permanent relevance for any civilized society. The oath on the witness stand along with the threat of punishment for perjury are attempts to maintain the principle.

The implication is that the same prohibition ought to govern personal relationships outside the courts, but oddly

enough there is no command against lying in general.
It was certainly understood because Hosea lists "lying"
along with "swearing, killing, stealing, and committing
adultery," clear references to the ten commandments (4:2).

No Coveting

Coveting is certainly one of the deadliest of sins, and
it may well be the most basic cause for human strife and
misery. Until human nature is changed, the prohibition
will always have relevance. As noted previously, this is
the one command which seems to stress the inner aspect
of man's being. This is undoubtedly so, and here Jesus
may have found his clue to the primacy of motivation. Yet
the Hebrew verb involves more than "desire." It can mean
"the attempt to appropriate the possessions of others."
Accordingly, both the inner and outer aspects of coveting
are included.

Whether the qualification "your neighbor's house" was
part of the original command is hard to prove, but logically
it would seem to be an addition because its intent is clearly
implied in the basic prohibition. One usually covets persons or things with which one comes in contact, and certainly this would apply to any attempt to appropriate the
objects of desire. In either case, E's reference to "house"
is more original than "wife" in D. A positive statement of
the command would be, "Acquire the things you desire
by legitimate means." The peoples of the world need this
message now more than ever.

The Decalogue and Revelation

One feature of the E tradition was the belief that God
had inscribed the commandments on the tablets with his
own finger (Exod. 31:18). While this claim cannot be
taken literally, it probably expresses Moses' awareness
of Yahweh's special help. It is evident that he had a revelatory experience on Mt. Sinai just as he had had earlier
at the burning bush.

The paramount insight was the realization that the
Hittite suzerainty treaty was an accurate analogy to express the relationship between Yahweh and his people.
With this understanding it was clear that Yahweh would
no more tolerate other gods than the Hittite suzerains

would permit their vassals to make treaties with other kings. This demand of exclusive worship, with its implicit prohibition of apostasy, was indeed "the commandment" (Deut. 5:30; 6:1). Equally revolutionary breaks with the religious customs of the time were the prohibition of images of Yahweh and the ban on the misuse of his name.

The general concept of a sabbath preceded Moses by centuries, but the insight that every seventh day was to be a day of rest devoted to Yahweh was distinctive. Similar ideas or counterparts to the remaining six commandments have been found in the literature of Mesopotamia and Egypt, and Moses probably took his clue from them. But again, concepts borrowed from the ancient world were raised to a new level of ethical insight when they were stated in the context of Yahweh's covenant with his people.

Most of the ingredients for the Decalogue were at hand, and in theory other peoples of the ancient Near East could have come to the same insights. The fact is, however, they did not! The crucial difference was Yahweh's revelation of himself. Moses was a brilliant person, but without the understanding of Yahweh as the holy, moral sovereign over all the earth and all the nations there would have been no Decalogue. It was Yahweh's revelation to Moses which accounted for the uniqueness of the first three commandments and for the new insights which the seven borrowed concepts acquired.

The Text of the Commandments

In the light of the discussion of the ten commandments it is suggested that the text of the two stone tablets was the Hebrew equivalent of the following version, and that the numbering represents the intended division of the original text:

1. You shall have no other gods in my presence.
2. You shall not make for yourself a graven image.
3. You shall not lift up my name in vain.
4. Remember the sabbath day, to keep it holy.
5. Honor your father and your mother.
6. You shall not kill.
7. You shall not commit adultery.
8. You shall not steal.

9. You shall not bear false witness (against your neigh-
    bor).
10. You shall not covet (your neighbor's house).

The Date of the Commandments

The claim has been made that the ten commandments
were the covenant stipulations at Sinai, but a further word
should be said about their antiquity. Because of the remarkable ethical quality of the commands, nineteenth-
century scholars, influenced by Wellhausen's theory of theological development, tended to assign a late date to the
collection in Exodus 20. But scholars have increasingly realized that to explain the people Israel it is necessary to
have a man like Moses with a high view of God. The
classical prophets of the eighth and seventh centuries B.C.
were not essentially innovators or creators of new ideas.
They were basically reformers, and as John Bright has said
of Amos, "His ethical protest was drawn from a well five
hundred years deep."[11] Aside from the early scholarly
prejudice, there is no reason to question the antiquity of
the commands because of their ethical content.

In discussing the date of the ten commandments, Noth
acknowledges that they derive from the time prior to the
classical prophets because (1) they contain no "social requirements in the narrow sense" as found in the prophets,
and (2) the writings of the prophets "appear to presup-
pose the commandments."[12] "But for the pre-prophetic
period," Noth declares, "all possibilities of dating are
open."[13] He observes that there is a kind of timelessness
about the commandments, and then he comments further,
"The Decalogue is the only legal entity in the Old Testament which indicates no certain reference to the conditions
of life in an agricultural community, but we cannot of
course conclude from this negative statement that the basic
material of the Decalogue came into being in the time before the conquest."[14] Noth is correct that an argument
from silence is not sufficient to prove a point, but this

---

[11] John Bright, *The Kingdom of God* (Nashville: Abingdon, 1953),
p. 65.
[12] Noth, *Exodus*, p. 167.
[13] *Ibid.*
[14] *Ibid.*

acknowledgment does not solve the problem. There is no certain reference to desert life at Sinai either, and since the commands have a timeless character about them, all arguments on the basis of lack of specific references cancel each other out.

The next step would be research in all the available evidence for clues as to the date of the commands. Apparently Noth thought he had done this because he states dogmatically, "There are no reliable criteria for answering the question of the age and derivation of the Decalogue."[15] This is a value judgment, of course, and the key word is "reliable." In 1954 Mendenhall published his study relating the Sinai covenant with the Hittite suzerainty treaty. As noted earlier, this new material offers a number of reliable criteria, and yet there is hardly a trace of Mendenhall's research in the three major works of Noth which should have dealt with the issue: *The History of Israel*, 1960 (based on the 2nd German edition, 1954); *Exodus*, 1962 (German original, 1959); and *The Old Testament World*, 1966 (based on the 4th German edition, 1964). It is hardly conceivable that a scholar of Noth's caliber did not know of Mendenhall's study; therefore he must have decided that the new material did not give "reliable criteria." Apparently his deep-rooted pessimism about the historicity of the biblical narratives prior to the conquest unconsciously foreclosed any possibility of viewing the new evidence objectively. For all his genuine concern to be fair, his scholarly agnosticism inclined him to mute the evidence supporting more traditional views.

Fortunately, biblical scholars in general recognize that the new criteria have undermined the old prejudice to the point where the burden of proof is on the scholar who takes a negative or noncommittal stance. Since the Sinai covenant was an adaptation of the suzerainty treaty, there had to be some stipulations or else there was no objective basis for the covenant. It is hardly likely that Israelite tradition lost or dropped these basic regulations, and so it would seem reasonable to look for them embedded in the biblical nar-

---

[15] *Ibid.*

ratives. The simplified list of commands proposed above
fits both the treaty context and the requirements of critical
scholarship.

Chapter 10

The Covenant Community at Sinai

It has been established that an actual covenant ceremony took place at Mt. Sinai and that the stipulations to which Israel vowed fidelity were at least the ten commandments. The D tradition claims that in addition to an explanation of the first command, "statutes and ordinances" were given to Moses at Sinai (Deut. 5:31). The E tradition seems to make the same claim: "Moses came and told the people all the words of Yahweh and all the ordinances" (Exod. 24:3). Yet in response to Moses' report the people answered, "All the words which Yahweh has spoken we will do." Then "Moses wrote all the words of Yahweh." The fact that the "ordinances" are not even mentioned in the latter two instances is a clear indication that the statement "and all the ordinances" is a scribal addition to verse 3. Furthermore, had ordinances been a part of the original narrative the account would probably have said "all the words and ordinances of Yahweh," because tradition considered them as much a part of Yahweh's instructions as the "words."

The Book of the Covenant

If the editorial comment is removed, then "the words of Yahweh" refer to the ten commands, which the people had heard. Moses repeats the words, and after the people's vow of obedience he writes them (presumably on a book or scroll). In the covenant ceremony he takes this "book of the covenant" and reads the stipulations to the people. They make the formal oath of obedience, and then Moses seals the covenant by throwing the blood on them.

Scholars have usually interpreted the Book of the Covenant to mean the collection of laws found in Exodus 20:22-23:33, but this is not necessarily so at all. The basis for the assumption is the reference to "ordinances" in 24:3 and in 21:1, the formal introduction to the collection of laws: "Now these are the ordinances which you shall set before them." There is a connection between the two references, but they do not identify the Book of the Covenant.

The Origin of the Book of Ordinances

What probably happened is that some editor, knowing the tradition about ordinances having been given at Sinai, inserted the collection of laws between the narrative about the commands and the account of the covenant ceremony. When this was done it was necessary to add "and all the ordinances" after "all the words of Yahweh" (24:3) so that the reader would understand that both categories of instruction were involved at the covenant ceremony.

A strong reason for doubting the reconstruction of the editor is that the collection of ordinances has many references to conditions and situations in the land of Canaan. The story of the covenant ceremony at Shechem fits into the picture nicely: "Joshua made a covenant with the people that day, and made statutes and ordinances for them at Shechem. And Joshua wrote these words in a book as God's law" (Josh. 24:25-26). Where is this book of ordinances? The stipulations of such a memorable covenant could hardly have been lost completely. A very probable explanation is that, allowing for some later additions, the collection in Exodus 20:22-23:33 represents essentially the law book of Joshua. An important question is whether or not any of these ordinances stems from Moses. Critical scholarship has tended to deny this possibility because the collection contains some laws which most certainly were formulated in Canaan. But any collection of laws has a long history, and later additions do not date all the material.

Exodus 33:7-11 has a very interesting passage about the "tent of meeting," as Moses called it. Almost without exception scholars have considered this section to be a very old tradition. Apparently any of the Israelites faced with a crucial decision could go outside the camp and seek Yahweh's counsel at the isolated tent. Primarily, however, the tent was used by Moses. Whenever he went out there the people would observe him from the entrances of their tents, and as the pillar of *anan*, that is, the cloud of manifestation, descended to the entrance of the tent of meeting the people would worship in front of their tents. Inside the tent Yahweh spoke to Moses "face to face, as a man speaks to his friend" (11), and probably these meetings with Yahweh gave rise to the name of the tent. Here the "face" of Yahweh probably refers to his mask *(anan)* because Exodus 33:20 is quite explicit that no one could see the actual face of Yahweh and live. No reason is given for these intimate conversations, but the strong implication is that Moses, like the people, was seeking Yahweh's advice on difficult matters.

As soon as the covenant ceremony was completed, Moses and the people faced the task of living by the stipulations. Everyday life at Sinai, regardless of how simple it was, involved all the issues highlighted by the ten commands, and Moses must have been called on to interpret the intent of the covenant requirements. It is logical to suppose that clarification of the problems came at a place where he could meditate and commune with Yahweh, and no more satisfactory location could be imagined than the tent of meeting described by tradition.

As noted already, there are a number of regulations, both direct (apodictic) commands and case laws, in the book of ordinances dealing specifically with issues of the ten commands. Critics have usually assigned these to the period after the conquest on the assumption that case laws were borrowed from the Canaanites. But the case law format, "If (When) ..., then ...," originated centuries before Moses, and knowledge of it had spread to Egypt as well as Canaan. It is rather presumptuous to assume that a man reared in the Egyptian court was ignorant of case law. If Moses knew of the suzerainty type treaty, he certainly knew something of the corpus of existing case law. It is no accident, therefore, that some regulations in the book of ordinances deal specifically with issues of the Decalogue. Rather, it is the natural result of trying to implement the covenant relationship.

From every point of view, therefore, it seems certain that Moses began the process of interpreting the commands, and that some of the statements in the book of ordinances originated with him. Thus the E and D traditions were correct in remembering that Yahweh gave

Moses some ordinances at Sinai. Where tradition was wrong was in assuming that the compilations of later times derived completely from Moses. Extreme views assign all or nothing to Moses, but as usual the truth is not an either-or. In all likelihood Moses began compiling the book of ordinances, Joshua extended it greatly by issuing statutes and ordinances relevant to conditions in Canaan, and then still later men like Samuel and Nathan carried on the interpretive process for their times.

The J Version of the Covenant

Whereas the E version of the covenant is fairly straightforward and in general agreement with the narrative up through Exodus 24:8, the J version (as indicated in Newman's reconstruction) involves a good deal of skipping around in order to make a logical sequence of the various incidents described. A crucial passage for any theory about Sinai traditions is 34:10-28. It is claimed that Yahweh delivered "ten words" (commands) to Moses and that Moses wrote them on the tablets of stone. The first difficulty is to isolate the comments and to identify the commands. The following list (with proposed numberings and notation of similar passages in Exodus) will indicate the problem:

1.	1.	1.	You shall worship no other god (34:14=20:3);
2.	2.	2.	You shall make no molten gods (34:17=20:4);
3.	3.	–	You shall keep the feast of unleavened bread (34:18=23:15a);
4.	–	3.	All that opens the womb is mine (34:19=13:12);
–	–	4.	You shall redeem the firstling of an ass with a lamb (34:20a=13:13);
–	–	5.	None shall appear before me empty (34:20b=23:15b);
5.	–	6.	You shall work six days (34:21a=20:9=23:12a);
–	–	–	You shall rest on the seventh day (34:21b=20:10=23:12b);
6.	4.	–	You shall observe the feast of weeks (34:22a=23:16a);

–	5.	–	You shall observe the feast of ingathering (34:22b=23:16b);
–	6.	–	All your males shall appear before Yahweh God three times a year (34:23=23:17);
7.	7.	7.	You shall not offer the blood of my sacrifice with leaven (34:25a=23:18a);
8.	8.	8.	You shall not leave the sacrifice of the feast of passover until morning (34:25b=23:18b);
9.	9.	9.	You shall bring the firstfruits of the ground to the house of Yahweh (34:26a=23:19a);
10.	10.	10.	You shall not boil a kid in its mother's milk (34:26b=23:19b).

If the commands which relate to the same issue are combined, it is possible (as indicated in the first column) to arrive at the number ten. But even then the arrangement is contrived, for if the Feast of Weeks and the Feast of Ingathering are combined, the Feast of Unleavened Bread ought to be included with them. The basic command is for all males to appear before Yahweh three times a year. This same series occurs in 23:14-17 (except that the feast of "weeks" is called the feast of "harvest"), and one would expect them to be listed together and in the same order. This would be true if verses 19-21 were deleted as a later insertion. Moreover, the number of commands (as noted in the second column) would still be ten. Another possibility is that the commands concerning the feasts were added later. In this case (as indicated in column three) the magic number ten could be obtained by considering the instruction to work six days as part of the command to rest on the seventh day. This alternative has the disadvantage of trying to explain why the festal instructions were inserted at different places; therefore the more likely possibility is that verses 19-21 were inserted later.

A further complication is the command "None shall appear before me empty." In Exodus 23:15 it appears abruptly after instructions for keeping the Feast of Unleavened Bread, but almost certainly it applies to the Feasts of Harvest (offerings from the early harvest, May-June) and Ingathering (produce from the last harvest, September-

October). Accordingly, the command would be more appropriate at the end of 23:16 or 17. The same command appears unexpectedly at the end of 34:20. There it applies to "all that opens the womb," that is, the firstborn of animals and humans. If verse 21 (work six days and rest on the sabbath) is deleted as an insertion, then the command not to appear empty prefaces the Feast of Weeks (Harvest) as in Exodus 23.

All of these inner difficulties indicate a very complicated history of editing and revision, and at this stage it is virtually impossible to determine the original wording of the list. It is clear, however, that the commands were compiled from material in Exodus 13, 20, and 23; for example, the designation "feast of harvest" in 23 has been revised to the later form "feast of weeks" in 34. It is equally certain that all of the "words," in any of the possible combinations, are apodictic in form. In this respect the list in Exodus 34 is similar to that in Exodus 20. Moreover, both tend to favor the negative statement: six in Exodus 34 and eight in Exodus 20. Further still, both lists seem to have had ten commands originally. Although no number is mentioned in Exodus 20, the basic commands total ten, and the specific reference to "ten" in Exodus 34 appears to be authentic.

The most striking feature, however, is the dissimilarity in content. Only with respect to idolatry, images, and the sabbath do the two lists agree. The concern in Exodus 34 is entirely cultic or ritualistic. The ethical aspect is implicit in some of the commands, but it is not made explicit like the great social commands in Exodus 20. Earlier critics considered Exodus 34 as the more original list of commands, which was displaced later by the ethical list of Exodus 20, but the reverse is more likely. As noted above, Exodus 20 fits the covenant context of Sinai admirably, whereas Exodus 34 includes statements which were probably formulated in Canaan. One of the Canaanite delicacies was a young goat prepared in the milk of its mother. This must have been a revolting practice for some of the Israelites because the ban appears three times (Exod. 23:19; 34:26; Deut. 14:21). Moses undoubtedly had some general knowledge of conditions in Canaan, and so he would have been concerned to warn the people and to set down some basic ground rules for life after the conquest.

But it is highly unlikely that the exotic Canaanite practice was a concern of Moses at Sinai. The specific regulation was evoked after the conquest when the Israelites began to develop a taste for the Canaanite delicacy.

But the recognition that Exodus 34 is a later compilation does not explain why it was compiled or what relation it had to Exodus 20. Tradition took the narrative quite literally and explained the Exodus 34 list as a summary of the main points in Exodus 20 and the book of ordinances. Since the latter two collections, according to the theory, were the stipulations for the first covenant ceremony, the summary in 34 was considered the basis for the renewal after the apostasy of the calf worship. But such a rationale is rather wishful. The book of ordinances did not figure in the first covenant ceremony, and by no stretch of the imagination can Exodus 34 be a genuine summary of Exodus 20. The explanation of Exodus 34 must be found elsewhere, but before this can be done it is necessary to consider Exodus 32-33 and the antecedents of the passage.

Exodus 32-33

Scholars are quite generally agreed that Exodus 34 represents the J tradition, but opinions vary considerably about 32-33. Older literary critics assigned about half of the material to J and the other passages to E. Beyerlin finds both traditions in 33, but he assigns practically all of 32 to E. Noth, on the other hand, thinks that the basic strand in both chapters is J. Since Beyerlin and Noth agree that the narrative in 32-33 is the resumption of the account found in Exodus 31:18 and 24:12-15a, the latter passages are assigned to E by Beyerlin and J by Noth. The reason for this wide-ranging disparity is that the material in 32-33 has been reworked and edited so many times the strands have been broken and thoroughly mixed. Difficulties in understanding some of the early material, and theological interests of various editors have resulted in one of the most complicated sections of the Old Testament.

At this point in the discussion, however, determining the narrative is more basic, and so the question of strand origin will be considered later. The immediate context of 32-33 is 31:18: "And he (Yahweh) gave to Moses, when he had finished speaking with him on Mt. Sinai, the two tablets of

the pact, tablets of stone, written with the finger of God."
As will be shown later, the long section 24:15b-31:17 is
an insertion by the P tradition; therefore Beyerlin and
Noth are correct in tracing the narrative back to 24:12-15a.
There Moses is instructed to come up on the mountain and
wait for the tablets on which Yahweh has inscribed his instructions for the people. Moses refers the elders to Aaron
and Hur during his absence, and then he ascends the mountain taking "his servant Joshua" with him. It is implied
that Joshua goes up only part way because only Moses
appears at the mountaintop.

The Golden Calf

When the narrative about the giving of the tablets is
completed, the story flashes back to what was going on in
the camp. The people assume from Moses' prolonged absence that he is lost, and so they look for other leadership
to deliver them from the wilderness. With fickleness of
heart they urge Aaron, "Up, make gods for us to go ahead
of us" (Exod. 32:1). Aaron suggests a collection of gold
and then he fashions a calf. In the ancient Near East a
young bull was the symbol of power and fertility, and no
doubt Aaron and the people knew of the bull-cult in Egypt.
In any case, the people exclaim, "These are your gods, O
Israel, who brought you up out of the land of Egypt" (4).
Aaron builds an altar in front of the calf image, and proclaims a feast to Yahweh. Then the people offer sacrifices,
eat, drink, and play (probably a reference to sexual
orgies).

Yahweh informs Moses that the people have corrupted
themselves, and in his anger he threatens to consume the
people and start over with Moses and his descendants. But
Moses rejects Yahweh's proposal, and he gives three reasons for his boldness: (1) in spite of their sin these are
still the people Yahweh delivered from Egypt; (2) the
Egyptians will have grounds for saying that Yahweh
brought them out with the evil intent of consuming them;
and (3) Yahweh should remember the covenant to Abraham, Isaac, and Jacob in which he swore to multiply their
descendants and to give them a land. Yahweh accepts
Moses' argument and decides not to consume the people.

Having assuaged Yahweh's anger, Moses descends the

mountain with the tablets (inscribed on both sides). When Joshua, whom Moses has apparently rejoined on the way down, hears the shouting from the camp he interprets it as a war cry. Moses has more discriminating ears, however, and realizes that the sound is that of singing. On seeing the dancing around the calf Moses' anger flares, and he throws the tablets to the ground. He burns the calf with fire, grinds it to powder, scatters it on water, and makes the people drink. Then Moses asks Aaron to explain what the people did to cause him to bring such a great sin on them. Aaron tries to cool Moses' anger by noting the evil intent of the people. With a very comical, but all too human, justification for his action, Aaron explains that he threw the gold into the fire and the calf just happened to come out (32:24).

A very odd feature about the story is that only one calf is made, and yet the term *elohim* ("gods") appears four times (32:1, 4, 8, 23). When the northern tribes rebelled against Judah and formed the kingdom of Israel, King Jeroboam made two golden calves (one for Bethel and one for Dan) in order to wean the people away from worship in Jerusalem. In explaining his action to the people he said, "Behold your gods, O Israel, who brought you up out of the land of Egypt" (1 Kings 12:28). Aside from the first word, this statement is identical with that in Exodus 32:4. Both at Sinai and Bethel, moreover, an altar is erected in front of the calf, a feast is proclaimed, and sacrifices are offered on the altar in connection with worship of the calf. Scholars have long recognized a definite relationship between the two accounts, but they have not agreed on the explanation for the similarity.

From start to finish the biblical editors considered Jeroboam's innovation as the great sin of the northern kingdom. Just as the idolatrous calf at Sinai resulted in the shattered tablets, the symbol of the broken covenant, so the calves of Jeroboam were proof of Israel's apostasy and breach of covenant. Since most conservative commentators take the biblical narrative and interpretations quite literally, they consider the use of "gods" as the biblical editors' way of stigmatizing both events as idolatry. They assume, of course, that there was a golden calf at Sinai and that

the original story referred to it as "god." Most critical
scholars, on the other hand, doubt that there ever was an
idolatrous calf at Sinai. They consider Exodus 32 as a piece
of Jerusalem propaganda against the religious practice of
the northern kingdom.

One of the simpler approaches to the problem is to consider the material out of which the calf was made. If the
text is correct that Moses burned the calf with fire, ground
it to powder, and scattered it on water, then the calf could
not have been of gold. It is possible to melt gold, but not
burn it. The ancients did not have the practice of grinding
or pulverizing gold, and most certainly it could not have
been scattered on water. The implication of making the
people drink the water is that it would serve as a curse or
lie-detector and produce visible effects on the guilty. Gold
at the bottom of a cup might have some psychological effect,
but this is hardly the implication of the story. A wooden
calf (whether overlaid with gold or not) could have been
burned and the ashes scattered on water, but how grinding
could have been involved is difficult to see. Albright has
suggested that the calf was made of limestone.[1] Although
the Jebel Musa region is largely granite, limestone is found
in the area, and limestone slackened in a fire could have
been pulverized and scattered on water. Drinking such a
potion would have indeed been a curse.

This possibility raises the question as to whether or not
a calf actually was fashioned and worshiped at Sinai. Noth
comments, "We can ask whether perhaps Exodus 32 contains an older tradition of a cultic apostasy of Israel even
on Sinai which was only later transformed into a polemic
against the 'golden calves' of Jeroboam. It is, however, impossible to find any concrete clues for such an assumption,
and so we must therefore reckon with the possibility that
the narrative of Exodus 32 was originally composed with
reference to Jeroboam's cult-politics."[2] In the Baal Epic of
Ugarit, dating from the fourteenth century B.C., the destruction of the god Mot (Death) by the goddess Anath is
described as follows:

[1] Albright, *Journal of Biblical Literature*, LVII, 1, 18.
[2] Noth, *Exodus*, p. 246.

> *With a winnowing sieve she scattered him,*
> *With fire she burned him,*
> *With a handmill she ground him.*

It is noteworthy that the same three verbs occur in the biblical text, except that "scattered" is last. This similarity can hardly be accidental, and therefore it is probable that Exodus 32:20 represents an early strand of the story.

Another indication of this probability is Moses' reply in verse 18: "It is not the sound of the victory shout, or the sound of the cry of defeat, but the sound of singing that I hear." This type of repetitive parallelism, so common in the Ugaritic epics, was not understood and employed later on in Israel's history; accordingly its appearance here is evidence that 32:18 is old. While verses 18 and 20 were apparently not considered "concrete clues" by Noth, they are strong indicators that the passage 32:15-20 is old. It is very unlikely that an editor in Jeroboam's time or after, could or would have antiqued the passage as it is; therefore Noth's "must" is a gross overstatement. The greater probability is that an actual apostasy occurred at Sinai and that the calf (young bull) was limestone, not gold.

Tradition and the Golden Calf

Some scholars assume that there was a tradition at Bethel, the important northern shrine, which Jeroboam employed as a sanction for the erection of the golden calves. If this be so, the story must have lost the negative aspects of Moses' condemnation and destruction of the calf, or else Jeroboam would have had no basis for appeal. Beyerlin solves the problem by considering only Exodus 32:1-6 as the Bethel tradition.[3] There was no stigma attached to the event because Aaron willingly accepted the wishes of the people and quite naturally fashioned a calf as the image. Only later on when the tradition was incorporated in the E account was it reinterpreted as an apostasy. According to Beyerlin, Jeroboam either used the Bethel tradition to authenticate his erection of a calf, or perhaps a calf cult was already in existence at Bethel and he set up a new golden calf to nationalize the existing worship.

---

[3] Beyerlin, *Origins and History of the Oldest Sinaitic Traditions*, pp. 126-130.

While this line of reasoning may have some basis in fact, it is virtually impossible to ascertain from available material precisely how tradition took the halfway step. What is quite evident is that finally some opponent of the calf cult edited the materials at hand so that the revised story served as a castigation of Jeroboam and his religious practices. The revision could have occurred in the south because the religious leaders in Judah were opposed to Jeroboam's calves, but certain circles in the north were indignant as well. Hosea, for example, snorts sarcastically, "Men kiss calves" (13:2), and he pronounces doom on the "calf of Samaria" (8:6).

Aaron and the Calf

One further question is whether Aaron was associated with the calf or not. Not only does Noth deny the historicity of a calf image in the desert, but he doubts that Aaron figured in the story when it was composed subsequent to Jeroboam's calf worship. He comes to this conclusion because the references to Aaron are so loosely attached to the story, and they seem to indicate two different periods of editorial activity.[4] Actually, Aaron is referred to implicitly or by name only in 32:1-5, 21-25, 35. It is odd that when Yahweh reports the incident to Moses on Sinai only the people are blamed for making the calf. There is no specific mention of Aaron and his willy-nilly association with the image. Admittedly, Aaron's attitude and role seem very much out of keeping, but some of the skewed vignettes may have resulted from the tension between opposing theological views.

Beyerlin, on the other hand, contends both for the authenticity of a calf incident in the wilderness, and for Aaron's role in it. As support he notes that Phinehas, a grandson of Aaron, cared for the ark when it was in Bethel, and that the Bethel priesthood considered itself as descending from Aaron.[5] This variant interpretation of the biblical material evidences itself still further in the assignment of sources: Beyerlin considers Exodus 32:1-6 as a unit incorporated within the E tradition, while Noth thinks it is a secondary addition to the J source. Such wide-ranging con-

[4] Noth, *Exodus*, pp. 244-245.
[5] Beyerlin, *op. cit.*, p. 129.

clusions from the same material indicate how exceedingly
complex the biblical narratives are, but even more signifi-
cantly they illustrate how much subjectivity is involved in
a chain of reasoning which attempts to solve inner details
of tradition and their development.

Ordination of the Levites

After the people have been compelled to drink the water
with the pulverized calf (32:20), there is no immediate
reference to the outcome of the water-ordeal or punishment. The nearest statement to anything of this sort is in
verse 35: "And Yahweh sent a plague upon the people because they made the calf which Aaron made." In between
are three units of material: 21-24, Aaron's naive answer to
Moses' rebuke; 25-29, the ordination of the Levites; and
30-34, Moses' second intercession for the people.

There are elements in all three passages which jog the
flow of the story. Moses most likely interrogated Aaron before destroying the calf and carrying out the water-ordeal;
thus 21-24 is a unit of tradition separate from the story in
15-20. The section 25-29 is still another tradition because
it backs up to the point where Moses first saw the idolatry:
"When Moses saw that the people had broken loose (for
Aaron had let them break loose to their shame among their
enemies), then Moses stood in the gate of the camp and
said, 'Who is on Yahweh's side? Come to me.' And all the
sons of Levi gathered themselves together to him" (25-26).
Each Levite is instructed to take a sword and go from gate
to gate, throughout the camp, killing his brother, companion, and neighbor. This they do and 3,000 men fall. Then
Moses declares, "Today you have ordained yourselves for
the service of Yahweh, each one at the cost of his son and
his brother, that he may bestow a blessing upon you this
day" (29).

According to the P tradition, Moses and Aaron consecrated the Levites (Num. 8:5-26). Moreover, aside from
the loosely attached editorial about Aaron, it is hard to relate the details of 32:25-29 to the preceding story. The
clear implication of Yahweh's report is that all the people
were involved and thus guilty. This is indicated when
Moses makes the people drink the water. Where were the
zealous Levites all this time? Had they participated in the

apostasy and then recanted? If only 3,000 were killed, it is implied that others were permitted to live. What was going on at the various gates that the Levites were ordered there? By what means were they to decide whom to kill? These and other questions are left unanswered in the account. Family and social ties were to be ignored because no guilty ones were to be spared. An oddity is the inner difference between Moses' instructions and his commendation: "brother, companion, and neighbor" become "son and brother." The clue to the placement of 25-29 is probably Deuteronomy 33:8-9. There the tribe of Levi is blessed by Moses because at some difficult situation near Massah and Meribah it obeyed Yahweh's covenant by not regarding father, mother, brothers, and children. The springs Massah and Meribah were in the region of Qadesh-barnea, and there is every reason to think that the incident described in Exodus 32:25-29 took place there, not at Sinai.

Moses' Second Intercession

Another indication of the intrusive nature of 25-29 is its complete incongruity with 30: "The next day Moses said to the people, 'You have sinned a great sin. Now I will go up to Yahweh. Perhaps I can make atonement for your sin.'" If the Levites have slain all the guilty, for whom is Moses to make atonement? Verse 30 makes far more sense following the water-ordeal in verse 20. In the first intercession Moses graciously refused to accept Yahweh's offer to make a new covenant with his family. In his second intercessory prayer his request for the forgiveness of the people is even more costly. He is willing to be erased from the book where Yahweh keeps the names of his own. But Yahweh rejects his offer: Moses will stay in the book, while the names of the sinners will be erased. Then Moses is instructed to lead the people (even though they are sinners), and he is given the assurance that Yahweh's messenger (angel) will go with him. Finally, Yahweh announces the postponement of punishment: "In the day when I visit, I will visit their sin upon them" (34). The implication is that Yahweh's visit will come at some indefinite period; yet the very next verse refers to a plague which Yahweh sent among the people because of the calf worship. Such jarring shifts indicate that many disparate units of tradition have been brought together in Exodus 32.

The Presence of Yahweh

Chapter 33 is another series of variant traditions, and the thread which holds them together is the theme of Yahweh's presence. Section 1-6 relates back to 32:33-34; therefore the reference to the plague (35) most logically follows as the aftermath of the water-ordeal in verse 20. The problem for Moses is how he can lead the sinful people when Yahweh will not forgive them and accompany them. In 33:1, as in 32:7, Yahweh refers to the people as those whom Moses brought up from Egypt. No reference is made to the usual claim that Yahweh brought the people out. Apparently the emphasis is psychological — Moses led them out and he has to continue leading them. He is reassured that Yahweh's messenger will go with him, and then he is instructed to go up to "a land flowing with milk and honey" (3a).

The positive, encouraging approach of Yahweh shifts suddenly to a negative outlook, and so some scholars consider 3b-6 as another tradition. Beyerlin assigns the section to E in contrast to J in 1-3a. Noth senses a break between the two parts, but he is inclined to assign 1-6 to the D tradition. In any case, Moses gets the message for the people: "You are a stiff-necked people. If for a single moment I should go up with you I would consume you. So take off your ornaments that I may know what to do with you" (5). The people mourn when they hear the news, and the narrative comments, "Therefore the people of Israel stripped themselves of their ornaments from Mt. Horeb on." By putting aside their ornaments the people show their penitence. Now Yahweh can do something with them, but he does not indicate what that might be. "Ornaments" in Hebrew is a general term including anything worn as adornment. This would include gold earrings of the people (both male and female); thus this would be further evidence that probably a collection of gold was not taken to make the calf.

The section about the "tent of meeting" (7-11), discussed earlier, is assigned to E by Beyerlin, D by Noth, and J by Newman. The theme of Yahweh's presence is clearly indicated, but precisely why the unit was inserted is a question.

Noth thinks the passage was included to show where Yahweh would inform Moses what he intended to do with the people. Beyerlin recognizes that the tent-sanctuary fits the desert context where men live in tents, but he is not sure how or why 7-11 was attached to 1-6. Newman attributes the unit to J because for him the tent of meeting was the dominant shrine in the J tradition. Noth's argument makes as much sense as any, but whoever added or inserted 7-11 was very successful in hiding his intent.

Whereas 7-11 is an enigma, most critics are agreed that 12-23 is J and that it continues the conversation between Yahweh and Moses. The latter replies, "Now you say to me, 'Bring up this people,' but you have not let me know whom you will send with me." This seems to throw doubt on the passages referring to the messenger (32:34; 33:2), but perhaps Moses is asking for the identity of the messenger. Here the issue is not so much the presence of Yahweh as it is the necessity of a human guide who knows the wilderness through which the people must go. The request seems to be related to Moses' insistence that Hobab go with the Israelites: "Do not leave us, I beg you, for you know where we ought to camp in the wilderness, and you will be our guide" (Num. 10:31).

In 12b-17, however, the concern is whether Yahweh will leave Sinai and accompany Moses and his people. Moses reminds Yahweh of his expressions of pleasure concerning his servant, and then he asks, "If I have found favor in your sight, show me your ways." This is bold language, but Moses is desperate and he must know what Yahweh really intends to do. He does not let Yahweh forget that the Israelites are his people too. This statement brings the assurance, "My presence (literally, face) will go with you, and I will give you rest" (14). Here "face" seems to be a reference to Yahweh's *anan*. Moses is still uneasy, nevertheless, and so he insists, "If your presence does not go, do not send us up from here." Finally Moses contends that any talk about favor for his distinct people is meaningless unless Yahweh actually accompanies them through the wilderness. Yahweh agrees: "This request you have made I will do because you have found favor in my sight, and I know you by name" (17).

The Special Theophany to Moses

The section 33:18-23 opens with Moses' ultimate request: "Show me your glory." This is even more audacious than asking to know Yahweh's plans. Furthermore, it does not seem to flow out of Yahweh's promise to accompany Moses and the people. Its position is evidently not determined by what proceeds but by what follows, because all the verbs are in the future tense. In other words, the section was inserted as anticipatory to Yahweh's special appearance to Moses on Sinai, and thus its relation to what precedes is accidental. There is good evidence, moreover, that the section is a compilation. Yahweh's answer to Moses is found in verses 19-23, and on the basis of many long quotations in the Old Testament one would expect the whole answer as a single quotation. But the appearance of "He said" in verse 20 and "Yahweh said" in verse 21 indicates that three separate statements of tradition have been joined together.

Yahweh promises to make his "goodness" pass by Moses and to make known his name "Yahweh." The latter was done previously near the burning bush at the foot of the mountain, but the new experience is to be a renewal of that awesome revelation. It is hard to see what "goodness" could mean other than "character," and so the two features seem to represent the visual and auditory aspects of Yahweh's revelation. Although he is granting Moses' request, he still wants him mindful of his sovereignty, and so he comments, "I will be gracious to whom I will be gracious, and I will have compassion on whom I will have compassion." There are limits to the visual revelation, however, because no man can look into God's face and live (33:20). In this instance "face" refers to the actual presence of Yahweh, not his mask *(anan)*. Moses will be on a rock near Yahweh's presence on the mountaintop, but Yahweh will have to protect him in the cleft of the rock while his glory passes by. When it has gone on, then Moses may view the back of Yahweh's glory. The experience of Elijah on Mt. Horeb has many similarities (1 Kings 19:8-18). Many scholars think that the Exodus account was influenced by the Elijah story. This may well have happened in some minor details, but the basic account about Moses was a well-known tradition and Elijah, like Moses, was seeking special reassurance to carry him over his period of depression and doubt.

Following his promise to accompany the people to Canaan, Yahweh instructs Moses, "Cut two stone tablets like the first, and I will write on the tablets the words which were on the first tablets, which you shattered" (34:1). Moses does so, and the next morning, following further instructions, he presents himself with the tablets at the top of the mountain. Yahweh descends in the cloud and takes his place beside Moses. Then he passes by Moses and exclaims, "Yahweh, Yahweh, a God compassionate and gracious, slow to anger, and abounding in steadfast love and faithfulness" (6). Verse 7 notes that Yahweh's covenant love will forgive all forms of sin, but that the results of the guilt will continue on to the third and fourth generations. The content of Yahweh's revelation of himself is found in a number of other contexts, so evidently it became a creedal statement which started with worship services at Sinai and continued thereafter.

It is apparently after Yahweh's declaration of his character that Moses sees the back of his glory, for he quickly bows his head to the ground and worships (8). The mention of Yahweh's steadfast (covenant) love brings to mind the people's guilty condition, and so Moses pleads, "If I have found favor in your sight, O Lord, let the Lord, I beg you, go in our midst. Although it is a stiff-necked people, pardon our iniquity and our sin, and take us for your inheritance" (9).

The Covenant in J

After hearing Moses' intercessory prayer, Yahweh declares, "Behold, I make a covenant." Then Moses is informed that marvelous things will be done with him in the presence of the people (10b). There is no hint as to when or where these events will take place. Normally, a historical survey of God's gracious deeds would appear at this point in the covenant proceedings, but in this case the covenant is primarily with Moses, and so the assurance of special help in the future is apparently more suitable as the basis for the covenant vow than a recital of past acts. Yahweh declares, "Observe what I command you this day" (11a), and then appears (with later comments) the list of cultic commands discussed earlier in this chapter.

After the stipulations, Yahweh instructs Moses, "Write

these words, for I have made a covenant with you and with Israel on the basis of these words" (27). Many scholars consider the comment "and with Israel" an editorial insertion. Be that as it may, the idea is clearly implied. Moses has interceded a number of times for the sinful people under his care, and he acts in their behalf. He has rejected Yahweh's offer to make a new covenant solely with himself and his descendants; therefore Moses understands that when the covenant is made with him he is the mediator of this renewed covenant.

A further question concerning the J tradition is whether or not the people had any part in sealing the covenant agreement. The story about Moses, Aaron, Nadab, Abihu, and the seventy elders going up the mountain and having a meal in God's presence (Exod. 24:1-2, 9-11) has been assigned to J by most critics. The oddity is that the name *Yahweh* appears in 1-2, but *Elohim* in 9-11. Both passages seem to refer to the same event, and the difference in the designation of God appears to be accidental. In any case, Beyerlin attributes both passages to E. Yet it seems very strange to have a covenant meal involving the leaders right after they and the people have sealed the covenant during the ceremony at the base of the mountain (3-8). On the other hand, the story of the meal does make a fitting conclusion to the J account because the leaders, representing segments from the entire camp, confirm the covenant which Moses has accepted in their behalf. The difficulty with this theory is trying to explain how the two pieces of the J tradition came to be where they are. No convincing explanation has been given, and so the suggestion must remain in the area of conjecture.

Covenant or Renewal

The discussion has gone full-circle, and now it is time to try putting the pieces together. Most critical scholars deny the historicity of the calf apostasy (at Sinai or elsewhere) in the desert wanderings of the Israelites. Since they recognize that Exodus 34 is the J account of the covenant, they think that the original form of 34:1 ended with the command, "Cut two stone tablets." The rest of the verse is deleted as the addition of the editor, who inserted the story about the calf and the broken tablets (Exod. 32). But the

sword of criticism is double-edged, and often the argument
can be reversed with equal effectiveness. It is the conviction of this writer that there was an actual apostasy at
Sinai involving the image of a young bull carved from limestone. The tradition that it was made from gold earrings
developed later and was incorporated into the story. Since
the tablets were intended as the official copy of the covenant stipulations, it was necessary to have them repro-
duced. In a real sense, then the covenant of Exodus 34 is
a renewal of the broken relationship and the shattered
tablets.

The Origin of the Commands in J

As noted earlier, the reference to "ten words" (34:28)
does not apply to the present list; therefore it is very likely
an authentic reference to the commands on the second set
of stone tablets, namely, the Decalogue found in Exodus 20.
The D tradition understood that Moses put the tablets in
the ark, the chest made of acacia wood (Deut. 10:5). The
P tradition does not mention the tablets explicitly, but they
are implied when Moses is told to put "the pact *(eduth)*"
into the ark (Exod. 25:16). There is no reason whatsoever
to doubt the tradition, because the only practical way to
care for the covenant stipulations would be to keep them
in a portable chest. Until its capture by the Philistines, the
ark remained in the area of the northern tribes; and so
both of the northern traditions, E and D, preserved scroll
copies of the ten commandments.

The original text of Exodus 34 had a similar list, but it
is very difficult to explain when and why the ethical Decalogue was replaced by the present cultic set of instructions.
Even granting the possibility that the religious leaders in
Judah lost their copy during the period of the Judges, they
had recourse to the other copies. Moreover, there is a specific statement in 1 Kings 8:9 that when Solomon had the
ark put into the most holy place of the temple, "there was
nothing in the ark except the two tablets of stone which
Moses put there at Horeb." It is granted that the death of
Uzzah (2 Sam. 6:7) gave rise to a theory of taboo concerning the ark, but the implication of 1 Kings 8:9 is that later
on the priests did inspect it. Thus the J tradition had access
to the wording of the ten commandments either from the

copies up north or the tablets in the temple. This is further evidence that the original compilation of J in Exodus 34 had the list of the Decalogue. In other words, the present list of cultic commands was an intentional replacement, not the attempt to compensate for the loss of the original list. The shift, therefore, must have occurred after the time of David and Solomon, when the J tradition was systematically compiled.

Why the substitution was made can only be a conjecture. It probably came at a time when the whole structure of ritual and practice was in danger. Some group with cultic concerns felt that the religious life of the people was doomed without a recovery of the experience of Yahweh's presence in corporate worship and everyday living. Pertinent regulations were selected from the old lists in Exodus 13, 20, and 23, and then given ultimate authority by being placed in the context of the covenant in Exodus 34. There were a number of periods of spiritual decline in the southern kingdom, but the most likely time for such an emphasis was the dark age of Manasseh's long reign. He sponsored the cult of his Assyrian overlords and reinstated the Canaanite worship of Baal and Asherah (2 Kings 21:3-6). More than that, he took the lives of those who opposed his pagan practices (21:16).

The Scroll and the Tablets

Another question needing clarification is the relationship between the Book of the Covenant and the stone tablets. As shown earlier, the Book of the Covenant was a scroll on which Moses wrote the Decalogue. The people had heard the words thundered forth by Yahweh, but their terror probably kept them from understanding the content. Accordingly, Moses was instructed to write the stipulations. Then they were read to the people before sealing the covenant with an oath of obedience. On the other hand, stone tablets were involved in the covenant in Exodus 34. Did the E tradition know about the stone tablets? If 24:12-15a, 31:18, and chapters 32-33 are assigned to J, as Noth does, then all references to the tablets come from the J strand. Yet this is hardly conceivable because the ark and the tablets remained in the north so long. Furthermore, the D tradition claimed that the tablets were in the ark. The fact that Joshua, a northerner from the tribe of Ephraim, is mentioned in 24:13 and 32:17 is very convincing additional evidence that the sections 24:12-15a and 32:15-20 stem from the E tradition, as Beyerlin and the older critics claim.

In 24:12 Moses is instructed to come up on the mountain and wait for "the tablets of stone and the law and the commandment." The words "and the law and the commandment" are very awkward. It sounds like three different documents are being given Moses, but actually the clumsy expression is an editorial comment intended to clarify for the reader what was inscribed on the tablets. Even so, it is not exactly clear what the editor meant by the terms. In D "the commandment" means the explanation of the first commandment. If that is what is meant here, then the editor claims that the Decalogue and the interpretation of the first command were inscribed on the tablets. What is certain, nevertheless, is that the stone tablets play a part in the E tradition. Thus the E strand has two sets of covenant stipulations, and no attempt is made to explain why both were necessary. The scroll copy served its purpose for the covenant ceremony, but in time the leather (or papyrus) would disintegrate. Yahweh's covenant was intended to be a permanent relationship, and so it was felt that the official copy, which was to be deposited in the presence of Yahweh, ought to be inscribed on stone. The covenant meal may have been the leaders' recognition of the stone tablets as the official copy of the covenant agreement.

The Inscribing of the Tablets

The special nature of the tablets may have given rise to the idea (basically E and D) that God had inscribed the tablets with his own finger (Exod. 24:12; 31:18; 32:16; 34:1; Deut. 5:22; 10:4). In 34:28, however, the antecedent of "he" is Moses, and so the basic claim in J is that Moses prepared the stone tablets and inscribed the ten commandments on them. This is undoubtedly what happened, and yet it is possible to see how Moses could have felt that Yahweh was guiding his hand as he selected and formulated the commandments out of his knowledge and experience. The E tradition claims (32:15) that the tablets were inscribed on both sides, and this could well have been the case. There is certainly nothing in the narratives to contradict this conclusion. Moreover, since the usual custom was to inscribe a stele (upright stone pillar) on one side only, inscription on both sides would mark it as an extraordinary text.

The Stay on Mt. Sinai

According to Exodus 24:18b, Moses was on the mountain "forty days and forty nights." Older critics assigned this information to the E tradition, but it seems to be part of the P strand. In either case, it applies to the first extended stay on the mountain. J makes the same claim for the second stay (34:28). Forty need not be taken too literally since it was considered a round number meaning a long time. J has the additional comment, "He neither ate bread nor drank water." Fasting for forty days is quite possible, but not without water. The people assumed that there was no water on the mountain and that Moses had not had a drink during his absence. Yet even today there is some water in the traditional valley of Elijah on the northern slope of Jebel Musa.

The P Version of the Covenant

Thus far the contributions of the E, D, and J traditions have been noted, but a more complete consideration of the P strand is necessary to gain an overall understanding of the stay at Mt. Sinai. After noting that the people of Israel arrived at the wilderness of Sinai (Exod. 19:1-2a), the P tradition seems to continue at 24:15b. The glory of Yahweh, which appears to the people like a devouring fire, settles on Mt. Sinai. At the same time, however, a cloud covers the mountain for six days. On the seventh day Yahweh calls to Moses, and he responds by ascending the mountain and entering the cloud. There he is given the detailed instructions for taking an offering and for constructing the tabernacle with all of its equipment. This extensive unit (25:1-31:17) is followed by the statement, "And he (Yahweh) gave to Moses, when he had finished speaking with him on Mt. Sinai, the two tablets of the pact *(eduth)*, tablets of stone, written with the finger of God."

But a literal interpretation of the text causes great difficulty. The clear implication is that the instructions for building the tabernacle were inscribed on stone tablets by God, and then given to Moses as the basis of a covenant *(eduth)*. But the length, form, and content of the passage have no relationship to any of the characteristics of a covenant. It is evident that the P tradition inserted 24:15b-31:17 on the conviction that Yahweh had given the instructions for the tabernacle. In order to gain unquestioned authority for the sanctuary and its cult it was necessary to identify the tabernacle instructions with the tablets of the covenant. The P editor made this identity complete by inserting "of the pact" (one word in Hebrew) into the text of 31:18.

Priestly Instructions

Following the prefatory command about an offering and the materials to be collected (25:2-9), the instructions begin with the most sacred and central piece of equipment: the ark and its related features, the cover (or, mercy seat) and two cherubim (25:10-22). In this connection two functional features are noted: "The (tablets of the) pact" are to be stored in the ark (16, 21); and Yahweh will meet Moses at the ark and speak with him from between the cherubim (22). The instructions move outward to the table for the bread of the Presence (23-30) and the lampstand (31-40). The pattern for the tabernacle is given in chapter 26, and the altar and court in chapter 27. The priestly garments are discussed in chapter 28, and the ordination services for Aaron and his sons in chapter 29.

After the introductory statement "Yahweh said to Moses" (25:1), the five chapters 25-29 appear as a single quotation, thus indicating that they are a unit of composition. Chapters 30-31, however, are a miscellaneous collection of priestly items. The instructions about the altar of incense (30:1-10) are out of place, because they should be at the end of chapter 25, after the instructions for the lampstand. The proof that chapters 30 and 31 are a collection is that the remaining six sections of miscellaneous material begin with the statement "Yahweh said to Moses": census and the half-shekel tax (30:11-16); bronze laver (17-21) has no details or measurements, and it should appear after 27:8; sacred anointing oil (22-33); incense (34-38); Bezalel and Oholiab (31:1-11); and the sabbath (12-

17). The purpose of the last section is to show God's concern for keeping the seventh day holy. Even work on the sacred house of God will be punished by death.

The P version continues at 34:29. Moses descends the mountain with the two tablets of the pact, but he does not realize that his face has taken on a radiant glow due to his conversation with God. Aaron and the people are afraid to approach him, and so Moses has to call to them. They return and he reports to them the commands which Yahweh has given. From that time on Moses wears a veil when he is around the people, but when he goes in to speak with Yahweh he removes it.

In 35:1 Moses assembles the people and commands them, "These are the things which Yahweh has commanded you to do." Then follows a long section (35:2-40:38) explaining how the previous instructions to Moses were carried out. Much of the material in 35-40 is identical with 25-31, except that the future tenses of the instructions are changed to the past tense in the report. In some respects the order is inverted. The warning about the sabbath appears first (35:2-3). After the offerings are received (4-29), the craftsmen Bezalel and Oholiab appear on the scene (35:30-36:7). Construction begins with the prefabrication of the tabernacle (36:8-38), and then the pieces of equipment and the court units are made (37:1-38:20). A summary of the gold, silver, and bronze used (38:21-31) is followed by the fashioning of the priestly paraphernalia and garments (39:1-31). All the components and pieces of equipment are presented to Moses (39:32-43), and then the tabernacle is erected (40:1-33). The date given is the first day of the first month of the second year (40:17); and since the Israelites came to Sinai on the first day of the fourth month of the previous year, the tabernacle was erected nine months after their arrival.

When Moses finishes outfitting the tabernacle and the court, the cloud of Yahweh's glory fills the tabernacle. The experience is so awesome Moses dares not enter (34-35). Mention of the cloud evokes a look into the future when the cloud by day and the fire by night will guide the Israelites and determine when they depart on the various stages of their journey (36-38). There is an indication that chapters 35-40 are a later grouping of priestly materials than 25-31 because some of the items which are out of place in the instructions (incense altar and bronze laver) are incorporated in the proper order in the report.

The Claims of the P Tradition

Just as the insertion of 25-31 gives the impression that the instructions for the tabernacle were on the first set of tablets, the placement of 35-40 right after Moses' descent implies that the second set of tablets contained Yahweh's commands to build and erect the tabernacle. But some of the instructions (for example, the ordination of Aaron and his sons) and related matters are not mentioned in 35-40; therefore the account of the establishment of sacrificial ritual and everyday practices is carried on throughout the book of Leviticus and the first ten chapters of Numbers.

The new element is the claim that Yahweh's additional instructions were given to Moses at the tent of meeting (Lev. 1:1). There is some substance in P's belief that the previous instructions were given to Moses on the mountain. During the period of formulating the ten commandments and meditating about the implementation of the covenant, it was inevitable that Moses should be concerned about the functional elements. It would be necessary to hold meetings for instruction and discussion of camp affairs, and so some kind of assembly place was necessary. In the desert, a large tent would be the most practical, and the most natural designation would be "the tent of meeting (assembly)." There would be need for a receptacle for the stone tablets, and there, with the covenant stipulations, would be the most natural place for the invisible God to manifest his presence and to give further instruction.

Certainly Moses anticipated breaches of the covenant, and so he must have wrestled with the problem of atonement. For him this would involve animal sacrifices, which in turn would mean a priesthood and the means for performing the ritual. There would be times of worship recalling the great mercies of Yahweh and praising him in song and words. In short, he must have contemplated the rudiments for the proper functioning of the covenant community. To this extent the P tradition is correct, but it goes too far in claiming that detailed instructions were given to Moses on the mountain and inscribed on the tablets. Elaboration and ex-

pansion of the initial instructions and regulations probably
came when Moses went to the tent of meeting to contem-
plate new situations and problems. In this respect also, the
P tradition is correct, but again it claims too much when it
implies that all the instructions and regulations in Leviticus
and Numbers came to Moses at Sinai.

The Book of Leviticus

Chapters 1-7 deal with the various kinds of sacrifices and
offerings (burnt, cereal, peace, sin, and guilt). Chapters
8-9 describe the ordination of Aaron and his sons according
to the instructions in Exodus 29. In 10:1-7 Yahweh slays
Nadab and Abihu, Aaron's eldest sons, because they offer
improper incense (Exod. 30:34-38). This story explains
why the priestly line of succession continues through Eleazar and Ithamar, the third and fourth sons. Moses becomes
angry with the latter when they do not eat their portion of
the sin offering at their first performance as priests (10:16-
20), but they do not die.

Laws distinguishing ceremonially clean and unclean animals and people occur in chapters 11-15. Included are the
regulations concerning "leprosy," which were noted in connection with the signs given to Moses at the burning bush.
Yom Kippur ("Day of Atonement") is discussed in chapter
16. Because of the transgressions of the people, atonement
is made annually for everyone (including Moses, Aaron,
and the priests), and even for the holy place, the tent of
meeting, and the altar. Chapters 17-26 represent another
collection of instructions governing everyday actions of the
covenant people. The major theme occurs in 19:2, "You
shall be holy for I, Yahweh, your God, am holy." Because
of this motif scholars have designated the section "The
Holiness Code." The collection appears at a most fitting
place: immediately following the atonement and the new
start on life. Although there are many regulations which
have ceased to have relevance, the presuppositions of the
covenant resulted in direct (apodictic) commands of eternal value; for example, "You shall not hate your brother in
your heart, but you shall reason with your neighbor, lest
you share in his guilt. You shall not take vengeance or bear
any grudge against the sons of your own people, but you
shall love your neighbor as yourself. I am Yahweh" (19:17-

18). Jesus linked this passage with D's interpretation of the first command (Deut. 6:5) as expressing the essence of all of God's instructions, but he went a step further and extended the word "neighbor" to include all people with whom one comes in contact, not just one's inner circle of relatives and associates.

Leviticus closes with a collection of regulations concerning vows and tithes (chap. 27). At the end the editor comments, "These are the commandments which Yahweh gave Moses for the Israelites at Mt. Sinai." The Revised Standard Version, the New Jewish Version, and the New English Bible translate "on Mt. Sinai." The Hebrew preposition can have either meaning in this context, but if the editor intended "on," then the comment is at variance with Leviticus 1:1.

The P Tradition in the Book of Numbers

Numbers opens with further instruction from Yahweh in the tent of meeting. On the first day of the second month, that is, just a month after the erection of the tabernacle, Moses is told to take a census. This he does, and the final count, according to the usual interpretation of the passage, comes to 603,550. A better understanding of the census report, as discussed earlier, indicates 598 clans with a total of 5,550 men of fighting age. Allowing for the old men, women, teen-agers, children, and the tribe of Levi, a total of about 16,000 would be fairly accurate.

The Levites have been excluded from the census because they are to be the custodians and guards of the tabernacle. As such they are to camp around it in the center of the community. During any movement of camp they are to take down the tabernacle, transport it, and then set it up again (1:47-54). Chapter 2 outlines the camp arrangement and the order of march. On the east, the favorite side, are Judah, Issachar, and Zebulun, and they are to be the first company out on the march (3-9). Reuben, Simeon, and Gad camp on the south, and they are the second group on the march (10-16). The Levites and the tabernacle, in the center of the camp, leave as the third company (17). On the west side are Ephraim, Manasseh, and Benjamin, and they follow the Levites during the march (18-24). Dan, Asher, and Naphtali, on the north, bring up the rear of the procession (25-31).

Aaron and his sons Eleazar and Ithamar are from the tribe of Levi, but since they have the special function of performing the sacrificial ritual, they are distinguished from the other Levites, who are to assist the priests in their duties and to care for the furnishings of the tabernacle (3:1-10). There is no reference to the self-ordination of the Levites by their zeal for Yahweh (Exod. 32:25-29). In fact, no reason is given for the choice of the Levites, but their special status is explained as Yahweh's exchange of the Levites for the firstborn males (3:12). Instead of the first son being devoted at the age of one month to lifelong religious service, a Levite will take his place, and so the family of the ransomed son has the responsibility of providing the means of support for the Levite.

The one-for-one exchange necessitates one census for the Levites (3:15-39) and another for the firstborn males (40-43), both ranging from a month old upward. The Levitical census is tabulated according to the three major groupings:

Gershon	7 clans with	500, or	7,500
Kohath	8 clans with	600, or	8,600
Merari	6 clans with	200, or	6,200

Total Levites	21 clans with	1,300, or	22,300

The 1,300 total, obtained by reinterpreting the numbers, seems more in line with the facts. The firstborn males are not listed by tribe, but a total of 22,273 is given. Oddly enough, the total for the Levites is given as 22,000 (3:39), even though the group figures total 22,300. Inasmuch as the accepted totals indicated an excess of 273 firstborn males over the male Levites, they had to be redeemed. At five shekels each, this meant 1,365 shekels for Aaron and his sons (3:44-51). In connection with the census report is the notation of their location in the camp: Kohath is to be on the south side of the tabernacle; Gershon on the west, behind the tabernacle; and Merari on the north. Moses, Aaron, and his sons are to camp on the east, the prime place in front of the tabernacle, because they have charge of the rites carried on in the sanctuary.

Another Levitical census occurs in chapter 4, but this

one is to determine how many are thirty to fifty years of age, and thus eligible for duty at the tabernacle. The total is 8,580, and the group tabulations reinterpret to 1,580, but this is more than the total number of Levites in the previous census. There seems to be no satisfactory answer to these figures.

The duties of the three Levitical groups are interspersed within the census reports in chapters 3-4. Since the Kohathites are in charge of the most holy objects (ark, table, lampstand, altars, sacred vessels, and veil of the screen), they are listed first. Actually, however, the priests must take down and wrap the holy objects. Only then may the Kohathites enter the sanctuary and carry them out. They are warned not to touch or take a look because they will die. The Gershonites are responsible for the tent covering, the court curtains, and the screens at the entrance of the court and the tabernacle. The Merarites have custody over the tabernacle framework and the supports for the court. Thus each group specialized and developed as a separate craft union.

Various laws concerning a woman suspected of adultery comprise chapter 5, and the laws for the Nazirite, one who vows to separate himself wholly to Yahweh, occur in chapter 6. At the close of the collection in 5-6 appears the famous priestly benediction, "May Yahweh bless you and keep you. . . ."

A new section of P begins with chapter 7. Here the story reverts back to the day Moses erected the tabernacle. The leaders of the twelve tribes bring their offerings to Yahweh: a covered wagon for each two tribes and an ox for each tribe. Yahweh instructs Moses to accept them and to give them to the Levites for transporting the tent of meeting. The Gershonites receive two wagons and four oxen to pull them, while the Merarites get four wagons and eight oxen. The Kohathites get no wagons because they must carry the holy objects on their shoulders. Then after the dedication of the altar the leaders, one a day, bring their offerings of silver and gold dishes, and various sacrificial animals (10-88). The chapter closes with the remark that when Moses entered the tent of meeting Yahweh spoke to him for the first time from the cherubim over the ark (89).

After a statement designating the priests to light the lamps (8:1-4), the consecration of the Levites is described (5-22). The unit 23-26 seems to be a later ruling because the eligible age for service of the Levites is 25-50 instead of 30-50 as in 4:3. The section 9:1-14 is a collection of regulations concerning passover. Inasmuch as the first anniversary of passover was to be celebrated on the fourteenth of Nisan, the supplemental laws are dated on the first of Nisan, the day the tabernacle was erected. In anticipation of the departure from Sinai the unit 15-23 picks up the theme of Exodus 40:36-38 about the fiery cloud and discusses it in great detail.

In 10:1-10 Moses is commanded to make two silver trumpets, and instructions for their use is given. The priests are to blow them, and if both are used, all the people are to assemble at the tent of meeting. But if only one is blown, then only the leaders are to respond. The trumpets can be blown in another way (which is not explained) to sound an alarm. At the first alarm the camps on the east side are to set out first, and at the second those on the south. The other groupings are not mentioned, but the regular order of march is implied. The trumpets are to be used for war, but also for the glad days of the festivals.

At long last the cloud is taken up and the Israelites "set out by stages from the wilderness of Sinai" (10:11-12). The date is the twentieth of the second month: nineteen days after the census, and ten months and nineteen days after arriving at Sinai. After jumping ahead to note that the cloud settled in the wilderness of Paran, the lengthy collection of P material closes with a description of the departure (13-28). The order is that prescribed in chapter 2, with one very interesting exception. Instead of all the Levites marching in the center of the procession, the Gershonites and the Merarites, carrying the units of the tabernacle and court on their wagons, leave after the first group has set out. Then in the middle, following the southern camps, come the Kohathites carrying the holy things on their shoulders. This variation in order certainly represents a different time or journey than that of chapter 2. The rationale of the change seems to be that the tabernacle would be erected when the Kohathites arrived so that they could put the objects in place immediately.

The Authenticity of the P Tradition

Notwithstanding P's voluminous records and apparent concern for detail, there are some genuine difficulties in the material. Attention has already been drawn to erroneous claims and variations within the text, but the wealth and skill needed to build the tabernacle are fantastic for a struggling desert community. It is claimed that a talent of silver (about seventy-five pounds) was used for each of the hundred bases for the tabernacle frames (Exod. 38:27). The editor is ingenious with figures. By exacting a half-shekel of silver from each of the 603,550 Israelites (who are not counted until Num. 1) the silver collection comes to 301,775 shekels. Since 3,000 sanctuary shekels make a talent, the silver offering comes to 100 talents and 1,775 shekels. The talents were used for the bases and the remaining shekels for hooks. A talent of gold would be worth $42,000 today (about 1,200 ounces at thirty-five dollars an ounce), and yet P reports the gold offering as 29 talents and 730 shekels. The collection of bronze comes to 75 talents and 2,400 shekels. To top it off, over 5,500 square feet of material, some beautifully embroidered, are necessary for the various curtains. The craftsmen needed to carry out this project pose another problem. Most of the Israelites had been slaves and their skill was making bricks.

Difficulties such as these drove early critical scholarship to deny the historicity of the P tradition. The tabernacle was interpreted to be a dream in the minds of some priests during the Babylonian exile. But here again the truth is between the extremes of those who take the whole account literally and those who deny practically all of it. The frequent references to acacia wood, which grows in the desert, fit the Mosaic period and not later, when olive and cedar are used. The *qubbah,* an ancient portable tent made of red leather, suggests that the tabernacle covering of tanned rams' skins (probably dyed red) stems from a desert tradition as well.

Just as significant is *mishkan,* the specific designation used by the P tradition for the tabernacle. It derives from the verb *shakan,* meaning originally "to tent." The term, therefore, embodies the idea of a place where deity "tents" with his people. Moses had been confronted by Yahweh and

had experienced the immanence of Israel's God; therefore
the most likely origin for the idea implied in *mishkan* was
Moses himself. Perhaps he coined the term and then the
P tradition carried it on.

The overall structure of the priestly tabernacle involves
a court for the assembly of the people, a holy place for the
priests, and a most holy place, which only the chief priest
could enter. Critics used to consider the theology back of
this layout as a very late development. But the experience
of the people at Sinai would lead to this triple approach to
God. The people observed from the foot of the mountain,
the elders and priests ate the meal on the slopes, but only
Moses went to the top and communed with Yahweh. There
is good reason, therefore, for believing that Moses and
Aaron originated a sanctuary complex with degrees of approach to God.

Earlier critics thought that some of the names in P's lists
were artificial, and thus late. The reverse has proven true.
In Numbers 1:5-15 the leaders of the twelve tribes are
listed by name along with the name of the ancestor (father
or grandfather). Three examples are interesting: 1:5, Elizur the son (descendant) of Shedeur; 1:6, Shelumiel the
son of Zurishaddai; 1:12, Ahiezer the son of Ammishaddai.
The names of the tribal leaders involve the elements *El*
("God") and *Ah* ("brother"), whereas their ancestors have
names with *shaddai*, the old name for God. Names with this
element do not appear elsewhere in the Old Testament, but
the name *Shaddaiammi* ("Shaddai is my kinsman") has
been found in a fourteenth- or thirteenth-century Egyptian
inscription. Accordingly, the inverted form (Ammishaddai) in 1:12 must be ancient as well. Names with *zur*
("rock") stem from this period also: Elizur ("God is my
rock"), and Zurishaddai ("Shaddai is my rock").

Much more evidence could be given, but the foregoing
lines of reasoning are enough to show that the roots of the
P tradition go back to Sinai and Moses himself. The detailed camp assignments may be a precision developed over
the years, but certainly there must have been some people
assigned to guard and care for the tabernacle, regardless
of how simple it was. It must have been equally necessary
to provide for transporting the sanctuary and guarding it
en route. When the items of the P tradition are considered

without the frills and expansions of later times, it becomes evident that the rudiments of Israel's cultic institutions (sanctuary, priesthood, and ritual) were formulated at Sinai. The mediating point of view is well expressed by Frank M. Cross, Jr.: "While the Priestly account is schematized and idealized, and while the Priestly writers read the theological interpretations and historical developments of later ages into their system, nevertheless, Priestly tradition must be deemed an important historical witness to the Mosaic Age."[6]

The Tent of Meeting and the Tabernacle

One problem which does require some clarification is the relationship between the old tent of meeting and the tabernacle described in P. In addition to *mishkan*, P refers to the Israelite sanctuary as "the tent of meeting," just as E and J do. In the priestly tradition, therefore, the tabernacle and tent of meeting are equated. Outside of P there are only four early incidents about the tent of meeting: the people and Moses seek instruction from Yahweh (Exod. 33:7-11); the seventy elders receive some of Moses' spirit (Num. 11:16-30); Moses is vindicated in the presence of Aaron and Miriam (Num. 12:1-8); and Moses commissions Joshua (Deut. 31:14-15). A number of features are common to all the references: Yahweh descends or appears in a (pillar of) cloud which hovers at the entrance to the tent; the tent is a place of revelation because Yahweh expresses his will; and there is no explicit reference to the ark being in the tent.

The Exodus 33 passage appears first in the narrative, and it seems to represent the oldest tradition about the tent: "Now Moses used to take the tent and pitch it outside the camp, far off from the camp, and he called it the tent of meeting" (7). The Hebrew verbs indicate that this was Moses' customary action, but when did he start the practice of pitching "the" tent outside the camp? Was it prior or subsequent to the covenant? After noting that anyone who wanted to seek Yahweh would go out to the tent, the rest of the passage speaks only of Moses' use of it. Perhaps Moses set it up for general use, but after the covenant he

---

[6] Frank M. Cross, Jr., "The Priestly Tabernacle," *The Biblical Archaeologist Reader, 1,* p. 209.

had much more reason to seek Yahweh's aid in interpreting the covenant regulations. Scholars cannot agree why Moses put the tent outside the camp. If fear of Yahweh's glory were the reason, who would have dared go out to seek him? It is easy to understand why Moses would want to remove the tent after the desecration of the camp by such sins as the calf worship, but this does not explain Moses' habitual practice. No convincing reason is possible because the evidence is so meager.

According to the biblical editors, the first three passages about the tent describe incidents prior to Israel's arrival at Qadesh-barnea, and there is no good reason to doubt their judgment. In each of them the use of the verb "to go out" clearly indicates that the tent was outside the camp. In Deuteronomy 31:14, however, the simple verb "to go" is employed, and the implication is that the tent is in the camp. It could well be that at the early stages of Israel's experience the tent was pitched outside the camp, but that during the long stay at Qadesh-barnea it was brought inside and a new camp arrangement set up. In short, the three early references to the tent are by no means proof that the tent was outside the camp throughout all of Israel's desert experience. It is not valid, therefore, to consider the tent of meeting and the tabernacle as absolute contradictions. Since, as has been noted, the description of the tabernacle involves later developments, the tent of meeting could well represent the early phase of the tabernacle.

The Tent of Meeting and the Ark

Numbers 10:33-36 (mixed JE) mentions that "the ark of the covenant of Yahweh" went before the Israelites when they left Sinai, and so this passage agrees with the P tradition that the ark was constructed at the camp before leaving Sinai. The various traditions agree, therefore, that both the tent of meeting and the ark originated with Moses at Sinai. The P tradition goes further, however, by claiming that Moses "brought the ark into the tabernacle" (Exod. 40:21). Some more recent critics have taken exception to this statement. The late Gerhard von Rad (1901-1971), the foremost exponent of this dissenting opinion, declares, "Tent and Ark were two cult objects existing independently of each other in the earlier period as the cultic foci of two completely distinct groups."[7] The tent, according to von Rad, represents a theology of manifestation in which Israel's transcendent God abides in heaven, but on occasions of his choosing he comes down in the form of a cloud and makes his appearance at the entrance to the tent. The ark, on the other hand, is the theology of God's immanence. Since his dwelling is over the ark, his presence among the people hinges on their possession and care of it.

The date of the merging of these two "heterogeneous streams of tradition" can no longer be determined, in von Rad's opinion, but he concludes, "All that can be said is that there can hardly have been any actual cultic event corresponding to this union; it is rather the result of a theoretic recasting of the old traditions by the priests."[8] But von Rad hinges his either-or in a cultic event. The prior question is whether the experience of the people demands this kind of polarization. Undoubtedly the prior tradition was one of manifestation because Yahweh made his appearance at Sinai in the form of a cloud which settled down on the peak. The same was true in the early stages of the tent of meeting, but gradually the idea of immanence was associated with the tent.

A key statement is Exodus 33:11b: "When Moses would return to the camp, his attendant Joshua, the son of Nun, a youth, would not leave the tent." Whether one holds that the references to Joshua are later additions or not, they do witness to a tradition that he was a trusted assistant of Moses. In this instance Joshua is on constant vigil, but what is he guarding? When the ark was at Bethel, Phinehas, the grandson of Aaron, served (literally, stood before) it, and implicitly he watched over it (Judg. 20:27). At Shiloh the boy Samuel was the attendant keeping vigil over the ark (1 Sam. 3:3). Although Beyerlin doubts that Joshua was actually at Sinai, on the basis of these passages and Joshua's connection with the ark he is convinced that tradition understood the ark to be in the tent of meeting.[9] But as stated earlier, Moses must have had someone in

---

[7] Gerhard von Rad, *Old Testament Theology* (New York: Harper, n.d.), I, 235.

[8] *Ibid.*, p. 238.

[9] Beyerlin, *op. cit.*, p. 120.

training to succeed him, and there is no better candidate than Joshua. In spite of the claims of Alt and those who follow him, the case against Joshua is far from a proven fact. At this point, tradition and Beyerlin's recognition of it are both to be taken seriously: Joshua was guarding the ark in the tent of meeting at Sinai.

The mixed JE tradition in Numbers 10:33-36 claims that when the Israelites left Sinai the cloud of Yahweh's presence was over them and the ark was leading the march. Because the tent was bulky, it was folded and carried by the Levites, while the more portable ark, with the covenant tablets, was placed at the head of the procession. Since the ark followed the movements of the cloud, the people gradually associated the cloud with the ark. It was inevitable, therefore, that the tent would begin to lose some of its distinctiveness. Inasmuch as the ark was put within the tent when the people camped, descent of the cloud would be reported as being at the entrance of the tent (as in Num. 11:25; 12:5). But with the shift of roles in the minds of the people, the ark would be considered the primary object of Yahweh's concern while the red-leather tent would be thought of as the distinctive cover for the ark.

During the wilderness wanderings, therefore, the ark gradually assumed the role which the tent of meeting had had. Moreover, since the cloud was with them during their travels, the people realized that Yahweh was not tied to Mt. Sinai. This led to an increasing awareness of Yahweh's immanence, and most naturally they associated that presence with the ark. In this way, then, the actual experiences of the people were responsible for the shift of emphasis from the tent to the ark, and from the concept of manifestation to the idea of immanence. Accordingly, Moses could say "Arise, O Yahweh" whenever the ark set out, and "Return, O Yahweh" when it rested (Num. 10:35-36).

It is doubtful that the ark was originally overlaid with pure gold inside and out (Exod. 37:2), and it is uncertain whether the cherubim were part of it at this time. If so, they were not of hammered gold, but probably of acacia wood like the ark itself. In any case, the *essence* of the P tradition is *not* in contradiction to JE. The ark is in the tent, and here Yahweh meets Moses and talks with him (Exod. 25:22; 29:42; Num. 7:89). The use of the verb "to meet" implies that Yahweh is not residing over the ark, but that he, like Moses, moves to the trysting place at the ark. Thus, some aspect of manifestation is retained even in P. The dominantly immanent concept that Yahweh was enthroned over the ark seems to come from the period of the Judges, and it carries over into the monarchy. In 1 Samuel 4:4, for example, the ark is referred to as "the ark of the covenant of Yahweh of hosts, who is enthroned on the cherubim." But even in this period the problem of transcendence-immanence was not resolved as a complete immanence. Yahweh's call and appearance to Samuel were considered exceptional events because "the word of Yahweh was rare in those days — there was no frequent vision" (1 Sam. 3:1). If Yahweh were dwelling over the ark, he was strangely inconspicuous and silent.

It is not in the nature of human experience to have a tradition emphasize a certain point of view without evoking its alternative. This is especially true of very complex issues which have no simple, once-for-all answers. Varying conditions give rise to different perspectives and new understandings of a problem. Certainly the issue of transcendence-immanence comes within this category, and it seems overly simple to argue that two separate groups could divide the issue with each carrying on one facet of the truth in monolithic isolation.

The Fate of the Tent of Meeting

The materials out of which the tent of meeting was made most certainly deteriorated during the desert sojourn and early days in Canaan. Since the ark had become the dominant sacred object, there was little, if any, reason to mention the tent. Nevertheless, there are three later references to it. Joshua 18:1 (usually assigned to P) claims that the Israelites "assembled at Shiloh and set up the tent of meeting there." But in 1 Samuel 1:9 and 3:3 the sanctuary housing the ark is called a *hekal* ("temple"), the same word used for Solomon's temple and his palace. Archaeology and the biblical narratives indicate that the amphictyonic center at Shiloh was quite simple. In this context the term "temple" can hardly refer to a permanent building. More likely it was a frame for a tent, maybe the old patched tent of meeting. 1 Samuel 2:22 refers to the tent of meeting, but it is an obscure passage about some women serving at its entrance. In view of the designation "temple" on either side of this passage, if one takes the reference seriously, it indicates that the ark was kept in a different sanctuary. When the Philistines captured the ark and destroyed Shiloh, the frame sanctuary and any remnants of the tent of meeting must have been devastated along with the town. For this reason the reference in 2 Chronicles 1:3, that the tent of meeting was at Gibeon, where God appeared to Solomon, seems rather remote. The passage appears to be more of a rationale to explain why the great king would go to a high place.

David's Tent and the Tabernacle

It is certain, on the other hand, that David decided to take the ark (which had been returned from the Philistines) and house the sacred object from the north in a new sanctuary in his newly acquired capital, Jerusalem: "They brought the ark of Yahweh and set it in its place inside the tent which David had pitched for it, and David offered burnt offerings and peace offerings before Yahweh" (2 Sam. 6:17). The reference to "its place" appears to indicate a special place within the tent, perhaps the most holy place. Furthermore, David's offerings imply an altar and priests to carry out the ritual. Unfortunately, the Samuel narrative gives no details about David's tent, but the description of the tabernacle in the P tradition fits this context admirably. The wealth and skill necessary to construct the tabernacle were available in David's time, and the type of construction was a logical step between the old tent of meeting of the desert tradition and the splendor of Solomon's temple.

The Exodus and Sinai

Before attempting to summarize the Sinai experience, one more area of scholarly debate needs to be considered. Even though von Rad is more cautious in his skepticism, yet he agrees with Noth that the people who participated in the Exodus were different from those who had the covenant experience at Sinai. On the basis of the reference to Egypt in the historical prologue to the Sinai covenant (Exod. 20:2), Beyerlin contends, "It may be assumed, therefore, that the Decalogue originated somewhere where we can count on the presence of those who experienced *both* the Exodus *and* (italics his) the meeting with God on Sinai."[10]

This issue is a very instructive illustration of the necessity for checking a theory from every conceivable perspective. As Noth extended his tradition-history approach over the years he began to put more and more reliance on his findings. This hardening of position resulted in less attention to other approaches, especially when the new evidence ran counter to his conclusions. It has been noted that in three of his major works where he discusses Sinai there is virtually no recognition of the Hittite suzerainty treaty and its relationship to the Mosaic covenant. Inasmuch as Mendenhall made this material available to the scholarly world in 1954, Noth could have taken advantage of the new insight in his works or their revisions. This he did not do, however. His intricate theory involves a number of inferential steps, each one on increasingly slippery footing. The risk of erecting such a shaky structure, regardless of the acumen and ingenuity involved, is that one solid fact can topple part of the theory.

The Covenant Community at Sinai

Although the J, E, D, and P traditions have different emphases and include later materials which are in contradiction, they all root in a series of events at Mt. Sinai (Horeb). While it is impossible to reconstruct in any detail the various incidents and the order in which they occurred, the essence of the experience can be outlined. According to the dates given, the Israelites were at the sacred mountain for ten months and nineteen days. This allows time for the formation of the covenant and the establishment of community life and worship, and it fits well within the total period of wilderness wanderings.

After arriving at Mt. Sinai, Moses most likely set up a tent for use in seeking instructions for Yahweh. Here he probably received the call to ascend the mountain, and in this connection he was given a preview of the covenant with instructions for consecrating the people and restrict-

---

[10] *Ibid.*, p. 145.

ing them from the mountain. He reported to the people, they expressed their desire to enter into the covenant, and they prepared to meet their God. At the long blast of the trumpet Moses led the people to the base of the mountain. Just then Yahweh appeared in the form of a terrific storm. The fire of his presence flashed at the top of the peak, and the mountain shook at his thunderous voice. The people cringed in fear at the delivering of God's commands, and they begged Moses to mediate for them lest they die. He entered the dark cloud shrouding the mountain and communed with Yahweh about the guidelines for the covenant.

On returning to the camp Moses reported the basic commands of God and the people promised to obey. After writing the Decalogue on a scroll, he built an altar and young men, not designated as priests, offered animal sacrifices. Then Moses read the covenant stipulations aloud to the people, and when they took the oath of obedience he sealed the covenant by sprinkling the blood of the oxen on the altar and the people. Either here or after the renewal of the covenant, the seventy elders, Aaron, Nadab, Abihu, and Moses confirmed the covenant relationship by eating a meal on the slopes of Jebel Musa. On the beautiful, sapphire-blue base of the sky they envisioned the majesty of their God.

Moses was called to the mountain again, but this time he took two stone tablets on which to inscribe the official copy of the covenant agreements. Apparently Joshua accompanied him partway up. While on the mountain Moses meditated on the implications for the community. There would need to be a chest for the tablets, means for atonement, a ritual, and a core of priests to function in sacrifice and worship. As he inscribed the ten commandments he probably thought of the task of teaching and interpreting them. During his prolonged stay he realized that all was not well in the camp, and so he descended quickly, picking up Joshua on the way. The idolatrous orgies were so foreign to the covenant stipulations that Moses was righteously indignant and he shattered the tablets on the ground as a symbol of the broken covenant. After rebuking Aaron for his spineless role, he pulverized the slackened limestone calf and made the people drink water with the particles.

Moses was angry, but he would not consent to Yahweh's

proposal to form another covenant solely with him and his descendants. While he was a man of violent temper, he had great compassion as well. He interceded for the people and Yahweh agreed to carry on the old plan. This meant cutting another set of tablets and going to the top of the mountain again. There he wrestled with the problem of atonement and the question of Yahweh's presence with his sinful people. During his continued intercession he received the assurance that God's presence would go with him to lead the people. Yahweh showed Moses the back of his glory and then renewed the covenant with him in behalf of Israel. After returning to the camp with the tablets, he had a chest made from acacia wood, and put the tablets in the chest. Then he placed the chest in the tent of meeting and assigned Joshua to guard it.

Perhaps in the tent Moses received more explicit ideas as to the form of service for atonement and worship. In any case, he consecrated Aaron and his sons as priests, and in turn Moses and Aaron consecrated other Levites to assist Aaron and to care for the tent of meeting and its furnishings. Implementation of the covenant meant a number of interpretations and guidelines, and no doubt Moses kept some kind of record of the ordinances which he issued.

But once the community was functioning in a fairly orderly manner it was time to set its face toward Canaan. Then Moses and the people received Yahweh's instruction, "You have stayed at this mountain long enough. Start your journey" (Deut. 1:6-7).

Chapter 11

To Qadesh and Beyond

In looking to the future, Moses inquired diligently of Yahweh whom he would send as a guide through the wilderness (Exod. 33:12). The answer is found in Numbers 10:29, where the JE narrative continues after the exceedingly long collection of P tradition material. According to the traditional translation of the verse, Moses is speaking with "Hobab son of Reuel, the Midianite, father-in-law of Moses."

Hobab and Moses

Jethro, the old priest of Midian and father-in-law of Moses, has gone back to his home. Moreover, it is unlikely that he would have been able to serve as a guide had he been there, because he was quite old. The solution to the problem seems to be the one suggested by Albright: Reuel is a clan name, and so Hobab is not the same person as Jethro. Since vowels were not inserted into the Hebrew text until after A.D. 600, they are not as authoritative as the consonantal text. As recent translations have indicated, the original meaning of the Hebrew can be ascertained at times simply by changing vowels. In the instance of Hobab the Hebrew term *hoten*, traditionally translated "father-in-law," is from a verb root meaning "to be related by marriage." By changing *hoten* to *hatan* the meaning can be either "brother-in-law" or "son-in-law." The NEB accepts the former interpretation; that is, Hobab was the brother of Zipporah or the brother of Zipporah's sister. Albright goes a step further by translating "son-in-law"; that is, a member of Zipporah's clan who married a daughter of Zipporah and Moses. This conjecture is quite possible because, as Albright explains, most of the west-Semitic clans were endogamous (that is, they married within the clan).

In Judges 1:16 and 4:11 Hobab is called a Kenite, a member of a guild of metal-workers or smiths. Evidently he knows Midian and the Sinai wilderness because of his travel between the copper mines of the region. Moses urges him, therefore, "Come with us, and we will do you good, for Yahweh has promised good to Israel." Most surely the reference is to some land in Canaan. Hobab declines the offer with the intention of returning to his home area, but in poetic form Moses pleads, "Do not leave us, I beg you, for you know where we ought to camp in the wilderness, and you will be our guide" (10:31). Hobab's answer is not given, but it is implicit that he accepted. The two passages in Judges indicate that Hobab, the smith from the Reuel clan of Midianites, did indeed accompany Moses and settle in Palestine.

The Route from Sinai

In the log of Israel's journey, twenty camp sites are listed between Sinai and Qadesh (Num. 33:16-36). Elath (later Ezion-geber), verse 35, has been located at the northern end of the Gulf of Aqaba. Hazeroth (17) may have been at Ain Khadra, northeast of Mt. Sinai, and Jotbathah (33) at Tabeh on the western shore of the Gulf, seven miles south of Ezion-geber. Dhahab, on the Gulf of Aqaba, directly east of Mt. Sinai, seems to have been the site of Dizahab, mentioned in Deuteronomy 1:1. It is strange, however, that so few of the sites named have any narratives associated with them. The log is not fictitious, but it may be a list of camp sites used by pilgrims going to Sinai, just as Elijah did.

An old tradition in Deuteronomy 1:2 states, "The journey from Horeb to Qadesh-barnea via the hill country of Seir takes eleven days." Seir is the usual designation of Edomite country east of the Arabah, but the Edomites refused to let the Israelites cross their territory, and so Seir in this instance must have included some of the area west of the Arabah as well. The same understanding is found in Deuteronomy 1:44. Small bands of pilgrims may have made the journey to Qadesh in eleven days, but it undoubtedly took Moses and the Israelites much longer.

The first leg of the journey took three days, and Hobab, accompanied by the ark, went ahead to find a suitable camp site. But the difficult country wearied the spirits of the people, and they complained as they had done from Egypt to Sinai. Two such incidents comprise most of Numbers 11. Although no specific complaint is mentioned in the first instance, the murmuring of the people results in the fire of Yahweh striking at the fringes of the camp. The people beg Moses to intercede with Yahweh, and he does so. When the fire abates, the place is named *Taberah* ("Burning").

"Give Us Meat"

The "rabble," a motley group of escapees who came out of Egypt with Moses, were assimilated to some extent during the stay at Sinai, but the pressures of the journey got to them. It is manna time again and they have had their fill, but they are not satisfied. By sowing discontent throughout the camp they evoke in the people a craving for meat. Yahweh is angry with their complaints, then Moses adds his: "Why have you brought trouble on your servant? What have I done that you lay the burden of this people on me? Am I their mother?... Must I carry them in my bosom like a nurse with her babies?... Where am I to get meat for all this people?" (11:11-13). The burden of carrying the people alone has become too great for Moses, and he asks Yahweh to take his life at once if no help is forthcoming. The analogy of Moses as the mother of the people is most interesting because it implies that Yahweh was really their mother. This is a rarity because the biblical writers carefully avoided the concept of mother or consort with respect to Yahweh. It is of further interest that the description of manna (11:7-9) is much fuller than that found in Exodus 16:14, where one would expect the more complete description.

After Moses' complaint, Yahweh instructs him to assemble seventy of the registered elders at the tent of meeting. He promises Moses that the people will have meat for a whole month until it comes out at their nostrils and makes them nauseated. Moses is aghast at the promise and wonders where the animals and fish could be found to do this. "Is there a limit to Yahweh's power?" Yahweh asks (11:23). When the elders assemble at the tent of meet-

ing outside the camp, Yahweh appears in a cloud and puts
some of Moses' spirit on them. Since they are to share
the burden of leadership, they must share his spirit. This
distribution of authority results in a prophetic ecstasy
which they never experience again. At the same time, the
spirit comes on Eldad and Medad, two elders who had
remained in the camp because they were not included
among the seventy, and they prophesy as well. When news
of the event reaches Moses, his attendant Joshua commands
indignantly, "Stop them, my lord Moses" (11:28). Moses
rebukes him by wishing that Yahweh would put his spirit
on all the people.

After Moses and the elders return to the camp, "a wind
from Yahweh" brings quails from the sea. They cover the
face of the ground for miles around the camp. In October,
quails from Europe migrate south to Africa and Arabia.
After the long flight over the Mediterranean, they fall
exhausted on the northern shores of the Sinai Peninsula
and are easily caught. On the return trip in the spring the
flight from the south is not normally as taxing as the long
Mediterranean leg, but apparently a stiff breeze wearied
the quails as they flew up the Gulf of Aqaba, and so they
came down in the area of the Israelite camp. Psalm 78:26
refers to this incident, but it complicates matters by attributing it both to an east wind and a south wind.

In any event, the people spend two days and a night
gathering the quails and spreading them around to dry.
The least amount gathered is ten homers (about forty
bushels), a fantastic supply. Perhaps this hyperbole is
intended to show the excessive greediness of the people.
Before their hoard is consumed, and while the meat is still
between their teeth, a plague strikes. It may have resulted
from spoiled meat, but no description is given. They bury
the dead and name the place *Kibroth-hattaavah* ("Graves
of Greediness"). In connection with the P account of the
stay at the wilderness of Sin (Exod. 16) it was noted
that the references to meat or quails (vss. 3, 8, 12-13)
were probably intrusive because the main narrative refers
only to manna. The story is more appropriate for Kibroth-
hattaavah, which is the first camp site after leaving Sinai
(Num. 33:16). Since there is no reference to travel after

the Taberah experience, and the name is not mentioned in the list, it may be that the incident is some aspect of the quail story and that actually Taberah is the same place as Kibroth-hattaavah. The journey on to *Hazeroth* ("Enclosures, Courts"), the second name on the list, is noted in Numbers 11:35 with the further comment that they remained there.

Miriam and Aaron Speak Against Moses

Numbers 12 relates two incidents at Hazeroth where Miriam and Aaron speak against Moses. One complaint is directed at the Cushite woman Moses has married. They do not complain directly to Moses. Rather, it is implied that they whisper their objection throughout the camp. Another complaint is made by asking leading questions of the people: "Is it only through Moses that Yahweh has spoken? Has he not spoken through us as well?"

Normally "Cush" refers to Nubia, south of Egypt; and since the grandson of Aaron was named Phinehas ("the Nubian"), Albright accepts the tradition that Moses is married to a Nubian woman. Other scholars find the solution of the problem in Habakkuk 3:7, where Habakkuk's prayer mentions "Cushan" in connection with "Midian." Zipporah, Moses' first wife, was a Midianite, and so these scholars believe that he took a second wife from a tribe in the Sinai region similar to the Midianites. No previous reference has been made to this marriage, but it is stressed by the additional comment "for he had married a Cushite woman." If Zipporah were still living, the second wife would be further indication of the biblical claim that Moses was a man of exceptional vigor. Inasmuch as the Midianites were on friendly terms with the Israelites at this time, and since Miriam did not complain about Zipporah, it may be implicit that there was some bad feeling between the Israelites and the Cush(an)ites.

Miriam had functioned as a prophetess after crossing the Reed Sea (Exod. 15:20), and thus she had some basis for challenging Moses' unique role. Aaron, on the other hand, was the spokesman for Moses. Never is he credited with receiving Yahweh's message directly, and so Miriam probably originated the objection. This second complaint implies that Moses has made quite a point about his unique relationship with Yahweh. The implication is countered with a comment that Moses was "a man of great humility, the most humble man on earth" (12:3). This humility was expressed when he pleaded with Hobab to accompany him. Even as Yahweh's servant he was a man who needed help.

Although Miriam and Aaron have been whispering in the camp, Moses is informed of their actions and instructed to bring them to the tent of meeting. Yahweh comes down in a cloud and asks Aaron and Miriam to come forward. He informs them that visions and dreams are the means he uses to speak through an ordinary prophet, but that Moses is different. Yahweh treats him more as an equal, speaking clearly face to face, and not in riddles (8). Yahweh is angry with them and asks, "Why were you not afraid to speak against my servant Moses?"

When the cloud rises Miriam is white with leprosy. Here, as with Moses in Exodus 4:6, some skin malady like psoriasis is probably involved. The fact that Miriam is punished indicates that it was probably she who started the talk and that Aaron went along with her. He suffers, however, when he sees her plight. He admits that they have acted foolishly and sinned, and then he begs Moses to intercede in behalf of Miriam. Moses may feel burdened and even angry with those who cause him so much trouble, but when the situation gets desperate his compassion comes to the fore. Here also he resumes his role as intercessor by praying that Yahweh will heal Miriam (13).

It was the custom to shame or put a curse on offenders by spitting in their face (Deut. 25:9). Yahweh commands Moses to put Miriam outside the camp for seven days because if she had done such a thing to her father he would have spit in her face and put her away in shame for seven days. In spite of the punishment, however, it is implied that she was healed immediately because the minimum period of exclusion and testing in the case of arrested leprosy was seven days (Lev. 13:4). There is no indication what, if any, provision was made for her, but she is put outside the camp, and the people wait until she returns.

Then the Israelites move on from Hazeroth and camp in the wilderness of Paran. This is the area where, according to P (Num. 10:12), the cloud first settled after leaving Sinai. But the P narrative, in contrast to P's camp list in Numbers 33, is rather condensed; therefore there is no reason to question the intermediate stages noted in the JE narrative. Moreover, the "wilderness of Paran" seems to be a very extensive designation. Wadi Feiran, to the west of Mt. Sinai, apparently preserves the name, and from other uses of the expression evidently the wilderness was equivalent to the southern two-thirds of the Sinai Peninsula. In this instance, however, the context limits the action to the area east and northeast of Sinai.

Spies Sent to Canaan

The story of the spies and the abortive attempt to enter Canaan from the south appears in Numbers 13-14. The narrative is replete with details and duplications, and it is certain that two different traditions have been woven together. Critics are generally agreed that the strands are P and J. The D account of the story is found in Deuteronomy 1:19-46. The traditions do not agree explicitly as to the camp site from which the spies were sent. The D account definitely locates the people at Qadesh-barnea, and J seems to do the same. In the narrative P uses the amorphous "wilderness of Paran," but an editorial addition in 13:26 identifies it with Qadesh. Furthermore, the camp list of P in Numbers 33 states that after leaving Eziongeber the Israelites came to "the wilderness of Zin, that is, Qadesh" (36).

Qadesh ("Holy Place") was a common name in ancient times because there were a number of old sanctuary sites. The one designated "Barnea" was between the Mediterranean and the Gulf of Aqaba, almost in line with the Brook of Egypt (Wadi el-Arish) as it runs northwest toward the Mediterranean. The area is still distinguished by a cluster of three springs a few miles apart. Ain Qoseimeh is rather small and flows only part of the year. Ain Qedeis, which retains the name "Qadesh," is larger, but Ain Qudeirat (perhaps En-mishpat of Gen. 14:7) has the greatest supply and flows all year round. This area was the major camp site during the wilderness years, and in all likelihood the Israelites were here when they sent out the spies. The region to the northeast was called "the wilderness of Zin," and apparently "the wilderness of Paran" was to the south and southwest.

The P account begins the story. Yahweh instructs Moses to send out leaders, one from each tribe, to explore the land of Canaan. The names of the twelve are listed (13: 4-15), including Caleb from Judah and Hoshea from Ephraim. The remaining ten are unknown otherwise, because none of them appears in the list of leaders in Numbers 1:5-15. The most honored leaders of the tribes were the elders, which by definition means that they were older men. The rigors of an exploratory trip dictated that younger men, potential leaders, be sent. The names seem to be later in form; therefore Noth contends that the list, contrived by an editor, has no authenticity. Yet the priestly tradition had great interest in names and genealogies, and it took great care to preserve such lists. There were probably some editorial shifts and additions (as we shall see), but it is doubtful that the entire list is a fraud. One difficulty is the ancestry of Caleb. While P classes him with the tribe of Judah, other passages refer to him as "Caleb the son of Jephunneh the Kenizzite" (Num. 32:12), or as the older brother of Kenaz (Josh. 15:17; Judg. 1:13). The Kenizzites were one of the groups of peoples in Palestine during the time of Abraham (Gen. 15:19), and Kenaz is listed as an Edomite chief (Gen. 36:11). Very likely Caleb was a non-Israelite who accepted the worship of Yahweh and married into the tribe of Judah. Perhaps the Kenizzite clan was adopted by the tribe of Judah later on.

The P account has the spies explore the whole land of Canaan from the wilderness of Zin up to Rehob Lebo-hamath (21). If Rehob means Beth-rehob (Judg. 18:28), then it was located somewhere in the region of Mt. Hermon. Lebo-hamath (usually translated "the entrance of Hamath") refers to ancient Lebo in the valley (Beqa) between the Lebanon ranges. Since it was within the borders of the Hittite province of Hamath at one time, it acquired the name "Lebo of Hamath." It is exceedingly doubtful that any of the spies got up this far. The land from Qadesh to Lebo constituted the Egyptian province of Canaan at the time, and this became the dream of the Israelites. The command to explore "the land" was interpreted by a priestly editor as the entire country, and so he appended the boundaries of the ideal Canaan.

The J account, on the other hand, mentions only the

Negev and the hill country, especially the region around Hebron (17, 22). The spies are to check on the people who occupy the area, the fertility of the land, and the conditions of the cities. Near Hebron they find "Ahiman, Sheshai, and Talmai, the descendants of Anak," men of great stature. Some editor wanted to indicate the antiquity of Hebron, and so he added "Hebron was built seven years before Zoan in Egypt" (22). Most scholars consider the archaeological note as an authentic piece of information, but Noth, with his pessimism, thinks the editor was guilty of one-upmanship: Zoan was old, but Hebron was older, and so he added seven years, a traditional cycle of time. In any case, the spies come to the Valley of Eshcol ("Cluster") and take samples of the grapes, pomegranates, and figs. The Hebron area was very fertile, even as it is today, but the story must have been expanded a bit to have a cluster of grapes so large it had to be carried on a pole between two men (23).

The Report of the Spies

In P the spies are gone forty days (meaning a long time), and they report to Moses, Aaron, and the congregation (25-26). J does not indicate how long they were gone, but they report to Moses. The land "flows with milk and honey," and they exhibit the fruit samples as proof, but then comes the sad news. The large cities are fortified, the giants are there, and various other strong peoples occupy the land. If they attempt to enter the country they will meet the Amalekites in the Negev, the Hittites, Jebusites, and Amorites in the hill country, and the Canaanites along the coast and in the Jordan valley (29). Apparently the people are listening in on the report to Moses because Caleb tries to quiet them: "Let us go up at once and occupy the land, for we are well able to conquer it" (30).

Joshua is never mentioned in this connection, as is true in the whole J account. It is the P tradition which ties Joshua with Caleb, and of course this raises the question whether Joshua actually did participate as a spy. In Joshua 14:6-13 (perhaps the D tradition), Caleb comes to Joshua at Gilgal and reminds him of the promise which Yahweh made to Moses concerning both of them. Then Caleb summarizes his part in the story. After noting his good report, he adds, "My companions who went up with me discouraged the people, but I completely followed Yahweh my God." Joshua makes no objection to the claim, nor does he indicate that he had any part in the spy journey. In fact, he blesses Caleb and allots him the Hebron area. Deuteronomy 1:36 exempts Caleb only, and so both D passages agree with J. Joshua was certainly at Qadesh assisting Moses, and it is implicit, of course, that he sided with him. It would have been a bit risky, however, to send Joshua on the exploration; yet after the conquest it was assumed that the great Ephraimite was the spy for his tribe. By noting that Joshua's name was formerly Hoshea (13:16), it was possible for the P tradition to equate the spy Hoshea with Joshua. This in turn led to the inclusion of Joshua throughout the story. Deuteronomy 1:38 explains why Joshua did not die in the wilderness. His faithfulness as Moses' assistant, not as a spy, resulted in his being commissioned to take the people into the land.

After Caleb's encouraging exhortation to take the land, the other spies claim, "We are not able to go up against the people because they are stronger than we" (31). Moreover, the land "devours its inhabitants," evidently referring to the results of the incessant wars between the various groups in the land. The Nephilim, from whom the descendants of Anak came, are so large that the spies confess, "We felt like grasshoppers, and so we seemed to them" (33).

The Reactions of the People

In the P account the people believe the majority report and spend the whole night weeping in fear (14:1). They wish they had died in Egypt or en route to Qadesh, and they wonder why Yahweh brought them to Canaan to die by the sword. They fear that their wives and children will become a prey to the enemy, and they think in terms of going back to Egypt. Verse 4 breaks in between the expressions of the people and the reactions of Moses and Aaron, and it may be a part of the J account. Here fear hardens into rebellion as the men say to one another, "Let us elect a leader and go back to Egypt." This represents a total rejection of Yahweh's covenant and Moses' leadership. Whether Moses and Aaron heard of this rebellious

attitude is uncertain, but when the people suggest re-
treating to Egypt in fear, Moses and Aaron prostrate themselves on the ground. In desperation Joshua (?) and Caleb
try to encourage the people to take the good land. They
beg them not to rebel against Yahweh, nor to fear the
people, but their pleas fall on deaf ears. They are on the
verge of being stoned by the people when the glory of
Yahweh appears at the tent of meeting (10).

Moses' Intercession

In the J account Yahweh asks Moses, "How long will
this people despise me? How much longer will they refuse
to believe me in spite of all the signs I have done among
them?" The "signs" probably refer to the plagues, and
the provision of food and meat in the desert, but the unique
sign was Yahweh's covenant with the people at the very
place where he had appeared to Moses. All of this was
forgotten in the dark hour at Qadesh, and so Yahweh
declares, "I will strike them with pestilence, and disinherit
them, and I will make of you a nation greater and mightier
than they" (12). In a scene reminiscent of Exodus 32:
11-14, Moses pleads with Yahweh. If the Egyptians, who
know what Yahweh has done for his people, hear that
he has blotted out his people, then they will say, "Yahweh
could not bring this people into the land which he promised
them by oath, and so he destroyed them in the wilderness"
(16). To this persuasive argument Moses adds his appeal
to Yahweh's steadfast love and willingness to forgive, and
then he prays, "Pardon the iniquity of this people, I beg
you."

Yahweh's Judgment

Moses' petition is answered and Yahweh acknowledges
pardon of the people, but this does not negate the punishment. All those who have despised Yahweh and put him
to the test "ten times" (22) will not see the promised land.
Some scholars take "ten" literally, but most likely it has
the idea "quite a few." Caleb is to be the exception because he has "a different spirit."

The judgment of Yahweh is expressed more harshly in
the P account. He is tired of the "murmurings" of the
people, and he instructs Moses to tell them, "As I live,

what you have said in my hearing I will do to you: your
dead bodies shall lie in this wilderness" (28-29). With the
exception of Caleb and Joshua, no one twenty years (the
eligible age for military duty) and older will be privileged
to see the promised land. The young ones, for whom the
men had such concern, will see the land despised by their
parents. But they will have to suffer as "shepherds in
the wilderness" because of their elders' faithlessness. The
length of the wilderness years is set at forty, one for
each day of the journey by the spies, but a far more basic
reason for the long judgment is that within the period all
the faithless leaders will die. After implying a gradual
death of the rebels, the P account closes with a sudden
statement that the spies who brought up the evil report
"died by plague before Yahweh" (37).

J continues the story with a very important passage
(39-45). On hearing the dire words of Moses, the people
mourn all night. By early morning they evidently feel that
Yahweh will change his mind, because they confess that
they have sinned and start toward the hill country as proof
of their faith. But Moses warns them, "Why do you keep
disobeying Yahweh's command? This will not succeed. Do
not go up, lest your enemies defeat you, for Yahweh will
not be with you" (41-42). They persist, however, even
though the ark and Moses do not leave the camp. The
nomadic Amalekites and the Canaanite settlers combine
forces to defeat them at Hormah. The name was probably
understood to mean "Destruction," because it has the same
consonants as the verb "to devote to destruction." This
popular etymology is found in Judges 1:17, where Judah
and Simeon attack the Canaanites at Zephath and rename
the city Hormah after its destruction. The exact location of
the site has not been determined, but scholarly opinion has
settled on Tell el-Meshash or Tell el-Milh, both a few
miles east of Beersheba.

Part of Yahweh's judgment on the people in the J account
is the following command to Moses: "Since the Amalekites
and the Canaanites dwell in the valleys, turn tomorrow
and march into the wilderness by way of the Sea of Reeds"
(14:25). The verse seems to be intrusive because it does
not fit the context in any sense. It contradicts 14:45, where
the Amalekites and the Canaanites dwell in the hill coun-

try; and, moreover, the Israelites do not leave Qadesh for many years. Some editor inserted the verse in anticipation of the promise to Caleb that he and his descendants would possess the land he explored. The "Sea of Reeds" means the Gulf of Aqaba since, as noted earlier, the designation was extended at a later time to include the Red Sea and its two arms. The intrusive comment is important, however, because it indicates a tradition that the Israelites went back down to Elath (Ezion-geber), and then circled around Edom and Moab on the east.

More Priestly Regulations

Numbers 15-19 is a collection of priestly materials with some additions from other sources. The block of material interrupts the narrative; therefore it is implicit that the editor thought that the contents derived from the sojourn at Qadesh. This is impossible to prove, however, and so the better part of wisdom is to recognize that there is a mixture of materials from Qadesh and elsewhere. Chapter 15 is a hodgepodge of regulations which seem to have no relationship to each other. The common denominator is that they seem to be supplemental to laws noted earlier. The unit 1-16 prescribes the cereal and drink offerings which are to accompany the burnt offerings (Lev. 1) and peace offerings (Lev. 3). In 17-21 the law of firstfruits is extended to include a cake made from the first grindings of the coarse meal.

The matter of unwitting sin is discussed in 22-31. The commandments given by Yahweh to Moses at Sinai and thereafter are to be the standard. This verse (23) is important because it recognizes supplemental Mosaic regulations, and it implies that Yahweh will issue more later ("throughout your generations"). Unwitting sin by the congregation will require a young bull and a male goat, whereas an individual will offer a year-old female goat. The implication of the whole sacrificial corpus is that only unwitting sins can be forgiven. This is made explicit in verse 30 in that the one who does anything "with a high hand," that is, defiantly or presumptuously, has reviled Yahweh, and as a result must be cut off from the people.

A man found gathering sticks on the sabbath becomes the occasion for another regulation (32-36). Yahweh instructs Moses to have him stoned to death, and this the people do. It has been declared unlawful to kindle a fire on the sabbath (Exod. 35:3), and now gathering sticks, preparation for a fire, is ruled out as well. The last unit (37-41) requires tassels at the corners of their garments (evidently meaning the four corners of material worn as an outer robe). The tassels are to be reminders of Yahweh's commandments.

Dathan and Abiram

Numbers 16 is an exceedingly complex mixture of strands, and scholars differ greatly in their interpretation of the chapter. The Hebrew text of verse 1 is difficult, but recent translations indicate that four people challenge Moses' authority: Korah, a Levite; Dathan and Abiram, Reubenites; and On, another Reubenite. Since there seem to be four different charges made against Moses, Newman finds four strands woven together in Numbers 16.[1]

Early P tradition (1a, 2b-7a, 18-24, 27a, 32b, 35, 41-50) involves Korah with 250 leaders of the congregation and the charge, "Why do you exalt yourselves above the assembly of Yahweh?";

Late P tradition (7b-11, 16-17, 36-40) involves Korah with 250 Levites challenging the exclusive prerogatives of the Aaronic priesthood;

E tradition (1b, 12, 14b, 25, 27b, 32a, 32b, 34) involves Dathan and Abiram complaining that Moses has not given them their inheritance of fields and vineyards;

J tradition (1b, 13, 14a, 15, 26b, 27c, 28-31, 33a) involves On with a challenge of the religious authority of Moses.

Noth accepts the two priestly traditions, but he combines Newman's J and E strands, assigning all the material to J.[2] Coats recognizes the variant aspects of P, but he assigns the basic Korah material to P, and thus he finds two main strands in the chapter: P and J.[3] Before evaluating this variety of critical opinion it is necessary to look at the essential features of the story. The section 2-7 involves Korah and 250 well-known "leaders of the congre-

---

[1] Newman, *The People of the Covenant*, pp. 95-97.
[2] Noth, *Numbers*, p. 121.
[3] Coats, *Rebellion in the Wilderness*, pp. 162-163.

gation, chosen from the assembly." They confront Moses
and Aaron and declare that Yahweh is with the congregation, and that all the people are holy. Moses and Aaron
have gone too far, they claim, by exalting themselves above
the assembly of Yahweh. Moses challenges them with a
test. The next day they are to take bronze, shovel-like
censers with hot coals and incense, and approach Yahweh.
The one whom Yahweh chooses will be the holy one.

In the section 8-11 Moses addresses Korah and his group
as "sons of Levi," and he charges them with ingratitude
for desiring "the priesthood" when Yahweh was gracious
enough to select them from the congregation to serve as
Levites. Moses warns them that their rebellion is against
Yahweh, not just Aaron. The contention in 8-11 seems
quite different from that in 2-7; therefore 8-11 is usually
considered either a secondary priestly addition, or a separate priestly tradition.

The JE story appears in 12-15. Apparently Dathan and
Abiram have been sowing discord among the people, and
so Moses calls them to give an account. They refuse and
inquire defiantly, "Is it a small thing that you have brought
us out of a land flowing with milk and honey to kill us
in the wilderness? Must you also make yourself a prince
over us?" Moreover, they add, Moses has not fulfilled his
promise to settle them in a land of milk and honey. Their
lack of faith is shown in that Egypt, not Canaan, is the
land flowing with milk and honey. As a parting shot they
ask, "Will you put out the eyes of these men?" The expression probably infers that Moses has fooled the majority of the people and thus blinded them to the real
situation. The New English Bible expresses the idea well:
"Do you think that you can hoodwink men like us?" Moses
is very angry at their refusal to come and he commands
Yahweh, "Do not respect their offering." The word for "offering" is not "incense offering," and so the verse cannot
be part of the Korah story. This implies that originally
Dathan and Abiram were involved in some kind of sacrificial test as well.

The Korah story resumes in 16-24. Korah and his 250
supporters take censers and stand at the entrance to the
tent of meeting. Aaron is there with his censer also. Yahweh's glory appears, and Moses and Aaron are instructed

to separate themselves from Korah and his group so that Yahweh may "consume them instantly." Moses and Aaron fall to the ground pleading, "O God, God of the spirits of mankind, if one man sins will you be angry with the whole congregation?" Then the members of the congregation not involved with Korah are told to get away from "the dwelling *(mishkan)* of Korah, Dathan, and Abiram" (24). Unless *mishkan*, P's term for "tabernacle," refers to the tent of meeting, the scene has shifted to Korah's personal dwelling. The addition of "Dathan and Abiram" appears to be an editorial glide to 25-31, where the story of the Reubenites continues.

Moses and the elders go out to the dwellings of Dathan and Abiram, and then Moses instructs the people to get away from "the tents of these wicked men." Verse 27, noting that they move away from "the dwelling of Korah, Dathan, and Abiram," seems to be a scribal attempt to harmonize the story with verse 24. After Dathan and Abiram and their families make their appearance in front of their tents, Moses announces, without Yahweh's prior authority, the conditions of the showdown. If the rebels die a natural death, then Yahweh has not sent Moses; but if Yahweh creates a new thing and the ground swallows them alive, then everyone will know that the rebels have despised Yahweh. When he finishes speaking, the earth opens up and swallows them and their households. Included in the judgment are "all the men that belonged to Korah and all their possessions" (32). The words "that belonged to Korah" involve only two words in Hebrew, and the question arises whether this is another scribal addition, or whether it may preserve a tradition that Korah suffered the same fate as Dathan and Abiram. In verse 35 the original story of Korah and the 250 leaders concludes: "And fire came out from Yahweh, and consumed the 250 men offering the incense." Korah is not mentioned, however. Is it because he died in the yawning chasm?

In Coats' discussion of Numbers 16,[4] he accepts the tradition that Korah was swallowed up by the earth, and that Dathan and Abiram had group backing (14) and were involved with a sacrificial ordeal (15). He notes the great

---

[4] *Ibid.*, pp. 156-184.

similarity between the basic outline of the stories, and then concludes, "The two narrative threads in this chapter are interdependent; i.e., a single common tradition lies behind both accounts."[5] Coats considers the J account with Dathan and Abiram as the oldest form of the tradition. Later on the P tradition, at a time when the priesthood was threatened, used the story to support its cause; but in doing so it substituted Korah the Levite as the villain, and then had the rebellious Levites die by fire. This reconstruction is quite plausible, and certainly the difficulties involved are no more formidable than those resulting from the theory that two completely separate stories have been interwoven.

With either reconstruction, however, there is the tradition that the earth opened up and swallowed the rebels. If one assumes that there was a literal earthquake with large fissures, it is difficult to see how the people would escape without some of them suffering the same fate. A more probable explanation is that a poetic oral version was taken literally in the prose version, just as the heaps of water from Yahweh's nostrils (Exod. 15) became walls of water in the narrative (Exod. 14). The psalmist prays that his enemies will "go down to Sheol alive" (Ps. 55:15), and the robber is pictured as saying, "Let us swallow them alive like Sheol" (Prov. 1:12). Isaiah 5:14 and Habakkuk 2:5 speak of Sheol, the grave or underworld, opening wide its throat. The ancients knew quite well that at times people in the prime of health suddenly die, and, as it were, "go down to Sheol alive." In the story of Dathan and Abiram, both the prediction and the event refer to going down alive to Sheol (30, 33). Later on, this poetic description of their drastic fate was taken literally.

The question of location is another difficult matter. Most scholars consider the story as an example of the rebellion which took place during the long stay at Qadesh. It may be related to the decline of Reuben, the oldest tribe according to tradition. It is known that soon after the Reubenites settled in Transjordan they ceased to function as an effective tribe, and consequently the tribe of Gad, to the north, occupied their territory.

---

[5] *Ibid.,* p. 174.

Priestly Warnings

After the death of the 250, Eleazar is instructed to scatter the holy fire of the censers. Then the censers are hammered down and worked into a bronze plate to cover the altar. This would serve as a warning that only priests are to burn incense to Yahweh (40). The next morning all the people murmur that Moses and Aaron have "killed the people of Yahweh," but when they confront them with the charge they notice that the glory of Yahweh has appeared at the tent of meeting. Again Yahweh's wrath flares, and he instructs Moses to move away so that he can "consume them instantly" (45). They fall to the ground again, but this time Moses instructs Aaron to carry incense and make atonement for the people because a plague is already under way. Aaron stands "between the dead and the living" (48), but in the meantime 14,700 are dead. This enlarged figure is a little less than a fortieth of the 603,550 of the first census, and so the editor indicates that the plague was a serious one moving quickly among the people. What actually happened in this instance is impossible to determine. It is clear, however, that since Aaron had made atonement and stayed the plague, the story was used as further authentication of the priesthood.

A final warning to any rebels occurs in 17:1-11. Twelve rods are to be taken, one for each tribe, and the name of the tribe or leader is to be inscribed. Aaron's name is to be on Levi's rod because he is the chief representative of the tribe of Levi. This is reverting to the old style before Levi was set aside for special duty, and so Manasseh and Ephraim inscribe both of their names on one rod or else they use their father's name, Joseph. The twelve rods are put before the ark in the tent of meeting, and behold, the next morning Aaron's rod has sprouted, grown buds and blossoms, and finally yielded ripe almonds. All the rods are produced for the people to examine, and then Aaron's miraculous rod is placed back in front of the ark to be kept as a sign for the rebels. Again the core event is difficult to determine, but the story, like the other two, speaks eloquently of occasions when the Aaronite priesthood was in serious jeopardy and felt it necessary to use all means to authenticate its position. There is no reason to doubt that feelings between the priests and the Levites became tense during those frustrating years at Qadesh, and that the stories came in useful many times later.

Further Priestly Regulations

The unsettled cultic conditions, especially the death of the 250 with incense, unnerve the people and they inquire of Moses, "Are we all to perish?" (17:13). This leads into chapter 18, which specifies the responsibilities of the priests and the Levites. The priesthood is Yahweh's gift to Aaron and his sons, and the Levites are his gift to the priests. The unit 18:8-20 explains that in lieu of inheritance of land the priests are to gain their support from the offerings made by the people. Certain parts of the offerings can be eaten only at the tabernacle, but other portions may be shared at home with their families. Since the Levites have no land either, they are to receive all the tithes (the tenth of all the produce from the land) of the people (21-24). In turn, the Levites are to make an offering to Yahweh as well. This tithe of the tithe is to be given to the priests (25-32).

Numbers 19 describes the details for cleansing persons or things defiled by a corpse. The unit 1-10 explains how to prepare the ashes for the removal of defilement. Eleazar appears in the first part of the instructions, but thereafter only "the priest" and other unnamed individuals are mentioned. It seems to be an old custom which the P tradition tried to incorporate into standard Israelite practice by inserting the name "Eleazar" in two verses (3, 4). A red heifer, without blemish and unworked with a yoke, is brought outside the camp and slain in Eleazar's presence. Then he sprinkles some of the blood seven times toward the front of the tent of meeting. The context implies that the heifer was slain outside the camp at a point with a view to the front of the tent, and that the sprinkling toward the tent was invoking the holiness of the sacred precinct. Some scholars contend that the whole process took place in the court of the tabernacle, where sacrifices normally took place, but there is no mention of an altar or sprinkling blood on it.

The whole animal is burned in the presence of the priest,

and during the process he puts some "cedarwood, hyssop, and scarlet thread" into the blaze. These same three items are mentioned also in connection with the cleansing of a leper (Lev. 14:4). Then another person gathers the ashes of the heifer and deposits them in a clean place outside the camp. The priest, the man who burned the heifer, and the one who collected the ashes must wash their clothes and bathe, and they remain unclean until evening. Priests did not become unclean by officiating at regular sacrifices; therefore the anticipated use of the ashes must have made the heifer unclean from the very beginning. This would be another indication that the burning took place outside the camp.

The continuation of the instructions appears in 14-22. Whenever a man dies in a tent, the tent and every person and thing within it become unclean. Spring (running) water is poured into a vessel with some of the ashes of the red heifer, and then on the third and seventh days after the contamination "the water for impurity" is sprinkled by means of hyssop on the tent and all the persons and things within it. Since the ashes are the agent for removing ritual uncleanness, the P tradition describes them as "ashes of a burnt sin offering" (17), because for the priestly mind ritual impurity was equal to sin.

The cleansing process (like that of the water-ordeal for suspected adultery, Num. 5:16-22) has overtones of taboo or magic. Originally it may have been a part of a ritual for the dead. Even though the custom was adapted for use within Israelite circles, there is no other biblical reference to the burning of a red heifer. Numbers 31:19-24 refers to the custom of cleansing, and "the ashes of a heifer" (Heb. 9:13) has Numbers 19 clearly in mind. It is interesting to note that the Mishnah (*Parah* 3.5) in the Talmud claims that the last killing of the red heifer took place during the office of the high priest Ishmael ben Phabi (about A.D. 58-60). The Samaritans continued the ritual until the fourteenth century A.D.

With the close of the long section of priestly regulations and concerns, the P narrative continues in 20:1: "In the first month the whole congregation of Israelites reached the wilderness of Zin and stayed some time at Qadesh.

There Miriam died and was buried." Unfortunately, no year is mentioned. If "third" is assumed, then the people got to Qadesh more than ten months after leaving Sinai, but this is hardly likely. The old conservative scholars Karl F. Keil and Franz Delitzsch held that the fortieth year was implied; that is, thirty-nine years after leaving Egypt the Israelites returned to Qadesh, where thirty-seven and a half years before Yahweh had consigned them to forty years of wandering.[6] This seems to be the intent of the priestly editor because in 20:22 the P narrative relates the departure from Qadesh en route to Transjordan. Still further evidence for this reconstruction is the comment in Numbers 33:38 that Aaron died at Mt. Hor in the fifth month of the fortieth year. The explicit claim of 20:1 is that Miriam died at Qadesh and was buried there.

Water at Meribah

Following the cryptic verse 20:1 is the story about water from a rock at Meribah (2-13). There are many similarities to the account in Exodus 17:1-7, and it appears that the latter is the JE account whereas the Numbers version is basically P with some harmonizing elements from Exodus 17. It was noted in connection with the discussion of Exodus 17 that Rephidim was not a likely place for the water miracle because the rock is granite, and that the probable locale was in the region of Qadesh-barnea. Since the Meribah story appears immediately following the reference to Qadesh, it is implied that Meribah was at Qadesh. If this be true, then the incident must have occurred at Ain Qoseimeh or Ain Qedeis during the dry season when they dried up. Deuteronomy 32:51 refers to the incident "at the waters of Meribah at Qadesh, in the wilderness of Zin."

The people confront Moses and remark contentiously, "Would that we had died when our brethren died in Yahweh's presence." This could be a reference to Dathan and Abiram, or the spies who gave the evil report. Still another possibility would be those who have already died because of Yahweh's judgment. The people wonder why Moses has brought them out of Egypt to die in the wilderness.

[6] Keil and Delitzsch, *Biblical Commentary on the Old Testament* (Grand Rapids: Eerdmans, 1949), Vol. III of the Pentateuch, p. 128.

The place is evil because it is not fit for "grain, figs, vines, or pomegranates, and there is no water" (5). Moses and Aaron go to the entrance of the tent of meeting and prostrate themselves. The glory of Yahweh appears and he instructs Moses to take "the rod," assemble the people, and command the rock to yield its water. Moses takes "the rod from the presence of Yahweh," implying that it is Aaron's rod which was deposited near the ark. It is not explained why the rod was necessary if only Moses' command was needed to provide water.

Moses and Aaron assemble the people at the rock, but instead of commanding the rock, Moses turns on the people, "Listen, you rebels, shall we get water for you from this rock?" (11). Then he raises his hand and strikes the rock twice with the rod, and water flows freely. Moses has been angry before, but for Yahweh's name, honor, and cause. This time, however, his anger stems from frustration with the contentious people. There is even a hint of doubt that water would come forth. Yahweh informs Moses and Aaron that because they have not trusted him enough to honor him in the presence of the people, they will not be permitted to lead them into the promised land. Then an editor comments, "These are the waters of Meribah (Contention) where the people of Israel contended with Yahweh, and he manifested his holiness among them" (13). Since the Hebrew word "to be holy" is *qadash*, it seems that the editor is using a word play to connect the incident with Qadesh ("Holy Place").

There is no reason to doubt the essential historicity of the event. Water from limestone is a fact, and the unrighteous anger of Moses shows his humanity. Considering the frustrations of taking the people through such difficult country it is remarkable that he did not lose control of his anger before. A matter for question is whether Yahweh's judgment was made known immediately to Aaron and Moses, or whether the P tradition, knowing of Moses' sin, read the judgment back into the story to explain why Aaron and Moses did not lead the Israelites into Canaan.

The Sojourn at Qadesh

The length of the sojourn at Qadesh is not spelled out, unfortunately, and so it is necessary to read between the lines of a number of isolated passages. The P tradition claims that the Israelites left Sinai about thirteen months and five days after departing from Goshen. The arrival at Qadesh is not dated, but a time about fifteen months after leaving Egypt would be reasonable. The judgment of wandering for forty years took place at Qadesh, apparently about a month or so after arriving there. If Numbers 20:1 is a summary verse and refers to the first month of the fortieth year, then the P tradition implies that the Israelites left Qadesh after God's judgment and wandered in the wilderness areas of Paran and Zin for about thirty-seven and a half years, only returning to Qadesh after most of the condemned generation have died in the desert.

The D tradition presents a complex picture. After mentioning the return to Qadesh following the defeat at Hormah, the Hebrew text of Deuteronomy 1:46 states literally, "And you dwelt in Qadesh many days, according to the days which you dwelt." It seems to imply that in relation to the total time in the wilderness, much of it was spent at Qadesh. The next verse (2:1) notes that they journeyed into the wilderness toward the Reed Sea (Gulf of Aqaba), according to Yahweh's command. This too seems to point to a long stay at Qadesh, but it must be understood in the context of Deuteronomy 2:14: "The journey from Qadesh-barnea to the crossing of the wadi Zered took thirty-eight years, until the whole generation of fighting men had passed away as Yahweh had sworn that they would."

If the portions of the D tradition are to have any consistency, the departure from Qadesh noted in 2:1 must be a reference to Yahweh's command to Moses, "Turn tomorrow and march into the wilderness by way of the Reed Sea" (Num. 14:25). As far as one can tell from the narrative, the next morning was the ill-fated departure for Canaan. Certainly Moses waited for the despondent remnant after the defeat at Hormah; however, there is no indication that he carried out Yahweh's order at that time. But apparently the D tradition understood that after an additional stay of seven or eight months (up to the second anniversary of the departure from Egypt) the Israelites left Qadesh in accordance with Yahweh's command. After wandering many days in the region around Mt. Seir (probably the southern part of the wilderness of Zin, and the Arabah down to the Gulf of Aqaba), Yahweh instructed Moses to go northward. He led the people away from the Edomites and the Arabah region, circled to the east of Edom, and then headed north toward the wilderness of Moab (Deut. 2:8). According to the D tradition, therefore, the Israelites stayed at Qadesh for about nine months all told, leaving there just two years after their departure from Egypt.

While the P and D traditions seem to agree that the Israelites left Qadesh soon after the defeat at Hormah, they differ radically in the time it took to travel from Qadesh to Moab: P about eight months (allowing a month to get to Mt. Hor), but thirty-eight years in D. In the J tradition the spies are sent out from Qadesh and the Israelites are still there when they send messengers to the king of Edom in preparation for departure. In his message to the king, Moses says, "Now here we are at Qadesh, a city on your border" (20:16). The implication is that the people have been at Qadesh the whole time, and there are no other references in J to indicate otherwise.

In the light of these varying and inconclusive statements about the length of the Qadesh sojourn, it is necessary to turn to other evidence to help resolve the issue. The remarkable fact is that there are so few narratives about the wilderness period. This lack has been traditionally attributed to the low ebb of morale during the bleak years of death's creeping judgment. But this theory of the lost years is based on a literal interpretation of the forty-year condemnation. It is true that in the cases of David and Solomon the number 40 seems to be a fairly precise indication of the length of their reigns. In the majority of instances, however, the number 40 is an expression of a complete period of time, or an approximation for one generation. The terrific toll on physical energy must have increased the death rate in the wilderness, and so an actual figure of twenty-five years would be nearer the truth.

The dates for the early years after leaving Egypt fit into the total context quite well, and there is no reason to question them. It is clear, on the other hand, that the data for determining the close of the wilderness period derived from biblical editors with a literal understanding of forty. The death of Aaron was set in the fifth month of the fortieth year because it occurred during the last leg of the journey to Moab. The D tradition, however, reckoned that Israel left Qadesh soon after the defeat at Hormah, and it subtracted two from forty, thus assigning thirty-eight years for the journey to Moab.

Another important factor is Yahweh's vow that none of the murmurers would come into the land which he had sworn to give them. All of the definitions of the promised land refer to territory west of the Jordan. Settlement in Transjordan was never part of the original plan; therefore the crossing of the Jordan, not the wadi Zered, should have marked the end of the wandering years. The number of narratives about the conquest and settlement of the areas of Sihon and Og, as well as the stay in the lowlands of Moab east of the Jordan, indicate that a fairly long period was involved. If ten years were allotted for this period, and ten years for the stay at Qadesh, the remaining five years or so would amply account for the sojourn at Sinai and all the travels involved between Egypt and Moab.

The Israelite Community at Qadesh

Whether the stay at Qadesh was ten years or not, the site was very crucial in the development of Israelite traditions. Most certainly the tent of meeting and the ark served as the center of the community at Qadesh, and the development of ritual and legal practices must have continued. Deuteronomy 33 is Moses' blessing of the tribes just prior to his death. The Hebrew of the introduction in verse 2 is difficult in places, but it seems to say, "Yahweh came from Sinai, and dawned on them from Seir. He shone forth from Mt. Paran, and he came from the myriads of holy ones." The last phrase in Hebrew is *meribeboth-qodesh,* and with slight changes it could read *memeribath-qadesh* ("from Meribah at Qadesh") (as the name appears in Deut. 32:51). With three place names it is quite possible that the fourth member of the parallelism was a proper noun. Whether this be true or not, God did indeed make himself known at Meribah. The gracious gift of water, in spite of the murmurings of the people and the temper of Moses, was the symbol of Yahweh's presence at Qadesh.

Meribah was equally important as the symbol of the contention which characterized the sojourn there. The pressures of finding enough food and water must have worn down the spirits of the people, especially those who did not have genuine faith in Yahweh. The grumblers complained and challenged Moses, and no doubt they were at odds with each other at times. The story of the Levites' zeal (located near Meribah by Deut. 33:8-9) indicates some life and death struggle at Qadesh. Here Miriam died, and here Aaron grew old and weary.

Since Qadesh plays a very important role in the reconstructions of most critical scholars, it is necessary to examine some of the basic theories in the light of the biblical evidence. When Jephthah tried to negotiate with the Ammonites he sent messengers summarizing Israel's history. In this account Jephthah notes, "When they came up from Egypt they went through the wilderness to the Reed Sea and came to Qadesh" (Judg. 11:16). On the strength of this verse, a number of scholars over the years have contended that the Israelites came directly across the middle of the Sinai Peninsula, and settled at Qadesh. Older critics holding this theory were inclined to locate Mt. Sinai in the area, but the highest hills of the region hardly account for the data about the Sinai experience.

Beyerlin gets around the problem by having the Egyptian slaves go directly to Qadesh, and then subsequently to take the eleven-day pilgrimage south to Mt. Sinai. After their worship with Yahweh and their vow of obedience, they return to Qadesh where the Decalogue is formulated and the covenant-treaty enacted on the basis of the Sinai experience.[7] Beyerlin sees the organization of the social, legal, and religious aspects of the community during the sojourn at Qadesh because, in his view, it is here that Jethro officiates at sacrifices and advises Moses. This combination theory is quite plausible, but its biggest drawback is the assumption that most of the material in Exodus 15:22-18:27 describes experiences at Qadesh. It has been granted that Exodus 17:1-7 seems better fitted for the Qadesh context, but the rest of the material is best accounted for by assuming a southern route.

---

[7] Beyerlin, *op. cit.*, pp. 145-147.

Rowley's Theory of the Conquest

Rowley was very conscientious in dealing with biblical material, and he tried to take into account every bit of evidence, but he came to the conclusion that there was no way to harmonize the details. The theory which seemed to reckon with the most data was one which allowed for two separate conquests of Palestine involving two different groups of people.[8] Starting with 1 Kings 6:1, Rowley holds that some of the Hebrew (Apiru) tribes associated with the reigns of Tuthmosis III and Amenophis II came out of Egypt about 480 years before Solomon began to build the temple (that is, about 1440 B.C.) and sojourned at Qadesh. There the four older Leah tribes (Reuben, Simeon, Levi and Judah) associated with Yahweh-worshiping Kenites and other groups like the Calebites and Othnielites, and over a thirty-eight-year span they formed a religious community oriented around worship of Yahweh.

The picture in Judges 1 is a conquest of Canaan by individual efforts of various tribes. The editorial heading places the action "after the death of Joshua," but since there is some question about the note, Rowley takes the chapter to be a combination of information about an early conquest (1-20) and a later one (21-36). The people ask Yahweh, "Who shall go up first to fight against the Canaanites?" Judah is Yahweh's choice, and he says to his brother Simeon, "Come up with me ... that we may fight against the Canaanites." Simeon agrees (3), and the two take Jerusalem (8), Hebron (10), Debir (11), Zephath, which was renamed Hormah (17), and finally Gaza, Ashkelon, and Ekron in the coastal plain (18). Caleb and Othniel are noted in 12-15 and 20, and the Kenites appear in 16. In the Song of Deborah, the tribe of Reuben seems to be in the central hill country west of the Jordan (Judg. 5:15b-16), and therefore Rowley thinks Reuben was involved in this early conquest. Reuben was not mentioned in Judges 1, according to Rowley, because it did not gain a strong foothold on the west bank. Therefore it had to share Gad's territory in Transjordan, after which it soon vanished as an effective tribe. Levi, as a secular tribe, was involved in the

---

[8] Rowley, *From Joseph to Joshua*, pp. 106-107, 109-164.

early conquest as well, but later when it was set apart for
religious duties it had no inheritance of land, and thus was
not mentioned in Judges 1.

On this line of evidence and reasoning, Rowley contends
that about 1400 B.C. the group at Qadesh began a gradual
conquest of Canaan from the south. Judah was more cautious in gaining a footing, but Simeon and Levi moved
north quickly and captured Shechem (Gen. 34:25-29). They
were not able to hold the city, however, and were forced
south. Some of each tribe found refuge with Judah, but
the rest went all the way to Egypt to join other Hebrew
tribes there. Rowley finds biblical basis for this reconstruction in Jacob's comments about the tribes, "Simeon
and Levi are brothers, their swords are weapons of violence. . . . Cursed be their anger, for it is fierce; and their
wrath, for it is cruel. I will divide them in Jacob and
scatter them in Israel" (Gen. 49:5, 7).

While the Qadesh group was moving north, some of the
small northern tribes were moving into their territory
from the north or northeast. Dan, son of Bilhah, Rachel's
maid, moved clear down to the coastal plain, but it had to
retreat north to the Mt. Hermon region later on. Zebulun,
one of the younger Leah tribes, and Asher, son of Zilpah,
Leah's maid, gained their footing in the fourteenth century
B.C.

Joseph was taken into Egypt about 1370 B.C. at the
beginning of the reign of Akhenaton (Amenophis IV),
under whom he rose to power. Oppression of the Hebrews
began about 1300 B.C. during the reign of Ramses II.
Moses was born about 1290, and he fled in 1260 to a Kenite
kinsman of his mother. About 1230, during the reign of
Merneptah, Moses led the Rachel tribes (Ephraim, Manasseh, and Benjamin) and the rest of Simeon and Levi out
of Egypt. Yahweh, the God of Jethro, the priest of Midian,
was made known to the people by Moses and they entered
into a covenant. The ethical Decalogue of Exodus 20 was
formulated. After a few months Moses led his group
directly to Transjordan, where he died. Then, just two
years after leaving Egypt, Joshua led the group across the
Jordan to begin the conquest of central Palestine.

Rowley's reconstruction is very intriguing and, as he

claims, it seems to have a great deal of biblical support. He is correct that the conquest was a much more complicated affair than the biblical narrative indicates, and that the evidence seems to point to at least two waves of invasion. However, his late dates for Joseph and the Shechem incident involve a good deal of conjecture and shifting of evidence. Morover, it is hardly true that the combined story in the Bible can or need be separated into two completely different events all the way along. Notwithstanding his claim, the narratives do not say that the people stayed thirty-eight years at Qadesh. Moreover, splitting the forty years between the two groups seems very artificial.

Newman's Reconstruction

Newman presents a different combination and interpretation of the data used by Rowley.[9] He holds, with Noth, that the Leah tribes (Reuben, Simeon, Levi, Judah, Zebulun, and Issachar) once comprised a six-tribe amphictyony at Shechem, but that it was broken up at a later time. Judah, Simeon, and part of Levi came south and settled at Qadesh along with the Caleb and Othniel groups. The Kenites, who worshiped Yahweh, were in the area, and they introduced the others to Yahweh worship. Some of the Levi tribe went to Egypt, and later Moses, one of their number, led them and the Rachel tribes (Ephraim, Manasseh, and Benjamin) out of Egypt to Mt. Sinai. After the covenant experience there, Moses led the people to Qadesh, and the Levites were reunited.

Basic to Newman's reconstruction is the assumption that Exodus 15:22-18:27 originated at Qadesh. Hobab got in touch with Jethro, who came to see Moses and helped set up systems of justice and worship. The two communities lived together for a while, and apparently the Kenite group accepted the experience of the exodus group, even to the point of joining the covenant and adopting the Decalogue. But with the increased population there was a shortage of food and water. This plus varying outlooks on life led to serious tension and disputes. Since, in Newman's view, the Kenites were the original worshipers of Yahweh, they set up the priesthood, which apparently Aaron headed. Thus

---

9 Newman, *op. cit.*, pp. 72-101.

they had a rather authoritarian, dynastic outlook. The exodus group, on the other hand, had a more charismatic, democratic approach. Both groups claimed Moses, evidently, and he was caught in the middle trying to mediate between the opposing forces.

Finally, the situation came to a desperate showdown, as implied by the story of the Levites' zeal (Exod. 32:25-29). Moses sided with the Rachel tribes, and most of the Levites followed him. They actually had a blood battle with their Levite brethren from the other group, resulting in a complete split between the two factions at Qadesh. Newman, following older critics, understands the two spy stories (Num. 13-14) as traditions about two conquests. The P tradition, with its stress on the whole land of Canaan, indicates the larger conquest, while the J account, covering only southern Palestine around Hebron, depicts the conquest from the south by Judah and the related groups.

Archaeological surveys indicate that there was a wall of Canaanite forts across the northern Negev, and the defeat at Hormah proved the effectiveness of the defense. Because of this fact Newman believes that the Judah contingent did not attempt its conquest until after the Rachel tribes, under Joshua, broke up the Canaanite control of southern Palestine. The biblical account of this southern conquest, according to Newman, is found in Judges 1:1-20. A basic issue is the relationship between Judges 1 and Joshua 10, the account of Joshua's conquest of southern Canaan. Traditionally they have been taken to be variant accounts of Joshua's southern campaign. Newman, however, holds that the campaign route south from Jerusalem to Hebron and then west is a scribal revision of the original record of the conquest from the south in order to make the data fit the theory of a unified conquest from the east under Joshua. This reconstruction is possible because Judges 1:1-20 consists of a number of separate units which have been put together by an editor. It is equally possible, however, that Judges 1 represents various campaigns which, as G. Ernest Wright suggests,[10] were carried out later on during the period of the Judges, when the Israelites repossessed some

[10] G. Ernest Wright, *Biblical Archaeology* (Philadelphia: Westminster, 1961), p. 70.

sites they had temporarily lost to the Canaanites. The available evidence is not strong enough to substantiate the idea of a conquest from the south; therefore the concept still remains a theory with the burden of proving its case.

Another major factor in Newman's reconstruction is the theory that after the breakup of the Qadesh community the ark and the tent of meeting were separated. The ark, with the Levites in charge, remained the holy object of the exodus group, while the tent of meeting, with the Aaronic priesthood, became the center of the cult of the Judah group when it established its amphictyony at Hebron. Newman avoids the extremes of Rowley, Noth, and von Rad by contending that the Qadesh community involved both groups and both cult objects, but by positing the tent of meeting as the cult object of the southern group he does so more on faith than on evidence. It is true, as has been noted, that there is little reference to the tent after the desert period, but when its function was assumed by the ark it became merely a covering, and there was hardly any need to mention it. The issue requires more than the silence about the tent up north to prove that it was down south. In fact, the argument from silence is the weakest link in Newman's theory. There is not one bit of evidence to show that the tent was ever in the south, let alone the amphictyonic shrine at Hebron.

A final query about Newman's reconstruction concerns the place of Moses. One of the major themes of the J tradition was the authority of Moses. Newman accepts the biblical tradition, which even Noth did not doubt, that Moses died in Moab. If in the bitter struggle at Qadesh Moses threw in his lot with the Rachel tribes, is it feasible psychologically to explain the role which he played in the J tradition? In summary, the tentative nature of the major factors in Newman's reconstruction raises the question whether a rigid either-or does not create more difficulties than it solves.

The Composition of the Qadesh Community

There is much to be said for Noth's theory that the earliest organization of the Hebrew tribes was the six-tribe amphictyony of the Leah group in the central hill country. Leah was the first wife of Jacob, and whenever the twelve tribes are listed the Leah group appears first. Something must have happened to the confederation, however, because much of the area it occupied was taken over later by the Rachel tribes. If in the theories of Rowley and Newman some of the Levites went down to Egypt at the destruction of the Leah amphictyony, there is no reason why some of Reuben, Simeon, and Judah could not have done the same, especially if Joseph is dated early. It is a question how many of the later Leah tribes (Issachar and Zebulun) and the concubine tribes (Gad and Asher from Zilpah, Leah's maid, and Dan and Naphtali from Bilhah, Rachel's maid) were in Egypt. An answer is not pressing since most of them were in the northern part of Palestine and none of them played a major role in Israel's later history.

While there may be reasons for positing two conquests, there is no evidence for two exoduses from Egypt. Accordingly, it is the contention of this writer that Israelite traditions are best explained by a representative group of tribes (at least Reuben, Levi, Judah, Ephraim, Manasseh, and Benjamin) sharing together the exodus, Sinai, Qadesh, and Transjordan experiences. In addition, non-Israelite groups like the Kenites and Calebites formed part of the group from Qadesh on. This is not to say that portions of the tribes could not have gone south after the breakup of the Leah confederation, and then circled through Transjordan to enter Canaan from the southeast just as the major group would do later under Moses.

Routes to Transjordan

The details about the journey from Qadesh to Amorite country in Transjordan are sketchy at best, and the placement of the narrative sections adds to the confusion. Over and above these difficulties there are two traditions about the route traveled. It will be helpful to clarify this issue before describing the events en route.

The J tradition, in accordance with Yahweh's command in Numbers 14:25, recalls that from Qadesh the route went through the wilderness (part of Zin, and down the Arabah) to the Reed Sea (Gulf of Aqaba) because the king of Edom would not permit the Israelites to go through his country. From there Moses led them east around the southern end of Edomite territory and then north through the fringes of the desert east of Edom and Moab.

Portions of the D tradition recall the same route. After wandering around the Mt. Seir region for a long time, Moses is told, "You have been going around this mountain country long enough. Turn northward" (Deut. 2:3). The command is clarified by 2:8-9: "Then we moved on, away from our kinsmen, the descendants of Esau who live in Seir, away from the Arabah road from Elath and Ezion-geber, and we turned and went in the direction of the wilderness of Moab." Elath and Ezion-geber seem to be successive names for the same place. At least both were not in use when the Israelites came through. Moses went east, away from the Arabah route extending north from Elath, and circled around Edom. But the instructions in Deuteronomy 2:4-6 seem to rely on the route of the P tradition. Moses informs the people that they will be going through the territory of Esau. Their kinsmen will be afraid of them, but the Israelites are not to fight with them because Yahweh has not given them even a footprint of Esau's land. They are to purchase food and water as they pass through. According to Deuteronomy 2:29, both Edom and Moab let Israel pass through and purchase food and water en route. Quite clearly, D combines features of two traditions.

The route in the P tradition goes via Mt. Hor, Zalmonah, Punon, Oboth, and Iye-abarim on the border of Moab (Num. 33:37-44). Zalmonah and Oboth are uncertain, but the anchor site of the route is Punon (Feinan), the great Edomite copper-mining center, almost due east of Qadesh-barnea. Since Mt. Hor is located on the border of Edom and Iye-abarim is on the border of Moab at a favorable point to cross the wadi Zered, it would seem that the P route goes through the heart of Edomite country.

What is to be done with these variant traditions? Noth solves the problem with a stroke of the pen. P's list of camp sites is simply a pilgrimage route, from the period of the monarchy, which some editor reversed and applied to the Israelites. But saying so does not necessarily make it true. Notwithstanding the difficulties involved with the P tradition, the central route should not be discounted too quickly. This is hardly the way the major group of tribes went, but it could have been the route of some groups in the fifteenth or fourteenth century B.C. before the Edomites were organized into a society with a king. Noth recognizes that a number of the tribes entered Canaan from the southeast; therefore some of the people from the Leah confederation could have come this way in an attempt to regain the territory they lost.

Departure from Qadesh

The section Numbers 20:14-21 tells of Moses' attempt to seek passage through Edom. It has none of the distinctive characteristics of the P tradition, and yet there are doublets and inner variations of detail. Noth explains this as the first clear-cut appearance of the E tradition since the book of Exodus. Yet the strands are so interwoven he designates the section as JE. In his message to the king of Edom, Moses calls himself "your brother Israel." He relates briefly the Egyptian experience and then adds, "Here we are at Qadesh, a city (actually a town) on the edge of your territory." The use of "city" for Qadesh is very odd, and so is the location of Qadesh on the border of Edomite territory. Moses promises to stay on the "King's Highway," the ancient north-south superhighway in Transjordan on which the king and other officials could travel with chariots and wagons. He offers to pay for the water used en route, but the answer is "No!"

Then the narrative states, "Edom came out against them with many men and with a strong force. Thus Edom refused to give Israel passage through his territory, so Israel turned away from him." This show of strength was hardly put on for the benefit of the messengers, and so the story shifts from the negotiations in the previous verses to an actual confrontation. It would appear that Israel left Qadesh hoping to go through Edom; therefore at a camp site on the border messengers were dispatched to the king. To back up his refusal the king ordered the army out in force. Since, as the D tradition makes clear, the Israelites were not to fight the descendants of Esau, they turned south and began their long detour around Edom.

The actual departure from Qadesh is noted in a unit of P tradition material (20:22-29). The people come to Mt. Hor and Moses is told of Aaron's imminent death due to his rebellion against Yahweh's command at Meribah. Moses takes Aaron and Eleazar to the top of Mt. Hor, where Eleazar is dressed with the priestly garments stripped from Aaron. Aaron dies there, but there is no reference to his burial. When Moses and Eleazar return to report his death, the people mourn for thirty days.

The JE section 21:1-3 relates that when the Canaanite king of Arad in the Negev heard that Israel was coming by "the way of the Atharim," he fought them and took some captives. Excavations at Tell Arad indicate that it was not occupied during the thirteenth century. There were two Arads, however, so the Canaanite Arad was probably Tell el-Milh, as Yohanan Aharoni suggests.[11] But this is far north of the route taken from Qadesh. It seems to be another report about the ill-fated attempt to enter Canaan through the Negev. "The way of the Atharim" does not occur elsewhere, in or out of the Bible, but ancient versions translate "the way of the spies," and most likely it was the route from Qadesh through the Negev up to Hebron in the hill country. Following this defeat in the Negev the Israelites vow that if Yahweh will give the land of Canaan into their hands, they will "utterly destroy their cities." Then the editor jumps ahead to the event in Judges 1:17 (where Judah and Simeon destroy Zephath and rename it Hormah) and comments that Yahweh heard the vow and the place was called Hormah because of the destruction of the Canaanites.

The editorial note in 21:4 places the story of the bronze serpent (5-9) during the difficult journey down the Arabah and around Edom. Again the people become impatient, and they speak against "God" (perhaps another indication of the E tradition) and Moses. There is no water and they loathe "this worthless food," which apparently is a reference to manna, but the narrative has not mentioned it for a long time. Yahweh sends "burning *(saraph)* serpents," which bite the people and cause many deaths. The idea of "burning, fiery" probably refers to the poisonous bite and not the bright coloring of the snakes. The people confess their sins, Moses intercedes, and Yahweh instructs him to

---

[11] Yohanan Aharoni, *The Land of the Bible* (Philadelphia: Westminster, 1967), pp. 184-185.

make a *saraph,* apparently a likeness of the snake. Then, according to the text, Moses makes a bronze serpent and puts it on a pole so that everyone suffering from snake bite can look at it and be healed.

There is no indication that the serpent was kept after it served its purpose, but during Hezekiah's reform a bronze serpent named "Nehushtan" was broken in pieces (2 Kings 18:4). The biblical editor identifies the serpent as the one Moses made, and then he notes that the people had been burning incense to it. In Hebrew *nahash* means "serpent," *nehosheth* means "bronze," and *nehushtan* is the name of the bronze serpent. Clearly a play on words is involved. Inasmuch as poisonous snake bites take effect fairly soon, the fashioning of a bronze serpent could hardly have been done in time, even with Hobab, the metal worker, on hand. Yahweh's instructions to Moses do not tell him to make a bronze serpent. The point of the story is that the likeness of the snake, regardless of what it was made, served as a symbol of Yahweh's healing power, not an object of worship. Almost certainly the bronze serpent of Hezekiah's time, which had practically served as a snake-god, was attributed to Moses to give sanction to the incense offerings. This in turn led to the editorial note in 21:9 that Moses made a bronze serpent.

The passage 21:10-20 is an editor's attempt to bridge the gap between the circuit around Edom and the conquest of the territory of Sihon the Amorite. It consists of little pieces of information and ancient poetry. References to the camp sites of Oboth and Iye-abarim, on the southern frontier of Moab (10-11), are from the priestly list (Num. 33:43-44), but the Israelites were further to the east when they came north. If, as 21:12 states, the next camp was at the wadi Zered, this would have meant a journey south; therefore this is another indication that verses 10-11 are out of place.

The next camp is in the wilderness (called Qedemoth in Deut. 2:26) to the northeast of the wadi Arnon, the boundary between Moab and the Amorites. The D tradition has Israel crossing the Arnon at Ar, west of the wilderness, but this is based on the assumption that they came up the King's Highway. As elsewhere, D has mixed traditions so that its narrative is not consistent. The mention of the Arnon and Moab is the occasion for inserting an old, and very obscure, piece of poetry from the Book of the Wars of Yahweh (14-15). This is the only time the old book is mentioned in the Old Testament. The RSV translates: "Waheb in Suphah, and the valleys of the Arnon, and the slope of the valleys that extends to the seat of Ar, and leans to the border of Moab." The NEB tries to make more sense by taking the first part of the poem as part of the introduction: "That is why the Book of the Wars of the Lord speaks of Vaheb (Watershed) in Suphah and the gorges: Arnon and the watershed of the gorges that falls away towards the dwellings at Ar and slopes towards the frontier of Moab." An indication of the antiquity of the quotation is the use of the letter "m" to bind two words into a unit. The original *nahale-m Arnon* ("the Valleys of the Arnon") was read later as *nehalim Arnon*, which is grammatically impossible.

The next camp site is Be-er ("Well, Water-hole"), the place where Yahweh said to Moses, "Gather the people together and I will give them water" (16). This event is mentioned nowhere else, but the people sang a song: "Spring up, O well — Sing to it — the well which the princes unearthed, which the nobles of the people dug with scepter and staves." From Be-er the itinerary continues to Mattanah, Nahliel, Bamoth, and finally to the valley in Moabite country below the summit of Pisgah. But inasmuch as this refers to the big camp on the east side of the Jordan, the editor has gotten ahead of the story, and we must return to pick up the account about Sihon the Amorite.

Chapter 12

In Sight of the Promised Land

At the wilderness of Qedemoth, northeast of the Arnon, Moses and the Israelites were near the end of their long, weary journey. They had safely skirted along the eastern edge of Edom and Moab, and now only the territory of Sihon the Amorite separated them from the Jordan valley.

Sihon Conquered by Israel

As they had done with the king of Edom, the Israelites send messengers to Sihon requesting passage through his territory. They promise to stay on the King's Highway and not to endanger his fields, vineyards, and wells. In the D tradition Moses urges Sihon to sell them food and water and to let them pass through on foot as the Edomites and Moabites had done (Deut. 2:28-29). But this is in contradiction to the JE account as well as D's own claim in Deuteronomy 23:4 that regulations against the Moabites were for their refusal to let Israel have bread and water. JE and D agree that Sihon refused the peaceful offer, but D comments, "Yahweh your God hardened his spirit and made his heart stubborn that he might give him into your hand" (Deut. 2:30). Sihon backs up his refusal by marching with his army out into the wilderness to confront his supposed enemy. At Jahaz he attacks the intruders, but they prove to be more than a match and he is slain.

The Israelites rout his forces, take possession of all his territory from the Arnon to the Jabbok, and settle in his cities and towns, including Heshbon, Sihon's capital. This conquest included Jazer and its environs, but they went no further because Jazer bordered on the small Ammonite state at the upper reaches of the Jabbok. Since Sihon had wrested his territory from the king of Moab, the Moabites and the Ammonites were not very friendly to him. In view

316

of Yahweh's instruction that Moses not fight with the Moabites and Ammonites, it is quite possible that Moses made some kind of nonaggression agreement with them in the event of difficulty with Sihon.

At the mention of Heshbon the editor includes a favorite ballad of the singers in the area (Num. 21:27-30). The poetry is quite difficult at times, and scholars are not agreed whether the ballad tells of Sihon's conquest of Moab and the construction of his capital Heshbon, or whether the poem was composed by the Israelites as a victory song over Sihon. The RSV assumes the former interpretation:

> *Come to Heshbon, let it be built,*
>   *let the city of Sihon be established.*
> *For fire went forth from Heshbon,*
>   *flame from the city of Sihon.*
> *It devoured Ar of Moab,*
>   *the lords of the heights of the Arnon.*
> *Woe to you, O Moab!*
>   *You are undone, O people of Chemosh!*
> *He has made his sons fugitives,*
>   *and his daughters captives,*
>   *to an Amorite king, Sihon.*
> *So their posterity perished from Heshbon,*
>   *as far as Dibon, and we laid waste*
>   *until fire spread to Medeba.*

Noth, on the other hand, is convinced that the Israelites composed the ballad:

> *Come to Heshbon, let it be rebuilt,*
>   *let the city of Sihon be established!*
> *for fire had gone forth from Heshbon,*
>   *a flame from the city of Sihon,*
> *it had consumed the cities of Moab,*
>   *devoured the heights by the Arnon.*
> *Woe to you, O Moab,*
>   *you are ruined, O people of Chemosh!*
> *He has made his sons fugitives,*
>   *and his daughters prisoners of the Amorites.*
> *But we have gained the upper hand, Heshbon is*

*ruined and we have further kindled a fire
against Medeba.*[1]

It seems far more probable that Israel would have preserved portions of its own victory song rather than that of
Sihon's, but perhaps the issue cannot be settled until further evidence is forthcoming. Hopefully the current excavations at Tell Hesban (Heshbon) will produce that
information.

The Defeat of Og

Once the Israelites are settled in Sihon's territory they
move north of the Jabbok to occupy the northern part of
Gilead. Then they continue on to Bashan, the fertile country flanking the upper reaches of the wadi Yarmuk. Og,
the king of Bashan, learns of the invasion, and so he comes
south from his capital at Ashtaroth and attacks the Israelites at Edrei (Num. 21:33). The fate of Sihon becomes his,
and the Israelites occupy his territory. The names Sihon
and Og have not been found in any nonbiblical records, and
some scholars doubt the historicity of the stories. Egyptian
records covering the century 1450-1350 B.C. refer to a
number of city-states in Bashan (Hauran) and upper
Gilead. By 1300 the Edomites and the Moabites, as vassals
of the Midianites, consolidated their areas, and there is
every reason to believe that Ramses II, who at that time
was fighting the Hittites, was favorable to such regional
states as buffers to his enemy up north. The kingdoms of
Sihon and Og fit the thirteenth-century trend from city-
states to regional confederations, and so there is good
reason to accept the narratives even though nonbiblical
references have not been found as yet.

The D tradition notes that Og was the last of the
Rephaim, a race of giants in Transjordan. The editorial
note cites as proof the gigantic iron bedstead of Og which
the Ammonites were displaying at Rabbah. It does not say
how the Ammonites got the bed if the Israelites conquered
Og, but it gives the measurements as nine cubits long and
four cubits wide, that is, thirteen and a half by six feet
(Deut. 3:11). It so happens that the Babylonian god
Marduk is reported to have had a bed of the same dimen-

[1] Noth, *Numbers*, p. 161.

sions in the bedroom of his temple Esagil in Babylon. Perhaps the ceremonial bed found its way indirectly to the Ammonite capital. Later on, knowledge of its gigantic size led to its association with Og.

The Occupation of Transjordan

The references to possessing the land of Og (21:35) and to settling in the cities of the Amorites (21:25) seem to indicate a rather extended stay; yet in 22:1 the people set out and camp in the "lowlands of Moab" on the east side of the Jordan valley, across from Jericho. This is a rapid shift in location and point of view, and perhaps the transition is explained in Numbers 32. There the tribes of Reuben and Gad come to Moses, Eleazar, and the congregation to request permission to stay on the Transjordanian plateau rather than go over to Canaan. They have many cattle and the land is suited to their needs. If this be true, it indicates a considerable time of settlement and stock breeding because they most certainly did not have them during the long journey in the wilderness. In any case, Moses inquires, "Shall your kinsmen go into war while you stay here? Why do you discourage the heart of the Israelites from going over into the land which Yahweh has given them?" (6-7). Then Moses likens them to the spies who discouraged the people and brought such disastrous results (14-15).

Reuben and Gad counter with a pledge (16-19). If Moses will permit them to get their animals and families settled, the men of military age will go and help conquer Canaan. They will stay until the task is done and they will request no land there because their inheritance will be on the east side of the Jordan. Moses accepts the idea (20-22), instructs Eleazar and Joshua (28-30), and allots the land of Sihon to the two tribes (33-38). Half of the tribe of Manasseh is assigned north of the Jabbok (39-42), even though it was not involved in the original request. Perhaps it is after this agreement that most of the Israelites move from the high plateau down to the lowlands in the Jordan valley. While the adolescents and older men were probably able to protect the settlements scattered on the plateau, they could not completely control the territory taken from

Sihon. Undoubtedly Moabites filtered back to settle where they could and to worship at the old shrines.

Balak Sends for Balaam

Numbers 22-24 relates the interesting story of the attempt of Balak, the king of Moab, to stop the Israelite expansion by hiring the seer Balaam to pronounce a curse on them. Moses is not mentioned once in the three chapters and the Israelites play no active role. They are oblivious to Balak's evil intent, but Yahweh is very active in their behalf. The whole story was transmitted through the early sources JE. Interspersed among the prose sections are four major discourses of Balaam, all in poetic form. The latter have very archaic forms at times, and in general they represent a far older tradition than the prose sections. Noth finds the main section of the E tradition in 22:41-23:26 and J in 23:28-24:19. While some of the prose has the appearance of being in doublet form, the pairs of poetic discourses have very little in common. Furthermore, "Yahweh" appears about twice as many times as "God" in the so-called E account. It is more probable that the JE story had the four poetic sections from the beginning.

Moab sees what Israel has done to the Amorites and becomes very fearful. After consulting with the elders of Midian, Balak sends messengers to "Balaam the son of Beor at Pethor, which is by the river, in the land of the sons of his people" (22:5). This description of Pethor's location is very odd, and many scholars have contended that the Hebrew text is inaccurate. In Balaam's first oracle he describes himself as being "from Aram" and "from the eastern mountains" (23:7). Deuteronomy 23:4 notes that he was from *Aram-naharaim* ("Aram of the Two Rivers"), that is, the land between the Tigris and Euphrates rivers. Another designation of Aram is the Greek term *Mesopotamia* ("Between the Rivers"). The "eastern mountains" seems to be a reference to the Jebel el-Bishri range in Syria. Yet this is a very long way to go for a seer, and since "Aram" and "Edom" are very similar in Hebrew, a number of scholars have taken Edom to be the home of Balak.

The conjecture has proven unnecessary, fortunately, because new evidence shows the accuracy of the consonantal Hebrew text. The inscriptions of the Assyrian king Shalmaneser III (858-824 B.C.) provide part of the answer in noting a town "Pitru" on the Sagur River above its junction with the Euphrates. The Idrimi stele (about 1450 B.C.) mentions four provinces in what is now Syria, one being "Amaw," along the Euphrates River. An inscription from the time of Amenophis II (about 1435-1420 B.C.) tells of Pharaoh capturing a Syrian land named "Amaw." The two fifteenth-century inscriptions confirm that there was a province of Amaw along the Euphrates, and the ninth-century text locates Pitru within that area. Since names tend to persist, it is reasonable to assume that in the thirteenth century there was a Pitru in the province of Amaw. By changing only the vowels of the Hebrew text back of "his people" the name "Amaw" appears, and so 22:5 can be translated intelligently: "Pethor, which is by the Euphrates, in the land of the sons (people) of Amaw."

Balak's message to Balaam makes clear why he went so far to seek help: "I know that those whom you bless are blessed, and those whom you curse are cursed" (6). Mesopotamian diviners were famous, and apparently Balaam had an exceptionally good record. It is impossible to say what kind of diviner he was. Perhaps he had worked both as a *baru* ("seer") (a technical diviner using animal livers to determine, for example, which road the army should take), and as an *apilu* ("answerer") (a prophet working alone, or on the staff of a temple, who delivered oracles on request from the king or other officials). As far as Balak was concerned, Balaam was to function as an *apilu*.

The elders of Moab and Midian come to Balaam with the request and the fees for divination. He requests that they remain overnight, then he will give them an answer. During the night God comes to Balaam, evidently in a dream-vision, and commands him not to go because he is not to curse the blessed people (12). Balaam informs Balak's officials, and they return to inform the king. Balak sends a greater number of officials of higher rank with the message, "I will surely show you great honor, and whatever you say to me I will do. Come, curse this people for me" (17). Balaam informs them that even Balak's house full of silver and gold would not be enough for him to go beyond the command of Yahweh his God. Again he requests that they remain overnight. This time God tells

him to go with the officials, but he is warned to do only
what God tells him to do (20).

Balaam's Donkey Talks Back

In the section Numbers 22:21-35 Balaam departs with
two of his servants on a 400-mile donkey ride, but God is
angry with him, and so the messenger (angel) of Yahweh,
with drawn sword, stands in the path as his adversary
(Hebrew *satan*). In order to avoid the messenger the
donkey strays into a field, crushes Balaam's foot against
a wall, and finally crouches down under him. Each time
Balaam strikes his donkey, and finally she inquires why he
has done it. "Because you have been making a fool of me,"
replies Balaam. "I wish I had a sword in my hand, for
then I would kill you." The donkey reminds Balaam that
she has never acted this way before, even though she has
carried him for years. Yahweh opens Balaam's eyes, and
seeing the messenger he prostrates himself. He is informed
that his actions are perverse, and then the messenger says,
"If she had not turned away from me, I would surely have
slain you just now and let her live" (33). Balaam confesses
his sin and volunteers to return, but the messenger says,
"Go with the men, but speak only what I command you."
And so "Balaam went on with the princes of Balak" (35).

The story of Balaam's donkey is well written and teaches
theological truths in a very interesting way. Yet its presence in the text raises some problems. In verse 12 God
refuses to let Balaam go, in 20 he grants his permission,
but with a warning, and then in 22 he is very angry with
Balaam for having gone. The older commentators deny
that God is whimsical or inconsistent here. He uses this
apparently contradictory way to teach Balaam a lesson.
Notwithstanding his statement placing obedience above
silver and gold, Balaam (according to these expositors)
is greedy for the large honorarium because otherwise he
would not have asked God's opinion the second time. Yet
the older interpreters did not reckon with the fact that
professional diviners sought the will of their gods at every
important juncture of life regardless of what had happened
previously.

But all of this jumping through hoops to preserve God's
integrity is unnecessary if it is recognized that the story

about the donkey is a separate unit. The designation "God" appears four times in verses 7-20, and aside from an editorial use of "God" in 22, "Yahweh" appears all the way through verses 21-35a. The story was transmitted through the J tradition and then incorporated at a later time into the larger story about Balaam. Further indication of this fact is that the officials of Balak play no real part in the story. They appear only as editorial blends at the beginning and end of the story. Accordingly, it is fruitless to speculate about their reactions to the curious interplay between the donkey and Balaam. The officials were not there. Moreover, the type of literature indicates that it is a folk tale, whereas the regular story is quite straightforward and factual. Finally, the point of view is different. In verse 21 Balaam leaves on his own volition, and so Yahweh is just in his anger and confrontation of Balaam. In verse 20, however, God grants his permission to go with Balak's officials, and in 35a Yahweh's messenger does the same. The wording is very similar and both temper the permission with the same warning. Whereas the two accounts differ in perspective at the outset, they both come to the same point, and the story continues in 35b: "So Balaam went on with the princes of Balak."

Balaam Blesses Israel

Balak hears that Balaam is coming, and he shows honor by going to the border of Moab to meet him. Balak asks Balaam why he did not come. He replies that he has come, but that he can speak only what God commands him. They come to Kiriath-huzoth, where Balak sacrifices sheep and oxen and invites Balaam and the officials to a meal. Unfortunately the town is not mentioned elsewhere in the Bible, and so there are no definite clues as to its precise location. The next day Balak takes Balaam to *Bamoth-baal* ("High Places of Baal"), where he can see the Israelite camp. Apparently Balak skirted past the Israelite settlements to a vantage point along the edge of the plateau. The purpose of giving Balaam a view of the Israelite camp was to ensure a more effective curse. Although the high place probably had an old altar for worshiping Baal, Balaam requests seven new altars as well as seven bulls and seven rams. Balak grants the request, and together they offer a bull and a ram on each altar. Balaam asks Balak to stand by his offering while he goes to a bare height nearby and inquires of God what to say. Balaam gets his message and returns to Balak and his officials.

His oracle (23:7-10) features assonance of verb forms: "How can I curse whom El has not cursed? How can I doom whom Yahweh has not doomed?" Balaam sees the people from his lofty vantage point and declares, "Who can count the host (dust) of Jacob, or number the hordes (dust-clouds) of Israel?" Then he closes with an implicit blessing, "Let me die the death of a just man, and let my end be like his."

Balak is aghast, and after denouncing Balaam he takes him to the field of *Zophim* ("Spies"), at the top of Pisgah. The view is excellent, as the name implies, and Balak hopes that seeing the Israelites from a better vantage point will encourage Balaam to pronounce a curse. The same sacrificial routine is carried out, and again Balaam seeks Yahweh's word. Having received his second oracle (18-24) he commands Balak's attention and declares, "El is not a man that he should lie, or a human that he should change his mind" (19). Balaam states that he was instructed to bless Israel and that he cannot revoke it. Yahweh, with royal majesty, is in Israel's midst, and they have "the horns of the wild ox," that is, the power to destroy, just as the victorious ox raises its horns after subduing its opponent (22). In old-style poetry Balaam affirms, "For there is no omen against Jacob, no divination against Israel." Those who have seen God's care for his people will say, "What has El done!"

Balak retorts, "You do not curse them, then do not bless them," but the blessing has been given and Balak must try again. He takes Balaam to the top of Peor which overlooks Yeshimon, the wilderness of the lower Jordan valley. Again the sacrificial routine is carried out, but this time Balaam knows that Yahweh will bless Israel, and so he does not resort to divination as he has twice before. As he looks toward the wilderness he can see the camp of Israel at the foot of the peak Peor, and the "Spirit of God" comes upon him with his third oracle (24:3-9). Among the blessings which Balaam pronounces is one declaring, "His king shall be higher than Agag, and his kingdom shall be exalted"(7). For many years critical scholars have interpreted this to be a reference to Saul and his victory over Agag, the king of the Amalekites (1 Sam. 15:7-8), and consequently they have dated the poem late. But Agag is the traditional name for the king of the Amalekites, and it functions more like a title. Perhaps Balaam spotted in the region some groups related to the Amalekites because he pronounces an oracle on them in 24:20. Moreover, Balaam's blessing is a general statement predicting Israel's dominance over her enemies, even the hated Amalekites. Albright has suggested translating the passage, "So may his kingdom be higher than Agag, and may his royalty be exalted!"[2]

Furthermore, conclusive evidence that the third oracle is very old is the style of poetry. In typical Canaanite form Balaam declares, "The oracle (vision) of Balaam, the son of Beor, the oracle of the man whose eye is sure." Then he adds, "The oracle of him who hears the words of El, who sees the vision of Shaddai." Finally Balaam invokes, "Blessed be everyone who blesses you, and cursed be everyone who curses you."

Balak is so angry at this third blessing he slaps his hands together and orders Balaam to head back home. Balaam says that he will go back to his people, but as his parting word he gives Balak an unsolicited oracle (24:15-19). The first two verses are quite similar to the introduction of the third oracle, but in addition to El and Shaddai the oracle is from one "who knows the knowledge of the Most High (Elyon)." Thus three of the old designations of God occur together. Balaam foresees that "a star shall come forth out of Jacob, and a scepter (or, comet) shall rise out of Israel" (17). This new leadership will "crush the foreheads of Moab and the skulls of the sons of Sheth." The sons of Sheth are really the *Bene Shut,* an old designation for the Moabites. Then in perfect Canaanite format (abc:acb') Balaam states, "And Edom shall be dispossessed, and dispossessed Seir shall be." Older critics understood these blessings as references to David's rise as king and his dominion over Moab and Edom. But

---

[2] Albright, "The Oracles of Balaam," *Journal of Biblical Literature,* LXIII, 3 (September 1944), 225.

David conquered the Ammonites and other groups in Transjordan, which are not mentioned here. The blessings are
general in nature and apply to Israel's experiences with
Moab and Edom in the thirteenth century.

For good measure Balaam adds three short oracles (20-
24). One predicts the destruction of the Amalekites, another
is against the Kenites, apparently a reference to the non-
Israelite group in the camp, and the last foresees that ships
from Kittim will afflict Asshur and Eber, that is, the people of Syria and Mesopotamia, Balaam's own neighbors.
The term "Kittim" originally designated the inhabitants
of Kitium on Cyprus, but eventually it meant anyone from
the island. Later on it referred to various other groups
coming into the Near East from the Mediterranean islands
or through Asia Minor, for example, the Greeks and Ro-
mans. Balaam's oracle makes no sense at this late date,
but recently it has been shown that the Philistines were
entrenched in eastern Cyprus by 1225 B.C. Word of their
prowess and determination probably made the inhabitants
of Syria and Palestine rather apprehensive, and by 1175
B.C. these fears came true. It is possible that this oracle,
involving Syria, was attributed to Balaam since he came
from that area. Be that as it may, after completing his
appended oracles Balaam returns home, and Balak goes
his way never to be heard of again. Although there are
still many obscurities about the circumstances of the Balaam story and the oracles, the style and content of the
poetry indicate that Balaam was an ancient Syrian diviner
who had some contact with Israel. He may have become a
convert to Yahweh through his futile attempts to pronounce a curse. He became famous because of his oracles,
and since the Israelites considered them as coming from
the "Spirit of God" (24:2) they were transmitted quite
carefully. They are an authentic witness to the presence
of the Israelites in Moab in the thirteenth century B.C.

The Apostasy to Baal at Peor

From their camp at Shittim (actually *Abel-shittim*,
"Meadow of the Acacias," Num. 33:49) the Israelites could
probably look up to the high place on Peor (Beth-peor, Deut.
3:29) where Baal was worshiped. Chemosh was the national god of the Moabites, but local shrines worshiped

Baal as the god of fertility. The rites involved sacred prostitution in which the human pair assisted the divine couple in promoting the fertility of the flocks and crops. In time the Moabite girls invite the Israelites to come up to Peor and share in the meals associated with the sacrifices. Eventually they participate in the fertility rites of Baal. Yahweh becomes furious, and he commands Moses to hang the chiefs of the people out in the sun to assuage his wrath. Evidently the leaders had not exercised very good care over the people; therefore they are held accountable. Then Moses instructs the judges to slay everyone who has been worshiping Baal of Peor. Nothing more is said about the chiefs or the slaughter of the idolaters because the JE account ends abruptly.

The unit 25:6-9 presupposes some such event as described in 1-5, but if it is a continuation it is a variant account because there are a number of differences. The language and focus of the unit are similar to the P tradition. In full view of Moses and the people one of the Israelites brings a Midianite woman to his tent while the congregation is weeping at the entrance to the tent of meeting. Phinehas, the son of Eleazar, is incensed at the brazen act, and pursues the couple with a spear. He finds them having intercourse in the inner room, and he pierces both of them with the spear. The plague, which has not been mentioned previously, is stayed, but 24,000 have died already. Undoubtedly sorrow for the dead and penitence over some great sin account for the weeping at the tent of meeting.

In the next passage (10-13), which is similar in theme to the ordination of the Levites (Exod. 32:25-29), Yahweh gives to Phinehas his "covenant of peace" because he has atoned for the people by his zeal. The covenant is defined further as "the covenant of a perpetual priesthood," probably meaning the line of chief priests. Supposedly the succession for the high priesthood has been determined by Aaron's dynasty, but theory must not have worked out as well in practice, otherwise there would have been no need to make this defense.

The two slain by Phinehas are identified as a Simeonite and the daughter of a tribal leader of the Midianites. Then Moses is commanded by Yahweh to harass and smite the

Midianites. The reason for this holy war is that the Midianites have beguiled the Israelites in the Peor and adultery incidents. This tradition, therefore, blames the Midianites for the apostasy, whereas the JE tradition faults the Moabites.

The Holy War Against Midian

The implementation of the ban on the Midianites is described in Numbers 31, and since 31:1 is a recapitulation of 25:16-18 it is certain that the two sections form one narrative. The five chapters 26-30 consist largely of priestly materials, and apparently the editor inserted the collection after chapter 25, instead of after 31, because it made reference (26:1) to "the plague," the same event noted in 25:18.

Yahweh commands Moses, "Avenge the Israelites on the Midianites. Afterward you shall be gathered to your people." Holy wars were the custom for Near Eastern nations in the thirteenth century B.C.; therefore it comes as no surprise that one of the last acts of Moses was the war with Midian. The theory in such wars was that each side devoted its opponent to its own god. In this case Moses devotes the Midianites to Yahweh with the intent of completely slaughtering the males, taking the women captive, and gathering the booty as holy trophies for Yahweh. An armed force of 12,000 (1,000 from each tribe) is sent out with Phinehas, who has the sanctuary vessels and the trumpets for sounding alarms. Remarkably there is no mention of the ark, which elsewhere is always at the head of the army in a holy war.

The Israelites are successful and return with the women, children, and booty. Moses is angry, however, when he sees the women, for they caused the apostasy at Peor. The virgins are kept as slaves and concubines, but the rest of the women are slain. Even the boys are killed, evidently in an attempt at genocide. All the soldiers and the booty go through the seven-day cleansing process, and the metal objects are purified by fire. The booty is divided into two parts: one for the warriors, who give a fifth of one percent of their share as a gift to the priests; and the other for the congregation, which gives two percent of its part to the Levites.

Discounting the offerings made to the priests and Levites, if the remaining portion of the booty is divided evenly, the amount captured by *each* of the 12,000 warriors comes to about fifty-six sheep, six cattle, five asses, and three virgins. In addition to the difficulty of such extensive spoils, the number of soldiers is way out of proportion to the total number of the Israelites. Again, the word *eleph* has been taken to mean 1,000, but each tribe probably supplied a much smaller number of warriors. Certainly the claim "they slew every male" (31:7) is an armchair editorial which superimposed theory on fact. In spite of many vicious wars and attempts at genocide within the period of more detailed reporting and record keeping, there has never been a complete destruction of a people, and there is no reason to think that it was so in the case of the Israelite attempt. The best proof of this is the biblical witness itself: during the period of the Judges the Midianites were back haunting the Israelites. Most uses of "all," "every," and "none" represent the oversimplification of later generations. This is true of the Midianite battle because "all" is used with respect to the cattle, flocks, goods, cities, encampments, booty, women, and young girls.

Although the account of the holy war with Midian evidences accretions from later times, there are indications that the story stems from the Mosaic period. It is very interesting, as Albright observes,[3] that the list of booty does not mention one camel. Camel-riding Midianites harassed the Israelites for a number of years around 1100 B.C. (Judg. 6:1-6), and from that time on inscriptions from the Near East refer mostly to camels for carrying goods and people. Numbers 31, accordingly, describes an event prior to that time at least.

Otto Eissfeldt has shown that during the thirteenth century B.C. the Midianites exercised a kind of protectorate over the vassal states Moab and Edom.[4] They, like the Nabateans 1,000 years later, controlled the great caravan

---

[3] Albright, "Midianite Donkey Caravans," *Translating and Understanding the Old Testament: Essays in Honor of Herbert Gordon May* (Nashville: Abingdon, 1970), pp. 197-205.

[4] Eissfeldt, "Protektorat der Midianiter über ihre Nachbarn im letzten Viertel des 2. Jahrtausends v. Chr.," *Journal of Biblical Literature*, LXXXVII, 4 (December 1968), 383-393.

routes from Arabia. Albright suggests that Queen Hatshep-
sut's successful expedition to Punt (Somaliland) about
1480 B.C. probably created a demand for spices and exotic
items like myrrh and frankincense. Around 1400, therefore,
the Midianites, working in conjunction with the caravaneers of Dedan, Saba, and Hadramot, inaugurated donkey caravans to South Arabia in order to supply the mar-
kets in Egypt and Syria.[5] It was a long, weary journey,
however, and the loads had to be shifted to fresh animals
a number of times en route. Camels were more naturally
suited for such a task, and by 1150 approximately, the
nomadic Midianites had domesticated enough of them to
replace the donkeys in the caravans. But the process of
domesticating and training a large number of camels must
have taken a number of years; therefore the story of Numbers 31 appears to go back to the thirteenth century B.C.

A startling detail in the account of the war against
Midian is that Balaam, the son of Beor, was among the
slain (8). He is accused of counseling the Midianites to
defeat the Israelites by the wiles of religious seduction
(16). Old conservative scholars like Hengstenberg sur-
mised that when Balaam was dismissed by Balak without
his honorarium he went to the Israelite camp and related
his oracles to Moses with the hope of gaining the reward
which Balak had withheld. After having his offer rejected,
he went to the Midianites (since they had been involved
in seeking his services) and got revenge on Israel by ad-
vising them to subdue the Israelites through the seductive
rituals of the Moabites. While this reconstruction may be
too neat, it has some basis. Balaam, in his oracles, seems
to imply that he is a believer in Yahweh, but he could
have reverted just as many converts have done. The cou-
pling of the blessing of Israel with the apostasy of Israel
(Num. 24 and 25) is quite unexpected, and this sharp
contrast seems to fit in with the tradition of Balaam's
apostasy.

One of the difficulties in the narratives of the stay in
Moab is the change of attitude the Midianites experienced
with respect to the Israelites. Zipporah and Hobab were
Midianites, and there is no indication that the Israelites

---

[5] Albright, "Midianite Donkey Caravans," *op. cit.*, pp. 204-205.

had any difficulty in their journey around Edom and up along the desert even though it was Midianite territory. According to the biblical narratives, the two peoples were on friendly terms until after the defeat of Sihon. Joshua 13:21 lists Evi, Rekem, Zur, Hur, and Reba as the five "princes of Midian" whom Moses defeated, and then it makes the interesting observation that these had been "princes of Sihon." In Numbers 31:8 the same five are named and called "kings of Midian."

The story of Balaam indicates that Israel's defeat of Sihon and the Amorites struck fear into the hearts of the Moabites (22:3), and so they expressed their fear (apparently through Balak, the "king of Moab") to the "elders of Midian" (4). As a result "the elders of Moab and the elders of Midian departed with the fees for divination in their hand, and they came to Balaam" (7). It is quite evident that the "king of Moab" and the "elders of Moab" were subservient to the "elders of Midian." In other words, the "elders" were actually supervisors the Midianites had stationed within the territory of Moab to guarantee that the vassal king did not get out of line. This same situation held true apparently even when Sihon conquered the northern part of Moab, because the Midianite "princes" are described as the "princes of Sihon, who dwelt in the land" (Josh. 13:21), that is, at Heshbon, the capital city of Sihon. Accordingly, the terms "elders," "princes," and "kings" are simply variant designations for the Midianite representatives in the land of Moab.

The control of the Midianites was so extensive and it involved so many segments that being on good terms with one or two groups within the Midianite federation did not guarantee the same treatment elsewhere. When the Israelites defeated Sihon and began to settle some of their people in the land, evidently the Midianites, like the Moabites, interpreted these successes as a threat to their welfare. The supervisors and the local leaders took joint action in seeking the aid of Balaam, and when he failed to pronounce a curse on the Israelites, they resorted to religious seduction to accomplish their goal. It is readily apparent how the complex political situation in Transjordan would lead to two parallel traditions, one attributing the apostasy of Israel to the Moabites and the other blaming the Midi-

anites. The fact that Midian was the object of Israel's holy
war indicates the leading role of the Midianites.

The Second Census

After the plague resulting from the apostasy at Peor,
Moses is commanded to take a census of all the men twenty
years old and up who are able to go to war (26:2). The
purpose is to determine Israel's fighting strength and the
size of each tribal allotment in Canaan. One significant
difference between this census and the one in Numbers 1
is that here Manasseh precedes Ephraim, in the order of
their birth (Gen. 48:8-22), whereas in 1:32-35 Ephraim
is first, representing the situation at a later time when
Ephraim was the dominant tribe. This variation probably indicates that the two census reports came through
different traditions, or from different periods.

Following the completion of the census Moses is told to
apportion the land according to the number of names; that
is, a large tribe was to get a large inheritance, etc. (26:
53-54). Yet in the next verse the land is to be "divided
by lot." The two methods are harmonized by a further
command, "Their inheritance shall be divided according to
lot between the larger and the smaller" (56). Accordingly,
certain large and small territories were to be specified and
the lot used to determine which specific area of a category
each tribe got. Such an idea was admirable in theory, but
aside from assigning each tribe an area to attack, the
actual conquest (according to the book of Joshua) did
not work out as neatly in practice. Even though the lot is
mentioned in 14:2, there is no report of a drawing of lots
or of a survey of the land. The big three (Judah, Ephraim,
and Manasseh) occupy what territory they can, and then
the rest of the land is surveyed and divided into seven sections, which are then assigned by lot at Shiloh (Josh.
18:8-10).

Zelophehad's Daughters

Numbers 27 is an excellent example of how case law
develops over a period of time. A basic principle of Israelite patriarchal society was inheritance by the males.
Another feature was the inviolable nature of inherited land:
it was to stay within the family and tribe (Lev. 25:10, 23).

At the time these principles were issued the problem of a man with no sons was not foreseen. Zelophehad was the father of five daughters, but he died during the wilderness years before he could beget a son. The girls approach Moses with their problem, "Why should the name of our father be taken away from his family because he had no sons? Give us a possession among our father's brothers" (4). Moses agrees that it is not fair to let Zelophehad's inheritance pass on to his brothers; therefore he orders that it be shared by the five daughters. This new case leads to an extended law in which Moses anticipates a number of situations in which there might not be an heir: if no sons, the daughter; if no daughter, the man's brothers; if no brothers, the man's uncles; and if no uncles, the kinsman next in line (8-11).

But still all possibilities have not been covered, and so in Numbers 36:1-12 another case and the resultant regulation are noted. Members of Manasseh, the tribe of Zelophehad's daughters, urge Moses to make another ruling because if any of the girls marries outside the tribe, then the inheritance will shift to the tribe of the husband, thus violating permanent tribal inheritance. Moses agrees again, and he issues another regulation permitting heiresses to marry within the tribe. The girls marry their cousins, and so their inheritance remains within the tribe of Manasseh.

The Commissioning of Joshua

In Numbers 27:12 Yahweh instructs Moses to go up to Mt. Abarim (the hills at the edge of the Transjordan plateau, of which Mt. Nebo is specified in Deut. 32:49) and view the land which the Israelites are to inherit. This will be his only experience of the land because, as a result of his rebellion against Yahweh at Meribah, he is to be gathered to his ancestors just as Aaron was. There is no indication here of Moses' feelings about being barred from the promised land, but the D tradition notes an attempt by Moses to change Yahweh's verdict. He is convinced that the Meribah affair was the fault of the people and so he pleads, "Let me cross over to see the good land on the other side of the Jordan, the fine hill country, and the Lebanon" (Deut. 3:25). But Yahweh is angry with him and commands him never to speak of the matter again.

Before Yahweh can get to the topic of a successor, Moses pleads, "Let Yahweh, the God of the spirits of all flesh, appoint a man over the congregation ... that the congregation of Yahweh may not be as sheep without a shepherd" (16-17). Yahweh instructs Moses to select Joshua, who has the spirit (that is, the gift to lead), and to delegate some of his authority to Joshua so that the people will obey him. This Moses does in the presence of Eleazar and all the people (23). There is one big difference, however. Whereas Moses received Yahweh's word directly, Joshua will receive it from Eleazar, the priestly mediator. The account of Joshua's commissioning in Deuteronomy 31: 14-15, 23 is usually assigned to JE. Here Yahweh calls Moses and Joshua to the tent of meeting. From the pillar of cloud Yahweh commissions Joshua: "Be strong and be courageous, for you shall bring the Israelites into the land which I swore to give them, and I will be with you."

Supplementary Regulations

Following the account of the commissioning of Joshua there are nine chapters (Num. 28-36) of miscellaneous laws with imbedded narratives. These seem almost anticlimactic, and maybe they represent a supplementary collection. In Deuteronomy the command to Moses to go up to Mt. Nebo and view the promised land (32:48-52) is placed quite near the account of his death (34:1-8), and the implication is that the same was originally true for the P tradition (Num. 27:12-14).

Numbers 28 and 29 constitute the most complete ritual calendar in the whole Old Testament. The general offerings are noted first: the daily sacrifices (28:3-8); then the sabbath offerings (9-10); and finally the (lunar) monthly sacrifices (11-15). Next the sacrificial requirements for the specific feast days are described: Passover and Unleavened Bread (16-25); Pentecost (26-31); New Year's Day (29:1-6); Day of Atonement (7-11); and the Feast of Booths (12-38). The completeness of the calendar and the fact that the sabbath offerings are mentioned only in this collection indicate that it is relatively late.

Numbers 30 deals with the topic of vows made to Yahweh. As a general rule vows were permanently binding. This was true for everyone with freedom for self-deter-

mination: men (2); and widows or divorced women (9).
If a father disapproved of a vow made by his daughter,
she was released from the vow and forgiven (5). The same
was true of a wife whose husband disavowed her "thought-
less utterance" (8).

Following the account of the holy war against Midian
(Num. 31) and the settlement of Reuben, Gad, and half
of Manasseh in Transjordan (Num. 32) is the long list of
Israel's camp sites (Num. 33). At the close of the list
(50-56) is a warning to drive out the inhabitants and to
obliterate their idol worship. Included is another note
about inheriting by lot according to the size of the tribe.

The theme of inheritance is carried over into Numbers
34. The four boundaries of the promised land are listed:
on the south, from the southern end of the Dead Sea around
the wilderness of Zin and Qadesh-barnea over to the wadi
of Egypt and the Mediterranean (3-5); on the west, the
Mediterranean (6); on the north, from some indeterminate
point on the Mediterranean over to Lebo-hamath, and then
down around Mt. Hermon (7-9); and finally on the east,
more or less down the Great Rift from Mt. Hermon to
the end of the Dead Sea (10-12). The southern boundary
agrees almost word for word with that found in Joshua
15:1-4. On the other hand, Joshua 19:41-46 describes only
the southern territory of Dan, and there is no clear idea
of the northern boundary. However, Ezekiel's dream of the
reoccupation of Canaan describes the northern boundary
(47:15-17) and relates it to the northern boundary of Dan
(48:1). Evidently Numbers 34 preserves the boundary
list for the period after Dan's shift up north; that is, it
dates from the period of the Judges, not from Moses. Moreover, even though David and Solomon controlled all this
territory, the ideal promised land was never occupied
completely by the nine and a half tribes as the inherited
land. In 34:16-29 are listed the twelve tribal leaders who,
along with Joshua and Eleazar, are to form the commit-
tee for supervision of the land.

Numbers 35 outlines the plan for Levitical cities and the
cities of refuge. Since the Levites have no inheritance
they are to be located in forty-eight cities (with surrounding pasture lands) apportioned according to the size of
the tribes (2-8). Six of the forty-eight are to be cities

of refuge, three in Canaan and three in Transjordan (14).
The intent of these cities was to check abuses of the old
tribal law of blood revenge. Under this law a kinsman
of the slain person was duty bound to kill the murderer or
a close relative, but often the element of intent was ignored. The cities of refuge are to be asylums for the innocent manslayer, thus preventing the avenger from re-
taliating before the congregation has a chance to decide.
Guidelines for determining murder are outlined in 16-21
because in such cases the guilty person is turned over to
the avenger, who then carries out the execution.

Guidelines for determining innocence are noted in 22-23,
with the stipulation that the manslayer must stay in the
city of refuge until the death of the high priest (25), when
the right of blood revenge expires. Should he leave the
protection of the congregation and the city before that time
he runs the risk of being slain by his avenger, in which
case the latter bears no guilt (26-27). On the death of
the high priest the manslayer is free to return to his own
land (28). Nothing is said about a grudge which ignores
the expiration and takes the life of the freed manslayer.
It is implicit that the avenger would then be guilty of murder and thus subject to being killed by the avenger from
the other family.

Further guidelines (29-34) provide that at least two
witnesses are necessary to pronounce a death sentence.
No ransoms are to be accepted in the case of murderers
or of those manslayers wishing to return home before the
death of the high priest. Care in carrying out the details
of the system is based on the premise that blood pollutes
the land and no expiation can be made for the blood shed
on it except by the blood of the murderer (33-34).

After the supplementary regulation permitting heiresses
to marry within a tribe, the book of Numbers closes with
the following summary: "These are the commandments
and the ordinances which Yahweh issued through Moses
to the Israelites in the lowlands of Moab by the Jordan
across from Jericho." The Israelites first camped at this
site in 22:1, and so all the intervening material is probably covered by this concluding statement. Some of the
contents are narratives, of course, and some of the material in the collections dates from later times, but there

is no reason to doubt that Moses did continue to update the corpus of case law right to the end of his life.

Beyond the Jordan

The book of Deuteronomy begins with the editorial note "These are the words that Moses spoke to all Israel beyond the Jordan in the wilderness." Then further specifications follow: "in the Arabah opposite Suph, between Paran and Tophel, Laban, Hazeroth, and Dizahab." Suph seems to be an abbreviation of Yam Suph ("Reed Sea") (Gulf of Aqaba). Tophel and Laban are uncertain, but Hazeroth is where Miriam and Aaron challenged Moses, and Dizahab is perhaps the site east of Mt. Sinai along the western shore of the Gulf of Aqaba. This enigmatic list seems to summarize sites where special events occurred. Sad experiences were associated with Paran and Hazeroth, but the reason for the selection of the others is a mystery. Then the editor notes that it took eleven days to travel from Horeb (Sinai) to Qadesh-barnea. Evidently this is to show by contrast how quickly the Israelites could have come to Qadesh and on to Canaan if they had had faith in Yahweh. Moses' address to Israel is placed after the defeat of Sihon and Og, and it is dated the first day of the eleventh month of the fortieth year after leaving Egypt.

In 1:5 the site of the address is reiterated: "beyond the Jordan in the land of Moab." The NEB has "in Transjordan" for "beyond the Jordan," and some conservative scholars have maintained for years that the Hebrew expression is really a proper name. There can be no question about the accuracy of the location, but what is missed in the proper noun is an important implication of the Hebrew expression. The term "beyond, on the other side" is used twelve times in Deuteronomy. A number of times it refers to Transjordan, but three times (3:20, 25; 11:30), which occur in the speeches of Moses, it means Canaan. It is quite clear, then, that originally "beyond the Jordan" was a relative expression. If the speaker was in Transjordan, the phrase referred to Canaan, and vice versa. Over the years, however, "beyond the Jordan" took on the overtones of the proper name "Transjordan" because most of the people using the expression in the biblical writings were on the west side of the Jordan.

But the variation of meaning in Deuteronomy indicates that 1:1, 5 are not simply geographic references. They clearly imply that the editor is in Canaan writing about Moses' addresses on the other side of the Jordan. The King James translators, clinging to the belief that Moses wrote the whole Pentateuch (even this introduction), translated "on this side Jordan" because they knew that Moses never got beyond Moab. It is utter futility, however, to continue defending the Mosaic authorship of the introductory verses because the editor is clearly in Canaan. The real question is to what extent the speeches of Moses are authentic discourses delivered in the camp at the Meadow of the Acacias.

The Covenant in Transjordan

As observed in connection with the discussion of the suzerainty treaty, the structure of Deuteronomy is really one extensive covenant ceremony. Yahweh is identified as suzerain, and his gracious acts from Horeb (Sinai) to Moab are summarized (1:6-3:29). Then Moses exhorts Israel to be faithful, and to strengthen his appeal he calls "heaven and earth" as witnesses to his warning that the people will be "utterly destroyed" if they anger Yahweh by doing evil in his sight (4:26). A brief recapitulation of Israel's experiences in Moab (4:44-49) is followed by the ten commandments and the story of their origin (5:1-33). The section 6:1-11:32 begins with an interpretation of the meaning of the first commandment. Then follows a series of exhortations (involving both blessings and curses) to obey Yahweh's commands because of what he has done. The long section 12:1-26:19 lists basic statutes and ordinances (both apodictic and casuistic), many of which have explanations and expanded details not found in discussions of the same laws elsewhere.

Deuteronomy 27 (which is in the third person) interrupts the sequence of the covenant renewal ceremony. It consists of instructions, purportedly from Moses, for a ceremony to be held at Shechem when the Israelites conquer the land of Canaan. On Mt. Ebal, north of Shechem, large stones are to be erected, plastered, and then inscribed with "all the words of this law" (27:3, 8). There an altar of unhewn stones is to be erected on which burnt and peace offerings are to be sacrificed (5-7). The tribes are to be divided into antiphonal groups: Simeon, Levi, Judah, Issachar, Joseph, and Benjamin on the flanks of Mt. Gerizim to pronounce the blessings; and Reuben, Gad, Asher, Zebulun, Dan, and Naphtali on the slopes of Ebal to recite the curses (12-13). The list of blessings is missing, but a series of twelve curses appears (15-26). These, however, are read aloud to "all the men of Israel" by the Levites, and at the end of each curse all the people say, "Amen." This latter ritual is certainly not the same as the antiphonal arrangement with the two groups of tribes; therefore the text has mixed two variant traditions again.

The conclusion of the renewal ceremony appears in Deuteronomy 28 with the rehearsal of the blessings and curses involved in the covenant. Following this rehearsal is an editorial note: "These are the words of the covenant which Yahweh commanded Moses to make with the Israelites in the land of Moab, in addition to the covenant which he had made with them at Horeb" (29:1). This comment is surely not intended to describe the covenant in Transjordan as another covenant. The preface in 1:5 notes that Moses undertook "to explain this law," meaning that what follows is an exposition of basic regulations. It is implied, therefore, that the explanations and interpretations involve laws previously given. The statement in 29:1, accordingly, must refer to a renewing of the old covenant by the new generation of Israelites. The use of the first person plural pronouns shows that the renewal was experienced as an actual re-creating of the scene at Horeb; therefore the new generation could say that they had been at Horeb too.

Judgment as to the historicity of this covenant renewal ranges from the extreme conservative view that Deuteronomy contains Moses' own account of what he said, all the way over to the extreme critical view that the book is a pious hoax of some zealous person who wanted to get Mosaic authority for his own theological views. Both of these alternatives are wide of the mark because they each ignore the body of evidence supporting the other conclusion. The truth of the matter is still between the extremes.

A number of reasons can be given for believing that Moses actually had a covenant renewal ceremony in Transjordan. A whole new generation was on the scene, and in preparation for the difficult years of conquest it would be necessary for them to experience the re-creation of the Horeb experience and to make the vow of obedience their own. Since Moses structured the original covenant ceremony in the form of a suzerainty treaty, there is every reason to believe that he would do so at the renewal. It is doubtful, in this connection, that a later editor would have understood the treaty form well enough to have antiqued the structure as accurately as it is. It is true also that within the shadow of death Moses would have been inclined to be more personal and to take greater pains in interpreting the law. From theological, archaeological, sociological, and psychological points of view there is good basis to support the D tradition memory that Moses officiated at a covenant renewal ceremony in Moab.

Deuteronomy and Later Tradition

On the other hand, it is fruitless to deny that later laws, traditions, and theological points of view have found their way into the account of the covenant renewal. The historical survey describes the Israelites' journey as going through Edom and Moab (buying food and water en route) and also around the southern end of Edom and north along the fringe of the desert. Moses did not lead his people over both routes; therefore the fact of dual traditions indicates that the present survey is a compilation from a period after Moses.

As noted earlier, the comments and explanations accompanying the Decalogue most likely developed after the issuing of the two stone tablets at Sinai. The Egyptian bondage is a very reasonable explanation for observing the sabbath (Deut. 5:15), and one could argue that Moses added the comment during the renewal ceremony, but with such an authoritative reason it is difficult to see how the rationale of the seventh day of creation week (Exod. 20:11) could displace it. The probability is that the two explanations developed within different Israelite traditions in Canaan.

Traditional interpreters have stressed the similarity of Deuteronomy with the books Genesis through Numbers, but the real test of the authenticity of Deuteronomy lies in the areas where it diverges radically from books which precede and follow it. One of the major contentions of

Deuteronomy is that Yahweh would choose a specific spot to make himself known. After the conquest the Israelites are to seek "the place" where Yahweh's name will dwell and all the worship and sacrificial ritual will take place (12:5-6). The holy site is not named, but it is generally assumed that Shechem was the intended location since the renewal of the covenant took place there. Others, however, believe Shiloh was envisioned.

Whether at Shechem or Shiloh, it is clear that after the discovery of the scroll in the temple in 621 B.C., Jerusalem was taken to be the site of Yahweh's only legitimate shrine. Yet in contrast, the E tradition gives instruction for the kind of altar to be built "every place where I cause my name to be remembered" (Exod. 20:24). This latter view certainly represents the early practice. Samuel officiated at a number of sacred sites, and Elijah built an altar on Mt. Carmel "in the name of Yahweh" (1 Kings 18:32). It is true that the major shrine was the one with the ark, but the idea that this would be the only legitimate site for all the worship life of the Israelites is certainly a later attempt to authenticate one holy place over that of others.

Another difference is the law of the tithe. In the P tradition all the tithes go to the Levites: "I have given every tithe in Israel to the Levites for an inheritance in return for their service" (Num. 18:21). In the D tradition, however, the tithe is to be eaten at "the place" which Yahweh will choose (Deut. 14:23). If it is too far to bring animals, grain, wine, and oil, then the tithe is to be exchanged for money. At the holy place the money is to be spent for "whatever the appetite craves" (oxen, sheep, wine, or strong drink, that is, beer), and there the Israelite and his family are to eat and rejoice before Yahweh (26). The Levite is not to be forsaken, however, and so every third year the tithe is to be stored in the towns for his use. In addition, the poor (sojourners, orphans, and widows) are to share with the Levites (28-29). The latter feature, about the Levites, was undoubtedly a supplementary regulation to care for the Levites in the rural areas since tithes collected at the main sanctuary apparently did not get disbursed throughout the land. But in the main the P and D traditions represent different theological approaches. Both could not have been practiced in the same area at the same time, and by no stretch of rationality can it be claimed that Moses issued both of them.

In Deuteronomy 17:14-20 the possibility of a king is anticipated. A request for a king will be acceptable as long as Yahweh chooses him. Five basic conditions are laid down: the king must be an Israelite; and he must not accumulate horses, wives, silver, or gold. When the king is enthroned he is to make for himself a copy of the law which is in charge of the Levitical priests. He is to read it daily so as to keep Yahweh's regulations, and thus to have a long reign In the narratives, however, there is no mention of such a scroll being prepared and presented to Saul and David. Samuel does prescribe the rights and duties of the king, but these written instructions are placed before Yahweh, that is, in the sanctuary at Ramah, since the ark was gone. Nothing more is known of this book, but certainly the copy in Ramah did Saul little good in his capital at Gibeah. David takes a number of wives and begins to amass a treasury of silver and gold, but he is not censored for doing so. Solomon violates the restrictions from the very start of his reign, and yet he is pictured as having Yahweh's blessing. It is only at the close of his reign, when he worships the gods of his wives, that Yahweh becomes angry with him.

In short, there is not one bit of evidence within the narratives to indicate that the law of Deuteronomy 17 was known in the early years of the monarchy. On the contrary, it was probably Solomon's flaunting excesses which evoked the restrictions. Copies of various laws were not dated in antiquity, and so later compilations tended to attribute unidentified laws to Moses, the original lawgiver. It is useless to conjecture that Moses originally gave the regulations about a king, but that they were lost for a while. If Yahweh had been concerned enough to give them to Moses in anticipation of the monarchy, he would most certainly have been concerned to convey the same ideas to Samuel and Nathan in order to forestall the tragic events of the early monarchy.

There are many more instances in which Deuteronomy is at variance with other parts of the Old Testament, but one more example will be sufficient to make the point. In

Deuteronomy 23:3-6 Moabites are restricted from the assembly of Yahweh up to the tenth generation because they did not meet the Israelites with bread and water, and because they hired Balaam to curse them. A closing statement even extends the limitations: "You shall not seek their peace or their well-being all your life for ever." Yet when famine struck the Bethlehem area during the period of the Judges, Elimelech and Naomi went to Moab to live. After Elimelech died, Naomi even permitted her two sons to marry Moabite girls. When David was being hounded by Saul, the king of Moab agreed to care for David's parents until his troubles were past (1 Sam. 22:3-4). Apparently a relationship already existed because David's genealogy was traced back to Ruth the Moabitess. There is no indication whatsoever that Naomi or David knew of any such regulation as given in Deuteronomy 23. It grew out of later periods of enmity between the Moabites and Israelites, and the earlier events were used as the justification for the prejudice.

Moses and the Pentateuch

The mixture of traditions in the book of Deuteronomy and the many ways it varies from the other biblical traditions constitute as conclusive proof as is possible that Moses did not write the book as we have it now. This raises the question as to how much of the Pentateuch was written by Moses. The first step is to check the five books to see what they say. There are only five passages where the narrative claims that Moses wrote some material. In Exodus 17:14 Moses is told, "Write this as a memorial in a book (scroll) and recite it in Joshua's hearing that I will completely blot out the remembrance of Amalek from under heaven." The writing seems to consist of Yahweh's promise to blot out Amalek, but the most that could be claimed is that the story of the battle with the Amalekites (8-13) was included.

Moses wrote the ten commandments on a scroll, and this "book of the covenant" was read to the people (Exod. 24:4, 7). According to Exodus 34:27-28, Moses wrote the ten commandments on the two stone tablets. It is claimed (Num. 33:2) that Moses kept a record of the camp sites of the Israelites, but this would not involve more than the rest of the chapter. The fifth reference to the writings of Moses occurs in Deuteronomy 31:9, 24-26. Moses wrote "this law" in a book and instructed the Levites to place it at the side of the ark of the covenant.

Tradition took "this law" to refer to all the preceding material; therefore it inferred that Moses wrote the Pentateuch to this point. Some old commentators went on to claim that the book included the rest of the material in Deuteronomy, even the account of Moses' death, which was revealed to him. Since the two tablets of the original covenant were already in the ark, the book placed alongside it would have been the copy of the regulations involved in the renewal ceremony. The covenant account ends with Deuteronomy 28, as the editorial note in 29:1 shows. Following the ceremony is an address by Moses (29:2-30:20) in which he exhorts the people to obedience and warns them of disobedience. Deuteronomy 31 begins the narrative of the last days of Moses; therefore the most that "this law" could include would be the first thirty chapters of Deuteronomy, that is, back to 1:5 where Moses undertook to explain "this law." The original scroll was much smaller, however, because later material found its way into the account. When all the sections which purport to have been written by Moses are added together, they do not amount to more than a fifth of the total Pentateuch. There are a number of places where Yahweh instructed Moses orally, and it is implied that he recorded them. But even here the amount must be reduced because regulations from later times were credited to Moses. Although he could well have started recording supplementary ordinances, the collection in Exodus 21-23 more likely represents the "statutes and ordinances" which Joshua wrote as the basis of the covenant renewal at Shechem.

In summary, Moses was the primary agent through whom Yahweh made himself known. He formulated the ten commandments, mediated the covenant, and began the process of rendering and codifying supplemental regulations for obeying the covenant stipulations. There can be little doubt that he kept some records and that they served as the core for the growing corpus of law and tradition. In a general sense, therefore, the first five books of the Old Testament can be described as Mosaic. Without him there would have been no Israel and no Pentateuch. But the traditional claim of the Mosaic *authorship* of the Pentateuch is untenable. It is more than the biblical text itself asserts. Moses was too well educated to have written an account with so many sudden shifts in content, form, and theological point of view. It takes more than all the genius of the harmonizers to explain how the great mind of the covenant mediator stuttered more in writing than his tongue did in speaking.

The Song and the Blessing of Moses

In Deuteronomy 31:1-8 Moses gives his final instructions to the people and Joshua. Then he writes "this law" and charges that every seven years at the Feast of Booths the copy of the law is to be read before all Israel (9-13). Joshua is commissioned (14-23), after which the elders and officials are assembled because of Moses' feeling that rebellion will occur in Canaan (27-30). Then Moses delivers in the form of a controversy psalm an account of Yahweh's faithfulness and Israel's infidelity (Deut. 32:1-43). There are many old features and expressions in the poem (usually called a song), but it is not as old as the Balaam oracles in Numbers 24. Albright dates the poem about 1025 B.C. and concludes, "We infer that Deut. 32 contains only echoes of true repetitive parallelism and that it dates from a time when assonance and paronomasia (puns) had become characteristic features of poetic style."[6] Someone wrote the poem to challenge Israel's rebellious ways, and then later it was attributed to Moses because it seemed to depict so many incidents of the wilderness years.

After an exhortation to heed the words of the poem, Moses is instructed "that very day" to ascend to Mt. Nebo (32:48). Since it is implied that the covenant ceremony took place in one day, "that very day" means the first day of the eleventh month of the fortieth year (Deut. 1:3), just six months to the day after Aaron died on Mt. Hor (Num. 33:38). As noted earlier, the stay in Transjordan must have been much longer, but the editor assumed that the events from Qadesh to Canaan occurred in the last months of an actual forty-year period.

---

[6] Albright, *Yahweh and the Gods of Canaan*, pp. 17-19.

As his final message to the people Moses gives a series
of blessings for the tribes. The poem is old, but only slightly earlier than Deuteronomy 32. Levi is commended because of his zeal at Meribah; therefore the blessing comes
from a period when the Levites were in favor. Inasmuch
as Samuel reacted against the family of Eli and the Levites
at the sanctuary in Shiloh, Albright dates the poem about
1050 B.C., just before the destruction of Israel's amphictyonic center.[7] Another reason for assigning the blessing
to a period after Moses is that Simeon is not mentioned.
By 1050 Judah dominated the southern part of Canaan
and Simeon had ceased to function as a separate tribe.
Verse 4 refers to the time "when Moses commanded us a
law." It is very unlikely that Moses wrote that line. On
the contrary, it probably explains why the blessing was
assigned to him. Nevertheless, the series of blessings is
important because it gives some key features about the
tribes during the period of the Judges.

In Sight of the Promised Land

At the conclusion of the blessing Moses ascends to the
top of Pisgah, a spur jutting out from Nebo and the Abarim, the hills along the edge of the plateau. Here Yahweh
shows him "all the land: Gilead as far as Dan; all Naphtali; the territory of Ephraim and Manasseh; all the land
of Judah as far as the western (Mediterranean) sea; the
Negev and the plain; and the valley of Jericho, the city
of palm trees, as far as Zoar" (34:1-3). Yahweh informs
him that this is the land which he swore to give to the
descendants of Abraham, Isaac, and Jacob. The view from
Pisgah is magnificent, and the thought of seeing the promised land must have been an awesome experience. But even
with undimmed eye, Moses could not have seen the Mediterranean and the northern and southern extremities of
Canaan. He had to envision those distant parts with his
mind's eye.

The fact that Moses could not go over, even though physically able, must have brought to mind that fateful incident at Meribah. He had failed once, but what about
the many times of intercession and the years of bearing

---

[7] *Ibid.*, p. 17.

the burden of the people? Tradition says that he was 120 years old with clear eye and unabated vigor (7), but he knew that he would never set foot on the promised land. In solitude he feasted his eyes, and then at the command (literally "mouth") of Yahweh he joined the patriarchs of old. Later Jewish commentators took "mouth" literally and suggested that Yahweh actually kissed his beloved servant. Moses had seen the back of Yahweh's glory, but the touch of that splendor was more than he could bear. The people never saw him after he ascended Pisgah; therefore his death and burial were shrouded in mystery. To the ancient mind the most horrible fate imaginable was not to be given a proper burial. It is interesting that the burial site is noted in connection with the last nine judges (Gideon through Samuel), and most likely their tombs, like those of other ancient notables, became shrines where pilgrims worshiped. The fact that tradition did not know precisely where Moses was buried suggests strongly that Moses planned it that way. When he ascended Pisgah he was alone, and he knew that he would never return to his people. As the humble servant of Yahweh he intended that the Israelites worship Yahweh in the land of Canaan and not at his tomb in Moab. How long he lived after the Pisgah experience and how and where he died are questions which we, like the Israelites, will never be able to answer. Tradition did declare, however, that Yahweh buried him in the valley opposite Beth-peor. The unbelief and rebellion of the people had led to the tragedy of Meribah, and it was most fitting that in the punishment of death Moses faced in condemnation toward the shrine of Israel's apostasy. Joshua and the people mourned for thirty days, as they had for Aaron, and then they prepared to enter the land of promise.

A word of praise is the fitting close of the story: "There has not yet risen in Israel a prophet like Moses, whom Yahweh knew face to face." Time has a way of painting halos on the portraits of great men, and Moses is no exception. Yet those passages which picture him as a giant are balanced by those in which he is portrayed as a human with all the limitations of mortal flesh. The leading role in the whole story is Yahweh's. Moses was a gifted man, but it was only by Yahweh's grace that he lived to exer-

cise those gifts. Out of the tragedy of his killing of the
Egyptian, Yahweh was able to work for good, and in spite
of the physical disability of a stammering tongue Yahweh
used him. What would Moses have been without the revelatory experience at the Burning Bush? From start to finish
the biblical narratives make it clear that Moses' greatness
was due to the personal, face-to-face relationship which
Yahweh had with him.

Because of the uniqueness of the role which Yahweh
assigned Moses he had to play a number of parts. As the
deliverer from Egypt he became the leader of the Israelites.
As the mediator of the covenant he became the founder
of the community of Israel. As the interpreter of the covenant he became its legislator. As the intercessor for the
people he became their priest, and although in his punishment on Pisgah he died because of his own sin, in a
sense he died in behalf of them, and thus he set the stage
for Yahweh's later acts in behalf of all mankind. Moses
had a special combination of gifts and grace which made it
impossible to replace him. Joshua and Eleazar tried, but
together they could not fill his shoes.

Moses ran the gamut of human experiences: from the
shining face of Yahweh's presence to the despair of doubt
and resignation. He was truly humble because he knew
that Yahweh was the source of gift and grace. He had an
understanding spirit and a forgiving heart because he knew
how much Yahweh had forgiven him. The later prophets
were great men and they spoke out of the spirit which
Moses had, but they were not called to play so many parts
and they did not have the unique relationship which Yahweh granted Moses. Truly, Moses was the greatest prophet
until the coming of him who went still further by atoning
for the sins of Israel and all of God's creation.

General Index

Index of Biblical Passages

364

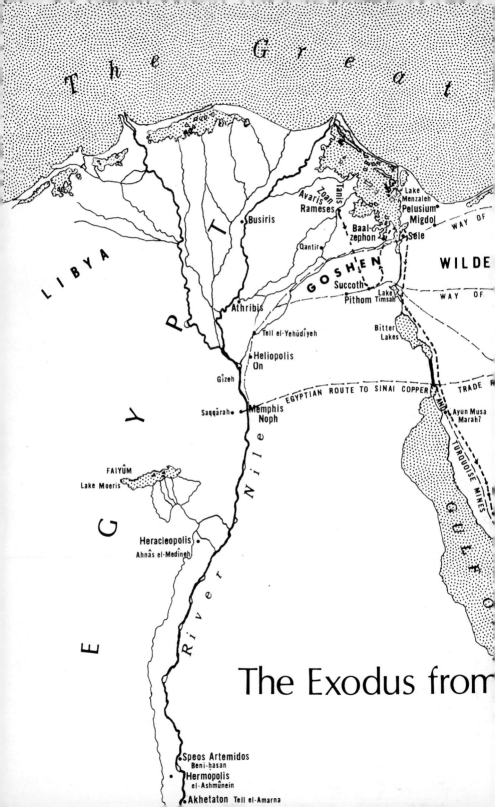

The Exodus from